2

THE CRUSADE
AGAINST
1830-1860 # SLAVERY

harper ⚲ torchbooks

EDITORS' NOTE: *A check-list of Harper Torchbooks, classified by subjects, is printed at the end of this volume.*

THE NEW AMERICAN NATION SERIES

Edited by HENRY STEELE COMMAGER *and*
RICHARD B. MORRIS

* *In preparation*

THE CRUSADE
AGAINST
1830-1860 SLAVERY

by LOUIS FILLER

HARPER TORCHBOOKS
The University Library
HARPER & ROW, Publishers
New York

Contents

Illustrations

These photographs, grouped in a separate section,
will be found following page 142

Maps

Editors' Introduction

IN THAT ferment of reform in which the generation of Americans before the Civil War participated, the movement to abolish the "peculiar institution" still holds the central place. It was an age of humanitarian preoccupations, in which reformers ranged over the whole spectrum of social change. They seldom advanced a single cure for all social ills. Instead, they turned from bankruptcy reform to public education, from women's rights to temperance and vegetarianism, from spiritualism to the abolition of capital punishment. Above all, the more earnest and courageous were ready and anxious to come to grips with the slavery question.

In the truest sense of that overworked term the reformer of that era was a radical, a radical in the sense in which Ralph Waldo Emerson would have used that term. In a famous public address delivered in 1841, Emerson declared that "the idea which now begins to agitate society has a wider scope than our daily employments, our households, and the institutions of property. We are to revise the whole of our social structure, the state, the school, religion, marriage, trade, science, and explore their foundations in our own nature; we are to see that the world not only fitted the former men, but fits us, and to clear ourselves of every usage which has not its roots in our own mind."

To these root-and-branch changes the reformer, notably the anti-slavery advocate, brought a sense of the vitality of American democracy, a broad humanitarianism, a Utopian vision, an evangelical fervor, and—it seemed to his opponents—a holier-than-thou attitude. To remodel his world he appealed to reason; he invoked the aid of religion; he engaged in enormous factual research; he fought his battles in the courts as well as in the press; he resorted to political action; he took grave personal risks; he engaged in conspiracies; and at times he even used violence. If he did not bring about a civil war he made that conflict appear irreconcilable. Recognizing slavery for what it was, an evil and morally indefensible institution, he invested the struggle over slavery in the territories and the enforcement of the fugitive slave law with moral overtones.

The learned author of this volume regards abolition as the ultimate reform, and tests the sincerity of reformers by their willingness to confront the supreme moral issue of that age. What unfolds in this book is the case against slavery, rather than an analysis of the institution itself, a subject which is reserved for another volume in this series. Admittedly, abolitionists were propagandists rather than objective reporters. They depicted slavery at its worst. They overemphasized plantation slavery and relied heavily on the slave code without adequate verification by reference to court records and common usage. They generally ignored the fact that a significant segment of the southern labor force of both races operated under varying degrees of compulsion, legal or economic, in a twilight zone of bondage. Many of them were blind to the iniquities of the system of "wage slavery" in their own back yards. Nevertheless, despite their partisanship and extravagance they roused the conscience of an important segment of the nation and dramatized the issues of human freedom and equality, still central problems of our own revolutionary age.

All those renowned for their impassioned battle against slavery are given their due in this volume, and many lesser figures have been rescued from undeserved oblivion. The author does not follow some recent scholars who would disparage Garrison and give a larger role to the western abolitionists. Garrison emerges from these pages as the seminal figure in antislavery, but significant roles are awarded to William Jay, Arthur and Lewis Tappan, Theodore Dwight Weld, the Lane Theological group and the Oberlin College group, among others, as well as such notable political abolitionists as John Quincy Adams and Joshua R. Giddings. Professor Filler has buttressed his conclusions by exhaustive research among the unpublished papers of antislavery leaders. He has uncovered little-known tracts and pamphlets, and delved through formidable files of abolition periodicals. His bibliography will be a treasure trove to future researchers in this field.

This volume, which is one of the New American Nation Series, a comprehensive and co-operative survey of the history of the area now embraced in the United States from the days of discovery to our own time, is concerned chiefly with the antislavery movement and only incidentally with other reforms of that age. These other humanitarian movements will come into larger focus in the volume dealing with the cultural life of the ante-bellum years. Other aspects of the times, such as western expansion, political issues, and constitutional problems, are each considered in separate volumes in the series.

HENRY STEELE COMMAGER
RICHARD BRANDON MORRIS

Preface

I N THE 1830's and after the winds of reform shook the United States more furiously than ever they had since the Revolution. Not only were there more causes than before, but, in an era of "the rise of the common man," they affected more people. In such an atmosphere of unrest, the status of the Negro, both enslaved and free, became an increasingly urgent and pre-eminent issue, and, in the end, divided the nation.

The abolition and reform movements were complex by nature, carrying emotional overtones, and associated with spectacular events. It was not possible to present disinterested analyses of their content and direction, either in their time or for a long time thereafter. The growth of free soil and the struggle to preserve the Union made reform seem less important, and confused the definition of abolition. In the post-Civil War period the reformers, once bound together by concern for the slave, by free speech, temperance, education, woman's rights, and other causes, tended to separate, each to pursue his own specialty. This growing emphasis on "specialists" made it increasingly difficult to accept the fact that one could agitate for woman's rights, *and* education, *and* the rights of the individual all at once—that many Americans had once done so. Hence, although there have been numerous biographies of pre-Civil War reformers, and monumental histories of woman's rights, temperance, education, and other crusades, their relevance *to each other* has been less persistently sought. The central hub of reform—abolition—has received fragmented consideration, for the most part, in the interest of one or another major figure.

It has been too readily assumed that the "moral struggle" against slavery in the 1830's became transformed, from 1840 to 1860, into a "political struggle" which diminished the value of the abolitionists. Whether true or false, the thesis requires re-examination. The present volume traces the relationship of antislavery to abolition, and probes their connection with the several reforms which dominated the period. It attempts to avoid merely mentioning names, to say nothing of name-calling. It seeks, rather, to discriminate among individuals and inquire into their purposes and worth. It endeavors to recapture a sense of the contemporary consequence which reformers enjoyed; and it may well be that such an attempt affects our judgment of their relevance to our own times.

The available materials are as numerous, as complex as our "dense-pack'd cities," as broad as our "myriad fields." The investigator who seeks to rise above the level of partisanship has a delicate task in seeking out representative materials intended to open inquiry, rather than to close it, while at the same time satisfying the reader's right to know how the author feels about his own findings.

Since 1960 when this volume was first issued, there have been developments in several aspects of the field, notably those affecting the role of the Negro in American and foreign civilizations generally, as well as in the antislavery movement. There have been new theses and special studies published, many of which have been assimilated into the footnotes of the present work, or reflected in revised passages of its text. There has been no occasion for drastic changes of statement; some of the new works published, for example, fill needs which were called for in the 1960 printing, as in the cases of studies of Benjamin Lundy, Elijah P. Lovejoy, and John Gorham Palfrey. Indeed, as noted in the bibliography, there is still much work to be done on individual Garrisonians and Free Soil figures, among others. And although we are now being given increased numbers of writings on individual Negroes and on developments among Negroes in the pre- and post-Civil War periods, a fine balance is yet to be sought and found with respect to their weight in national affairs. As the bibliography notes (p. 288): "The greatest loss [in modern historical writing] has been the lack of scholarly attention to white-Negro antislavery relations. Negroes and white people met at sensitive points of colonization, abolition, and political abolition proceedings."

Undoubtedly, the most important modern development has involved the much-bruited civil rights drive: a product of social, legal, and international turbulence and aspiration. This "second Reconstruction" is certainly momentous to the nation and to scholarship, and it has had its influence on both. The task of the responsible historian is, of course, to help place it in focus, rather than to exploit it for casual and possibly eye-catching purposes. We seek light, now as always, on the meaning to us of our public affairs. The manner in which we view our past experiences inevitably affects our current judgments.

All the more necessary is it, therefore, that our experiences be seen whole, with a minimum of wishful thinking, and with a will to approach reality. For example, have Negroes in fact, heretofore, been accorded insufficient place in the history of the antislavery drive of 1830–1860? Was or was not Frederick Douglass the first "sit-in"? How are modern civil libertarians best described? Are they "new abolitionists," and thus comparable to the older ones? As will be seen, the word "abolitionist" can be confusing, rather than enlightening, unless controlled by a clear view of actions and events. Fostering such a view can help us in our living affairs, as well as in our historical perspectives.[1]

In some ways the South emerges as momentous in this narrative as the Negro himself. Southern attitudes toward slavery, toward the Union, toward the Federal Constitution, and other issues which dominated the scene helped define the terms upon which adjustments and relationships were based. This study has, accordingly, striven, and continues to strive, to render them as faithfully as possible. Their uses are matters for readers to determine.

Louis Filler

Major Abbreviations Used

AHR—American Historical Review; APS—American Philosophical Society; BFHA—Bulletin of the Friends Historical Association; BPL—Boston Public Library; DAB—Dictionary of American Biography; HSP—Historical Society of Pennsylvania; JEH—Journal of Economic History; JNH—Journal of Negro History; JSH—Journal of Southern History; LC—Library of Congress; MVHR—Mississippi Valley Historical Review; NEQ—New England Quarterly; NYPL—New York Public Library; OAHQ—Ohio Archaeological and Historical Quarterly; PMHB—Pennsylvania Magazine of History and Biography; PSQ—Political Science Quarterly; SS—Science and Society; WMQ—William and Mary Quarterly; WRHS—Western Reserve Historical Society.

[1] The author has undertaken to define factors which affect both living affairs and historical ones in his study, "Dynamics of Reform: the Antislavery Crusade and Others; with Something about the Negro," *Antioch Review,* XXVII (Fall, 1967), 362–378. See also his article, "Negro Materials of the 1960's," *Choice,* V (April, 1968), 1–6.

CHAPTER 1

The Challenge of Slavery

THROUGHOUT the colonial period and after the American Revolution, slavery was accepted by most Americans as a normal and inevitable aspect of their affairs. True, it became more and more confined, as a working institution, to the southern states. True, also, relatively few Americans had a direct economic stake in its perpetuation. These few, however, included some of the most respected elements of society. They bought and sold slaves, rented them as laborers, and otherwise lived by money gained from their use. To no small degree, they involved in their fortunes non-slaveholding Northerners from whom they purchased goods and services and for whom they felt friendship. They enjoyed the good will of humbler classes of Southerners and Northerners who despised the Negro for his color or feared him as a possible competitor.

Yet curiously enough, during the decades which preceded the reform era, slavery inspired not one notable literary or legal defense. Many influential leaders of society assumed that it must ultimately give way to a more democratic order. Others deplored its workings and sought to hasten its end. Their compassion sometimes extended to the Indian, as well, who had also been marked for enslavement, though he was less tractable than the black man. In New England, back in the seventeenth century, John Eliot, "apostle to the Indians," had been stirred to his saintly labors of Indian conversion. In the South, the following century, Christian Priber, from Saxony, adopted the Cherokees in western Carolina; he died a prisoner of Oglethorpe,

English reformer and founder of Georgia.[1] Among others, Samuel Sewall, notable Massachusetts diarist and penitent judge of the Salem witchcraft hysteria, had been concerned over the right and wrong of slavery, and had undertaken to pay his own slave for services rendered.

It would later become a major assumption in American history that the frontier had fostered freedom. There is, indeed, persuasive evidence that the frontier encouraged the creation of democratic ideas and attitudes and helped push democratic leaders to the' fore, but it did not, on the other hand, help to undermine slavery. The frontier tended to reflect the prejudices and expectations of those who settled it. It permitted them almost unbounded opportunity, so that practical and experimental, progressive and patently reactionary, modes of behavior flourished according to the strength of their sponsors. Cosmopolitan Cincinnati in Ohio and Mormon Nauvoo in Illinois, Natchez with its Old South ways and atheistic New Harmony in Indiana—all were made possible by the open terrain.[2] It was part of the tragedy of the South that its rapidly tightening social system should have so dominated its own frontier as not to have permitted a leavening process between the new areas being developed in the South and the original states. Western Virginia—hilly, with few slaves, with large numbers of poor whites and individualists—was not able to modify Old Virginia's ways. Ultimately, they separated.[3]

The American Revolution and the years following excited new expectations that slavery must soon dwindle in strength and prestige. Such actual plans for ending it as maintaining high tariffs on the slave trade, or permitting slaves to buy their own freedom, were impractical.[4] But the spirit of the times seemed to favor an expansion of civil

---

[1] Robert B. Caverly, *Life and Labors of John Eliot* . . . (Lowell, Mass., 1881); Verner W. Crane, "A Lost Utopia of the First American Frontier," *Sewanee Rev.,* XXVII (1919), 48–61, Knox Mellon, Jr., "Christian Priber and the Jesuit Myth," *South Carolina Historical Magazine,* LXI (April, 1960), 75–81.

[2] Benjamin F. Wright, Jr., "Political Institutions and the Frontier," in Dixon R. Fox (ed.), *Sources of Culture in the Middle West* (New York, 1934), pp. 17 ff.; Stanley Elkins and Eric McKitrick, "A Meaning for Turner's Frontier," *PSQ,* LXIX (1954), 321 ff., 565 ff.; Avery Craven, "The 'Turner Theories' and the South," *JSH,* V (1939), 291–314.

[3] Ray A. Billington, *Westward Expansion* (New York, 1949), pp. 322 ff. For the "legacy" of slavery with which America was endowed, see David Brion Davis, *The Problem of Slavery in Western Culture* (Ithaca, 1966).

[4] Anonymous speech, 1759; Benjamin Dearborn to the American Philosophical Society, Feb. 4, 1803, APS MSS.

and other liberties. Leading Southerners freely expressed abhorrence of the foreign slave trade and domestic slavery. Not a few rewarded loyal slaves with manumissions for services during the Revolutionary War. Dr. Samuel Hopkins, noted theologian and a disciple of the great Jonathan Edwards, expressed himself in behalf of the slave, and contributed a vital *Dialogue Concerning the Slavery of the Africans* (1776) to the Revolutionary debate. After the Revolution had been fought and won, it continued to influence the American imagination; identification with it would strengthen a demand for a specific reform. The Negro's cause was seen as aided by his association with the Revolutionary effort, which was regarded as the most favorable era in Negro-white relations. In due course, antislavery views of the Revolutionary Fathers would be carefully collected and widely quoted.[5]

But with the war over, popular interest in the slave declined. Abolitionist petitions to the first Federal Congress were, according to one caustic observer, received "with a sneer" by John Adams, presiding, and with hostility by distinguished senators. Such acts as Virginia's, officially manumitting Negroes who had served the Revolution, did not contribute to a landslide of manumissions, although well into the nineties it was customary for slaveowners to manumit some of their faithful Negroes by will.[6]

The invention of the cotton gin by Eli Whitney in 1793 made slavery profitable in cotton cultivation; thereafter, the southern leadership became more assertive in defense of its rights. Representative Northerners unequivocally expressed their antislavery sentiments, but they did not speak for a section united on the issue, nor were they themselves clear about what should be done. Sensibilities on the subject took time to form in the North. William Jay, soon to be one of the most distinguished of abolitionists, was proud of the career of his father, John Jay, and of the latter's services as president of the pioneer

[5] "Revolutionary Soldiers in Prison for Debt," *Working Man's Advocate,* VI (June 20, 1835); William C. Nell, *The Colored Patriots of the American Revolution* . . . (Boston, 1855); George H. Moore, *Historical Notes on the Employment of Negroes in the American Revolution* (New York, 1862); Ezra B. Chase, *Teachings of Patriots* . . . *on Slavery* (Philadelphia, 1860).

[6] *The Journal of William Maclay* (New York, 1927), pp. 191–192. In 1782, Virginia repealed a law restraining manumissions, and within nine years 10,000 slaves had been freed. William Jay, *Inquiry into the Character and Tendency of the American Colonization and American Anti-Slavery Societies* (New York, 1835), pp. 27–28.

Society for Promoting the Manumission of Slaves. His biography of the first Chief Justice of the United States Supreme Court placed Jay's ownership of slaves in a special category:

> In the year 1798, being called upon by the United States marshal for an account of his taxable property, [John Jay] accompanied a list of his slaves with the following observations:
> "I purchase slaves, and manumit them at proper ages, and when their faithful services shall have afforded a reasonable retribution."
> As free servants became more common, he was gradually relieved from the necessity of purchasing slaves; and the last two which he manumitted he retained for many years in his family, at the customary wages.[7]

Thus, in this early period, antislavery leaders resorted to slaveowning for "humane" ends.

By 1825, North and South were clearly distinguishable in their attitude toward slavery, but not in their attitude toward the Negro. The celebrated visit of the Marquis de Lafayette, in that year, helped underscore how far the new nation had fallen from earlier expectations. The eminent Frenchman received an appeal from a public-spirited citizen to speak out against slavery, the latter having "a recollection of the notices in my early youth of thy generous efforts in the Cause of American liberty," and being convinced that the General's views would be received with enthusiasm.[8] But Lafayette himself was dismayed by the amount of anti-Negro prejudice he observed everywhere, and recalled that during the Revolution "black and white soldiers messed together without hesitation."[9]

Theodore Dwight and John Sergeant were typical of many Northerners who were sincerely antislavery in sentiment, but who inadvertently fell into the posture of mere sectionalists. Theodore Dwight, editor of the New York *Daily Advertiser,* not only favored the abolition of slavery; he denounced the flogging of soldiers, and cruelty toward Negroes, Indians, Eskimos, mental patients, and even lobsters. But besides being a reformer he was also an ardent Federalist, whose strictures on the virtues and vices of Thomas Jefferson were far from

---

[7] William Jay, *The Life of John Jay* (New York, 1833), I, 235; cf. Bayard Tuckerman, *William Jay and the Constitutional Movement for the Abolition of Slavery* (New York, 1894). For a general study, Edgar J. McManus, *A History of Negro Slavery in New York* (Syracuse, 1966).

[8] Joseph Churchman to General Lafayette, Aug. 6, 1825, APS MSS.

[9] Jay, *Inquiry into Colonization and Anti-Slavery Societies,* pp. 27–28.

dispassionate.[10] John Sergeant was an outstanding Philadelphia lawyer
and congressman who earned the denunciation of Robert Y. Hayne
of South Carolina as being "a distinguished advocate of the Missouri
restriction, an acknowledged abolitionist." There is no evidence, however, that Sergeant had any regard for Negroes as individuals or as
a people.[11] Having little firsthand knowledge of slavery's workings,
such partisans failed to acquire the information which would have
added sinews to their arguments opposing it. Of different mettle was
Benjamin Lundy, greatest of the pioneer abolitionists, who noted in
1826 that the governor of South Carolina had recommended that the
custom of burning slaves in capital cases be stopped. "Is it possible
that this has not been done long ago?" Lundy asked. "Will the cruel-
ties of slaveholders hence be denied, as they have, by slaveite
editors?"[12]

The majority of Lundy's fellow Northerners remained indifferent to
such practices; in fact, not a few of them were actively proslavery.
The line between anti-Negro sentiment and proslavery feeling was
sometimes shadowy, but Major Mordecai Manuel Noah, picturesque
and popular Jacksonian, did not beat about the bush. Noah preached
the rights of man, but also defended enslavement for the Negro. His
point of view was shared by numerous elements throughout the
North.[13]

Daniel Webster, in his greatest peroration, pleading in 1830 for
"Liberty *and* Union, now and forever, one and inseparable," observed
that suspicion had been fostered in the South against the North for
political reasons. The North was represented as "disposed to interfere

[10] Glover Moore, *The Missouri Controversy 1819–1821* (Lexington, Ky.,
1953), p. 74; Theodore Dwight, *The Character of Thomas Jefferson as Ex-
hibited in His Own Writings* (Boston, 1839).

[11] John Sergeant, *Select Speeches* (Philadelphia, 1832); Roy H. Akagi,
"The Pennsylvania Constitution of 1838," *Pa. Mag. of Hist. and Biog.*,
XLVIII (1924), 301–333; William M. Meredith, *Eulogium on the Character
and Services of the Late John Sergeant . . .* (Philadelphia, 1853); Philip S.
Klein, *Pennsylvania Politics, 1817–1832* (Philadelphia, 1940), *passim*.

[12] *The People's Press and Impartial Expositor* (Xenia, Ohio), I (May 24,
1826).

[13] Isaac Goldberg, *Major Noah* (New York, 1937), *passim*. Proslavery
thought in the North merits more comprehensive study than it has received.
See Lulu M. Johnson, "The Problems of Slavery in the Old Northwest, 1787–
1858" (Ph.D., State University of Iowa, 1941); Joel H. Silbey, "Proslavery
Sentiment in Iowa, 1838–1861," *Iowa Journal of History and Politics*, LV
(1957), 289–318; Howard C. Perkins, "The Defense of Slavery in the Northern
Press on the Eve of the Civil War," *JSH*, IX (1943), 501.

with them in their own exclusive and peculiar concerns." The charge was untrue, Webster averred: "Such interference has never been supposed to be within the power of government; nor has it been, in any way, attempted." Many other Northerners adopted an equally virtuous stand regarding their willingness to live with slavery as a system.[14] Their insensitivity was a major challenge, not only to abolitionists, but to other antislavery partisans now coming to be frustrated in their hopes that southern spokesmen would support programs for freeing slaves. But as Theodore Parker was to point out in sermon after sermon, the supporter of the slave system would not let the North alone. Horace Greeley was one day to sum up the problem brilliantly:

"Why can't you let Slavery alone?" was imperiously or querulously demanded at the North, throughout the long struggle preceding [the bombardment of Fort Sumter], by men who should have seen, but would not, that Slavery never left the North alone, nor thought of so doing. "Buy Louisiana for us!" said the slaveholders. "With pleasure." "Now Florida!" "Certainly." Next: "Violate your treaties with the Creeks and Cherokees; expel those tribes from the lands they have held from time immemorial, so as to let us expand our plantations." "So said, so done." "Now for Texas!" "You have it." "Next, a third more of Mexico!" "Yours it is." "Now, break the Missouri Compact, and let Slavery wrestle with Free Labor for the vast region consecrated by that Compact to Freedom!" "Very good. What next?" "Buy us Cuba, for One Hundred and Fifty Millions." "We have tried; but Spain refuses to sell it." "Then wrest it from her at all hazards!" And all this time, while Slavery was using the Union as her catspaw—dragging the Republic into iniquitous wars and enormous expenditures, and grasping empire after empire thereby—Northern men (or, more accurately, men at the North) were constantly asking why people living in the Free States could not let Slavery alone, mind their own business, and expend their surplus philanthropy on the poor at their own doors, rather than on the happy and contented slaves![15]

Perhaps the pre-bellum South never harbored the vast conspiracy its enemies conjured up and it was unfair of Southerners to consider the North a vast seedbed of antislavery agitation.[16] The fact is that

---

[14] Daniel Webster, *Speeches and Forensic Arguments* (Boston, 1848), I, 380.
[15] Horace Greeley, *The American Conflict* (New York, 1864–66), I, 354–355.
[16] Russel B. Nye, *Fettered Freedom* (East Lansing, Mich., 1949), discusses "The Great Slave Power Conspiracy" (pp. 217 ff.), yet notices that this had been "simply an alliance of common economic and political interests" (p.

one must distinguish conspiracies and conspiratorial methods from be-hind-door negotiations inseparable from politics. The latter were as common in the ante-bellum North as in the ante-bellum South. Thus, the entrance of Illinois into the Union, in 1818, was accomplished through the intrigues of pro- and antislavery leaders. The former agreed their state constitution must nominally come out against slavery, if it was to earn the approval of Congress. They believed, however, that they could then re-enact the old Territorial code of Black Laws which discriminated against Negroes. All this was planned with great secrecy. Antislavery elements won the constitutional bout, but Illinois law was to prove harsh and rigorous to the Negro.[17] The coming tragedy of Elijah P. Lovejoy might almost have been pre-dicted by the tenor of the Illinois debates.

The South was a way of life, and presumed to operate with laws of its own. It was not content to defend its mores. It found ways and means to create a picture in part borrowed from European sources, and in part infused with romantic notions—which presented them as splendid and desirable.[18] Though the South's poor whites and non-slaveholders were far more numerous than the slaveholders, they lacked program and organization, and chose to despise the Negro and adopt in exaggerated form the viewpoint of the patricians.[19] Slave-holders and nonslaveholders maintained their own version of freedom, supported by the slave system. Sincere and humane as many of them were, they found the economics of that system an irresistible and per-suasive force.

The abolitionist attack finally drove Southerners toward adopting a stern uniformity in outlook and a program of repressing liberal thought. But their stand was neither passive nor defensive. Beset by hostile criticism and bitter ridicule, they struck back with what were

---

249). See also Chauncey S. Boucher, "In Re That Aggressive Slavocracy," *MVHR*, VIII (1921), 13–79.

[17] Norman D. Harris, *The History of Negro Servitude in Illinois* (Chicago, 1904), pp. 18 ff.; Merton L. Dillon, "The Anti-Slavery Movement in Illinois, 1809–1844" (Ph.D., University of Michigan, 1951), pp. 73 ff., 115 ff.; John D. Barnhart, "The Southern Element in the Leadership of the Old Northwest," *JSH*, I (1933), 186–197.

[18] Rollin G. Osterweis, *Romanticism and Nationalism in the Old South* (New Haven, 1949); for a general discussion, Avery Craven, *The Coming of the Civil War* (New York, 1942), pp. 17 ff., 151 ff.

[19] Frank L. Owsley, *Plain Folk in the Old South* (Baton Rouge, 1949); Roger W. Shugg, *Origins of Class Struggle in Louisiana* (Baton Rouge, 1939).

often telling arguments in justification and rebuttal. Aside from the pseudo-science which supported white-supremacy arguments, and the promise that they could give "their" Negroes greater freedom if they were not harassed by meddling Northerners, they depicted in their literature a society wherein master and servants lived together harmoniously. They offered detailed reminders of the horrors of northern and British capitalism, its ignoble treatment of "white slaves," and took satisfaction in what they saw as the relative virtues of their own system.[20] Their arguments ignored notable reform movements, especially in Great Britain, concerning education, the suffrage, the right of laborers to organize, and the amelioration of conditions in the factories and mines.[21] Cruel as were conditions among British labor, the democratic process offered possibilities for improvement. But with so much evidence of disorder under freedom, southern leaders felt they needed to apologize to no one for the defects of slavery.

The South conceded—even insisted—that it was peculiar, but not that it was inferior. If it had its horror story of Lilburn and Isham Lewis, kinsmen of Thomas Jefferson, who in 1811 literally chopped a Negro slave to pieces—a gruesome event which abolitionists never permitted the South to forget—the North had such macabre characters as John White Webster. This Harvard College professor, a man of scientific and social standing, in 1849 dismembered the body of his long-time friend and creditor, Dr. George Parkman, and in other ways attempted to efface all presence of flesh and bone.[22]

The North, too, had a way of life, and advanced notions about poverty and Negroes which were often as sentimental and uninformed

[20] See, e.g., *An Appeal to the People of the United States, Shewing the Condition of the Slaves of the South, Contrasted with the Poor Laborers of Europe and America* (Charleston, 1835). For a thoughtful consideration of the southern outlook and prospects, Eugene D. Genovese, *The Political Economy of Slavery* (New York, 1965). See also William Stanton, *The Leopard's Spots: Scientific Attitudes toward Race in America 1815–59* (Chicago, 1960).

[21] For an economic argument that the capitalism which Charles Dickens and others deplored was, in fact, raising the over-all standard of the British laborer, see T. S. Ashton, "The Standard of Life of the Workers in England, 1790–1830," in F. A. Hayek (ed.), *Capitalism and the Historians* (Chicago, 1954), pp. 127–159. It is doubtful that this analysis of prices and staples shakes appreciably the traditional interpretation; cf. E. L. Woodward, *The Age of Reform, 1815–1870* (Oxford, 1949 ed.), pp. 10 ff.

[22] Robert P. Warren, *Brother to Dragons* (New York, 1953), a striking and perceptive poem based on the Lewis tragedy; Richard B. Morris, *Fair Trial* (New York, 1953), pp. 156–203.

as those which could be found farther South. Divided on numerous sectional and religious principles, the North proved a stumbling block to antislavery reformers. Before they could come to grips with the slaveholders, they must needs build a common denominator of interests between the rest of the North and themselves. The crises which the antislavery agitators precipitated revealed these divisions in northern society as clearly as they did the irreconcilable differences between the two sections of the country.

CHAPTER 2

Abolition Before Garrison

ABOLITION seemed suddenly to burst upon the public in the 1830's, but this was only because a new and more radical ingredient had been added to older antislavery elements. These had once seemed a natural concomitant of slavery. Virginia long remembered that she had once taken the lead in condemning slavery and the slave trade in colonial times and been overridden by the Crown. Most laws defining the state of slavery dated only from about 1700, and included some relatively liberal provisions.[1] Southerners had been active in promoting the colonization of Negroes. They had even been ready in 1820 to compromise the slavery issue in the territories. Now extremists on both sides took increasingly rigid positions.

To sanguine observers, it was a mere accident of economics which allowed the northern states first to inaugurate gradual abolition. Vermont proclaimed it in 1777. Massachusetts (including Maine) wrote abolition into its state constitution in 1780, according to judicial interpretation,[2] and New Hampshire in 1783. Gradual abolition was won in Pennsylvania in 1780, in Rhode Island (which had large-farm slavery) and Connecticut in 1784, in New York in 1799, and in New

---

[1] John H. Franklin, *From Slavery to Freedom* (New York, 1947), and Clement Eaton, *Freedom of Thought in the Old South* (Durham, 1940), take differently the possibilities of freedom within the slavery system. For an over-all view, Arthur Zilversmit, *The First Emancipation* . . . (Chicago, 1967). See also Lorenzo J. Greene, *The Negro in Colonial New England* (New York, 1942).

[2] Walker Case (1783), Henry S. Commager (ed.), *Documents of American History* (New York, 1958), I, p. 110.

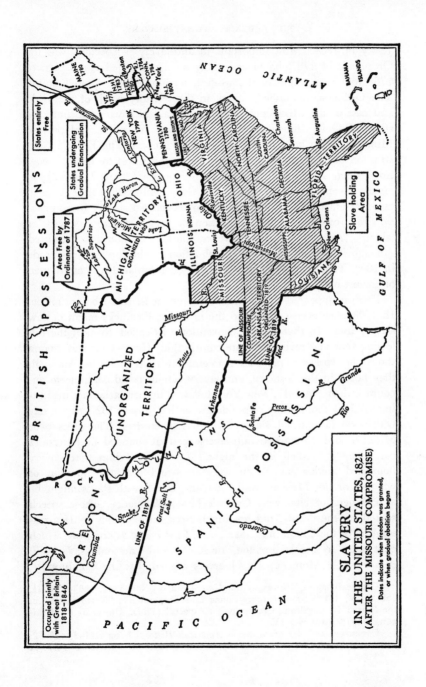

SLAVERY
IN THE UNITED STATES, 1821
(AFTER THE MISSOURI COMPROMISE)

Dates indicate when freedom was granted,
or when gradual abolition began

Jersey in 1804.[3] Most important to antislavery perspectives was the Ordinance of 1787, based essentially on Thomas Jefferson's plan of 1784 for organization of the western territory of the United States. The Ordinance abolished slavery in the territory north of the Ohio and east of the Mississippi rivers: an area which would include the states of Ohio, Illinois, Indiana, Michigan, Wisconsin, and part of Minnesota.[4] To be sure, slavery held its ground. The Federal Constitution of 1787, though it did not mention slaves by name, recognized them as "three fifths of all other persons" (Art. I, sec. 2), in giving slaveholders representation in Congress based on slaves as well as on freemen. The Constitution also recognized slavery by implication in providing for the extradition of persons "held to service or labour" (Art. IV, sec. 2). However, the Constitution also permitted (though it did not require), the abolition of the foreign slave trade in 1808. That year, President Jefferson congratulated his countrymen on having outlawed the traffic.

Thus, it appeared that antislavery proponents could be optimistic. In 1798, they even entertained the idea that Kentucky might outlaw slavery itself. In that year, a convention was called, to meet the following year and revise the state constitution; Henry Clay was among those who worked to persuade it to end slavery in Kentucky. Although they failed in this instance, antislavery actions could continue to encourage them. In 1817, New York followed up her earlier act instituting gradual abolition by resoundingly setting July 4, 1827, as the day which would end all slavery within her borders. The crisis over Missouri in 1819 startled antislavery men; it sounded in Jefferson's ears like "a fire-bell in the night." It reminded him that slavery flourished among his closest associates, and that the question of whether or not Missouri could join the Union with slaves might be a harbinger of civil war. General James Tallmadge, whose speech stirred up the debate, did not flinch from the possibility: "If a dissolution of the Union must take place, *let it be so!* If civil war, which gentlemen so much threaten, must come, I can only say, *let it come! . . .*"[5] More hopeful observers argued that the Compromise,

[3] George Bancroft, *History of the United States* (New York, 1883 ed.), II, 268 ff.; V, 404 ff.; and *passim;* Emma Lou Thornbrough, "Negro Slavery in the North: Its Legal and Constitutional Aspects" (Ph.D., University of Michigan, 1946), Chapters I–IV.

[4] Commager (ed.), *Documents of American History*, I, pp. 121–3, 128–32.

[5] *Speech of the Hon. James Tallmadge of Duchess County, New York, in*

which forbade additional slave states above 36° 30', had created a vast area of freedom, and that in time, slavery would deteriorate in the South.[6]

Although there were always individual voices opposing slavery, the first group to take a stand on slavery had been the Quakers. Ralph Sandiford's *A Brief Examination of the Practice of the Times* (1729) was published at the press of Benjamin Franklin, without that cautious publisher's imprimatur. Sandiford was one of a number of conscience-ridden Friends who were disapproved by their coreligionists, many of whom trafficked in and owned slaves. Repudiated by them and ill, Sandiford died in 1733. His cause was taken up by the hunchbacked Benjamin Lay, whose *All Slave-Keepers That Keep the Innocent in Bondage, Apostates* (1737) equally offended the Quakers, who turned him away from their meetings.[7]

Such efforts as Lay's affected Quaker opinion, and the outbreak of war between the British and French in 1754 impelled the Quakers to reconsider their pacifist principles. It brought them closer to their coreligionist John Woolman, who had patiently been seeking light on slavery, its practice and its cure. His publication of the widely circu-

---

the House of Representatives of the United States, on Slavery (Boston, 1849), p. 11.

[6] Relatively few slaves were at stake in 1820. Virginia had the great bulk of them: 425,353, as compared with a white population of 616,222. South Carolina had 258,475. But border-state Kentucky, had it decided for emancipation, would have deprived the slaveholding tier of 126,732 slaves, and North Carolina, if her antislavery movement had been as strong as its Quaker partisans thought it was, of 205,017 slaves. Georgia counted 149,656; Alabama, 41,879; and Tennessee, 80,097. Maryland's 107,398 is the last considerable figure. Slaves were otherwise distributed as follows: District of Columbia, 6,377; Connecticut, 97; Delaware, 4,509; Illinois, 917; Indiana, 190; Louisiana, 69,064; Mississippi, 32,814; Missouri, 10,222; New Jersey, 7,557; New York, 10,088; Pennsylvania, 130; Rhode Island, 48; Arkansas Territory, 1,617. Free Negroes ran approximately 10 per cent additional. To appreciate their significance, it is important to compare these figures with white populations. *Census for 1820* (Washington, 1821).

[7] Lay was intransigent in his religious views and spectacular in his expression of them. He kidnaped some children of Friends so that they could feel sympathy for slaves deprived of their own children. At one Quaker meeting, Lay rose to give his testimony and thrust a sword through a bladder of red liquid hidden in the hollowed-out book, spraying his shocked audience as he spelled out for them the symbol of blood which slavery exacted from its victims; Roberts Vaux, *Memoirs of the Lives of Benjamin Lay and Ralph Sandiford* . . . (Philadelphia, 1815). See also Thomas E. Drake, *Quakers and Slavery in America* (New Haven, 1950), pp. 36 ff.

lated *Some Considerations on the Keeping of Negroes* . . . (1754) was, like so much he wrote, notable for beauty of expression as well as message. Untiring in his devotion to antislavery, Woolman won attention far beyond the Quaker fold, and in England as well as in America. The Huguenot Quaker Anthony Benezet, too, was effective in pressing his antislavery views upon his associates. Friends ceased buying slaves; in the 1760's, they began the slow process of freeing their slaves as a body. Some individual Quakers undertook modest "gradualist" crusades against slavery. The long-concerted experience of Friends gave them numbers and authority in the field; the pioneer Society for the Relief of Free Negroes Unlawfully Held in Bondage, organized in Philadelphia in 1775, counted sixteen Friends among twenty-four original members.[8]

Antislavery elements other than Quaker developed no small tradition of their own. In addition, there was no time in which some Negro slaves, at least, failed to display a taste for freedom. The problem these presented helped to trouble uneasy consciences North and South. Even within the confines of servitude, Negroes found ways for self-expression: by appealing to law, when they could, by hiding or threatening suicide, by pretending to be foolish, by seeking to keep or find desirable masters, or by being contrary. "I sold Jack [a recalcitrant slave] this morning at $1800," wrote an angry overseer to his employer, "the amount in bank for you[. I]t would have provoked you to have heard Jack's lies of his inability &c." Another slaveholder could not understand why Negroes were so "absurd," being unable to make the simplest decisions for cutting tobacco before the frost could get it.[9]

Negro revolts were trifling, compared with Latin American revolts, but the expectation of social control in the United States gave them significance.[10] In 1800, a serious uprising took place in Haiti against

[8] Edward Needles, *An Historical Memoir of the Pennsylvania Society, for Promoting the Abolition of Slavery* (Philadelphia, 1848); Amelia M. Gummere (ed.), *The Journal and Essays of John Woolman* (New York, 1922), and George S. Brookes, *Friend Anthony Benezet* (Philadelphia, 1937); cf., Herbert Aptheker, "The Quakers and Negro Slavery," in *Toward Negro Freedom* (New York, 1956), pp. 10 ff.

[9] John R. Commons *et al.*, *A Documentary History of American Industrial Society* (New York, 1958 ed.), II, 33–34, 40–41; Herbert Aptheker (ed.), *A Documentary History of the Negro People in the United States* (New York, 1951), *passim;* Raymond A. and Alice H. Bauer, "Day to Day Resistance to Slavery," *JNH,* XXVII (1942), 388–419.

[10] Arthur Ramos, *The Negro in Brazil* (Washington, 1939), pp. 24 ff., 54

the rule of Napoleon, decimating a proud French army. This event discouraged Bonaparte's hopes for an empire in America, and led directly to his sale of Louisiana to the United States. In that same year, the plot of Gabriel, a Virginia slave, was discovered. It resulted in no less than thirty-five executions, and proved that a more efficient southern policy toward slaves would have to be formulated.

Since 1794, the various abolition societies, most numerous in the South, had been meeting irregularly in convention to discuss their modest program. They petitioned state legislatures and Congress, encouraged schools for Negroes, and published antislavery essays. They aided free Negroes who found themselves in jeopardy from slaveholders under the Fugitive Slave Act of 1793, and they protested the African slave trade. The abolitionists undoubtedly aided fugitives to escape.[11]

Antislavery forces North and South failed signally to utilize the free Negro, despite the fact that his own efforts in behalf of slaves probably exceeded those of all others. By 1850, there were 434,495 free Negroes as against 3,204,313 slaves—approximately one in eight, a considerable proportion to give leadership to Negroes of lesser status.[12] Yet they were universally despised, and held to be degraded and a "nuisance"—a popular term never clearly defined. They were in constant danger of being themselves remanded to slavery, and their field of work was accordingly limited. The purchase of other Negroes

ff. Cf. Dorothy B. Porter, "The Negro in the Brazilian Abolition Movement," *JNH,* XXXVII (1952), 54–80; Herbert Aptheker, *American Negro Slave Revolts* (New York, 1943); for a striking report on white encouragers to rebellion, Lionel H. Kennedy and Thomas Parker, *An Official Report of the Trial of Sundry Negroes . . . [and] of the Trials of Four White Persons on Indictments for Attempting to Excite the Slaves to Insurrection* (Charleston, 1822), pp. 189 ff. See also Davidson B. McKibben, "Negro Slave Insurrections in Mississippi, 1800–1865," *JNH,* XXXIV (1949), 73–90; Wendell G. Addington, "Slave Insurrections in Texas," *JNH,* XXXV (1950), 408–434.

[11] Typical personalities and deeds appear in Mary S. Locke, *Anti-Slavery in America, 1619–1808* (Boston, 1901); Alice D. Adams, *The Neglected Period of Anti-Slavery in America, 1808–31* (Boston, 1908); and John S. Bassett, *Anti-Slavery Leaders in North Carolina* (Baltimore, 1898). See also William R. Leslie. "The Fugitive Slave Clause, 1787–1842: a Study in American Constitutional History and in the History of the Conflict of Laws" (Ph.D., University of Michigan, 1945), pp. 139 ff.

[12] *Census of 1850* (Washington, 1853), xxxviii, xliv. See also Carter G. Woodson (comp. and ed.), *Free Negro Owners of Slaves in the United States in 1830* (Washington, 1924), and, more particularly, *Free Negro Heads of Families in the United States in 1830* (Washington, 1925), with its valuable introductory essay.

was their one direct means of service to slaves, when slaveholders permitted it. One abolitionist discovered, when visiting Cincinnati in 1834, that of its almost three thousand Negroes 75 per cent had "worked out their own freedom," and that of some thirty families he visited one week half were saving formidable sums of money to purchase relatives. Others made public tours—or, on a more humble basis, door-to-door appeals—to raise funds.[13]

Distinguished and even wealthy free Negroes were found in the early national period, and in the South as well as the North. Many of them, like Benjamin Banneker of Maryland, astronomer and surveyor, and Richard Allen of Philadelphia, the first organizer of Negroes and founder of the African Methodist Episcopal Church, were ornaments of their race rather than notable antislavery workers. Paul Cuffe of Massachusetts was a seaman and a Quaker, having been accepted by a meeting in 1808. He pioneered colonization plans to Sierra Leone in Africa, and himself paid the passage of thirty-eight Negroes to that land, spending freely out of what was not, after all, a great fortune. James Forten of Philadelphia, a wealthy Revolutionary veteran, was a pillar of Negro organization and antislavery exertion, as was Robert Purvis, also a wealthy merchant of that city. Dr. David Ruggles, though blind and an invalid, was a successful practitioner, founder of a famous water-cure establishment in Northampton. He claimed to have "had the pleasure" of helping six hundred fugitives from slavery.[14]

Most free Negroes in the South lived in squalor. To what degree they enjoyed better conditions in the North is uncertain. A Quaker survey of Philadelphia's 10,000 Negroes showed that they lived in dire need as late as 1838. At least one free Negro from South Carolina, who had left to reside in Philadelphia and was restrained by law from returning, pleaded with a white protector to help him. Many others,

---

[13] *Genius of Universal Emancipation*, XIV (May 1934); *Xenia* (Ohio) *Torchlight*, VII (March 27, 1845). For slaves kept by Negroes in the South, largely for fraternal reasons, see Luther P. Jackson, *Free Negro Labor and Property Holding in Virginia, 1830–1860* (New York, 1942), pp. 187 ff.

[14] Carter G. Woodson, *The Negro in Our History* (Washington, 1928), *passim;* Hallie Q. Brown, *Homespun Heroines and Other Women of Distinction* (Xenia, Ohio, 1926); Charles H. Wesley, *Richard Allen, Apostle of Freedom* (Washington, 1935). Henry N. Sherwood, "Paul Cuffe," *JNH*, VIII (1923), 153–232, is a notable study. For a free southern Negro and slaveholder, see Edwin A. Davis and William R. Hogan, *The Barber of Natchez* (Baton Rouge, 1954).

he said, were in his predicament. It was commonly held among Ne-groes that "Run-away slaves are welcome everywhere in the North, but free Negroes are met with an interdict as far as Oregon."[15]

Thus, during a period of population growth when the number of Negro slaves was increasing by half a million each decade, the forces of abolition were undermanned and ineffective. Most perplexing were the careers of abolitionists in the South, upon whom the future of southern abolition depended. The Reverend George Bourne came from England and weathered seven years as pastor of a Virginia congrega-tion. In 1815, he expressed himself openly on "man stealing" and determined to fight the "monster" of slavery. No man, he asserted in the face of local disapproval, could be a Presbyterian or a Christian at all, and a slaveholder.[16] The following year, Bourne published *The Book and Slavery Irreconcilable* (1816) and was condemned by the Presbyterian Council for heretical views. Bourne was driven to leave the state and take up antislavery and ministerial work in the North.

Death, rather than persecution, ended the promising labors of Elihu Embree, a Tennessee manufacturer who in 1812, aged thirty, became a Friend and antislavery advocate. With another Friend, Charles Osborn, and the Reverend John Rankin, a Presbyterian, Embree helped build the Manumission Society of Tennessee, and when they left the state he persisted in his mild but steadfast crusade. In 1819, a year before his death, Embree established the weekly *Manumission Intelligencer*, succeeded by the monthly *Emancipator;* they were the first American periodicals devoted exclusively to abolition.[17]

[15] Quoted in Frederic Bancroft, "Schemes to Colonize Negroes in Central America," in Jacob E. Cooke, *Frederic Bancroft, Historian* (Norman, Okla., 1957), pp. 194–195. See also Carter G. Woodson (ed.), *The Mind of the Negro . . .* (Washington, 1926), pp. 10–13, and *The Present State and Condition of the Free People of Color, of the City of Philadelphia . . .* (Philadelphia, 1838). Cf. *A Statistical Inquiry into the Condition of the People of Colour, of the City and Districts of Philadelphia* (Philadelphia, 1849); Edward Needles, *Ten Years' Progress: or A Comparison of the State and Condition of the Colored People in . . . Philadelphia from 1837 to 1847* (Philadelphia, 1849); *On the Condition of the Free People of Color in the United States* (New York, 1839).

[16] Rev. George Bourne to Rev. A. B. Davidson, Harrisonburg, Va., July 28, August 10, 25, 1815, HSP MSS.; Theodore Bourne, "George Bourne, the Pioneer of American Anti-slavery," *Methodist Qu. Rev.*, LXIV (1882), 68–91.

[17] Asa E. Martin, "Pioneer Anti-Slavery Press," *MVHR*, II (1916), 509–528; *The Emancipator . . . [with] a Biographical Sketch of Elihu Embree* (Nashville, 1932); Matilda W. Evans, "Elihu Embree, Quaker Abolitionist, and Some of His Co-Workers," *BFHA*, XXI (1922), 5 ff.

Most important of all such figures was John Rankin, whose *Letters on Slavery* (1826), addressed to his brother, a Virginia merchant, constituted a landmark in American abolition. A native of Tennessee, he argued against slavery in all but "immediatist" terms. Lacking the support of published writings, he developed his own arguments from Biblical sources and elsewhere, and his own version of compensated emancipation, urging that part of the public domain be set aside for the purchase of slaves. Rankin was not forced to leave the South—he departed with his Paris, Kentucky, congregation in 1822—but he could hardly have done, while among slaveholders, the work which made him famous. In Ripley, Ohio, overlooking the Ohio River, he developed the best-known of all "underground railroad" stations: it was here, early in the 1830's, that the real Eliza crossed the ice, as described in Harriet Beecher Stowe's *Uncle Tom's Cabin,* and it was Rankin who received her.[18]

There were many other deviants from a norm of proslavery attitudes in the South. Zephaniah Kingsley of Florida in 1828 published a small pamphlet, *A Treatise on the Patriarchal, or Cooperative System of Society, with Its Necessity and Advantages.* Kingsley was a slaveholder and a former slave trader who favored a division, not between Negro and white, but between freeman and slave. He himself married a Negro and admired abolitionists.[19] Yet despite such individualists, there is little evidence that the South was building an efficient antislavery movement.[20] True, in 1827, of some 130 antislavery societies, all conciliatory in approach, claiming about 6,625 members throughout the country,[21] no less than 106 were in the slave states.

---

[18] Andrew Ritchie, *The Soldier, the Battle, and the Victory . . . the Work of Rev. John Rankin in the Anti-Slavery Cause* (Cincinnati, n.d.); Paul R. Grim, "The Rev. John Rankin, Early Abolitionist," *OAHQ,* XLVI (1937), 215–256; Richard F. O'Dell, "The Early Antislavery Movement in Ohio" (Ph.D., University of Michigan, 1948), pp. 362 ff.

[19] L. Maria Child, *Letters from New York* (New York, 1857 ed.), pp. 153 ff. Kingsley was the uncle of Anna Matilda McNeill Whistler, the artist's mother. Public pressure in 1835 forced him to send his wife and children to Haiti; Philip S. May, "Zephaniah Kingsley, Nonconformist (1765–1843)," *Florida Hist. Qu.,* XXIII (1945), 145–159.

[20] Charles S. Sydnor, *The Development of Southern Sectionalism, 1819–1848* (Baton Rouge, 1948), pp. 77 ff. Such works as Ruth Scarborough, *The Opposition to Slavery in Georgia Prior to 1860* (Nashville, 1933), must be read in terms of the actual balance of antislavery and proslavery forces.

[21] Exclusive of about a dozen societies in Illinois, "of which not much is known." *Genius of Universal Emancipation,* VII (October 14, 1827).

But the actual influence of these societies was small, their strength an illusion. Most promising seemed the North Carolina Manumission Society, strongly staffed by Quakers, which at its peak had forty-five branches. It advocated Negro education, antislavery and colonization activities, and the use of women in the antislavery movement. A newspaper, *The Patriot,* expressed its point of view. Proslavery opinion, however, in the 1820's rose without serious resistance even in this state, and laws repressing free Negroes and slaves were instituted as early as 1824. The society went into decline in 1828, years before William Lloyd Garrison came upon the scene to further—or inhibit —the spread of antislavery sentiment.[22]

A member of the American Union for the Relief and Improvement of the Colored Race—an unsuccessful effort to compete with Garrison —later met Southerners on his travels in behalf of his society who complained that the northern abolitionists had undermined the antislavery work they had been accomplishing among their neighbors.[23] Numerous Southerners, some influential, undoubtedly hated slavery.[24] There were areas in the South which had nothing to gain from it: eastern Tennessee, for example, was much like western Virginia, and like the latter found use mainly for free and independent farmers. Nevertheless, in view of the claims made by those who felt that the South would rid itself of slavery, and without interference from Northerners, it is noteworthy how rapidly antislavery efforts in the South were frustrated; how regularly antislavery protagonists found it expedient to depart from the deeper South to the border states, and thence to the north.

[22] H. M. Wagstaff (ed.), *North Carolina Manumission Society, 1816–1834* (Chapel Hill, 1934); cf., Bassett, *Anti-Slavery Leaders in North Carolina, passim,* and *Slavery in the State of North Carolina* (Baltimore, 1899), pp. 30, 104–105.
[23] Ethan A. Andrews, *Slavery and the Domestic Slave Trade* (Boston, 1836), pp. 85, 156–157, 179–180. Andrews was a Latin scholar who had once lived in the South. See also *Exposition of the Object and Plans of the American Union for the Relief and Improvement of the Colored Race* (Boston, 1835); *Report of the Executive Committee of the American Union . . .* (Boston, 1836).
[24] See, for example, *Speech of the Rev. Wm. H. Brisbane, Lately a Slaveholder in South Carolina; Containing an Account of the Change in His Views . . . Delivered before the Ladies' Anti-Slavery Society* (Hartford, 1840). Dwight L. Dumond, *Anti-Slavery Origins of the Civil War in the United States* (New York, 1939), emphasizes the alleged strength of antislavery in the South, but does not distinguish it from abolition. Ulrich B. Phillips, *The*

Before the era of reform, antislavery workers in the North had to face the competition of the American Colonization Society, which absorbed antislavery enthusiasm and, at first glance, seemed practical and desirable. It was evident to the Society's leaders that slavery was a national responsibility. They were therefore eager to avoid recriminations against slaveholders, and they agreed that economic and other penalties should not afflict one portion more than another of the white population which was doing something about slavery.

Late in December of 1816, the legislature of Virginia passed resolutions asking the governor to correspond with the President of the United States "for the purpose of obtaining a territory on the coast of Africa, or at some other place not within any of the states or territorial governments of the United States," to receive free or emancipated Virginia Negroes. A few days after, there was a meeting in Washington, composed almost entirely of Southerners. Judge Bushrod Washington, nephew of the late President—but who had not, like his famous kinsman, manumitted his slaves—presided. Present also were Henry Clay, John Randolph of Roanoke, and others of mark. They set up the American Society for Colonizing the Free People of Colour of the United States, and in the face of skepticism quickly built up impressive support. Societies were organized in all the states except South Carolina. Manumissions and gifts to the Society multiplied. In 1819, Congress passed an Anti-Slave Trade Act, inspired by a memorial from the Board of Managers of the Society, and intended to suppress the slave trade by returning Negroes from captured slavers to Africa.[25] The federal government appropriated $100,000 for the Society's use. The American Bible Society, founded also in 1816, aided the Society's missionary workers. In 1820, a first shipload of eighty-eight colonists departed for the West African coast, and two years later Liberia was founded. Fourteen state legislatures favored colonization and instructed their congressmen to work for it. In 1825, the *African Repository* was founded, an excellent publication which kept the Society's aims before the public and carried news of its prog-

---

Course of the South to Secession (New York, 1939), pp. 110 ff., distinguishes antislavery from "outright abolition." It treats in one context those who sympathized with the slave, and those who were primarily defending southern interests.

[25] Early L. Fox, *The American Colonization Society, 1817–1840* (Baltimore, 1919), p. 54.

ress. Its prestige was international, colonization being endorsed by the grand old men of English emancipation, among others.

Colonizationists recognized that the presence of free Negroes troubled white people North as well as South, and inhibited manumissions. Let the Negroes develop colonies elsewhere (so their argument ran): in the West Indies—in Haiti, in Santo Domingo—where Negroes like themselves were actually administering affairs, and where they would be welcome. Let them go to Africa, which could be home again to many of them. It was later observed that this plan contained contradictions: colonizationists who despised free Negroes at home were willing to imagine them socially competent in Africa. But the argument had a logic of its own. It attempted to recognize the real, if unhappy, status of the free Negro in the United States, and it ventured to hope other climes and circumstances would give the Negro a chance not otherwise available to him. It assumed that the Negro's success abroad would raise his prestige in the United States and encourage more and more manumissions. It planned to enlist public support by giving the several classes of slaveholders and Negroes what each wanted: compensated emancipation for those who thought they deserved it, an opportunity to others who wished to free their slaves to do so without fear for the future of the Negroes. The colonizationists thought they would gain freedom for those Negroes in bondage and, for those who were already free but unwelcome, a haven of opportunity.

The free Negroes were frightened and antagonistic. They felt impelled to create a movement of their own for self-protection. They were Americans, the Negroes declared, and their destiny was on this continent, rather than in Africa. They raised money for colonies of their own, for schools, for speakers who would plead their cause. Their conventions gave some unity to their harassed followers, and became meeting grounds for various Negro personalities and programs.[26]

As one free Negro expressed it: "[T]he Colonizationists want us to go to Liberia if we will; if we won't go there, we may go to hell."[27]

[26] Bella Gross, *Clarion Call: the History and Development of the Negro People's Convention Movement in the United States from 1817 to 1840* (New York, 1947); see also Leon F. Litwack, *North of Slavery: the Negro in the Free States, 1790–1860* (Chicago, 1961).

[27] Woodson (ed.), *Mind of the Negro,* p. 142. No less tragic was the excitement word of the Society stirred in slaves eager to go to Africa whose masters

The sweeping contempt and hatred for free Negroes shared by many colonizationists effectively separated the Society from antislavery. As the later Governor Henry A. Wise wrote, unofficially, for a branch of the Society in Virginia which included among its directors such proslavery stalwarts as John Tyler, Abel P. Upshur, and William C. Rives: "The Colonization Society must now maintain that great original principle upon which it was founded:—'Friendship to the SLAVE-HOLDER. . . .' It stands in direct contrast to that [of] . . . the abolitionists . . . —'Philanthropy to the Slave!' "[28]

As late as 1834, an antislavery partisan would claim that "[t]ill the organization of the New-England Anti-Slavery Society in 1832, there was scarcely a rill of pity for the slave which was not diverted to the EXPATRIATION OF THE FREE."[29] Although not quite accurate, the statement reflected the attitude of abolitionists who were dissatisfied with the vague hopes and verbal victories of the colonizationists. David Walker, Joshua Leavitt, and Benjamin Lundy represented three separate abolitionist approaches to the problem.

Walker was a free Negro, formerly from North Carolina. He had come to Boston in 1828, and a year later had printed *Walker's Appeal in Four Articles, Together with a Preamble to the Colored Citizens of the World, But in Particular and Very Expressly to Those of the United States.* A bitter view of the wrongs Negroes had suffered, it called plainly for violence and revolt. Walker, until his mysterious death in 1830, kept his pamphlet in circulation among Negroes and white sympathizers. He even sent copies into the South itself. The response of Southerners was impressive, even though hostile legislation had been a staple with them for years, and Walker's challenge only advanced an already mature process of repression. Now the South outlawed Negro education and threatened heavy reprisals for the circulation of incendiary publications.[30]

---

had no intention of freeing them; for such letters from a slave to the Society, *ibid.,* pp. 15 ff. See also John B. McMaster, *History of the People of the United States* (New York, 1895), IV, 560 ff.; Louis R. Mehlinger, "The Attitude of the Free Negro toward Colonization," *JNH,* I (1916), 276–301; Samuel E. Cornish and Theodore S. Wright, *The Colonization Scheme Considered in Its Rejection by the Colored People* (Newark, 1840). For a significant life in colonization, Hollis R. Lynch, *Edward Wilmot Blyden, Pan-Negro Patriot, 1832–1912* (London, 1967).

[28] Va. Colonization Society, *Seventh Report* (Richmond, 1838), pp. 22 ff.
[29] *First . . . Report . . . Anti-Slavery Society* (New York, 1834), pp. 39–40.
[30] Clement Eaton, "A Dangerous Pamphlet in the Old South," *JSH,* II (1936), 323–334; Henry H. Garnet, *Walker's Appeal, with a Brief Sketch of*

Walker used religious language, but was mainly concerned for the wrong of slavery. Outstanding Negroes were ministers and appealed to Christian conscience, but their needs kept them close to the edge of secrecy and action. Their church was, indeed, a social as well as spiritual instrument, and the slave states recognized this by forbidding their bondsmen to convene for religious purposes, sometimes even though there might be white people present to supervise them.[31] The Negroes' very songs often mixed a vibrant emotionalism with double meanings of classic profundity, though they were encouraged to sing with cheerful inconsequence. Songs could be used as signals indicating meeting places, warnings, times for escape.[32] Especially for the desperate and daring, escapes from slavery, avoidance of slave catchers, and restrictive ordinances in the free states were matters for constant preoccupation. In Ohio, for example, the Black Laws were intended to keep Negroes out of the state, or discourage them from staying. Such laws plagued Negroes from their passage in 1804 until their final repeal in 1849, and they did not cease to struggle against them. As an abolitionist, himself heavily involved in antislavery matters, observed, in the case of a runaway slave who was being hidden: "Such matters are almost uniformly managed by the colored people. I know nothing of them generally till they are past."[33]

If Negroes emphasized action more than creed, white antislavery workers did the opposite. "I do not depend on any man as an abolitionist who does not act from a sense of religious obligation," wrote William Jay. Experience justified his attitude. Freethinkers showed small serious regard for antislavery, though they were often evangeli-

---

His Life (New York, 1848). For a modern comment, see Charles M. Wiltse, ed., *David Walker's Appeal* (New York, 1965).

[31] W. E. B. Du Bois (ed.), *The Negro Church* . . . (Atlanta, 1903), p. 22.

[32] George P. Jackson, *White Spirituals in the Southern Uplands* (Chapel Hill, 1933), and *White and Negro Spirituals, Their Life Span and Kinship* (New York, 1943), attempted to demonstrate that Negro spirituals merely copied those of whites. In effect, the author and his followers held spirituals to be ludicrous or "pathetic," as well as ignorant, reflections of songs of the dominant culture. Cf. Miles M. Fisher, *Negro Slave Songs in the United States* (Ithaca, 1953); Russell Ames, "Protest and Irony in Negro Folksong," *SS*, XIV (1950), 193–213.

[33] Dwight L. Dumond (ed.), *Letters of James Gillespie Birney, 1831–1857* (New York, 1938), I, 376. See also Frank U. Quillan, *The Color Line in Ohio* (Ann Arbor, 1913), pp. 13 ff.; Francis P. Weisenburger, *The Passing of the Frontier, 1825–1850* (Columbus, Ohio, 1941), pp. 467, 471–473, vol. 3, in Carl Wittke (ed.), *History of the State of Ohio* (6 vols., Columbus, Ohio, 1941–4); O'Dell, "Early Antislavery in Ohio," pp. 96 ff., 128 ff.

cal about atheism. "The Anti-Slavery movement . . ." another abolitionist asserted, "was at its commencement, and has ever since been,
thoroughly and emphatically a religious enterprise."[34]

Of Joshua Leavitt it could be said that the religious impulse was
a paramount motivation. Leavitt was a New Englander who graduated from Yale College in law, in 1814. He felt the need to return
and take a course in divinity. Ordained, he filled a pulpit for several
years, then took up writing and reform. He was general agent of the
Seamen's Friend Society and edited its magazine as well as a *Seamen's Devotional Assistant, and Mariners' Hymns* (1830). He became
the country's first temperance lecturer, and prepared an evangelical
hymnal, *The Christian Lyre*. By 1825, he had discovered the slavery
issue. If his articles about it for the *Christian Spectator* produced a
"violent sensation" in Charleston, South Carolina, it could only have
been because such discussion was then not anticipated at all in religious publications. For Leavitt was not yet the ardent advocate of
personal liberty he later became. Minors, idiots, and drunkards ought
to be restricted, he then thought, and a Christian could exact services
of slaves without feeling "a pang of self-reproach *merely on account
of his holding slaves.*"[35] Leavitt also contributed to the *Journal of
Public Morals* in this first phase of his career; he was one of its editors
and chairman of the American Seventh Commandment Society.

Leavitt combined special qualities of personality with Puritan rigor
and preparations for the Last Judgment, qualities which quickly began to affect the course of abolition. Although he absorbed ideals of
peace from his Federalist elders, he also urged his younger brother to
assume militia duty. We have to give up privileges, he explained, "for
the good of the whole." It was a tenet which would in due course
enable him to accept extremely painful responsibilities in order, as he
thought, to advance antislavery. Still later, he would esteem it "a
duty and a privilege" for northern youths to enter the federal army

[34] Charles K. Whipple, *Relations of Anti-Slavery to Religion* (New York,
1856), p. 1. Albert Post, *Popular Freethought in America, 1825–1850* (New
York, 1943), cites only one notable abolitionist who became a freethinker:
John A. Collins, who, however, left the antislavery field when he repudiated
religion (pp. 181–182). Free thought received some support from among
British immigrants drawn to the United States after the Panic of 1819. Atheists
tended to be poor, though they received some financial aid from better-off
individuals (*ibid.*, p. 32).

[35] Leonard Bacon, *Slavery Discussed in Occasional Essays from 1833 to
1846* (New York, 1846), pp. iii ff.

to preserve the Union. Meanwhile, in the 1830's, with abolitionism looming large on the American scene, he edited the *Evangelist* in New York and with his program of causes, including a mild version of abolition, won it 10,000 subscribers. In this way, he helped revolutionize religious journalism. The depression of 1837 forced the sale of the *Evangelist,* but Leavitt reappeared as editor of the *Emancipator,* a vehicle of the American Anti-Slavery Society. Therein he not only expounded the tenets of its creed but also championed cheap postage, free trade, and American international relations. A powerful wheelhorse of abolition, Leavitt influenced many of its major figures long before he himself achieved major status.[36]

The giant among antislavery precursors, however, was Benjamin Lundy, whose work constituted a one-man setting of the soil for abolition. A New Jersey Quaker, Lundy was a saddler whose travels to Wheeling, Virginia, a thoroughfare for slave traders, first drew him toward antislavery. In 1815, aged twenty-six, and settled in St. Clairsville, Ohio, Lundy organized the Union Humane Society, which, beginning with five members, soon had five hundred. He had come to know Charles Osborn, a fellow Friend, who had worked with Elihu Embree in Tennessee, but who now lived in Mt. Pleasant, some ten miles from St. Clairsville. There Osborn had begun to issue the *Philanthropist,* which dealt with antislavery among other reforms—and, indeed, with such topics as the polar regions and agricultural implements.[37] Lundy aided Osborn in his work, and later accepted Osborn's proposal that he join him in Mt. Pleasant. Lundy went to St. Louis to liquidate his own business. There he wrote on the Missouri question, then before the country. He returned home after having traversed seven hundred miles: a harbinger of travels which took him to Texas, to Canada, and to numerous points in between on antislavery business.

With the failure of the *Philanthropist* and the death of Embree, Lundy determined to issue a new antislavery paper which he called the *Genius of Universal Emancipation.* Its first number came out in January 1821; it was to continue, with some irregularity, until Lundy's death in 1839. During the first months of publication, the paper was

[36] Louis Filler, "Liberalism, Anti-Slavery, and the Founders of the *Independent,*" *NEQ,* XXVI (1954), 300–301.

[37] Ruth A. Ketring, *Charles Osborn in the Anti-Slavery Movement* (Columbus, Ohio, 1937).

printed in Steubenville, twenty miles from Mt. Pleasant, and carried home on Lundy's back. Lundy soon walked to Tennessee, where he could use Embree's press. He was the first delegate from Tennessee to the American Convention for the Abolition of Slavery. In 1824, he moved to Baltimore, where the *Genius of Universal Emancipation* became a weekly. Lundy's travels took him to North Carolina and Virginia and resulted in the organization of a number of antislavery societies.

Lundy's dream was a movement for emancipation combined with colonizing projects which would establish the Negro as self-supporting and respectable. In 1825, he settled a number of freed North Carolina Negroes in Haiti—it was the first of many such visits for him. In 1830–31, he visited Canada during the winter, traveling north in disguise, and Texas and Louisiana in summer, seeking aid for his colonization plans. Lundy feared that Texas, now in the hands of aggressive and not too scrupulous white colonizers, might be committed to slavery. He later made two other trips to Texas and parts of Mexico, negotiating land grants and agreements for Negro settlements.[38]

Haitian colonizations, the legal emancipation of slavery in Central America, the possibility that Frances Wright's Nashoba, Tennessee, settlement might succeed—this feminist had made an abortive effort, in 1825, to organize a co-operative venture involving white people and Negroes[39]—these and other projects aroused Lundy's enthusiasm. On a walking tour north in 1828, Lundy became acquainted with Arthur Tappan in New York. This New Englander had, with his brother Lewis, become a highly successful New York businessman. The Tappans were interested in such causes as temperance and religious salvation, but they were also becoming known, or notorious, for their single-minded opposition to slavery.[40] In Boston, Lundy met William

[38] Lundy sought to stimulate interest in the project by describing opportunities in the region. A sorrowful detail he felt bound to record was the American habit of profanity: natives frequently remarked, on passing a stranger from the United States, "That is Mr. G—— D——." *A Circular, Addressed to Agriculturists, Manufacturers, Mechanics, &c., on the Subject of Mexican Colonization; with a General Statement Respecting Lundy's Grant, in the State of Tampaulipas* . . . (Philadelphia, 1835), p. 14.

[39] A. J. G. Perkins and Theresa Wolfson, *Frances Wright: Free Enquirer* . . . (New York, 1939); William R. Waterman, *Frances Wright* (New York, 1924).

[40] Lewis Tappan was the more significant personage of the two, certainly after 1843, when Arthur was bankrupted. Lewis worked with pen and personality, as well as with money. His book about the relatively narrow-minded

Lloyd Garrison, who though only twenty-one years of age, was the veteran editor of two reform publications. Several Quakers of character and moderate talent helped Lundy to issue the *Genius* while he was away.

Despite the mildness of his approach toward slavery problems, Lundy was assaulted in 1828 and all but killed in Baltimore by resentful slave traders. An effort to prosecute the offenders failed, the presiding judge believing that Lundy had received no more than his deserts. Lundy thought he had suffered relatively little harassment, and that the antislavery tide was mounting. What he did not take into account was the fact that the proslavery tide was also rising.[41]

Arthur gave the latter an unwarranted priority among scholars; see [Lewis Tappan] *The Life of Arthur Tappan* (New York, 1870). For an appreciation, see Eugene P. Southall, "Arthur Tappan and the Anti-Slavery Movement" (M.A., University of Chicago, 1929). All references, hereafter, are to Lewis Tappan unless otherwise stated.

[41] Most of Lundy's papers were lost when Pennsylvania Hall, in Philadelphia, was burned by a mob in 1838. See [Thomas Earle, comp.] *The Life, Travels and Opinions of Benjamin Lundy* . . . (Philadelphia, 1847); William C. Armstrong, *The Lundy Family and Their Descendents* . . . (New Brunswick, 1902), pp. 349–407; George A. Lawrence, "Benjamin Lundy, Pioneer of Freedom," *Jour. Ill. State Hist. Soc.*, VI (1913), 183–205; Annetta C. Walsh, "Three Anti-Slavery Newspapers. . . ," *OAHQ*, XXXI (1922), 172 ff.; Fred Landon, "Benjamin Lundy, Abolitionist," *Dalhousie Rev.*, VII (1927), 189–197; O'Dell, "Early Antislavery in Ohio," pp. 197 ff. William Birney, *James G. Birney and His Times* (New York, 1890), Appendix B, credits Lundy with achievements he believes to be slighted in the biography of Garrison by his children.

CHAPTER 3

Abolitionists and Reformers

A T THIS time a great many persons might have regarded themselves as reformers. They possessed all the superficial attributes.
They deplored slavery, worried about the sincerity of the religious
professions of others, and sought in various ways to elevate individual
and public standards of behavior. The attitude that slavery was deplorable was common enough to qualify a good many slaveholders as
being antislavery in sentiment. The mark of the true reformer, however, was his compulsion to probe, to question, and to agitate. In the
eyes of less dedicated individuals he might well seem "arrogant,"
"malignant," "belligerent," and, above all, "impractical."[1] At this
stage in his development, the reformer now found that friends and
associates tended to desert him, and the good will he originally encountered from others often turned into impatience, if not active opposition.

Although abolition became the reform of reforms, it took its shape
from its particular relations with other reforms. Some historians have
seen fit to challenge the view that antislavery was a sincere reform
movement, and have contended that it was no more than an effort
on the part of formerly dominant elements of society to reassert their
waning authority over the country. In the opinion of their critics, the
abolitionists were no more than partisans of rural and conservative
interests, largely of Congregationalist-Presbyterian background, whose

---

[1] Joseph C. Stiles, *Modern Reform Examined; or, the Union of North and
South on the Subject of Slavery* (Philadelphia, 1857), summarizes such views,
and in addition finds abolitionists wanting in charity and true religion.

prestige had been undermined by social upstarts and a newly influential industrial class aligned with the slaveholding interest, and
whose women had been deprived of dignified marriage opportunities.
Accordingly, they hit upon abolitionist, woman's rights, and related
reforms in order to re-establish themselves as arbiters in public affairs.[2]
The evidence hardly substantiates such generalizations. The fact is
that abolitionism was not confined to particular sects or particular
social groups. Antislavery crusaders could appeal to almost three times
the number of Methodists and Baptists—to speak only of them—as
to Congregationalists and Presbyterians combined.[3] Certainly the abolitionist movement was basically rural, but this was because the nation
was overwhelmingly rural; the program which did not appeal to the
farmer could elect no one, accomplish nothing.[4] Other reforms were
no more a mask for envy and ambition than was abolition. Feminist
leaders were not demonstrably frustrated or declassed spinsters; most
of them were not spinsters at all. Nor were New Englanders, as some
historians have suggested, easily divided into nobodies who had become rich through industry, and formerly distinguished families
turned by failure into reformers. The Lowells produced Francis Cabot
Lowell, who pioneered American cotton manufacture, and also James
Russell Lowell, who became a major singer of reform. Such undis-
tinguished families as Beecher, Wright, Bovee, Burritt, Stone, Follen,
Rose, and Lewis produced, not pushing businessmen, but forceful reformers who proved that reform was a problem for all the states and
classes.

Northern society after the War of 1812 had, indeed, been confused
by its loss of young people to western frontier expeditions, by new
accessions of immigrant poor, and by newly matured elements of the
middle class. A new nationalism labored (as in Daniel Webster's
matchless oratorical flights) to overcome sectional feelings and a pro-

---

[2] David Donald, "Toward a Reconsideration of Abolitionists," in *Lincoln
Reconsidered* (New York, 1956), pp. 19 ff.; cf. Merle Curti, *Growth of
American Thought* (New York, 1951 ed.), pp. 376 ff.

[3] For the abolitionist strength of non-Congregationalists and non-Presby-
terians, see, for example, Weld to Birney, September 26, 1835, Dumond (ed.),
Letters of James Gillespie Birney, 1831–1857 (New York, 1938), I, 246.

[4] Even Locofocoism, the "radical" movement of the middle thirties, which
had its center in New York City, the extreme left wing of Jackson Democracy,
with its hard-money, anti-monopoly, anti-Bank program, had a rural program,
in spite of its urban constituency; Carl N. Degler, "The Locofocos: Urban
'Agrarians,'" *JEH*, XVI (1956), 322 ff.

vincial frame of mind. Older forms of American self-expression and
social relation required overhauling. Reforms offered one method,
painful but therapeutic, toward modernizing social understandings and
modes of operation.[5]

Calvinist tenets and Puritan law had once held the northern community together and prepared it to endure the worst a hostile frontier
could offer. But the old, integrated New England congregation was
no more, nor could its children who had departed for new homes
elsewhere sustain themselves with old maxims. Increased population
and industry multiplied material goods and diversions, and weakened
Calvinist authority. But only wishful liberal thinking would permit
Oliver Wendell Holmes to assert he had buried it, in the merry sym-
bolism of his poem "The Deacon's Masterpiece." Holmes likened
Calvinism to a coach designed to hold together forever, but:

> First a shiver, and then a thrill,
> Then something decidedly like a spill,—
> And the parson was sitting upon a rock,
> At half past nine by the meet'n-house clock. . . .
> What do you think the parson found,
> When he got up and stared around?
> The poor old chaise in a heap or mound,
> As if it had been to the mill and ground!
> You see, of course, if you're not a dunce,
> How it went to pieces all at once,—
> All at once, and nothing first,—
> Just as bubbles do when they burst.
>
> End of the wonderful one-hoss shay.
> Logic is logic. That's all I say.[6]

Yet Calvinism was far from dead. Although liberal religious thought
was stimulated by changing times, and stirred interest and excitement,
pillars of orthodoxy were also roused to act in their own behalf. Thus,
western New York, built up rapidly by the Erie Canal, attracted not
ignorant immigrants from overseas but civilized Easterners who were

---

[5] Reform is seen as "essentially a pragmatic growth in a pragmatic society,"
paying "more attention to hurried cures than to slow preventatives" in Allan
Nevins, *Ordeal of the Union* (New York, 1947), I, 119. For a valuable study
of reform, Clifford S. Griffin, *Their Brothers' Keepers: Moral Stewardship in
the United States, 1800–1865* (New Brunswick, N.J., 1960).

[6] O. W. Holmes, *Complete Poetical Works* (Boston, 1895), pp. 159–160.

receptive to religious innovations. They were given the anxious attention of the traditional denominations. When Congregationalists and Presbyterians formed the American Home Missionary Society, their first report, issued in 1827, recorded 169 missionaries in the entire country, 120 of them in New York State.[7] The Baptists preached their own gospel through the American Baptist Home Missionary Society, and the Methodists, most numerous of all the sects, by way of the circuit rider and the camp meeting. With both of these last denominations as powerful in the South as in the North, their enterprises were bound to influence sectional differences.[8]

The sons and daughters of Puritans and of other religious strains who felt a need to remodel the world they inhabited felt also a need for a more vigorous and enveloping faith. Lewis Tappan was typical of self-made men who could not make themselves comfortable in liberal religious circles. As a rising young businessman in Boston, he had been a Unitarian; but then, as he explained: "For many years I have seen, that the Unitarian denomination did not give equal evidence with the Orthodox of their spirituality and liberal giving. I have been persuaded, from my own observation, that they did not, in an equal degree, consider themselves as stewards, and their property as consecrated to the cause of Christianity; and that they were deficient in a devotional frame of mind."[9]

What was it that Tappan missed in the Unitarian fellowship? A more intensive type of prayer, he said, observance of the Sabbath, and serious purpose and missionary zeal. Such needs as Tappan felt others felt, and sought to satisfy among many sects, including the Unitarian. The churches gave the reformers attitudes and ideas, and offered

[7] Whitney R. Cross, *The Burned-Over District: the Social and Intellectual History of Enthusiastic Religion in Western New York, 1800–1850* (Ithaca, 1950), pp. 22, 47 ff., and *passim*.

[8] William W. Sweet, *Religion on the American Frontier: The Baptists, 1783–1830; a Collection of Source Material* (Chicago, 1931), I, 58 ff., cited hereafter by denominations; *ibid., The Methodists* (Chicago, 1946), 31 ff. Other volumes deal with the Congregationalists and Presbyterians.

[9] [Tappan] *Letter from a Gentleman in Boston to a Unitarian Clergyman of That City* (Boston, 1828), p. 6. This was the third edition. Rev. Henry Ware of the Harvard Divinity School, in his response, noted the "exultation which has attended the conversion to Orthodoxy of an active Unitarian layman, and the triumphant zeal with which his letter is scattered by thousands over the country" (*Reply of a Unitarian Clergyman* . . . [Boston, 1828], p. 5). For events attending Tappan's change of views, see "Chronological Summary" of his life for the year 1827, Tappan Papers, LC.

them personalities around whom they could rally. Typical and contrasting figures who held spiritual authority in the North, and whom reformers necessarily took with the utmost seriousness, were such ecclesiastical giants as Lyman Beecher and Charles Grandison Finney. Both veered between Presbyterian and Congregationalist principles. Both were endowed with great physical energy and were among the most influential evangelists. Yet Beecher is memorable chiefly for having sired an extraordinary family, and for his robust attacks on liquor, Unitarianism, and Catholicism. The source of Finney's greatness is more difficult to define. John Humphrey Noyes, who was a close student of religion and reform as well as an innovator in both fields, emphasized Finney's strength as a revivalist.[10] But what explained the impressive residue at his meetings after the stormy sessions were done, and the shaken and exhausted crowds had retired? Finney had a splendid presence, a clear, logical mind—he had been a lawyer before beginning his career of "calling down fire." There were intimations of action and accomplishment in his work. As a result, he won a dedicated following among well-educated and responsible people in western New York and New York City.

Finney had been converted by the Reverend George Washington Gale, himself a noted Presbyterian revivalist, from whom Finney derived social as well as spiritual inspiration. In 1824, Gale had retired to a farm at Western, in New York State, where he instructed students in divinity. The students paid their keep with manual labor. Out of these associations grew the Oneida Institute at Whiteboro, New York, which Gale headed from 1827 to 1834, and where the union of work and study was maintained.[11] Gale's most remarkable pupil, the eloquent and magnetic Theodore Dwight Weld, whom Finney converted, was soon sent out to preach the gospel of manual labor and to raise money for that cause. A few years after, Gale founded Knox College in Galesburg, Illinois—a college which included antislavery with its other purposes.[12]

[10] John H. Noyes, *History of American Socialisms* (Philadelphia, 1870), pp. 24 ff. Beecher and Finney are reviewed in Bernard A. Weisberger, *They Gathered at the River* (Boston, 1958), pp. 69 ff.

[11] Robert S. Fletcher, *A History of Oberlin College* (Oberlin, Ohio, 1943), I, 37. Indispensable are the *Memoirs of Rev. Charles G. Finney. Written by Himself* (New York, 1876).

[12] Hermann R. Muelder, *Fighters for Freedom: the History of Anti-Slavery Activities of Men and Women Associated with Knox College* (New York, 1959), treats Gale and his followers in detail, and relates them to antislavery in the West.

All these interests and activities impressed themselves on Finney and were reflected, directly or indirectly, in the evangel which he proceeded to preach with extraordinary success. Many factors combined to make western New York the region in which Finney became great, a leader to Weld and many others who soon peopled the abolitionist ranks. Many of the New Yorkers were transplanted New Englanders, but with a sense of freedom from old restraints. They had been joined by deviants from other Protestant sects, who helped give a tone of religious multiplicity to the region. Thoroughgoing individualists, they tended toward "distinct peaks of fervor" and toward "eccentricity of opinion and extremity of temper." The rapid social and economic development of western New York deepened their qualities and sharpened their susceptibility to such religious and emotional appeals as Finney directed at them.

"My heart was fixed on the millennium, and I resolved to live or die for it," wrote John Humphrey Noyes, whose destiny was also in western New York, in what was called the "Burned-Over District": an area in the vicinity of Rochester which was peculiarly sensitive and responsible to revivalism and religious experimentation. The religious spirit was often deliberately whipped up by revivalists in the course of protracted meetings; as one of them put it: "I hope we look to God, but we must have means." Such deliberate manipulation of human emotions and religious hopes may well have, to an extent, wasted "a potent motivation which if applied to the political, economic, and social problems of the era might have accomplished great things."[13] But to the extent that Finney patently inspired numerous reformers and joined them in some of their work, his reputation is secure.

Gentler than Finney but no less effective was the Reverend William Ellery Channing, leader of the Unitarians, strong in New England but influential elsewhere as well. His chief claim to a place among reformers before the 1830's lay in his advocacy of peace. His sermon opposing the War of 1812 was a landmark for pacifists, and the Massachusetts Peace Society had been organized in his study in 1815. True, the war had been unpopular with New England merchants,

---

[13] Cross, *Burned-Over District*, pp. 12, 73, 183, 356. For an account of revivalism, though of the century before, which emphasizes its virtues, see Leonard W. Labaree, "The Conservative Attitude toward the Great Awakening," *WMQ*, 3rd ser., I (1944), 331–352. Weisberger, *They Gathered at the River*, pp. 151 ff., draws up a "balance sheet of revivalism."

who had nursed grievances against southern agitators for war and
built up in their minds a case against Jefferson and others of the
"Virginia dynasty" whom they blamed for New England's social and
financial troubles. But practical motives which made pacifists of businessmen only lightened the way for Channing's crusade. His *Discourses
on Wars* (1816) and *Second Discourse* (1835) provided pacifist arguments which would reappear in later social crises and in more disinterested peace crusades. Channing was sincerely conciliatory toward
the South. A year and a half spent as a tutor in Virginia had given
him insight into southern attitudes. He mixed sympathy for slaveholders who disliked slavery with fear of war which self-righteous
slaveholders might be willing to wage. An ill man, burdened with New
England reserve, he was a mediating figure between such differing
personalities as Ralph Waldo Emerson, whose concern for individualism limited his usefulness to reform movements, and Samuel J. May,
a young Unitarian minister whose commitment to organized abolition
was somewhat at the expense of his insight into the varied aims of
American social groups. Channing's influence was on all his generation, and his own career was to illustrate the relation between religion
and abolition, as well as between abolition and reform.

The reform period recognized the existence of a "woman problem"
and was to have stormy occasion to discover its connection with abolitionism. To the advocates of equal rights for women, their need for
justice was such that only blindness or bigotry could explain any unwillingness to deprive them of their due. Clearly, as a sex, they had
low standing before the law, were meagerly served in education, were
denied positions in commerce and the professions, could not avail
themselves of divorce for the most part, and were subject to the
double standard of morality. Practice, to be sure, modified the dramatic import of these generalizations;[14] nevertheless, faced with a
common choice of having to serve either father or husband, and

---

[14] For example, women were widely employed in commercial pursuits
(Arthur W. Calhoun, *A Social History of the American Family* . . . [Cleve-
land, 1918], II, 182); there were numerous means for educating girls (Thomas
Woody, *A History of Women's Education in the United States* [New York,
1929], pp. 88 ff.); and various conditions permitted divorce (Theodore D.
Woolsey, *Essay on Divorce* [New York, 1869], *passim*. See also George E.
Howard, *A History of Matrimonial Institutions Chiefly in England and the
United States* . . . (Chicago, 1904).

bound by laws which were made and interpreted by men, women could—and would—be compared with slaves. Indeed, the militant women would refuse in 1866 to endorse the Fourteenth Amendment to the Constitution, which defined the civil rights of male Negroes, because it did not also legislate for women.[15]

Yet women had endured their subordinate status and found compensations, and more, therein. For that matter, even in earlier generations, American conditions which had created opportunities not available in other lands had served women as well as men.[16] In addition, whether their relatively unequal position before the law rendered the lot of women any more or less contemptible than that of any of their male counterparts among the Irish or the Negroes, for example, is questionable. Whether love, intelligence, personality, and prestige had served more men than women was debatable. Whether feminine "rights," in short, were, indeed, the same as male rights was a question of time and place at least as much as of absolute judgment.

Fathers and husbands, brothers and male connections and friends, were not all agents of oppression to womankind. Elizabeth Cady Stanton, when a young girl in western New York, met feminists, antislavery advocates, and general reformers at the home of her cousin Gerrit Smith, always the active reformer in nearby Peterboro. She had been permitted to read intensively in her father's law offices, and there had taken note of cases of injustice to women which were to inform her later actions as a militant feminist. Other male relatives and connections had helped her prepare for the role she was to assume. No more had Lucretia Mott's career been retarded by her social circumstances. She was an "acknowledged minister" among the Philadelphia Friends as early as 1817, and in that capacity preached temperance, peace, woman's rights, and antislavery. Her husband, James Mott, a successful businessman, was sympathetic to her views and inseparable from her work. Susan B. Anthony, too, met abolitionists and feminists at the house of her father, a Quaker cotton manufacturer, and her aunt was a Quaker preacher. Lucy Stone had, more than any of the other leaders of feminism, to contend against adverse circumstances before she managed to work her way to and through Oberlin College. Yet

---

[15] Elizabeth C. Stanton et al., History of Woman Suffrage (Rochester, 1889 ed.), II, 90 ff.; Calhoun, "Social Subordination of Woman," II, 79 ff.

[16] Richard B. Morris, "Women's Rights in Early American Law," in Studies in the History of American Law . . . (New York, 1930), pp. 126 ff.; cf. Mary S. Benson, Women in Eighteenth Century America (New York, 1935).

her educational odyssey was, in sum, no more painful than that which many an aspiring male had to endure.

Woman's rights, then, were no simple matter of law. Suffrage advocates would point with pride to women in education, journalism, literature, and other pursuits—women who, for the most part, had little regard for their feminist movement. The frontier was hewn and shaped by pioneers who divided tasks with their womenfolk; Caroline M. Kirkland was not only such a pioneer but, by inditing her classic account of life in the West, *A New Home—Who'll Follow?* (1839), she indirectly contributed to the arguments favoring feminism, which she herself did not advocate. Opportunities for expanded female social activities were not necessarily equivalent to reform. Thus Sarah J. Hale became editor (or editress) of *Godey's Lady's Book* in 1837, and of no small fame and consequence. Yet she did not approve of Lucretia Mott's career, or of her aims:

> It is evident that Mrs. Mott places the "true dignity of woman" in her ability to do "man's work," and to become more and more like him. What a degrading idea; as though the worth of porcelain should be estimated by its resemblance to iron! Does she not perceive that, in estimating physical and mental ability above moral excellence, she sacrifices her own sex, who can never excel in those industrial pursuits which belong to life in this world? . . .
>
> [B]ut nature is more potent than her reasoning . . . [and] Mrs. Mott deserves an estimation higher than her public displays of talent and philanthropy have ever won.[17]

Women in the 1830's were not driven by new humiliations to organize in their own interests, as the agitation of their foremost spokesmen would have suggested. Rather, expanded social needs and opportunities all but forced many of them to become active, alongside their men or alone. The causes in which women came to participate, including woman suffrage, were not peculiar to them. Woman's rights had the quality of all true reform of the time, of stressing principles instead of opportunistic needs. This was both the strength and limitation of the woman's rights campaign. It exploited the sorrows of oppressed and ruined women, but it did little to alleviate them; it demanded the suffrage which was to many of them no more than a dry husk. It indignantly carried the fight for woman's rights to abolitionists who

---

[17] Sarah J. Hale, *Woman's Record; or Sketches of All Distinguished Women from the Creation to A. D. 1868* . . . (New York, 1870), p. 753.

loaded their meetings with men as chairmen and managers; it was less idealistic in finding leaders for women's meetings who were true representatives of the humble and oppressed sisterhood: the leadership of the suffrage movement, though female, was almost totally white and economically comfortable. All reformers represented in combination elements of radicalism and conservatism. It was doubtless inevitable that those reformers whose programs cut across classes rose to the top rank. Thus the Married Woman's Property Bill, which became law in New York in 1848, was supported by Dutch aristocratic ladies and their sires, whose fortunes had in some cases fallen into the hands of blackguards and fools.[18] Women without property had less to gain from such a victory, although in the long run it served all women.

Education, temperance, prison reform, work with the blind, and antislavery were not the property of any one group or sex. In 1852, prim Susan B. Anthony would wear the notorious Bloomer costume as a matter of principle, but without enthusiasm, because it took. attention from her speeches and gave it to her clothes. She was ungratefully to conclude that "to be successful a person must attempt but one reform."[19] But by then it had become possible for a determined woman to stand up and speak only of woman's rights. In earlier days, she and others like herself gained public attention by the simple technique of identifying themselves with other, recognized causes.

[18] Stanton, *Eighty Years and More* (New York, 1898), p. 150; this is also Volume One of Theodore Stanton and Harriot S. Blatch, *Elizabeth Cady Stanton, as Revealed in Her Letters* [,] *Diary and Reminiscences* (New York, 1922). Labor reformers had thought of this means for protecting women and children years before, while questioning bankruptcy laws and imprisonment for debt; *New York Sentinel, I* (February 24, 1830). This reform was also effective in the South; Sydnor, *The Development of Southern Sectionalism*, pp. 98–99. For contrast between woman's rights advocates and working women, see Hannah Josephson, *The Golden Threads: New England's Mill Girls and Magnates* (New York, 1949), which describes the evolution of the mills from their "romantic" beginnings in the 1830's, when they seemed an open door for farm girls who wished to better themselves, to the early 1840's, when abrupt changes were made by the mill owners, who lowered wages, among other "reforms" intended directly to improve their profits.

[19] Ida H. Harper, *The Life and Work of Susan B. Anthony* . . . (Indianapolis, 1898), I, 117. "The 'Bloomer costume' consisted of a tunic loosely belted at the waist, a skirt not much more than knee length, and—the most sensational feature—Turkish pantaloons which reached to the ankle"; Eleanor Flexner, *Century of Struggle* (Cambridge, Mass., 1959), p. 83. The costume was not originated by Amelia Bloomer, but popularized by her.

The suffragists' need to receive democratic opportunities ensured a genuinely democratic tone in their circles. There were few Negro women prominent in them, true, and the best-known women's rights advocates among Negroes were men. But this was not because Negro women were unwelcome in woman suffrage groups; it was, at least in part, because the antislavery movement appealed to Negro women as the more urgent cause. So it was with the gracious young Charlotte Forten, granddaughter of the Philadelphia Negro philanthropist and abolitionist; so it was with the eloquent Sojourner Truth, who had been a slave in New York State and was now a vibrant and unique testament against slavery;[20] so it was with other socially conscious Negro women in Philadelphia, New York, Rochester, Boston, and other centers.

Of all the reforms relevant to the antislavery crusade, none cast a larger net than temperance. In 1826, when the American Society for the Promotion of Temperance was formed, a number of significant agencies concerned for spiritual and moral well-being had been ambitiously inaugurated. The American Home Missionary Society, the American Peace Society, the American Tract Society, the Society to Improve the Condition of the Sailors—these and others sought to instill Christian principles into Americans. The Temperance Society was, in considerable degree, an offshoot of these other missions. But temperance possessed a characteristic quality of reform that none could match—that combination of zeal with a program for change. There had been temperance efforts of a more than merely regulatory type for decades. Increased population and multiplying communities made for increased drinking, for deteriorated social standards of dignity and diminished social controls. William Cobbett, who should have been sufficiently inured to the Hogarthian scenes of drunkenness in England, was impelled to remark, during his second stay in America, in 1817–1819:

There is one thing in the Americans, which . . . I have . . . *kept back* to the last moment. . . . [T]hey *tipple:* and the infernal spirits they tipple, too! The scenes that I witnessed at Harrisburgh I shall never forget. I almost

[20] Ray A. Billington (ed.), *The Journal of Charlotte L. Forten* (New York, 1953); *Narrative of Sojourner Truth; a Bondswoman of Olden Time . . .* (Boston, 1875 ed.); Arthur H. Fauset, *Sojourner Truth, God's Faithful Pilgrim* (Chapel Hill, 1938).

wished (God forgive me!) that there were Boroughmongers here to *tax* these drinkers: they would soon reduce them to a moderate dose. . . .

To see this beastly vice in *young* men is shocking. . . . Well-dressed, well educated, polite, and everything but *sober*. What a squalid, drooping, sickly set they looked *in the morning!*[21]

The "rich, the well-born and the able," though they could use irresponsible drinking as an added charge against democracy and the poor, had stakes of their own in temperance. Its remarkable features during the reform era were its influence on the antislavery crusade and the fact that it embraced a great number of groups and classes which otherwise were opposed to one another. The "world's" temperance convention which met in New York in 1853 furnished a case in point. Before the convention's hectic sessions concluded, the feminist Reverend Antoinette L. Brown, though a regularly elected delegate, had been silenced because she was a woman; Dr. J. McCune Smith had been barred because he was a Negro; and Wendell Phillips, as earnestly for temperance as for abolition, had been expelled on specious grounds.[22] All believed that the fight against liquor was essential to the progress of their separate causes: that women suffered by the intemperateness of their men, that Negroes ought to arm themselves in sobriety for the advancement of their race, and that drinking was part of the moral corruption which sustained slavery. Yet there were also dedicated Southerners, to whom slavery was justified by religion, who sought to array their fellow patriarchs in the moral armor of temperance, as well as to curb the drinking habits of their Negroes. There were merchant-temperance societies, and women's temperance societies, and young men's temperance societies: the Tappans, especially Arthur, were busy organizers of such agencies.

Temperance inspired antiliquor actions. A celebrated case was that of the Reverend George Barrell Cheever, who later became a prominent New York minister, and still later an abolitionist. In 1835, while a minister in Salem, he published his tale, "Inquire at Amos Giles' Distillery," a dream of intemperance and retribution which dealt with a real distiller and an actual distillery. For having, as it was claimed, perpetrated a libel, he was publicly assaulted, fined, imprisoned, and gained national notoriety.[23]

[21] William Cobbett, *A Year's Residence in America* (Boston, n.d.), pp. 158–159.

[22] Nevins, *Ordeal of the Union*, I, 115.

[23] Robert M. York, *George B. Cheever, Religious and Social Reformer,*

Numerous Americans held that temperance was (often along with opposition to tea, coffee, snuff, and tobacco) a cornerstone of moral principle. P. T. Barnum, among others, considered it an essential part of "The Art of Money-Getting." Orthodox factions argued whether wine could, properly, be part of religious ceremonies.[24]

The career of temperance during the reform period was given a fateful form by being equated with prohibition. In due course, it would be identified by antiprohibitionists with intolerance and aristocracy. The rising Democratic party was careful in this respect not to offend the numerous poor, and profited by its prudence. Not until 1840 would the Whigs learn to meet the Democrats on the level of demagogy with their famous "Hard Cider" campaign. But the grounds for the movement to curb the consumption of alcohol were firm ones. Perhaps the estimates were biased, but in 1830 it was contended that intemperance cost fifty thousand lives a year, in a population of about twelve and three-quarters million.[25]

Temperance served the cause of abolition directly in many ways. It helped give respectability to its agitators, who might have been called fanatical, but not corrupt. The demand for "immediate" temperance added an argument to abolitionist appeals for "immediate" abolition. The belief that addiction to drink was "white slavery"—a term also employed by laborites—helped impugn slavery. The temperance movement also offered another avenue to Negroes and women seeking testing grounds for acceptance.[26]

"If temperance prevails," Horace Mann was to write, "then Education can prevale [sic],—if Temperance fails, then Education must

---

1807–1890 (Orono, Maine, 1955), pp. 72 ff.; George I. Rockwood, "George Barrell Cheever, Protagonist of Abolition . . ." in *Proc. of Amer. Antiquarian Soc.*, new ser., XLVI (1937), 97–113; *A Defence in Abatement of Judgment for an Alleged Libel in the Story Entitled "Inquire at Amos Giles Distillery"* . . . (New York, 1836).

[24] For a map showing the distribution of temperance societies in 1830, see John A. Krout, *The Origins of Prohibition* (New York, 1925), p. 130. Father Edward Johnson Taylor, who became "Father Mapple" in Melville's *Moby Dick* and who was a founder of the Seaman's Aid Society, fiercely opposed Arthur Tappan for wishing to replace wine at the Sacrament with what Taylor called "raisin water"; Rev. Gilbert Haven and Hon. Thomas Russell, *Father Taylor, the Sailor Preacher* (Boston, 1872), pp. 255–256.

[25] "Temperance," *New York Sentinel*, I (March 25, 1830).

[26] [Warren Burton] *White Slavery: a New Emancipation Cause* . . . (Worcester, 1839); John W. Campbell, *Biographical Sketches* . . . (Columbus, Ohio, 1838), pp. 196–198; Krout, *The Origins of Prohibition*, pp. 217–218.

fail."[27] Nevertheless, education was sought by groups uninterested in the temperance platform, as well as by antislavery leaders. To the labor reformers knowledge was, first of all, power, and they sought to acquire more schools at the public expense. Samuel Lewis, outstanding Ohio educational reformer, later distinguished among political abolitionists, had a quite different approach, though he achieved the same objectives.[28] Oppressed by the condition of the poor, including what seemed to him their low spiritual state, he took time from his study of the law to teach at the primary level; as he wrote a relative:

You will perceive that my path is not one that will lead to fortune; but it is sure to lead to happiness. . . . [I]f you could visit the Sabbath schools that are in operation in this place for the benefit of poor children, you would think there is a reality in it. By the exertions of a few of us young men, with the aid of a few young women, we keep us three different schools composed of about two hundred and fifty scholars from six to sixteen years of age. You will no doubt wonder that in a country so fertile there should be so many ignorant. But you must know that we have no advantages of public schools, as the lands appropriated by Congress do not yield a sufficient revenue to support them; and it is much to be lamented that the state legislature has never yet taken the subject into consideration.[29]

Education was the master reform: the "universal utopia."[30] In this pre-Darwinian period which still held hopes of the perfectibility of man, education was the key to unlock all doors. It would open light on darkness and inform the wise and powerful. On a less lofty plane, it would relieve sickness, reduce crime, and advance morality, industry, and thrift. It was resisted by those who continued to believe that people with means ought not to be taxed for the education of other people's children.[31]

[27] Horace Mann Diary, Sept. 20, 1838, typescript, pp. 102–103, Antiochiana Collection, Antioch College. See also, Louis Filler, ed., *Horace Mann and the Crisis in Education* (Yellow Springs, O., 1965), *passim*.

[28] See Harold E. Davis, "Social and Economic Base of the Whig Party, 1828—1840" (Ph. D., Western Reserve University, 1933), pp. 218-219.

[29] Arthur T. Carr, "Samuel Lewis: Educational and Social Reformer" (Ph.D., Western Reserve University, 1938), pp. 7–8.

[30] Arthur A. Ekirch, Jr., *The Idea of Progress in America, 1815–1860* (New York, 1944), pp. 195 ff.; cf. F. S. Marvin, *The Century of Hope: a Sketch of Western Progress from 1815 to the Great War* (Oxford, 1927 ed.), pp. 188 ff. For a thoughtful summary, see Morris Ginsberg, *The Idea of Progress: a Revaluation* (Boston, 1953).

[31] Frank T. Carlton, *Economic Influences upon Educational Progress in the United States, 1820–1850* (Madison, Wis., 1908), pp. 45 ff.; Filler, "Main

The concept of education as bringing light into darkness and exposing sin and error was basic to the program of reform in general and abolition in particular. To the extent that reform was part of a national process of democratization, it was related to, though separate from, the movement favoring mechanics' institutes, set up by elements of labor to encourage self-education. The lyceum was part of the same impulse, though directed at audiences on a higher economic level. This brought the famous and the mellifluent before interested or curious auditors from Boston to Cincinnati and beyond. Ralph Waldo Emerson, Wendell Phillips, Daniel Webster, and Edward Everett delivered their set orations, offering apostrophes to the Higher Life or more or less specific reform programs.[32]

There were notable Democratic advocates of universal education, including Walt Whitman in New York and Robert Rantoul, Jr., in Massachusetts.[33] But education as a complex operation, permeating society and building standards of quality, became largely the province of educators of Whig or otherwise conservative tendency. Thus, the Reverend Horace Bushnell viewed American life through what were in many ways the strictest conservative spectacles. He hated slavery, but had no use for the Negro.[34] He opposed woman suffrage as *The Reform against Nature* (1869) and was indifferent to the troubles of the poor. Yet his *Christian Nurture* (1847) was fought over as though it had been the work of a radical, and simply because he transgressed Calvinist assumptions by treating the infant as a Christian and concerning himself for its education.

Women's education was advanced, in the main by women, who were also innovators more than they were reformers. Notable among them was Catherine Beecher, whose Hartford Seminary, instituted in 1823, gained renown for its high standards and influence. Miss Beecher became the most influential of antifeminists and antiabolitionists, be-

---

Currents in Progressivist American Education," *Hist. of Education Jour.*, VIII (1957), 35–36.

[32] Carl Bode, *The American Lyceum: Town Meeting of the Mind* (New York, 1956). For portraits of lyceum favorites, see David Mead, *Yankee Eloquence in the Middle West, the Ohio Lyceum 1850–1870* (East Lansing, 1951).

[33] Florence B. Freedman, *Walt Whitman Looks at the Schools* (New York, 1950); Luther Hamilton (ed.), *Memoirs, Speeches and Writings of Robert Rantoul, Jr.* (Boston, 1854), pp. 67 ff.

[34] Charles C. Cole, Jr., "Horace Bushnell and the Slavery Question," *NEQ*, XXIII (1950), 19–30.

lieving they harmed all reform causes by their harsh tactics and radical aims.[35]

A reformer could argue that Miss Beecher was lending her great name to an unworthy argument, or attempt to derogate her educational ideas because of lack of sympathy for her other social attitudes. Few reformers attempted the latter; her major work was too patently progressive to be repudiated, and they themselves were unwilling to support more radical educational theory. Bronson Alcott's Temple School, in which he attempted to treat children as individuals, failed dismally. (One of his novelties was to have the children strike him, rather than he them, when they had been remiss.)[36] Abolitionists, feminists, and others among reformers preferred more conventionally organized schools.

None better than Horace Mann demonstrated, in his personal development, the intrinsic relation between education and antislavery. Education was not his first reform. As a young Massachusetts state legislator in the 1820's, he had preceded Dorothea Dix in his concern for the miserable lot of the insane. He was later to join with Dr. Samuel Gridley Howe and Charles Sumner, among others, in helping her to wage her battle to establish legal protections for the mentally ill. Mann was never a radical, his interest was less with the individual than with his social role. It was his republican aims, rather than his psychological depth, which made him a reformer and ultimately an antislavery spokesman.

In 1837, Mann accepted the secretaryship of the newly created State Board of Education, closed his law office, and set out to encourage the building of schools which would serve all children, and to establish institutes which would train competent teachers. Fortunately for his cause, Mann was cautious and respectable.[37] He largely ignored the slavery question during the years he was creating his program. He courted businessmen and opposed the trade unions and ignored labor conditions in the newly proliferated factories. He opposed sectarianism in the schools, and (though no bigot himself) undoubtedly capitalized

[35] Woody, *History of Women's Education in the United States*, I, 341 ff.; Catherine E. Beecher, *An Essay on Slavery and Abolitionism, with Reference to the Duty of American Females* (Philadelphia, 1837).

[36] Odell Shepard, *Pedlar's Progress* (Boston, 1937), p. 169. See also Elizabeth P. Peabody, *Record of A. B. Alcott's School* (Boston, 1874 ed.).

[37] Mann's aims and methods are explained in the introduction to Lawrence A. Cremin (ed.), *The Republic and the School: Horace Mann on the Education of Free Men* (New York, 1957).

upon Protestant antipathy to Catholic parochial schools. His understanding of literature was limited by his demand for moral lessons,
as Richard Henry Dana discovered for himself. Dana was already
renowned for his *Two Years before the Mast* (1840), an account of
his experiences as a common sailor, when Mann came to consult him
about republishing it as a textbook. Mann had already sent Dana
what struck him as a remarkable letter, informing him that "I would
make the book worthy of this honor, by amending it, giving it more
information, making it more useful, etc." Dana had answered ironi-
cally that the book belonged to the publishers, otherwise he would be
obliged for the opportunity:

Judge of my surprise to find that [Mann] had taken me literally. . . . He
gravely proceeded to state the defects of the work. . . . He thought the
book fell off in interest at the close, that the concluding chapter was wanting in the true, humane and philanthropic spirit (as an excuse for which he
kindly intimated that it was probably hastily written), and that the book
should contain more valuable information, which would be useful to young
persons, statistical information and facts as to the countries I visited, their
resources, productions and the habits of the people. . . .[38]

Yet this insensitivity to the needs of art, to the extent that it derived from an absorption in the problem of bringing education to the
people, on terms which they could grasp, helped give Mann the
strength which established the *Common School Journal* and the first
public normal school in the United States; and produced his masterly
annual reports from which much of American education derives. In
addition, there was a generosity in Mann which permitted him to
appoint the Reverend Samuel J. May, in 1842, as second principal of
the normal school, despite May's radical views on peace, equal rights
for women, and abolition. Mann was anxious about May's reformist
compulsions, and exacted a promise that he would hold strictly to
education, a promise May was unable to keep. There was, too, a
quality of statesmanship in Mann which made it possible for him to
enlist the support of ministers, politicians, and public figures of varying types for his educational projects.[39]

Above all, it was Mann's courage that enabled him to withstand
the hammerings of religious zealots. That courage was exemplified in

[38] Charles F. Adams, *Richard Henry Dana* (Boston, 1890), I, 118–120.
[39] See, for example, Mary P. Mann, *Life of Horace Mann* (Washington,
1937 ed.), pp. 100–101.

his epochal Seventh Annual Report. This report embodied his observations on education abroad, gathered during his wedding trip, and summarized the weaknesses of schools in Massachusetts—their languor, their incompetence, their inadequacy—as compared with the best that Scotland, Germany, France, and other nations had to offer. The subsequent retort of thirty masters of Boston schools set off a major battle which brought the actual weaknesses of their schools into sharp focus. It established the truth of Mann's charges and touched all American education, if not with millennial virtues, at least with modernity.

From all this, the antislavery cause ultimately gained. It required a wide concern for understanding in order to consummate its purposes. Its own river of propaganda, in the form of pamphlets, newspapers, and public meetings, never faltered. But as important were the many forms of education which bridged the gap between convinced abolitionists and the unresolved public. Wendell Phillips on the lyceum circuit, Samuel Lewis in Ohio pleading for universal education as well as antislavery measures, and the numerous schoolmasters and schoolmistresses who carried on the message of moral purpose and constitutional liberties were essential to the furtherance of antislavery. Ultimately, they turned Mann himself into a political abolitionist of force and influence.

At first glance, Horace Greeley's causes would seem to light up a flaming radical. Protemperance, antitobacco, anticapital punishment, an admirer of Emerson, Margaret Fuller, and Henry D. Thoreau, open-minded to woman suffrage, a medium for vivid writings about the conditions of the poor, and, above all, an ardent proponent of co-operative communities—Greeley was all these and a good deal more.[40] How his thought related to his actions was another matter. With abolition he would have no traffic; the mildest antislavery perturbed him, until the issue of free soil became unavoidable. His political ambition scarred and bent his career with the grossest expediency. His deeds in behalf of the poor were negligible.[41] He favored thrift, labor-employer negotiations, labor exchanges, education, work relief. But he feared mass action, and had no intention of spending govern-

[40] Glyndon Van Deusen, *Horace Greeley: Nineteenth Century Crusader* (Philadelphia, 1953), pp. 59 ff.
[41] Jeter A. Iseley, *Horace Greeley and the Republican Party, 1853–1861: a Study of the New York Tribune* (Princeton, 1947); Glyndon Van Deusen, *Thurlow Weed: Wizard of the Lobby* (Boston, 1947).

ment money on the needy. Greeley opposed trade unionism and the strike, and his unqualified demand for protection of American manufactures from foreign competition differed in no way from that of the manufacturer bluntly seeking government aid.

His greatness lay in his matchless sensitivity to the social currents which created reform, all of which he industriously reported. Greeley was a patron of reform rather than a reformer, and helped publicize it and give it a forum. Reform proper would be achieved by advocates more pertinaciously concerned about the difficulties which had to be overcome before progress could be achieved.

Part of the problem of reform lay in distinguishing it from the "reform," sponsored by political parties. The appeal of the new Democrats in the late 1820's was neither to the poor nor to the dispossessed. As one recent critic has pointed out:

> Around the lower middle class there collected a motley aggregation of landowners and farmers, who were taxed for roads and canals they neither needed nor wanted, "hard money" men who distrusted the banks and their paper money, artisans and master mechanics who resented the head-start that the "protected" industries had over their unprotected industries, "states rights" men, especially in the South, who feared that the concentration of power in the Federal Government might prove disastrous to the institution of slavery, faddists and fanatics of all sorts, and a few pure Democrats. This miscellaneous group was called by the Jacksonians "the democracy," "the people," "the working men," and various other similarly appealing names.[42]

Their "reforms"—like those of their opponent Whigs—took off from the level of high government policy, involving free trade, monopoly, attitudes toward banks, courts, and other institutions. It was the economic man, the political man, the sectional man who was wooed. Less consequential in this perspective was the individual, of whatever section or politics. It was the reformer who called attention to him.

The central objective of these reform movements was not antislavery, except where slaves were directly involved, but respect for the rights of the individual. Woman's rights, universal education, prison reform were all means for magnifying the individual's qualities. Judged by these standards, the truest reformer, in the period 1830–60, included the Negro in his program because he thought of him as a person rather than a cause. So moderate a reformer as Dana, during

[42] Joseph L. Blau (ed.), *Social Theories of Jacksonian Democracy* (New York, 1947), p. xiv.

his visit to John Brown at New Elba, noted how punctilious he was in his treatment of Negroes:

I observed that he called the negroes by their surnames, with the prefixes of Mr. and Mrs. The man was "Mr. Jefferson," and the woman "Mrs. Wait." He introduced us to them in due form, "Mr. Dana, Mr. Jefferson," "Mr. Metcalf, Mrs. Wait." It was plain they had never been so treated or spoken to often before, perhaps never until that day, for they had all the awkwardness of freed hands on a plantation; and what to do on the introduction was quite beyond their experience.[43]

But even when the Negro was the recipient of patronage, rather than respect, he gained from the movement toward individual fulfillment.

[43] Adams, *Dana*, I, 157.

CHAPTER 4

The Antislavery Concert

VIEWS of reform and calls to action vibrated continuously between groups and individuals in Great Britain and the United States. They were initiated either in one or the other, but took their color and content from domestic circumstances.[1]

Although the problem of slavery with which the British were concerned differed radically from that confronting Americans, the slave trade had been reprobated by both. The cruelty of African slave sellers and European and American slave buyers, the inhumane methods used of packing slaves into ships for transportation, and the treatment they received as merchandise on board ship and after being landed in the West Indies, Cuba, Brazil, and the southern American ports had disgusted observers and horrified humanitarians. It had appeared to the antislavery opposition that ending the foreign trade must be the first step to ending slavery itself. In part as a result of coincidence, in part because the movement against the foreign slave trade had gained strength and approval on an international scale, its demise had been voted officially in both Congress and Parliament in March 1807, to take effect the following year.[2]

---

[1] For an example of early intercontinental communication about antislavery, see *Extract of a Letter from Dr. Benjamin Rush of Philadelphia to Granville Sharp* (London, 1792); see also Michael Kraus, "Slavery Reform in the 18th Century: an Aspect of Transatlantic Intellectual Cooperation," *PMHB*, LX (1936), 53 ff.

[2] Thomas Clarkson, *The History of the . . . Abolition of the African Slave-Trade* (London, 1808), I, 283–284. Valuable for its collection of data and references is James Bandinel, *Some Account of the Trade in Slaves from*

In the United States, the slave trade had few friends to defend it, and many enemies, notably in Virginia, which had become a major area for breeding slaves for the market. As a result, it had fallen without a quiver. During the debate, a Mr. Stanton of Rhode Island had joined southern and northern congressmen in opposing the death penalty for nabbed slavers. "I cannot believe that a man ought to be hung," he had observed, "for only stealing a negro."[3]

The crusade against the slave trade had, in Great Britain, enlisted a wide variety of impeccably respectable personages, working under the restricted suffrage conditions of the time with caution and a strong regard for the rights of slaveholders. It had gained from the antislavery position of the Quakers, who offered concerted opposition to the slave trade; in 1783, they had presented to the House of Commons the first petition deploring its continuance. That same year, a number of them had formed among themselves the first British group which aimed to influence public opinion on the subject. Four years later, a society was formed to work for the abolition of the slave trade; of its twelve original members, nine were Quakers. Nevertheless, practically all the most distinguished leaders of the antislave trade and antislavery movements were to be outside that sectarian fold. This was doubtless in part because of their limited political influence on a subject which engaged the most powerful financial and social leaders in the realm. Most moderate, most formal in his approach had been the reformed dilettante and model Evangelical, William Wilberforce, the Parliamentary front for more active and radical workers of abolition. Wilberforce's conservatism and piety had won him a world-wide reputation, far exceeding that of Granville Sharp, Thomas Clarkson, Henry Brougham, Zachary Macaulay, and others among his more resourceful associates. He was even popularly credited with the abolition of slavery itself, though his efforts in this respect had been moderate and he had died before abolition was attained. In America he was esteemed as a philanthropic institution by many who had no regard for abolitionists.

Once the slave trade was driven outside the law, antislavery was

---

Africa as Connected with Europe and America . . . (London, 1842), though its statement of the "extinction" of the traffic is made meaningless by wishful thinking; cf. Thomas F. Buxton, *The African Slave Trade* (London, 1839 ed.).

[3] Henry Wilson, *Rise and Fall of the Slave Power in America* (Boston, 1872), I, 95.

put on the agenda. Here the British situation determined a different course of events from that which would unfold in the States. For the struggle in England was between Parliamentary factions, free to deal as they pleased with their Caribbean islands and their three-quarter million slaves. Once humanitarian considerations were raised in the course of the debate on the slave trade, legal slavery itself was morally foredoomed. On the other side of the water, however, in the American South, the states rights argument left no ground for compromise.

In 1823, the English began their civilized campaign for emancipation. The Anti-Slavery Society which they formed that year, and which superseded the transitional African Institution, was led in the Parliamentary phase of its labors by Thomas Fowell Buxton, wealthy brewer and brother-in-law of Elizabeth Fry, the Quaker prison reformer. Buxton himself was not a Quaker, but gained some antislavery inspiration from those in his family and from other Quaker associations. "He never set eyes upon the black thousands for whom he laboured, never visited either the country of their origin or that of their bondage. He seems to have looked on them in the light of human souls in danger of damnation rather than as human bodies in need of civil rights, congenial conditions and a more easy-going occupation."[4]

Friends in Great Britain, including William Allen, noted scientist and philanthropist, and James Cropper, a Liverpool merchant, maintained their antislavery work. Theirs was once again the first of many petitions, this time praying an end to slavery. Most notable among the Quakers was Joseph Sturge, a Birmingham manufacturer, whose long and radical career, involving personal dedication to numerous reform causes, was to make him a figure somewhat similar as a broad influence to Lewis Tappan in America. Indeed, Sturge would be well known to American abolitionists and reformers throughout the reform period. More immediately urgent to the struggle against British slavery, however, were the Parliamentarians, on the one hand, and the missionaries to the West Indies, on the other. The first formulated a patient set of demands upon the colonial administrators, from religious

---

[4] R. H. Mottram, *Buxton the Liberator* (London, n.d.) ; cf. C. M. MacInnes, *England and Slavery* (Bristol, 1934), p. 168. See also Lowell J. Ragatz, *The Fall of the Planter Class in the British Caribbean, 1763–1833* . . . (New York, 1928), esp. VIII, XII. See also David E. Swift, *Joseph John Gurney: Banker, Reformer, and Quaker* (Middletown, Conn., 1962).

instruction to slaves to controls over the type of punishment which could be inflicted on recalcitrant slaves, all of which demands they were able to persuade British leaders to accept and which helped undermine the prestige of the slaveholder as well as slavery as an institution. The missionaries, for the most part Wesleyan, by their exertions could be credited with having "done more to avert the dangers of emancipation than had been accomplished in ten years of popular agitation and parliamentary effort."[5]

Numerous acts of Parliament and of the colonial legislatures passed into law between 1823 and 1833, aimed to lighten the lot of slaves of Jamaica, Barbados, Trinidad, St. Lucia, and other of the British Caribbean islands. With the passage of the famous Reform Bill of 1832, which tripled the British electorate, it was no longer possible for the antiabolitionists to resist party demands or public opinion, and abolition was voted in the next year. A great compensation of £20 million was given to the slaveholders, and a period of "apprenticeship" set for the former slaves which varied with several classes of hands from six to four years, and which was intended to reassure white colonials against the dangers of social anarchy.

Abolition had yet a distance to go before it found even legal completion on August 1, 1838. Parliamentary questions were asked to determine whether the "apprenticeship" system which had been instituted was being carried out in good faith. Individual investigations, the most effective of which were those by Sturge and Thomas Harvey, incorporated in *The West Indies in 1837* (1837), revealed that oppression and slavery in fact continued. These revelations stirred up a new abolition movement which gave some limited attention to the well-being of the freed Negroes, and considered the incidence of slavery in other British possessions—estimated to involve over 800,000 slaves in British India alone.[6]

Precisely how British antislavery affected the American movement, it is difficult to say. "British Christians are aiding American emanci-

[5] William L. Mathieson, *British Slavery and Its Abolition, 1823–1838* (London, 1926), p. 114.

[6] *First Annual Report of the British and Foreign Anti-Slavery Society . . . Exeter Hall, June 24, 1840 . . .* (London, 1840); *Slavery and the Slave Trade in British India; with Notices of the Existence of These Evils in Ceylon, Malacca, and Penang. Drawn from Office Documents* (London, 1841). For a general history, see Mathieson, *Great Britain and the Slave Trade* (London, 1929).

pationists by their sympathy and their prayers," wrote one gentle chronicler of slavery and the English experience.[7] But their influence went much deeper. British abolitionists offered strength, support, and even money. Canada and England became havens for fugitive slaves, though in relatively small numbers. British visitors were praised or denounced for their views on slavery with a vehemence reserved for significant spokesmen. An important service was performed in 1824 by Elizabeth Heyrick, a British Friend, whose pamphlet, *Immediate, Not Gradual Emancipation,* gave the signal for the British campaign and the slogan which was available to all antislavery workers in the States, but which William Lloyd Garrison first dramatized.[8]

Numerous events contributed to the growth of a crisis psychology in both the North and South. There was the Andrew Jackson "revolution" of 1828, his election to the Presidency, which overturned established political alliances. The year 1829 teemed with incidents, including the official ending of slavery in Mexico, which caused the Yankee settlers of Texas to be concerned for their slave property. That same year saw a cruel riot against the free Negroes of Cincinnati which caused many of them to flee the city and state, clouded as it was by a Black Code. In 1829, too, there was a debate on the slave trade in the District of Columbia, which resulted in resolutions condemning the trade and even looking to the gradual abolition of slavery.

The real crisis was precipitated in August 1831 when a remarkable slave, Nat Turner, a religious fanatic, long convinced that he was destined to free his fellow bondsmen, led a revolt of some seventy Negroes in Southampton County in southeast Virginia.[9] Within twenty-four hours, almost all the men, women, and children of what had

[7] Esther Copley, *A History of Slavery and Its Abolition* (London, 1844 ed.), p. 647; see also Rev. Thomas Price (ed.), *Slavery in America: with Notes of the Present State of Slavery and the Slave Trade Throughout the World* (London, 1837).

[8] An American utterance demanding immediate emancipation appeared the same year: Rev. James Duncan, *A Treatise on Slavery* . . . (Vevay, Ind., 1824). Its force was weakened by an appendix which expected to keep the Negroes under control after they had been "freed." For other expressions of pioneer "immediatism," see Birney, *Birney,* pp. 389 ff., and Adams, *Neglected Period,* pp. 279 ff. Theodore Dwight preached unequivocal immediatism, by name, in *An Oration; Spoken before the Connecticut Society, for the Promotion of Freedom and the Relief of Persons Unlawfully Holden in Bondage* (Hartford, 1794), pp. 6–7.

[9] Aptheker, *Negro Slave Revolts,* pp. 293 ff.; cf. [Samuel E. Warner] *Authentic and Impartial Narrative of the Tragical Scene which was Witnessed*

been a quiet, rural area a few miles from the county seat, Jerusalem, to the number of fifty-seven, had been slaughtered. Advancing on Jerusalem, the insurrectionists were met by a volunteer corps of whites and forced to give ground. Later, heavy reinforcements of troops and militia suppressed the uprising. In a savage massacre many Negroes were killed without trial. This latest of major slave plots evoked memories, North and South, of the gruesome violence which had been reported during the struggles in Santo Domingo several decades before. It alerted Virginians to the dangers among which they lived, and to their need for guarantees against further insurrections.[10]

The Nat Turner affair inspired the fateful debates on slavery of 1831–32 in the House of Delegates. The issue was no longer, as it had so often been before, one merely involving meliorative measures concerning the slave. The new antislavery alliance was not partial toward Negroes; in the proceedings, humanitarians played an insignificant role. The contestants were now legislating for their lives. Such antislavery forces as there were in the Tidewater areas were strengthened by the underrepresented contingent from western Virginia—later, following secession, West Virginia. These spoke for farmers, poor whites, and frontiersmen of an area with few slaves and no desire for them. They continued their struggle, which had come to a head in 1829 in the Virginia Constitutional Convention, for representation in the state legislature based only on the white population.[11] The most widely approved program offered by the antislavery advocates was that of deporting the Negroes. When the dust of controversy had settled, and a motion calling for emancipation and expulsion of the Negroes from the country had been brought to a vote, proslavery was victorious by a decisive though not sweeping majority.[12] The basic weakness of the

in Southampton . . . (New York, 1831). Turner became a major symbol of Negro pride and controversy; cf. William Styron, *The Confessions of Nat Turner* (New York, 1967) and John Henrik Clarke, ed., *William Styron's Nat Turner; Ten Black Writers Respond* (Boston, 1968).

[10] John W. Cromwell, "The Aftermath of Nat Turner's Insurrection," *JNH*, V (1920), 208–234.

[11] *Proceedings and Debates of the Virginia State Convention of 1829–30. To Which Are Subjoined, the New Constitution of Virginia and the Votes of the People* (Richmond, 1830).

[12] Theodore M. Whitfield, *Slavery Agitation in Virginia, 1829–1832* (Baltimore, 1930); J. C. Robert, *The Road from Monticello: a Study of the Virginia Slavery Debate of 1832* (Durham, 1941). B. B. Munford, *Virginia's Attitude toward Slavery and Secession* (New York, 1909), attempts to demonstrate the antislavery record of Virginia and the evil effects of northern

antislavery alliance—its lack of a genuine program of emancipation, its unwillingness to bear the expenses of liberation—had been obscured by the eloquence it had displayed during the debate. The Richmond *Whig* had affirmed:

[T]he great mass of Virginia herself triumphs that the slavery question has been agitated, and reckons it glorious that this spirit of her sons did not shrink from grappling with the monster. We affirm that in the heaviest slave districts of the state, thousands have hailed the discussion with delight, and contemplate the distant but ardently desired result, as the supreme good which a benevolent Providence could vouchsafe to their country.[13]

The same paper was constrained to observe, a few days after, that a bill for deporting free Negroes to Africa had been killed, thanks to differences over the expenses involved: "All goes for nothing, a ludicrous *finale*, all things considered."

Had Virginia decided to free her slaves, or accepted any modification of the concept that slaves as property were necessary to her well-being, it is difficult to see how proslavery could have fastened itself on southern policy as it did. The southern states could not act without Virginia. It is even more difficult to see how abolitionist extremism could have come to dominate the antislavery movement. The failure of the antislavery forces in Virginia in 1832 spelled the total collapse of reform in that state as well.

The decay of reform there would extend not only to slavery, but even to Negro education, and this despite an allegedly friendly attitude on the part of the public.[14] The triumph of slavery was complete. It was not a result of northern aggression toward the South; it no more than fulfilled the rise of militant proslavery which could be clearly perceived from 1818 on.[15]

The policy which would thereafter dominate southern thought was voiced by Thomas R. Dew, professor of history, metaphysics, and political law at William and Mary College. His *Review of the Debate in the Virginia Legislature of 1831 and 1832* was an ambitious survey,

---

abolitionist intervention; see also Kenneth Stampp, "The Fate of the Southern Anti-Slavery Movement," *JNH*, XXVIII (1943), 10–23.

[13] *Niles' Weekly Register*, XLII (March 31, 1832), 78.

[14] *Educational Laws of Virginia: The Personal Narrative of Mrs. Margaret Douglass, a Southern Woman, Who Was Imprisoned for One Month in the Common Jail of Norfolk, under the Laws of Virginia, for the Crime of Teaching Free Colored Children to Read* (Boston, 1854).

[15] Bassett, *Slavery in North Carolina*, pp. 90–100.

both historical and analytical. After justifying slavery in ancient and modern times, Dew went on to examine proposals for freeing Negroes or colonizing them elsewhere, and found all suggestions false. Virginia, he thought, had no need to apologize for that which was good in nature and tradition. The *Review*'s appeal was largely to reason, except when Professor Dew was excited by the suggestion that insurrectionary slaves could be equated with revolutionary heroes: "And has it come at last to this," he asked indignantly: "that the hellish plots and massacres of [the Haitian] Dessalines, Gabriel and Nat Turner, are to be compared to the noble deeds and devoted patriotism of Lafayette, Kosciusko, and Schrynecki? and we suppose the same logic would elevate Lundy and Garrison to niches in the Temple of Fame, by the side of Locke and Rousseau."[16]

It is significant that he should have coupled the names of Lundy and Garrison, for though the first inspired the second, they had very different approaches to slavery. Southerners had become aware that slavery had to be defended or it would be undermined. Their decision to defend it turned them against antislavery in any form.

Garrison's achievement can best be measured by placing him beside the great figures of abolition. Among his followers, Wendell Phillips had greater literary ability, and a patrician heritage as well; Parker Pillsbury, from New Hampshire, had rugged eloquence and passion; Nathaniel P. Rogers was sensitive, earnest, appealing; Maria Weston Chapman came from high social circles, and was vibrant and arresting in her own right. Henry C. Wright was the radical of radicals: a creator of radicalisms and the originator of many of Garrison's formulas. The Garrisonians were varied, picturesque, able, yet none of them denied Garrison pre-eminence, and few withheld admiration even after they had broken with him.

Among the non-Garrisonians, Arthur and Lewis Tappan were central to literally hundreds of abolitionist actions. Gerrit Smith, one of New York State's wealthiest landowners, was unreserved in his commitment to reform. William Jay bore a great name and wrote with distinction and effect. James G. Birney was a prize catch for abolition, being a noted slaveholder who had turned against slavery: a lawyer

[16] (Richmond, 1832), p. 104; cf. Stampp, "An Analysis of T. R. Dew's *Review* . . ." *JNH*, XXVII (1942), 380–387, and William S. Jenkins, *Pro-Slavery Thought in the Old South* (Chapel Hill, 1935), pp. 87–88.

of ability, an abolitionist of courage and noble presence. And so many others, including Theodore D. Weld, whose biographer believed him to be "not only the greatest of the abolitionists, [but] one of the greatest figures of his time,"[17] and who was, certainly, a vital figure of the 1830's. Yet Garrison outranked them one and all as a subject for controversy and as an antislavery symbol, in his own time and after.

When Garrison began his crusade, he had neither family nor wealth nor a striking personality. The son of a demoralized sailor who deserted his family in 1808, Garrison was brought up in poverty in Newburyport, Massachusetts, by an intensely pious Baptist mother. The family broke up early, his mother to go to Baltimore, his elder brother to become a sailor and a disastrous drunkard. Lloyd was a sober, industrious, religious youngster. He bore the family troubles with fortitude, resisted being made a shoemaker and a cabinetmaker, and, in 1818, at the age of thirteen, was an apprentice on the Newburyport *Herald*. Here he learned the printer's trade and published effusions reflecting conventional opinions under the name of "An Old Bachelor." Having served his seven years, and being a seemly if nearsighted young man, neatly dressed and "quite popular with the ladies," he prepared to make a career.

Garrison read and experimented with literary compositions. He thought of joining the Greeks in their struggle with Turkey—inspired, in part, by the adventures of such Americans as Dr. Samuel Gridley Howe, who were aiding that cause—and also of entering West Point. There can be no doubt that Garrison yearned for glory and recognition, but one of his tenacity and moral fiber was not likely to fritter away his energies on empty dreams. He moved as swiftly to his work as did that other great New England youth, Horace Greeley.

Garrison and a second Newburyport printer, Isaac Knapp, issued *The Free Press,* which ran unsuccessfully in 1826 from March to September. It printed the first verses of John Greenleaf Whittier, who was then a shoemaker's apprentice, and whom Garrison sought out and directed into poetry and abolitionist journalism.[18] Garrison then

---

[17] Gilbert H. Barnes, in *DAB,* XIX, 627. The ensuing account of the rise of the antislavery movement may be compared with that in Barnes and Dumond (eds.), *Letters of Theodore Dwight Weld, Angelina Grimké Weld and Sarah Grimké, 1822–1844* (New York, 1934), Introduction, which undertakes to define Weld's title to greatness.

[18] Whittier later rejected Garrisonianism in favor of political abolitionism, but lived to accept Garrison's apotheosis in post-Civil War decades; see Cecil

went on to Boston, where he engaged in a bit of Whiggist newspaper controversy. There, too, he became associated with the Reverend William Collier, who had been issuing the world's first temperance newspaper, the *National Philanthropist*. In January 1828, Garrison became its editor. Piety, peace, total abstinence, and a general search for reform issues characterized his work and reflected his need for a moral universe. He had seen Lundy's *Genius of Universal Emancipation,* but failed to find in it a center for action. Lundy's visit to Boston crystallized his antislavery sentiments. Despite the fact that "gradualist" antislavery societies were strung along the border states, in the South, and, somewhat sparsely, in the middle states, New England boasted almost none. Of the few individuals Lundy managed to convene to discuss antislavery, only Garrison was enthusiastic. Five months' effort by Lundy to stir up interest and organization in New England convened no more than a meeting at a Boston church. Here Lundy mildly discussed the pros and cons of slavery, and recommended a petition campaign to abolish slavery in the District of Columbia.

The meeting was abruptly closed by the church's pastor, who denounced interference with matters of no concern to the assembly. Antislavery, then, was to be considered a sectional question only. Garrison took this proposition with him to Bennington, Vermont, where he had been offered the editorship of the *Journal of the Times.* It was intended to help re-elect John Quincy Adams to the Presidency, but it could also further antislavery, temperance, peace, and moral reform. Garrison's antislavery recommendations were moderate, but his tone was urgent. Lundy may have walked to Bennington to persuade him to come to Baltimore and lend his lively journalism to the erratically issued *Genius;* certainly he wrote with eager hope for Garrison's continued interest in antislavery.[19] On July 4, 1829, Garrison delivered, in Park Street Church, Boston, an oration in which he asserted "the right of the free States to demand a gradual abolition of slavery, because, by its continuance, they participate in the guilt thereof." By September he was in Baltimore, issuing the *Genius.* Between these dates, he had developed a program of immediatism in

---

B. Williams, "Whittier's Relation to Garrison and the 'Liberator,'" *NEQ,* XXV (1952), 248 ff., and letter, Walter M. Merrill, *NEQ,* XXVI (1953), 103–105.

[19] *Genius of Universal Emancipation,* IX (December 27, 1828).

abolition which still welcomed colonization but felt free to acknowledge its limitations. The refurbished *Genius* discussed a variety of antislavery matters, from the cruelty of a local slave trader to the harsh measures taken in the South in retaliation for the publication of Walker's *Appeal*. Yet it was Garrison's condemnation of a slave carrier from Newburyport, his own town, which brought him into court for libel. The court sentenced him to pay a fine of $50 and costs. In default, Garrison was sent to Baltimore Jail on April 17, 1830. The *Genius* had already ceased publication on a partnership basis.

Active and of good conscience, Garrison published *A Brief Sketch of the Trial of William Lloyd Garrison, for an Alleged Libel on Francis Todd, of Massachusetts,* and various communications.[20] He did not sit in prison unnoticed. Eventually, Arthur Tappan paid his fine, and Garrison went north with a plan to publish a vigorous journal in Washington. Investigating possible support in Philadelphia, New York, and elsewhere, he built up the aggressive style which would be his public trademark. In due course, he would be denounced as self-seeking, casuistic, and arbitrary in his dealings with others. Many flaws could be found in his viewpoint even when seen from his own perspective;[21] nevertheless, it must be judged against contemporary circumstances.

Garrison was met by a combination of silence and abuse which, out of his large store of self-righteousness and adroit polemical skill, he answered with effect. He relinquished respectability and fine prospects to issue a paper with a tiny circulation, and that largely among the free Negroes, and with no guarantees of success of any sort; and he kept it going despite notoriety and contempt. "The truth is," his major academic critic averred, "that the *Liberator* was made famous not by its Northern supporters, but by its Southern enemies."[22] This remarkable achievement was better appreciated in Garrison's own

---

[20] An attempt at refutation is contained in *Proceedings against William Lloyd Garrison for a Libel* (Baltimore, 1847).

[21] The copy of [Wendell P. Garrison and Francis J. Garrison] *William Lloyd Garrison, the Story of His Life Told by His Children, 1805–1879* (New York, 1885–1889) in the Antioch College Library belonged to Leonard W. Bacon, son of Leonard Bacon, and was carefully read in order to indict Garrison out of his own deeds and writings, with meager results. See also Leonard W. Bacon, *The Services of Leonard Bacon to African Colonization* (Washington, 1900), and Garrison to Tappan, February 29, 1836, Tappan Papers, LC, with respect to a doubtful financial arrangement.

[22] Barnes, *The Anti-Slavery Impulse, 1830–1844* (New York, 1933), p. 50.

time, which was impressed that a nonentity should have disturbed powerful southern interests—apparently less concerned about abolitionists who took a moderate tone toward slaveholders, the "practical" reformers who were presumably more of a real threat to slavery than were mere "madmen." Garrison was made by intransigent southern proslavery forces, but he did not create them; he unmasked them and their northern counterparts.

Garrison was unusual, too, for the notable set of coworkers he gathered about him. His effect upon people he met has been inadequately grasped. True, he later attracted hatred for having subverted serious abolitionist action. But in the beginning, certainly, when abolitionists were needed who would speak out their sentiments, he marshaled cohorts for the cause. "I remember very distinctly the first time I ever saw Garrison," wrote Lydia Maria Child, who had been a popular writer, author of such works as *The Little Girl's Own Book* (1831):

I little thought then that the whole pattern of my life-web would be changed by that introduction. I was then all absorbed in poetry and painting, soaring aloft on Psyche-wings into the ethereal regions of mysticism. He got hold of the strings of my conscience and pulled me into reform. It is of no use to imagine what might have been if I had never met him. Old dreams vanished, old associates departed, and all things became new.[23]

Garrison's maiden speech in Boston as an immediatist was attended by several churchmen, including Lyman Beecher. Present also was the Reverend Samuel J. May, then known as the only Unitarian minister in Connecticut, along with his cousin Samuel E. Sewall, a young Boston lawyer, and his brother-in-law, Bronson Alcott. The latter's magisterial impracticality has often been remarked. But May's faith in human nature was such that, being in the same room with a lunatic of murderous propensities, he went to sleep. He awoke to find himself threatened with a knife, soothed his companion, then went to sleep again.[24]

[23] *Letters of Lydia Maria Child* (Boston, 1883), p. 255. For her works, see Jacob Blanck (comp.), *Bibliography of American Literature* (New Haven, 1957), pp. 134–156. Her most important abolitionist writing was her first: *An Appeal in Favor of That Class of Americans Called Africans,* published in 1833. Although it did not circulate widely, thanks to her loss of popularity, it did impress Wendell Phillips, Charles Sumner, and the Reverend Dr. Channing, among others.

[24] Thomas J. Mumford (ed.), *Memoir of Samuel Joseph May* (Boston, 1873), pp. 254–256.

Stephen Foster,[25] a young printer and abolitionist, joined Garrison and his old Newburyport associate, Isaac Knapp, in issuing the first number of the *Liberator*, January 1, 1831. However, the *Liberator*, during its first months of publication, attracted only fifty white subscribers. James Forten sent $54 in advance for twenty-seven subscriptions, and other Negroes in Boston, New York, and Philadelphia supplemented the money Garrison received from Sewell and Ellis Gray Loring, his wealthy and aristocratic followers. Arthur Tappan subscribed $1,000 to the work.

The Nat Turner catastrophe suddenly raised Garrison to fame, as reports confused and connected Walker's *Appeal*, the *Liberator*, and the events in Southampton County. The South multiplied statutes, rewards, and denunciations to repel the abolitionists. Thanks to official communications between its governors and Massachusetts, the state became aware of Garrison, though its officials did not find it expedient or necessary to silence him. Garrison became a household word, yet the *Liberator* neither increased in circulation nor influence. Garrison's meetings to form an antislavery society were modestly attended. That of December 16, 1831, brought together only ten persons, including Garrison himself, the already persuaded Sewall, and Loring. Also attracted were David Lee Child, a young lawyer and editor, husband of Lydia, and Oliver Johnson, who was to be a Garrison stalwart and editor for almost half a century, and to defend him against detractors.[26] Later additions included Arnold Buffum, a Friend, long committed to gradual abolition; unlike the others a man of business, a hat manufacturer, who was to move from the Garrison camp to the Liberty party. The Reverend Amos A. Phelps would be one of the most effective of the more moderate Garrisonians until he broke with them in 1838. So would Amasa Walker, a Boston merchant and political economist, who would help found Oberlin College, teach there, work outstandingly in the peace reform, and serve in Congress. One

---

[25] Foster, who died soon after, is readily confused with the more important Stephen S. Foster, a revivalist and schoolteacher who joined the movement in 1839 and figured in sensational Garrisonian episodes; see Parker Pillsbury, "Stephen Symonds Foster," *Granite Monthly*, V (1882), 369–375. Lundy urged "friends of humanity" to hasten to the *Liberator*'s aid; *Genius of Universal Emancipation*, XI (February, 1831).

[26] Oliver Johnson, *William Lloyd Garrison and His Times* . . . (Boston, 1880), and "The Abolitionists Vindicated in a Review of Eli Thayer's Paper on the New England Emigrant Aid Company," *Proc. of the Worcester Soc. of Antiquity* . . . *1866*, XXV (1887), 17 ff.

of Garrison's most distinguished converts was Dr. Karl Follen, a German scholar and liberal who fled persecution and became a professor of German at Harvard College. His decision to adhere to abolitionists resulted in his professorship not being renewed. In 1840, his notable services as a minister, antislavery lecturer, and moral preceptor ended abruptly in the destruction of the steamboat *Lexington*.[27]

These were some of the men who concluded that the future lay in abolitionist action. But it must be borne in mind that a quarter of the original seventy-two names which were affixed to the new constitution of the New-England Anti-Slavery Society were colored men, some scarcely able to write.

This first immediatist society projected a full-bodied program,[28] which it lacked the sinews and opportunities to develop. Garrison's other achievement of the year, however, was fully as significant as the founding of the *Liberator* and the Society. His thick pamphlet, *Thoughts on African Colonization . . .* (1832), struck a hard blow at the movement it examined. Particularly incisive was his appended "Resolutions, Addresses and Remonstrances of the Free People of Color," revealing as they did the chasm separating the American Colonization Society from the race it was supposed to serve. That Garrison's was a rude blast, there can be no doubt, though in distinguishing between the Society's program and Lundy's own quixotic colonization efforts, Garrison was more subtle than anyone else on the scene. More important was the fact that he forced the colonizationists to clarify their real intentions and speak out about them. Some abolitionists Garrison disillusioned out of hand, as at Western Reserve College, where the president, Charles B. Storrs, and two professors, Beriah Green and Elizur Wright, Jr., turned immediately against colonization.[29] The Tappans were only two among the front-line aboli-

---

[27] E. L. Follen, *The Life of Charles Follen* (Boston, 1844); William E. Channing, *A Discourse Occasioned by the Death of the Rev. Dr. Follen* (Boston, 1840); Samuel J. May, *A Discourse on the Life and Character of the Rev. Charles Follen . . .* (Boston, 1840); George W. Spindler, *The Life of Karl Follen: a Study in German-American Cultural Relations* (Chicago, 1917). See also Eliza C. Follen, *The Works of Charles Follen . . .* (5 vols., Boston, 1842).

[28] Garrison defined his program as follows: "Urge immediate abolition as earnestly as we may, it will, alas! be gradual abolition in the end. We have never said that slavery would be overthrown by a single blow; that it ought to be, we shall always contend" (Garrisons, I, 228).

[29] Frederick C. Waite, *Western Reserve University: the Hudson Era* (Cleveland, 1943), pp. 95 ff.

tionists who thereafter washed their hands of colonization, Arthur himself purchasing a hundred copies of Garrison's pamphlet for distribution. One among many major efforts to defend the Society by a distinguished New Haven Congregationalist minister (later to have his own strategic place in the abolition crusade) succeeded only in calling attention to the points at issue.[30] The campaign which Garrison initiated culminated in the publication of *Jay's Inquiry,* as it came to be called, which no one could pretend to ignore.[31] Its high organization, dignified prose, and monument of data exposed the Society: its anti-Negro bias, its proslavery affections, and the brutal methods employed to force the migration of free Negroes to Liberia. It inspired a notable cry of pain which mixed fear of the harm Jay had done to colonization with fear of abolition.[32]

Garrison's great coup of 1833 was his trip to England, ostensibly to gather money for a manual training school for Negroes, but also to combat the efforts of the Colonization Society agent, Elliott Cresson, who was abroad. Garrison wished also to establish regular communication with British abolitionists. He arrived in a festive atmosphere: abolition had been proclaimed in Great Britain. It was a triumph qualified, to Garrison's mind, by the more than generous compensation of £20 million to the slaveholders. Garrison may have overdramatized his trip to England, which may have been less the result of popular demand than his own creation. In addition, no Negro school resulted from his trip. But he won the support of all the titans of British abolition, who knew him already by reputation (Buxton had imagined he was black); he won their expressed condemnation of colonization; and he returned the momentary leader of abolitionism in America.

Meanwhile, however, New York abolitionists were sensing that the time for organization had come. The East and Middle West were covered by a light mantle of abolitionists and abolition-minded groups

---

[30] [Leonard Bacon] *Review of Pamphlets on Slavery and Colonization . . .* (New Haven, 1833).

[31] It was, however, ignored in Fox, *American Colonization Society. Jay's Inquiry* went into three editions during its first year, as well as into an English edition, and was in its tenth edition by 1840. See also Jay's preface to G. B. Stebbins, *Facts and Opinions Touching the Real Origin, Character, and Influence of the American Colonization Society . . .* (Boston, 1853).

[32] David M. Reese, *Letters to the Hon. William Jay . . .* (New York, 1835).

and journals. New York City wanted an organization which could help lead the way to more ambitious programs. Joshua Leavitt, then editing the *Evangelist*, was a directing hand among the organizers, along with William Jay and the Tappans. So was William Goodell, who had been Garrison's successor on the *National Philanthropist*, and who had then edited first the *Genius of Temperance*, next the *Emancipator*, established by the Tappans in 1833. In 1835, Goodell was to go to Utica and there edit the *Friend of Man* and also co-operate with an active group of abolitionists who dreamed of political action.[33] Elizur Wright was also a luminary among the New Yorkers. Since leaving Western Reserve College, he had published *The Sin of Slavery and Its Remedy* and was about to turn all his writing and administrative ability to the cause. John Rankin, too—not the Reverend John Rankin of Ohio—was one of a number of New York merchant-reformers who gave time in abundance to abolitionism. And indefatigable in reform, even among his dedicated associates, was Isaac T. Hopper. In his Philadelphia period, he had served the Negroes on innumerable occasions. He was a leading Hicksite, radical among the Quakers. Hopper founded and kept active a society for employing the poor, was an overseer for the Benezet School for colored children, an unpaid teacher in a free school for Negro adults, and long an unpaid inspector of prisons. Abused apprentices, runaway slaves, and the friendless criminal and insane found a friend in Hopper. Moving to New York, he and his son-in-law James S. Gibbons continued their sometimes dangerous work.[34]

Such were some of the men who were to lead the new society. Arthur Tappan paved the way with the publication and distribution of antislavery tracts—most effectively, 5,000 copies of Whittier's *Justice and Expediency* (1833). Tappan and his colleagues announced that an antislavery society was to be formed on October 2 at Clinton Hall. Provocative notices brought a mob there, but the hall had been vacated owing to a trustees' decision not to make it available. Only Hopper calmly decided to stay on and see what the mob might wish to do. The others convened at the Chatham Street Chapel and concluded their business in time to disperse before the mob arrived.[35]

[33] *In Memoriam. William Goodell. Born in Coventry, N. Y., October 25th, 1792. Died in Janesville, Wis., February 14th, 1878* (Chicago, 1879).

[34] L. Maria Child, *Isaac T. Hopper: a True Life* (Boston, 1853), pp. 389 ff. and *passim*.

[35] [Tappan] *Tappan*, pp. 168 ff.; Johnson, *Garrison and His Times*, p. 145.

The "Martyr Age," as the English writer and visitor to America, Harriet Martineau, was to call it, had already begun. In the fall of 1832, a female boarding school had been opened in Canterbury, Connecticut, by Miss Prudence Crandall of Rhode Island. She had read the *Liberator* and been impressed by its message. A "pious colored female" having applied for admission, she accepted her. Miss Crandall was threatened and, after considering further, discontinued her school. In February 1833, she announced that she was opening a school for colored girls, and shortly after assembled some fifteen or twenty of them, with the aid of Garrison, whose advice she sought and received. To the Garrisonians, subsequent events were a living answer to the question why they did not carry on their agitation in the South, where the slaves actually were. The "moral cholera" of the North, they insisted, gave them more than enough to do at home. The Crandall case was a Garrisonian project from start to finish, though this fact was forgotten as its implications for civil liberties took the country's attention.

The Canterbury townspeople determined to rid themselves of the little school, and boycotted Miss Crandall and her children, who could purchase nothing in town. They were subjected to insults, the school doors and steps were smeared with filth, and the well fouled. An obsolete vagrancy law was resurrected making the children, after being warned to leave, liable to fines and to whippings "on the naked body not exceeding ten stripes." A warrant was served on one girl, but Miss Crandall was being supported by Samuel J. May, Arnold Buffum, and George W. Benson, soon to be Garrison's father-in-law. No effort was made to enforce the writ, which might as properly have been served on Yale College students who were residents of other states.

The issue was joined late in May, when the state legislature passed a law making illegal any such school as Miss Crandall's. Bells and cannon sounded in Canterbury to celebrate the victory. On June 27, the determined young woman was taken into custody. To the dismay

---

Inadequately explained, by friend or foe, has been Garrison, who arrived from England, September 29, possibly spent several days at quarantine, but was present at the Clinton Hall turmoil, though unrecognized by the bravos. Oddly, he did not make contact with the New York abolitionists but went directly to Boston. His name was loosely flung about by the rioters, but Garrisons, I, 380 ff., finds connections between him and the organization of the New York Anti-Slavery Society which are without foundation.

of her keepers, she and her advisers refused to provide bond, and the embarrassing ritual of imprisonment had to be completed, bond being given the following day.[36]

Arthur Tappan came to Canterbury, provided the money for the expensive court action in prospect, and recommended publicity; as a result Charles C. Burleigh was made editor of the extemporized *The Unionist* and, incidentally, turned from a law career of conventional promise into one of the memorable Garrisonian agitators. The resulting trials, which take high place in the legal history of civil rights, produced striking arguments on both sides.[37] One of the arguments offered by the prosecution was that free colored people were not citizens; for if they were, laws could not be passed discriminating against the children. This was the argument which William Gaston, speaking for the Supreme Court of North Carolina, was to reject in 1838.[38] Although the trials ended inconclusively, harassment continued, including an attempted burning of the school and a more successful assault upon it with clubs and iron bars. So it closed its doors, but it had shown the way to abolitionists and inspired their organization.

The later fight for the right of petition opened a road to attack slavery in its southern stronghold, and thus could appear a more realistic campaign than any being conducted in the North. Yet the petition fight could not have been waged before Northerners had reached an understanding of their own rights as citizens. The fight of the reformers, then, was not peripheral to the organization of great political issues; it was a necessary preliminary to them.

Such Philadelphians as Evan Lewis, an associate of Lundy, Dr. Edwin P. Atlee, and Abram L. Pennock, valid friends of the Negro though they were, were aware that the New Yorkers were more re-

---

[36] Her cell was "nicely cleaned and whitewashed, and had a comfortable bed put in it, and one of [Helen Eliza Benson's] sisters, Miss Anne Benson consented to go and spend a night with Miss Crandall." *Proc. of the American Anti-Slavery Soc. . . .* (New York, 1864), pp. 45–46. It helped the cause that the cell had lately been inhabited by a murderer. For primary accounts of the Crandall persecution, see Garrisons, I, 321. Samuel J. May, *Some Recollections of Our Antislavery Conflict* (Boston, 1869), pp. 39 ff., recaptures a sense of the crisis. See also Alfred T. Child, Jr., "Prudence Crandall and the Canterbury Experiment," *BFHA*, XXII (1933), 35–55.

[37] Helen T. Catterall (ed.), *Judicial Cases Concerning American Slavery and the Negro* (Washington, 1926–1937), IV, 413–417, 430–433.

[38] *Ibid.*, II, 82–83.

sourceful than themselves and better able to plead their cause before
the public. Evan Lewis was sent to New York to confer with the Tappans and to request them to send out a call for a national convention.
It was issued October 29, 1833, for a meeting to convene December 4
in Philadelphia. Of the sixty-two people who met amid local suspicion
and dislike, twenty-one were Friends. These included Lucretia Mott
and three other women, in itself a notable event. They comported
themselves modestly, and were not asked—nor did they expect—to
sign the convention's organizing document.[39] But every detail of their
presence and participation would be recalled during the later struggle
over women's rights in the antislavery movement.

Roberts Vaux, an affluent and conservative Friend, notable in prison
reform, was not in actual attendance; he was asked to preside but
declined. Time was lost considering other markedly respectable possibilities before Beriah Green made his ironic comment: "If there is
not timber amongst ourselves big enough to make a president of, let
us get along without one, or go home and stay there until we have
grown up to be men." Green, now president of Oneida Institute, and
a man of resolution and strength, became himself the presiding officer.
Garrison was chosen, with May and Whittier, to prepare a Declaration of Sentiments, and substantially drew it up. This and other
details of the proceedings justified his biographers in imagining him
as having "called the Convention into being." The Convention offered
Garrison eulogies; but abolition had expanded beyond his controls,
though not beyond his influence.

Now abolition became organization: a combination of evangelical
Christianity and antislavery, and of New England ideals, moved from
the Atlantic Ocean to the Mississippi River.[40] It was never precisely
known how many societies or members the American Anti-Slavery
Society possessed: "our 4 or 500 societies," Garrison called them late
in 1835. "What!" wrote Weld, early the next year, "another Convention for the formation of a State Anti-Slavery Society! Massachusetts, Vermont, Maine, New-Hampshire, Kentucky [an abortive effort],
Ohio, New-York, and now Rhode-Island!"[41] In 1835 alone, 328 ad-

[39] Anna D. Hallowell (ed.), *James and Lucretia Mott, Life and Letters*
(Boston, 1884), pp. 111 ff.; cf. Otelia Cromwell, *Lucretia Mott* (Cambridge,
1958), pp. 48–49.

[40] Lois K. Mathews, *The Expansion of New England . . . 1620–1865* (Boston, 1909).

[41] *Proc. of the Rhode-Island Anti-Slavery Convention . . .* (Providence,

ditional societies were reported, claiming 27,182 members in 254 societies, the others not reporting their membership. By 1838, the national society could officially claim 1,350 societies, with a membership of perhaps 250,000.[42]

"In 1832," said James Henry Hammond, the southern nationalist, bitterly, ". . . the New England Anti-Slavery Society was formed. This I believe was the first Society of this kind created on this side of the Atlantic. I remember well the ridicule with which it was covered when it was known that it had been formed by a meeting of eleven persons."[43] In 1837, it could claim 145 Garrison-led societies in Massachusetts alone; there was never any question but that Garrison was the leader of abolitionism in New England.[44] However, New York State had 274 societies and a virile state organization, while Ohio reported 213 societies and had the other most effective network of state affiliates. The New York-Ohio connection was firm and distinct. Its operation could best be seen in the chain of events which created Lane Seminary and Oberlin College.

Weld had been sent west to spread the gospel of temperance and manual labor, but his enthusiasm for manual training waned as his concern over slavery deepened, from colonization to immediatism.[45] He had also been instructed to find a proper site for a manual labor institution which would train young men for home missionary work, mainly designed to oppose Catholicism in the West. He visited Lane Seminary, already instituted by clergymen eager to save perishing Cincinnati; as the Reverend Amos Blanchard, deemed liberal in

---

1836). This Garrison-led assembly was brought together on a call signed by 850 citizens (*ibid.*, p. 3).

[42] For figures reporting growth, see *Annual Reports* of the Society for the years 1834–1839.

[43] *Remarks of Mr. Hammond, of South Carolina, on the Question of Receiving Petitions for the Abolition of Slavery in the District of Columbia. Delivered in the House of Representatives, February 1, 1836* (Washington, n.d.), p. 5.

[44] Figures for other New England states included Maine, 33; New Hampshire, 63; Vermont, 89; Rhode Island, 25; Connecticut, 39.

[45] The manual labor movement grew phenomenally, some sixty of the eighty colleges of the country assuming it, as well as many theological seminaries, several medical schools, and several hundred academies. By 1840, manual labor had been revealed as impractical and abandoned as a major educational program; see Waite, *Western Reserve University*, pp. 72 ff.; [Weld] *First Annual Report of the Society for Promoting Manual Labor in Literary Institutions* (New York, 1833); Earle D. Ross, "The Manual Labor Experiment in the Land Grant College," *MVHR*, XXI (1935), 513 ff.

theology, said, they were in an area containing four million people and able to sustain one hundred million; and in Cincinnati:

> The whole number of attendants in the 4 Presbyterian churches does not exceed 3,000. There may possibly be as many more in all the other evangelical churches. Six thousand subtracted from 28,000 leaves 22,000 who either do not attend anywhere, or only where *damnable* error is preached. . . . There is in this city a very large Roman Catholic cathedral, a Jew Synagogue, a Swedenborgian Church, 1 Unitarian, one Universalist, one Campbellite Baptist, and one Christian or New Light Society. The regular attendants at these poisonous fountains may possibly be 3 or 4,000. . . . Besides these nominal Christians, we have a large number of Infidels, Owenites, Atheists, and Fanny Wright men [sic] who with open mouth and daring front, lift high the arm and rant out aloud their blasphemies against God.[46]

Beecher was to head the new Seminary. Asa Mahan, a Finney associate, was a rugged and liberal minister among the trustees. Numerous students were convening from New York, from the Middle West, and from the South. Weld felt he need go no further; Lane was the proper place for their plans, he informed the Tappans, who opened their purse to it. Weld remained on, bringing a contingent of Oneida Institute students to it and helping to choose its professors. These soon included Calvin E. Stowe, formerly of Dartmouth College, who taught Biblical Literature. He was not yet married to the president's daughter Harriet.

The brilliant assembly of some ninety students, with more coming, included Henry B. Stanton of Rochester and James A. Thome from Kentucky, who several years before, as a student, had heard James G. Birney praise the Clarksons and Wilberforces of the world and hold them up for emulation. Others included William T. Allan of Alabama; Marius R. Robinson, who became an outstanding Ohio abolitionist;[47] and James Bradley, "a man of color," admitted to the Literary Department. Lane Seminary stirred with classes, manual labor, and Sunday School services for white people and Negroes.

Here, early in 1834, Weld brought about the most strategic act of his relatively brief abolitionist career. A powerful, humorless controversialist and leader, he had taken his place with the students, though

---

[46] Fletcher, *History of Oberlin College*, I, 47–48.
[47] Betty Fladeland, *James Gillespie Birney* . . . (Ithaca, 1955), pp. 41–42; Russel B. Nye, "Marius Robinson: a Forgotten Abolitionist Leader," *OAHQ*, LV (1946), 138–154.

he could have had a professorship. He now laid the ground for a major discussion on slavery. The Lane Debate, when it came, brought together all the students and most of the faculty, and even brought Beecher to some of the sessions. Nine days of discussion led by Weld resulted in an overwhelming affirmative vote on the question "Ought the people of the slave-holding states to abolish slavery immediately?" Nine days of further intensive argument spelled an end to colonization ideas at Lane. The students organized an antislavery society and set up an intensive program for Negroes.

During the summer, the trustees convened and concluded with a report which argued that "education must be completed before the young are fitted to engage in the collisions of active life."[48] Weld had already had occasion to notice that nine students of the Theological Department were between thirty and thirty-five years of age, and thirty were over twenty-six; but nevertheless, their extracurricular activities were to be ended. An issue as instructive as that which the Crandall case had presented was now debated by an awakening public. No less significant were the actions of the students themselves. In October forty of them, including Weld, resigned. Some of them scattered to other seminaries, or bent to authority and returned. A core of them held together and continued their studies at a nearby town.

In the northeast corner of Ohio was the little town of Elyria. Here the Reverend John Jay Shipherd, a Finney enthusiast, had set down the Oberlin Institute, intended to nurture ministerial talents which would ensure salvation to the Midwest. Opened in 1833, it quickly began to founder, and by the autumn of 1834 was in trouble. Shipherd made contact with Asa Mahan, who had vigorously defended Lane's militant students. A new beginning was projected for Oberlin. The Tappans could be counted on to provide funds if an antislavery stand was assumed by the college. Coeducation was already in its program. It was, surprisingly, the provision that Oberlin was to be opened to Negroes which roused protest among the Oberlin pioneers; Finney himself, who was part of the reinvigorated project, was a conservative on the subject. Painful arguments preceded the final an-

[48] Fletcher, *History of Oberlin College*, I, 150 ff. This chapter, "The Test of Academic Freedom," is the most balanced account of the Lane uprising. See also John Rankin, *A Review of the Statement of the Faculty of Lane Seminary, in Relation to the Recent Difficulties in That Institution* (Ripley, Ohio, 1835).

nouncements: that Mahan was to head Oberlin, that Finney had been made professor of theology, and that $10,000 had been received for buildings. The Lane rebels were at home, and Oberlin was at the beginning of its unprecedented career in abolition and reform.

It would misconstrue the abolitionist crusade not to appreciate its roots in ordinary people. The most famous reformers were merely elements of an advance guard of antislavery workers, made notable by accident or peculiarities. They were not different in kind from such a teacher in colored schools as one who reported her affairs from Mount Pleasant, Ohio, to her "Esteemed Cousins":

the Anniversary of the Ohio Anti-Slavery Society held its meetings at Short creek meeting house on the 27th 28th and 29th of last month, it was a very interesting meeting, I believe there were about two hundred and fifty delegates from the different Anti-Slavery Societies in the state and there were a great many in attendance who were not delegates, there were a hundred young women there who have been teaching coloured schools in different parts of this state there were two young women by the name of Wright have been teaching school in Chil[l]icothe they are sisters, there were two other sisters by the name of Wright who are teaching school in Cincinnati Axia Colburn is teaching school in Putnam Sarah Galbraith is teaching in Dayton Emily Robinson [wife of Marius] has been teaching in Cincinnati Phebe Weed has been teaching in Cincinnati Emeline McConnel has been teaching in Logan County Hannah Barker has been teaching in Brown County I heard her say there was not a white family within six miles of her she could have any intercourse with there were two young men here who have been teaching coloured schools one in Cincinnati the other in Canada, these that I have mentioned I believe are all the nigger teachers that I became acquainted with, the most of these have gone a great distance from home and have undergone a great many trials and have barely received enough to buy them provisions and some not enough there are but a few of them that could get boarding in white families some have boarded with coloured people but the most of them have rented rooms and boarded them-selves it is almost impossible for some to get rooms. . . .[49]

Despite such relatively routine activities by individuals who had no bizarre aims or desire to be offensive to their neighbors, the antislavery movement demanded that some of its partisans jeopardize their liveli-

[49] Eliza Ann Griffith to Jane and Rebecca Woolman, Damascus, Columbiana County, Ohio, "5th month 6th 1837," WRHS MSS.

hoods, their personal relations, and even their lives.[50] "The Martyr Age" was created by mobs and unsympathetic law-enforcement agencies. It was largely a northern phenomenon, though there were startling exceptions to this rule. Most startling, perhaps, was the brief sojourn of the Reverend George Frederick Simmons in Mobile, Alabama, in 1836. This was two years after the Reverend Joel Parker, in the liberal phase of his career, had been hanged in effigy at New Orleans for sentiments deemed offensive to slavery. "Will his elders persist in bringing him back to the city?" the *Louisiana Advertiser* had asked. "If they do the consequence be on their heads, for they can no longer doubt that disorders, riots, and perhaps bloodshed, will be the consequence."[51] Now came young Reverend Simmons, then a Unitarian, to "supply" a pulpit such as southern ministerial resources could not always fill. Simmons had already, in the North, defended Channing's new book on slavery from conservative New England criticism. In Mobile, Alabama, he spoke as earnestly on the character of Christ, as he conceived it, as he did on the proper treatment and due emancipation of slaves. He appears to have been more concerned for accurate interpretations of his argument than for the fact that he had not been far from death. It is significant that, much later, in Springfield, Massachusetts, and in a period which academic students would interpret as having seen the victory of free speech, his study would be "broken in by the note of riot," a result of local indignation because of the freeing of a fugitive slave: "It is well known [Simmons explained] that I have a degree of sympathy with the Abolitionists. But I do not know that this is a crime. In another place it *was* so considered, by the multitude who only heard of it abroad. But here, I trust, it is not reckoned a crime to share the opinions of Channing, of Franklin, and of Wilberforce."[52]

Simmons was a mere flaw in southern uniformity, but the North witnessed a succession of antiabolitionist actions. Weld's talents helped precipitate them. He himself was mobbed countless times, despite his

[50] [Harriet Martineau] *The Martyr Age in the United States of America, with an Appeal on Behalf of the Oberlin Institute in Aid of the Abolition of Slavery* (Newcastle upon Tyne, 1840).

[51] Quoted in *Working Man's Advocate*, VI (December 20, 1834); cf. Clarence Gohdes, "Some Notes on the Unitarian Church in the Ante-Bellum South . . ." in David K. Jackson (ed.), *American Studies in Honor of William Kenneth Boyd* (Durham, 1940), pp. 327 ff.

[52] George F. Simmons, Pastor of the Third Congregational Society, Springfield, *Public Spirit and Mobs, Two Sermons . . .* (Boston, 1851), p. 14.

manifest sincerity and power to persuade. One friend of abolition remembered how Weld "held increasing audiences at fever pitch, with his flashing eye, his clarion tones and marvellous eloquence, without manuscript or note, for sixteen successive evenings." But his voice was affected in 1836, and did not recover substantially before his full retirement from the antislavery movement in 1842.[53] However, he earlier turned his energies to the grand project of the American Anti-Slavery Society: to collect a host of agents to abolitionize the country. Weld instructed and inspired some seventy notable talents and sent them forth. Few, if any, escaped continuing insults and physical danger. Henry B. Stanton was mobbed at least two hundred times, and yet he had none of the unorthodox notions which Garrisonians developed.[54] The records of all the antislavery evangelists are strewn with their shattered meetings, tar-and-feathering incidents, and fearless appeals to civil rights which held completed tragedies to a minimum.

In 1834 there was a second riot at the Chatham Street Chapel, now host to the American Anti-Slavery Society, but one vastly more successful from the viewpoint of the rioters. It is possible that the presence of free Negroes added fury to the assault. The disturbance was the beginning of a three-day riot, during which the antiabolitionists themselves held a meeting; a stage production was broken up at the Bowery Theater on the rumor that the stage manager, a Britisher, had made anti-American remarks; Lewis Tappan's home was sacked; and several other churches were damaged on the assumption that their pastors were abolitionists.[55]

Riots the next year at Utica, where six hundred delegates had met to form a state antislavery society, inspired Gerrit Smith to receive the reformers at his vast estate at Peterboro. The riots were the final straw to one who had been heart and hand in colonization, even down to its casual prejudices. Smith was to lend his wealth and awkward

[53] Luther R. Marsh (ed.), *Writings and Speeches of Alvan Stewart* (New York, 1860), p. 35; Benjamin P. Thomas, *Theodore Weld* (New Brunswick, 1950), pp. 117 ff.; [Samuel Webb] *History of Pennsylvania Hall* . . . (Philadelphia, 1838), p. 8.

[54] An incomplete list of "The Seventy" is in Dumond (ed.), *Birney*, I, 357; Henry B. Stanton, *Random Recollections* (Johnstown, N.Y., 1885), p. 27.

[55] For an account by an eyewitness and all but victim, see Leavitt to his parents, July 12, 1834, Leavitt Papers, LC; see also "Defensor" [William Thomas], *The Enemies of the Constitution Discovered, or, an Enquiry into the Origin and Tendency of Popular Violence* (New York, 1835).

perfectionism to numerous reform causes, and he now joined the abolitionists.[56]

That same year of 1835, a significant step was taken by one who had become a key abolitionist. James G. Birney's path from acceptance as a reformer in the South to public prosecution as an abolitionist in the North was an epitome of the problem which faced moderate and extreme abolitionists alike. An Alabama lawyer of family, wealth, and prestige, in 1832 he made his final turn away from the life of a planter aristocrat. He had already been converted for a number of years, shown sympathy for the Indians, and engaged in the usual benevolences. He was opposed to slavery. It was the uncompromising stand of the South to the implications of Nat Turner's uprising which made Birney consider leaving for Illinois. The offer of the American Colonization Society to make him its agent for the Southwest seemed providential. Weld came south preaching temperance, and they gave each other strength; as Weld then put it, encouraging Birney in his work, "I am ripe in the conviction that if the Colonization Society does not dissipate the horror of darkness which overhangs the southern country, we are undone. Light breaks *in from no other quarter.*"[57] Weld had not made contact with Boston abolitionism at that time, but he could not be, and Birney had not been, unaware of its effect on proslavery opinion. Their attention centering on the conversion of slaveholders, they rejected Garrison's approach. Birney entered wholeheartedly into the task of winning his fellow slaveholders over to colonization. In 1833, he moved to Kentucky, and there organized the Kentucky Society for the Gradual Relief of the State from Slavery. Among disheartening neighbors, and with news from Lane Seminary and New York stirring him, conviction over colonization left him. "Its dead carcass . . . is still occasionally thrown before the community," he wrote Lewis Tappan sadly, "and all the Rabbis consult how it can be restored to life."

[56] Ralph V. Harlow, *Gerrit Smith: Philanthropist and Reformer* (New York, 1939), pp. 113 ff.; see also Octavius B. Frothingham, *Gerrit Smith, a Biography* (New York, 1878), pp. 165 ff.

[57] Weld to Birney, September 27, 1832, Dumond (ed.), *Birney*, I, 27; cf. Fladeland, *James Gillespie Birney*, p. 53. Barnes, *Anti-Slavery Impulse*, bent on proving Weld central to abolitionism, is inaccurate (pp. 39, 69). Incidentally, it underrates Birney, deemed "negligible . . . in the councils of the [abolitionist] movement . . . an admirable but not a great man" (p. 262).

Birney was now famous among northern abolitionists: a rehabili-
tated slaveholder who might create a wedge of antislavery sentiment
among his former associates. But Birney was losing his faith in old
anticipations. "I am more and more convinced," he wrote, "from
many of the proceedings at the north, that they are, in the main,
ignorant of the Slaveholder's *tenacity,* and of the moral obliquities that
Slavery has produced in him." Northern hopes that he would publish
an antislavery newspaper in Kentucky, though he made courageous
efforts to fulfill them, ended before the courteous but firm letter of
his neighbors, officially warning him "how you make an experiment
here, which no *American Slaveholding community* has found itself
able to bear."

Birney had suffered in fortune and family, had freed his own slaves,
and would later take his inheritance in slaves in order to free them.
He had come to the end of his resources for converting the South. He
retreated with the remnants of his family and household goods to
Cincinnati, at a time when Ohio abolitionists were ready to organize
on a state-wide basis. Present at their convention at Putnam were a
tried set of abolitionists. They included seasoned veterans like John
Rankin, as well as crusaders like Weld and Elizur Wright, who had
become widely known through the American Anti-Slavery Society.[58]

The South as well as the North stirred in self-defense against the
abolitionists. In 1831, Governor John Floyd of Virginia, father of a
later governor and statesman of the same name, sent a letter north.
Although it was addressed to the governor of New York, the letter
protested the incendiary views published by the "people of color" who
had met in Philadelphia, denounced an address which Garrison had
delivered in several states and then published, and expressed offense
because the *Liberator* could be published in Boston. Such writings,
wrote Floyd, were likely to arouse "feelings to be depricated [*sic*] in
friendly nations much less those who are members of the same confederacy." He hoped the northern states had laws "to restrain and
punish these libellous and incendiary papers: if not the law of nations
will fully warrant their persecution."[59]

[58] *Proc. of the Anti-Slavery Convention Held at Putnam* . . . (Cincinnati,
1835).
[59] John Floyd to the Governor of New York, December 3, 1831, Simon
Gratz Collection, HSP. Copies may have been sent to all governors of the
North; cf. Garrisons, I, 241, 311. For a general view, Henry H. Simms, *Emotion at High Tide: Abolition as a Controversial Factor* (Richmond, Va., 1960).

Thus the governor thought the suppression of the abolitionists ought to be a community project of the states. Southern law operated as informally. Amos Dresser, a young Lane student from New York State, decided to bring the Bible to the South. His reason for being in Tennessee in 1835 was professedly to earn money to complete his education. He also had with him abolitionist newspapers, for protecting his books, he said. He sold one copy of Rankin's *Letters,* and later claimed that he carried Bourne's *Pictures of Slavery* solely for his own use. There seems no doubt that Dresser was on a personal antislavery mission. Seized in Nashville and taken before a Committee of Vigilance, he asserted his antislavery principles, but denied any malicious intentions. He received twenty lashes before a large and approving gathering, and left in disguise after, he said, he had been taken in by strangers. Dresser was one of the famous "Seventy" who proselytized the backwoods in behalf of abolitionism. He later joined Elihu Burritt in the latter's peace enterprises before settling in Ohio as a pastor.[60]

Dr. Reuben Crandall was the younger brother of Prudence, and had settled in Washington to teach botany. In August of that ripe year of 1835, he was arrested and lodged in prison, charged with intent to circulate incendiary publications. Francis Scott Key, the district attorney, was pious as well as patriotic, an ardent Jacksonian as well as an associate of the Tappans in their campaign for Sabbath observance. He "avowed, from the first, his determination to subject [Crandall] to capital punishment."[61] Key was an active colonizationist, but vehement on the subject of Crandall and his "fiend-like" doctrines. Such was the spirit of the city that a friend of Crandall, Ransom G. Williams, of New York, whose testimony was important to Crandall's defense, did not dare to appear at the trial, having been warned that his life was endangered. Williams had published the view that "God commands, and all nature cries out, that man should not be held as property." For this he was indicted in Alabama, and its governor demanded of the governor of New York that he be extradited as a

[60] *The Narrative of Amos Dresser* . . . (New York, 1836); Henry W. Cushman, *A Historical and Biographical Genealogy of the Cushmans* (Boston, 1855), pp. 626 ff.

[61] William Goodell, *Slavery and Anti-Slavery* . . . (New York, 1852), pp. 437–438. Key avowed his desire that the prisoner receive "every advantage of a fair trial," but was very clear that the challenge of immediate emancipation was at stake, to be stopped at all hazards; see *The Trial of Reuben Crandall* (Washington, 1836), p. 46, and Edward S. Delaplaine, *Francis Scott Key, Life and Times* (New York, 1937), p. 308.

fugitive from justice.[62] Crandall was acquitted, but he had suffered eight months' imprisonment before being brought to trial. His lungs had been affected, and he died in Jamaica in 1838.

There were other famous cases, involving riot and the position of the law, which abolitionists reported in somber detail, linking their cause to that of civil liberties. Best known, and flashing with particulars made unforgettable by the literary ability of its chroniclers, was the Boston riot of October 21, 1835, the day of the Utica riot. Garrison's life was threatened because of the irresponsibility of "many gentlemen of property and influence," as they called themselves—a phrase Garrison and his associates never permitted them to forget.

The precise cause of the riot must be found in a combination of circumstances. There was increased distaste for Garrison, and dissatisfaction with the now lengthy stay in America of George Thompson, an outstanding Chartist and abolitionist, much like Garrison in sentiment and approach, who had made no effort to ameliorate his British phrases or reformist views to appease hostile auditors.[63] There was also indignation at the scheduled meeting of the Boston Female Anti-Slavery Society, an organization offensive to some masculine sensibilities; and, as tinder, an emotion-laden handbill calling the populace to end unseemly abolitionist activity. The rumor that Thompson was to address the ladies was succeeded by the no less aggravating information that Garrison was to be the speaker.

A mob forced its way into the hall where Garrison's women auxiliaries had assembled. A scriptural reading did not awe the visitors; Garrison's decision to leave and draw off the intruders did not slake their need for expression. Mayor Theodore Lyman urged the women to disperse: "Indeed, ladies, you must retire. It is dangerous to remain." This drew from Maria Weston Chapman her immortal retort:

---

[62] *Remarks of Henry B. Stanton . . . before the Committee of the House of Representatives, of Massachusetts . . .* (Boston, 1837), pp. 39–40.

[63] Garrison, *Lectures of George Thompson . . . History of the Connection with the Anti-Slavery Cause in England* (Boston, 1836). The excitement raised by Thompson aided political demagoguery and encouraged President Jackson to denounce him in the course of a message to Congress; James D. Richardson (ed.), *A Compilation of the Messages and Papers of the Presidents* (Washington, 1896), III, 175. Thompson was a leader in various reform movements, and on his visit to the United States during the Civil War received a public reception in the House of Representatives with Lincoln and his Cabinet present.

"If this is the last bulwark of freedom, we may as well die here as anywhere."[64]

The mob found Garrison and momentarily threatened his life. He was led through the streets of Boston with a rope about him, though not, as sometimes thought, for hanging purposes. The mayor put him in the jail for safekeeping, and the riot died out.

Garrison and his associates were doubtless correct to believe that the rioters should have been put in prison rather than himself. Moderate and religious sentiments were no safeguard against exasperated mob feelings. Garrisonians and anti-Garrisonians faced the problem of obtaining due consideration for their argument. The Garrisonian Stephen S. Foster termed churches "combinations of thieves, robbers, adulterers, pirates, and murderers, and, as such . . . the bulwark of American slavery"—the last being a phrase of Birney's. The Reverend Leonard Bacon, on the other hand, had been the author of a Connecticut resolution, presented to his General Association of Congregationalist Ministers, barring "itinerant agents and lecturers on various points of Christian doctrine and morals"—that is, antislavery speakers —from the use of pulpits. Both Foster and Bacon intended, in their own ways, to improve American society and to undermine slavery. Both felt the other harmful to his purposes. It is difficult to see that either lacked courage or relevance.[65]

It was in this atmosphere that Birney experienced his own trial by fire in Cincinnati. He had there been issuing the newspaper it had been his dream to address to southern readers. The *Philanthropist* was no agitational sheet, a fact which did not help it with those who, on July 15, 1836, placed the following on the scales of a "respectable and industrious tradesman":

Sir,—It is said that you profess friendship to the cause of abolition. We wish you immediately upon the receipt of this to put your answer in your window so that one or many may see it, and report the same. The simple word *Yes* or *No,* will suffice. Be sure you comply immediately. Anti-Abolition.[66]

[64] Garrisons, II, 15. This account must be supplemented by the equally filial, though useful, and even entertaining Theodore Lyman, 3d (ed.), *Papers Relating to the Garrison Mob* (Cambridge, 1870).

[65] Garrisons, III, 29; [Birney] *The American Churches the Bulwarks of American Slavery* (London, 1840); Theodore D. Bacon, *Leonard Bacon: A Statesman in the Church* (New Haven, 1931), pp. 251–252.

[66] *Narrative of the Late Riotous Proceedings against the Liberty of the*

Thus the people with whom Birney had to deal were both literate and convinced of the justice of their cause. Their assault on the *Philanthropist* culminated long conferences and negotiations, as well as minor destruction. When the storm broke on July 30, and the press was destroyed, Birney was fortunately away. His son proved quick-witted enough to deflect the mob and prevent their house from being burned. "I had but little idea," Birney later commented, "of the personal malignity of the mobcrats against myself." He found it wisest to stay away from Cincinnati until the antiabolitionist rage had simmered down. By August 10, he was able to "walk out into the street without concealment—except down towards the business part of the city near the river." Soon he was to leave Cincinnati for the larger purposes of the national society. The *Philanthropist* continued under Dr. Gamaliel Bailey. He was competent and conservative, yet his press was destroyed twice more before he himself left Cincinnati in 1847 for Washington, to edit the new antislavery *National Era*.[67]

It has entirely passed notice that Elijah P. Lovejoy was a bigot who believed, with little reason, that slavery was a papist product. He was a talented young man who had taken first honors at what became Colby College in his native Maine. He edited a Whig newspaper in St. Louis, became ardently religious as well as antislavery in sentiment, and returned east to enter the Theological Seminary in Princeton. His sense of mission accompanied him back to St. Louis, where in November 1833 he began the *St. Louis Observer* as a Presbyterian

---

Press, in Cincinnati. With Remarks and Historical Notices . . . (Cincinnati, 1836), p. 15.

[67] Bailey was born in New Jersey in 1807, attended Jefferson Medical College in Philadelphia, and sailed before the mast for health and a change for restlessness. In 1831, he edited *Mutual Rights and Methodist Baptist* in Baltimore, and advocated colonization. He next joined an expansionist expedition to the Northwest, which collapsed, leaving him stranded in St. Louis. He walked east to Cincinnati, where he became a practicing physician. He also kept his editorial experience alive by working with the *Western Medical Gazette*. The Lane debate changed his life. By 1835, he was a convinced abolitionist, and a capable secretary of the Ohio Anti-Slavery Society. A better editor than Birney, he gradually assumed responsibility for the *Philanthropist* as Birney increased his lecture and organization work. When Birney joined the Executive Committee of the American Anti-Slavery Society in New York, Bailey began his long editorship with the *Philanthropist;* see Joel Goldfarb, "The Life of Gamaliel Bailey, Prior to the Founding of the National Era; the Orientation of a Practical Abolitionist" (Ph.D., University of California, 1958). Bailey, as a significant, almost key abolitionist, merits further, as well as published, studies.

journal. Lovejoy was violently anti-Catholic, but also, to the embarrassment of his sponsors, as firmly antislavery.[68] He was crystal-clear on his rights as a citizen. Being warned to stop offending border-state prejudices, he declared his intention to send such publications as he chose through the mails, for "The truth is, my fellow-citizens, if we give ground a single inch, there is no stopping place. I deem it, therefore, my duty to stand upon the Constitution."[69]

He persisted against rising unpopularity, and his lively prose and editorial skill did not help him. St. Louis was not then the antislavery (though not pro-Negro) center which it became, thanks to the German Republican refugees who made it their home after 1848. Lovejoy's unpopularity was deepened by his fearless report of the burning in St. Louis of a mulatto sailor on May 5, 1836. This event was rendered more disturbing by the charge of Judge Luke E. Lawless, by an unfortunate mischance a Catholic, to the effect, in Lovejoy's bitter paraphrase, that "a crime, which if committed, by one or two, would be punishable with death, may be perpetrated by the multitude with impunity."[70]

Lovejoy had determined to leave St. Louis. He feared for his family, and he had been promised antislavery support, including the encouragement of the Reverend Edward Beecher, then president of Illinois College, and unlike his father a forthright opponent of slavery. Lovejoy's office was smashed up before he could leave St. Louis, and his press destroyed before he could begin work in Alton, Illinois, across the Mississippi River. He there met antagonism, but also fellowship which supported him despite the loss of two more presses. Lovejoy would not bend, though within the context of his convictions he was democratic, offering to resign his editorship if his sponsors preferred.[71] In addition, he was active in organizing a state antislavery society.[72]

---

[68] "Elijah P. Lovejoy as an Anti-Catholic," *Records of the American Catholic Historical Society of Philadelphia*, LXII (1951), 172–180. The subject is reduced to a note in John Gill, *Tide without Turning: Elijah P. Lovejoy and Freedom of the Press* (Boston, 1959), pp. 218–219, an eloquent work, the result of long study. Lovejoy's bigotry was not merely the result of nineteenth-century superstition; it was a substantial part, in his case, of the Protestant domestic missionary program; cf. below, pp. 147 ff.; see also pp. 230 ff.

[69] St. Louis *Observer*, II (November 5, 1835).

[70] *Ibid.*, III (July 21, 1836).

[71] Letter of September 11, 1837, sent after his death to Lewis Tappan; in "Arranged Chronology," etc., Tappan Papers, LC.

[72] *Alton Observer—Extra. Proceedings of the Ill. Anti-Slavery Convention.*

The final catastrophe was precipitated early in November 1837, when his fourth press arrived, and elements in Alton grimly determined that it should not function. Lovejoy died defending it with arms. His younger brother Owen vowed at his bier never to rest in his own war against slavery.[73]

The tragedy, as John Quincy Adams wrote, sent "a shock as of an earthquake throughout this continent." Abolition had its first martyr, ineradicably linked with the freedom of speech and press. Repeated countless times were Lovejoy's impassioned words, in declaring his inability to give up his fight and leave Alton, "Should I attempt it, I should feel that the angel of the Lord, with his flaming sword, was pursuing me wherever I went. It is because I fear God that I am not afraid of all who oppose me in this city."

In Boston, the Reverend Channing, though a pacifist, headed a committee which petitioned the mayor and aldermen for permission to use Faneuil Hall to memorialize Lovejoy. It was refused, but a more formidable appeal reversed the decision. Distinguished speeches at the meeting included one by Channing himself. But the most notable were those offered by the attorney general of Massachusetts, James T. Austin, and the then twenty-six-year-old Wendell Phillips, only recently admitted to the bar. The attorney general compared the rioters of Alton to the "orderly mob" which acted at Boston Harbor when the Tea Party was given, and asserted that the "presumptuous and imprudent" Lovejoy had "died as the fool dieth." Phillips then rose to unleash the eloquence which was to enchant his sometimes otherwise outraged hearers for almost half a century; in the most famous passage of his improvised speech:

Sir, when I heard the gentleman lay down principles which place the murderers of Alton side by side with Otis and Hancock, with Quincy and Adams, I thought those pictured lips [pointing to the portraits in the Hall] would have broken into voice to rebuke the recreant American—the slan-

---

Held at Upper Alton on the Twenty-sixth, twenty-seventh, and twenty-eighth October, 1837 (Alton, 1838).

[73] Gill, Tide without Turning, needs, for the many relevant insights not covered in this work, to be supplemented by such primary sources as Joseph C. and Owen Lovejoy, Memoir of the Rev. Elijah P. Lovejoy . . . (New York, 1838); Edward Beecher, Narrative of Riots at Alton (Alton, 1838); Henry Tanner, The Martyrdom of Lovejoy (Chicago, 1881); [William S. Lincoln] Alton Trials of Winthrop S. Gilman [and others] . . . for the Crime of Riot . . . (New York, 1838). For a general account, Nye, Fettered Freedom, pp. 115 ff.

derer of the dead. [Great applause and counter applause.] The gentleman said he should sink into insignificance if he dared to gainsay the principles of these resolutions. Sir, for the sentiments he has uttered, on soil consecrated by the prayers of Puritans and the blood of patriots, the earth should have yawned and swallowed him up.[74]

No less important to coming events was the response to Lovejoy's death said to have been made by a man of thirty-seven at a memorial meeting held in Ohio. This was attended by Owen Brown, an old-time abolitionist, and by his son John, who capped the ceremonies by rising to raise his hand and vow to consecrate his life to the destruction of slavery.[75]

[74] Wendell Phillips, *Speeches, Lectures, and Letters* (Boston, 1864), 1 ff.
[75] Edward Brown (cousin of John Brown), in article cited by John Newton Brown, in letter to *Nation*, XCVIII (1914), 157. Cf. Filler (ed.), "John Brown in Ohio: an Interview with Charles S. S. Griffing," *OAHQ*, LVIII (1949), 213–218.

CHAPTER 5

The Politics of Freedom

T HE OUTBURST of sectional feeling which had accompanied
the Missouri crisis had introduced the antislavery issue into
American politics. They were also affected by an increasing suffrage
which reached a climax in the elections of 1828. The Jackson "revolution" of that year overthrew the old system of presidential nominations by congressional caucus and elections geared to a relatively
restricted electorate. Under this system, four years earlier, no less than
four candidates had bid for the Presidency, and the final decision had
been thrown into the House of Representatives. The victorious Democratic machine now brought out a host of new personalities in national
affairs. Their irascible leader could act with unprecedented decisive-
ness; but this was only in part because he sensed the people's "will."
Jackson rode into the White House in large measure thanks to political intrigue, and on the strength of having exposed a "corrupt
bargain":[1] Henry Clay as having managed the election of John
Quincy Adams, Jackson's predecessor in 1824, and having in exchange
been made Secretary of State. Yet Jackson's clever managers had
won him the Presidency through an alliance with John C. Calhoun,
who was slated to succeed him. Undoubtedly, Jackson's rough-hewn
and autocratic personality satisfied deep popular needs, but none
which depended on his particular decisions. The Peggy Eaton affair
was, in itself, a vast inconsequentiality. Jackson's Maysville veto neither
saved nor damaged the Union. It is difficult, indeed impossible, to
prove that the "hard money" issue which attended Jackson's war on

[1] Charles G. Sellers, Jr., "Jackson Men with Feet of Clay," *AHR*, LXII
(1957), 537 ff.

the Second Bank of the United States retarded or advanced the interests of any single social stratum.[2]

Jackson spoke in the phraseology of the "common man," but he gained politically from the common man's political advancement, rather than perceptibly contributed to it. The bottom fact of Jacksonianism was not its thirst for democracy, but its high regard for the already largely completed white male suffrage which it courted. Exemplars of democracy Jackson had in plenty: the vitriolic Francis Preston Blair, from Kentucky, his journalistic alter ego; Martin Van Buren, the deferential upstate New York politician; Roger B. Taney, who seemed a southern radical of unrestricted proportions: Taney had once successfully affirmed the right of a minister to preach antislavery to a Maryland camp meeting in which some four hundred Negroes participated. In his speech to a jury of slaveholders, Taney had spoken with the utmost contempt of slavery, and of his hopes for its death.[3] Many other distinct personalities surrounded Jackson. But if "the working classes of the North were rendered explosive by a variety of broad frustrations and particular grievances . . ."[4] they could look for little more from the Jacksonians than from the Whigs. There were no representatives of the "working classes" in Jackson's official family. There were not even labor leaders available, in the post-Civil War sense of the term. Those who made bold to speak for labor were themselves capitalistic entrepreneurs. Laboring elements, to the extent that they could exercise influence, seem not to have voted in overwhelming favor of Jackson. And Jackson himself manifested no regard for them.[5]

[2] See especially, in this series, Glyndon G. Van Deusen, *The Jacksonian Era* (New York, 1959). For Jacksonian measures, see Commager, *Documents of American History*, I, 253–255, 270–277. Major studies of Jackson's economic policies include Bray Hammond, *Banks and Policies in America, from the Revolution to the Civil War* (Princeton, 1957), pp. 326 ff. (for a summary statement, pp. 740–742), and Joseph Dorfman, *The Economic Mind in American Civilization, 1606–1865* (New York, 1946), II, 601 ff. See also Marvin Meyers, *The Jacksonian Persuasion* (Stanford, 1957).

[3] Carl B. Swisher, *Roger B. Taney* (New York, 1935), pp. 95–98; William E. Mikell, "Roger B. Taney," in *Great American Lawyers*, ed., William D. Lewis (Philadelphia, 1908), IV, 91–92.

[4] Schlesinger, *Age of Jackson*, p. 33.

[5] Dorfman, "The Jackson Wage-Earner Thesis," *AHR*, LIV (1949), 296–306; William A. Sullivan, "Did Labor Support Andrew Jackson?" *PSQ*, LXII (1947), 569–580; Edward Pessen, "Did Labor Support Jackson: the Boston Story," *PSQ*, LXIV (1949), 262–274, cf. Robert T. Bower, "Note on 'Did Labor Support Jackson: the Boston Story,'" *PSQ*, LXV (1950), 441–444;

Needy there were; Jackson mounted in part on the wave of trouble stirred up by business conditions of 1826–29, as the more romantic elements of his movement were to ride out in the economic crash of 1837. The times created "loafers" who were without means, and susceptible to slogans. They received a more ready sympathy from the Democratic party than from the Whigs. But there was no more natural relationship between laborers and Democrats than between laborers and Whigs. The Rochester meeting in 1830 which raised the "tri-coloured flag of reform, representing the interests of the Farmers, Mechanics, and Working men" did not thereby set itself down as Democratic.[6] Workingmen's demands were essentially conservative. Labor did not seek to raise itself at the expense of other classes, or conceive vengeful plans to compensate for past injuries. It asked no more than something of the respect accorded the farmer, and the hope of rising out of the laboring classes.

In New York City, the choice before the worker in 1830 was clear enough. He could join the misnamed "agrarians," led by that forthright radical, Thomas Skidmore, who demanded an equal division of the land. This precursor of Henry George had "split" (the facts are controversial) the Workingmen's party of Robert Dale Owen and the British-born George Henry Evans. Skidmore had set up his Poor Man's party, which, however, attracted few supporters, poor or otherwise. More workers, "too easy-tempered and short-sighted," preferred the conservative hodgepodge which included Colonel William L. Stone of the *Commercial Advertiser*, Theodore Dwight of the *Daily Advertiser*, and Arthur Tappan "of Church and State notoriety," as the New York *Sentinel* angrily saw him. As an alternative to these figures, there was the powerful Democratic party and its agent Tammany Hall.[7]

Morris, "Andrew Jackson, Strikebreaker," *AHR*, LV (1949), 54–68; Harry R. Stevens, "Did Industrial Labor Influence Jacksonian Land Policy?" *Indiana Mag. of Hist.*, XLIII (1947), 159–167. For anti-Democratic sentiment among western workers, see Halvor G. Melom, "The Philosophy of Mississippi Valley Labor in the Age of Jackson: a Case Study of St. Louis to 1846," MS. read at MVHA annual meeting, 1949.

[6] New York *Daily Sentinel*, I (April 30, 1830).

[7] "Parties in New York," New York *Sentinel*, I, July 26, 1830; Thomas Skidmore, *The Rights of Man to Property* . . . (New York, 1829), a storehouse of radical thought, and Pessen, "Thomas Skidmore: Agrarian Reformer in the Early American Labor Movement," *New York Hist.*, XXXV (1954), 280–296; Gustavus Myers, *The History of Tammany Hall* (New York, 1901), and M. R. Werner, *Tammany Hall* (New York, 1928).

Tammany attracted the poor and the downtrodden Irish, as it had been doing as far back as the days of Jefferson and Aaron Burr. But its leaders were patent opportunists and even double-dealers. Their prototype was Ely Moore, an assiduous laborer in his own behalf, whose calculated phrases and deals won him Tammany support for Congress in 1834 and the presidency of the Trades Union of New York a year later.[8] Moore's calm readiness, as a state prison commissioner, to join in a report which countenanced convict labor—a sore point with free labor—won him the reprimand of labor, but did no harm to his fortunes. Labor, in these early days of organization, had no choice but to experiment with alleged leaders, and too little of a community of interest to develop a sophisticated sense of their worth. Thus, although public education was one of labor's major reforms, offering it the possibility of deserting for more elite circles, twenty-five out of the forty-five members of the Executive Committee of the Workingmen's party—that short-lived phenomenon—voted down a resolution favoring improved educational facilities on the grounds that it was irreligious, though one of them was reported "blunderingly" to have confessed that his party "did not choose to be taxed for the support of any general System of Education, as is unjustly done in the New England States. . . ."[9]

There was a labor movement, which had certain aims in common with those of the Jacksonian Democracy, even though all labor reformers, as in the case of the Philadelphia reformer Stephen Simpson, were far from necessarily being Jackson Democrats.[10] The program of the Workingmen's party in 1830 opposed monopolies, imprisonment for debt, capital punishment, the militia system, legislation on religion, and unequal taxes. It favored public education, as well as reforms in the legal and political systems. Generally, Jacksonians tended to advocate a separation of church and state, an antimonopoly position, at least in theory, and perhaps to emphasize technical issues of economics more than their opponents. But labor reformers had an interest in the

[8] Commons et al., Documentary History, VI, 146, 197 and passim; Commons et al., History of Labour in the United States (New York, 1918), I, 360, 369–370; Walter E. Hugins, "Ely Moore: the Case History of a Jacksonian Labor Leader," PSQ, LXV (1950), 105 ff.; Nevins, Ordeal of the Union, II, 272 ff.

[9] New York Sentinel, I (May 24, 25, 1830).

[10] Pessen, "The Ideology of Stephen Simpson: Upperclass Champion of the Early Philadelphia Workingmen's Movement," Pennsylvania Hist., XXI (1955), 328–340.

vital realities of labor struggle which separated them from the mere politicos.[11]

Unlike the moral reformers, the labor theoreticians were little concerned with abolition. They condoned lotteries, though they cost the public some $49 million in 1832, because they gave the poor the hope of otherwise unattainable gain. They approved amusements, rejected currently lugubrious modes of mourning, and generally upheld a this-worldly attitude quite at variance with millennial thought.[12] They praised Jackson for having vetoed Henry Clay's "Bribery consolidation bill," which would have kept up the price of public lands and increased the difficulty of getting it into the hands of would-be settlers.

Labor reformers came somewhat closer to moral reformers when they approved the experiments of Josiah Warren, who sought practical means of ensuring people the rewards of their labor. His "time store," set up in Cincinnati in 1827, was an effort to charge prices according to the cost of production, rather than scarcity. Warren caught the attention of a labor journal because "he has devised a plan by which types can be cast by any person of common intelligence, without apprenticeship, and without dependence on capital. His press can be made in five days and the art of printing acquired by females or children in a few hours." John Humphrey Noyes, in his own discussion of Warren, took pains to point out that Warren was not pressing cooperative ideas, but their obverse: "The Sovereignty of the Individual:"[13] It was economic advancement, then, which bemused labor; personal fulfillment which stood first with the moral reformer. Labor could not conceive of personal fulfillment apart from material objec-

---

[11] Pessen, "The Workingmen's Movement of the Jacksonian Era," *MVHR*, XLIII (1956), 428–444.

[12] The lottery, however, seriously offended public sensibilities, and offered extraordinary opportunities for knaves. It was banned in most of the states in the course of the 1830's and 1840's, though condoned in the territories, and required another campaign later in the century; McMaster, *History*, VII, 154 ff. Moral reformers came around, though slowly, to a less somber view of due earthly deportment; see Oliver Johnson, *Amusements: Their Uses and Abuses. Testimony of Progressive Friends* (New York, 1856), and Rev. Henry W. Bellows, *The Relation of Public Amusements to Public Morality, Especially of the Theatre* . . . (New York, 1857).

[13] New York *Sentinel*, I (March 16, 1830); Noyes, *History of American Socialisms*, pp. 94 ff. See also William Bailie, *Josiah Warren, the First American Anarchist* (Boston, 1906); George B. Lockwood, *The New Harmony Movement* (New York, 1905), pp. 294–306; and Rudolf Rocker, *Pioneers of American Freedom* (Los Angeles, 1949), pp. 49 ff.

tives; thus it emphasized the desirability of education, but as a weapon
to advance its status and competence at least as much as its understanding. There were few, if any, transcendentalists among labor
leaders.

On the subject of free lands labor reformers and moral reformers
stood on common ground. Take the case of Gerrit Smith's noteworthy
gifts of large tracts of land in New York State to Negroes and poor
whites. Smith had been denounced by George Henry Evans as one of
the greatest slaveholders in the nation because of his monopoly of so
much of the available terrain. Yet Smith thought of himself as an
agrarian, eager to turn his holdings over to the common people, but
fearful that they would end up in the hands of would-be monopolists.
In 1846, when Smith undertook his grand scheme of land distribution
—much of it of inferior, if workable, quality—he appointed Evans to
his committee charged with selecting worthy recipients. On the committee, too, was Isaac T. Hopper, representing the abolitionist interest. In due course, the land was parceled out: a notable deed in
abolitionist, as well as general, philanthropic annals, since Negroes
gained from the gift as well as white settlers.[14]

The laborer, seeking free land, was a potential farmer. He spoke
admiringly of the farmer's life, and wishfully of a farmer-labor alliance. In practice, there were limits to their sense of common aims:

> True it is that farmers, like other men, have their hardships and their
> crosses. . . . They find, perhaps, a ruinous competition, that sinks the value
> of their produce. . . . The village merchant, perhaps, when they go to his
> store, takes their pork and corn at half price, and sells them his own flimsy
> goods at cent percent profit. . . .
> But still they know little or nothing of the bitter suffering that visits the
> poor in large cities. They have no idea of men actually reduced to beggary,
> or driven to the almshouse, not because they are idle and have been im-
> provident, but because society cannot find any employment for them. . . .
> And, therefore, they may not feel, so sensibly as we of the city do, the abso-
> lute necessity of change and reform.[15]

Thus both laborer and farmer approved cheap land and opportunities for small farmers. If the Democrats boasted, among the cheap
land advocates, spokesmen like Andrew Johnson, representing the

---

[14] Commons et al., Documentary History, VII, 30–33, 352 ff.; Harlow,
Gerrit Smith, pp. 243 ff.; Frothingham, Gerrit Smith, pp. 102 ff.
[15] New York Sentinel, I (February 22, 1830).

poor whites of Tennessee, the Whigs could point to Horace Greeley, eager to settle the plains with free men.[16] The paradoxes these two figures incorporated are numerous; but Greeley, though he was a "moral reformer," was no less a politician than the Tennessee tailor and statesman, and responded to practical needs as much as to human principle.

"Political opportunism, perhaps [so Jackson's program has been described], but a thousand times more effective than the Channing program of regenerating individual souls."[17] The choice, however, need not have been—and was not, in practice—between opportunism and grace. For the Democrats, however, in the time of Jackson, "abolitionism was the great untouchable issue."[18] Jackson himself was, of course, a hearty buyer and seller of slaves, and had dealt in slaves.[19] As a symbol and partial figurehead, he had no need to spell out his sentiments on slavery, as did Calhoun, the other pillar of the first Jackson alliance. There were border-state Jacksonians who put union above slavery and would repudiate secession; but they suffered no agonizing choices during Jackson's time. Thomas Morris, the first antislavery United States senator, elected from Ohio in 1833 as a Democrat, was read out of the party for his antislavery declarations in Washington. It has been argued that Jackson's victory in 1828, which largely involved a congealing of aggressive proslavery southern politicians, signaled the suppression of the antislavery forces in the South.[20]

But what of the North? Here the report must be more complex. Democrats included not only such Tammany specimens as Mike Walsh, "a left-wing Calhoun leader," and Fernando Wood—for whom "majoritarian" seems an amusing euphemism[21]—but the intelligent and arrogant James Fenimore Cooper, a Democrat only in the most Platonic sense, and also Robert Rantoul, Jr., of Massachusetts, worthy son of a worthy father, whose career was studded with liber-

[16] Commons *et al., Documentary History,* VII, 211–216; VIII, 40–44, 49–51, 62–64, 71.

[17] Schlesinger, *Orestes A. Brownson* (Boston, 1939), p. 40.

[18] Schlesinger, *Age of Jackson,* pp. 190–191.

[19] *Genius of Universal Emancipation,* IX (September 28, October 4, 18, 1828); *A Brief Account of General Jackson's Dealings in Negroes* (n.p., 1828?).

[20] B. F. Morris (ed.), *The Life of Thomas Morris* (Cincinnati, 1856); Birney, *Birney,* pp. 72–73.

[21] Schlesinger, *Age of Jackson,* pp. 406, 408.

tarian causes. There was also William Cullen Bryant, great editor of the New York *Evening Post,* as well as poet, who took no pleasure in slavery but would take no principled stand against it. Walt Whitman's lack of true antislavery convictions has been obscured by passages in his poems which embodied abstract principles. William Leggett, ardently Jacksonian in sentiment, was probably as aggrieved by slavery as any Democrat in the north, and as helpless to express himself in opposition to it. As he wrote James G. Birney, who had urged him to contribute to the abolitionist agitation:

. . . I am an abolitionist not less zealous, than yourself, though my ideas of constitutional obligations may differ widely from yours; and I hope you may not consider it boasting if I add, that I have proved my sincerity and devotion to the glorious cause of equal liberty—of which the abolition of negro slavery is but a part—by personal sacrifices relatively as great as those encountered by any champion of human freedom. . . . I am at this moment just out of a sick bed, and have scarcely strength to write this letter to you—much less to write essays for the newspapers. And if I had, what newspaper, alas! would publish them?[22]

Less forthright was James K. Paulding, a writer of talent, a familiar of Washington Irving, and an early American novelist, whose *Letters from the South* (1817) were illuminating and unhesitatingly antislavery. William Jay had the unhappy duty of observing that the 1835 edition of this same work completely overturned Paulding's system of observations: it omitted the denunciations of slavery, and directed the author's contempt against the abolitionists and, for good measure, Englishmen, whom Paulding demagogically accused of contributing "foreign money" for incendiary purposes. Paulding deliberately tampered with the details of his own pages to serve newer purposes. He

[22] William Leggett to Birney, November 22, 1838, Dumond (ed.), *Letters of James Gillespie Birney,* I, 477. As editor of the New York *Evening Post,* Leggett had vigorously opposed the antiabolition riots of 1834. See also Hamilton (ed.), *Rantoul, passim;* Curti, "Robert Rantoul, Jr., the Reformer in Politics," *NEQ,* V (1932), 264–280; Howard R. Floan, "The New York Evening Post and the Ante-Bellum South," *American Qu.,* VIII (1956), 243–253; Nevins, *The Evening Post . . .* (New York, 1922), *passim,* and Parke Godwin, *A Biography of . . . Bryant* (New York, 1883), I, 345 ff.; Robert E. Spiller, "Fenimore Cooper's Defense of Slave-Owning America," *AHR,* XXXV (1930), 575–582; Lorenzo D. Turner, "Walt Whitman and the Negro," *Chicago Jewish Forum,* XV (1956), 5–11; Theodore Sedgwick, Jr. (ed.), *A Collection of the Political Writings of William Leggett* (New York, 1840), I, xii–xiv, 34 ff.; II, 36 ff.; and F. Byrdsall, *The History of the Loco-Foco or Equal Rights Party . . .* (New York, 1842), of which Leggett is the hero.

was a Navy functionary, with a prominent social background, as well as a Democrat. Whether or not he hungered for the Navy Secretaryship which Van Buren gave him in 1838, his shift of view undoubtedly helped him politically.[23]

The run of northern Democrats was symbolized by Silas Wright of New York, who, by the time of his death in 1847, had accepted slavery restriction as desirable, and was mourned not only by his large following but also by Whittier and Whitman. In 1836, Wright's interest in slavery was confined to keeping it out of public debate. He was reluctant to stamp out congressional discussion of it, on the grounds that this would help agitators. As proof that the South had nothing to fear from abolitionists, that the North was equally opposed to them, Wright cited the Utica riot of recent memory. Wright apparently deemed the rioters a legitimate expression of public opinion. When Calhoun contradicted him, and referred to an antislavery article which had appeared in a Utica paper, Wright pointed out that the newspaper office had been wrecked by a mob the day after the article's publication.[24]

Far more complex was the response of labor itself to slavery. A number of standard citations are often employed to demonstrate that it opposed Negroes and deemed abolitionist efforts no more than a hypocritical means for diverting attention from "white slavery" in the North. The problem is to determine when labor spokesmen did or did not speak for the ordinary laborer. Garrison's incarceration in Baltimore in 1830 was noticed and deplored in one outstanding labor journal, and anti-Negro riots in more than one. Several of them criticized southern attempts to stop freedom of the press, to encourage kidnaping of abolitionists by publishing gross rewards, and to halt western immigration. They disapproved the barring of "free blacks" from Texas and treated slave catchers with contempt. Even colonization, so convenient a cause for proslavery advocates, they dubbed a Tory-Whig subterfuge, used by schemers "who would be among the last to allow the people (black or white) to speak or think for themselves."[25]

---

[23] Jay, *A View of the Action of the Federal Government, in Behalf of Slavery* (Utica, 1844 ed.), p. 30. For a defense of Paulding which does not meet the issue, Floyd C. Watkins, "James Kirke Paulding and the South," *American Qu.*, V (1953), 219 ff.

[24] John A. Garraty, *Silas Wright* (New York, 1949), pp. 165–166, 406–407.

[25] Joseph Rayback, "The American Workingman and the Anti-Slavery Cru-

True, Evans, the author of this view of colonization, among other labor reformers, treated with heavy humor white persons who amalgamated with Negroes. They were so fearful of Negro competition that southern theoreticians were divided on whether to ally with labor against capital, or with capital against labor.[26] The Irish, on the lowest rung of the labor scale, competitors of the Negro, were intensely hostile to him. They even upbraided Daniel O'Connell, "the Liberator," because this fighter for Irish independence from Great Britain had joined with other Irish leaders to condemn American slavery. His manifesto was treated as emanating from a foreign source.[27] British sympathy with antislavery, which was always more articulate if not necessarily more effective than British sympathy with slavery, inflamed Irish hatred for Negroes and moral reformers.

In one field of labor, at least, workingmen met the Negro with a degree of camaraderie, if not co-operation. Brutalized, despised, toiling under conditions which differed only in details from that of the slave, with no status on shipboard and little before the law, the northern seaman had no logical reason to esteem himself the Negro's superior. The latter had a long tradition before the mast. His services had been praised by Captain Oliver Hazard Perry, when one-tenth of the upper-Lakes crews had been Negro. It was now estimated that one sailor in six was a Negro, and there were to be higher estimates. Later, the Negro was to break ground for the organization of seamen.[28] It is not surprising that Herman Melville, in his years of

---

sade," *JEH*, III (1943), 152–163; Bernard Mandel, *Labor: Free and Slave: Workingmen and the Anti-Slavery Movement in the United States* (New York, 1955), pp. 61 ff.; Foner, *A History of the Labor Movement in the United States* (New York, 1947), I, 249 ff.; Williston H. Lofton, "Abolition and Labor," *JNH*, XXXIII (1948), 249–283.

[26] Wilfred Carsel, "The Slaveholders' Indictment of Northern Wage Slavery," *JSH*, VI (1940), 504–520.

[27] "Loyal National Repeal Association, Daniel O'Connell, and American Slavery," *Pennsylvania Freeman* (Extra), June 17, 1843.

[28] Williams, *History of the Negro Race in America*, II, 28–30; Sidney Kaplan, "The American Seaman's Protective Union Association of 1863 . . ." *SS*, XXI (1957), 154–159. Charles H. Wesley, *Negro Labor in the United States* (New York, 1927), p. 49, estimates one-half of the American seamen in 1850 to have been colored. William McNally, *Evils and Abuses in the Naval and Merchant Service Exposed* (Boston, 1839), is filled with valuable detail, though skirting the Negro issue, except to raise the peculiarly inapposite cry of antislavery as a measure for skirting the problem of the seaman (pp. 128–129). See also Henry W. Farnam, *Chapters in the History of Social Legislation . . .* (Washington, 1938), pp. 242 ff., and Morris, "Labor Controls in Maryland in the 19th Century," *JSH*, XIV (1948), 385–400.

wandering at sea, should have pondered the meaning of Negroes, slavery, and the color black as disturbingly as he did—in too complex a fashion for the idealists of his time to fathom, who, like the abolitionists, sought tangible results.[29] Richard Henry Dana, less profoundly than Melville but with unexampled clarity, exposed, in famous passages of *Two Years before the Mast* (1840), the shocking tyranny which ruled the sea. That same year Dana began his conservative and humane career in law as the seaman's counsel, in politics as in antislavery. Father Taylor in 1833 helped found the Seaman's Aid Society, which offered a helping hand coupled with admonishments against the use of hard liquor. The salty preacher was originally from Virginia, and had an ease with Negroes he missed in white Bostonians.

The Negro seamen tended to look to themselves and to reformers more than to white workers. In 1822, Denmark Vesey's intended insurrection had been discovered, and horrified Southerners by its scope, the audacity of its leaders, and the close relations it revealed between slaves and free Negroes.[30] South Carolina leaders not only took steps to tighten controls over Negroes at home, but to resist infections from abroad. Free Negroes entering their state ports, in whatever capacity, or whatever their nationality, were to be imprisoned until their ship left. They had to pay the costs of their own retention, or be sold as slaves. Soon, forty-one ships had been deprived of one or more Negro hands, and one British trader lost almost his entire crew. Court action brought release of the Negroes, but, though congressional authority and a treaty with Great Britain were defied, the practice continued.[31] South Carolina's flouting cf the courts and the government represented an early and continued nullification of constitutional enactments.

[29] However, it is equally misleading to treat Melville in terms of mere "explication." He had a keen eye for detail, which was intended to carry direct messages, as in his *White Jacket* (1850), where he describes the "game" of "head-bumping" conducted on ship: "*Head-bumping,* as patronized by Captain Claret, consists in two negroes (whites will not answer) butting at each other like rams . . ." (Boston, 1892 ed.), p. 258.

[30] John M. Lofton, Jr., "Denmark Vesey's Call to Arms," *JNH,* XXXIII (1948), 395–417. The final words of one of Vesey's aides to the other conspirators were memorable: "Do not open your lips! Die silent as you shall see me do." The episode is controversially re-examined in Richard C. Wade, *Slavery in the Cities* (New York, 1964), pp. 228 ff.

[31] McMaster, *History,* V, 199 ff.; *Imprisonment of Colored Seamen under the Law of South Carolina. A Tract Containing the Cases of Manuel Pereira and Reuben Roberts; and of John Glasgow, a Free British Subject Who Was Sold into Slavery in Georgia* (London, 1854).

As northern sympathy rose for fugitive slaves, the South retaliated against free Negroes, who were so heavily involved in their escapes. South Carolina forbade emancipations; Mississippi required its free Negroes to give $100 bond or be sold for costs, and threatened Negro intruders from outside the state with slavery and the whip; Missouri also forbade free Negroes to enter her harbors. In 1835, South Carolina re-enacted her Negro Seaman's Law; a similar law ruled in Louisiana.

Demands upon the Massachusetts legislature by citizens of the state finally, in 1844, caused it to send to South Carolina an emissary, Samuel Hoar, an elder statesman and eminent lawyer, who accepted the appointment after two others had refused it. The hope was that South Carolina administrators would join him in seeking reasonable legal solutions to their problem. Americans found it hard to accept the fact that they were living under two social and legal codes—Hoar was genuinely surprised that his visit and representations aroused the animosity that it did: that the legislature passed resolutions directing the governor to expel him from the state; that a mob threatened to destroy the hotel in which he was staying; that a respectable deputation of citizens requested that he leave, and were prepared to put him on the boat themselves had he refused to leave voluntarily. It was at this point that Hoar gave over attempting to carry out his mission.[32]

Generally speaking, northern concern with the lot of the Negro was based upon a concern for liberty and the rule of law. The abolitionist alone combined religion, humanitarianism, and law to emphasize the Negro's rights as a person. The charge that abolition was intended to divert attention from the tragic conditions of the workers cannot be demonstrated.[33] Even Channing, following the depression of 1819, had helped organize the philanthropic Ministry at Large and continued to show awareness of the needs of the poor. Thoreau, in

[32] McMaster, *History*, VII, 259 ff.; Philip M. Hamer, "Great Britain, the United States, and the Negro Seamen Acts, 1822–1848," *JSH*, I (1935), 3–28, and "British Consuls and the Negro Seamen Acts, 1850–1860," *ibid.*, I, 138–168; George F. Hoar, *Autobiography of Seventy Years* (New York, 1905), I, 24–25; "Treatment of Samuel Hoar," *Senate . . . No. 31, Commonwealth of Massachusetts, February, 1845; Massachusetts and South Carolina: an Examination of the Controversy between Them. By a Member of Congress from South Carolina* (Washington, 1845).

[33] The view that abolition was a conservative "plot" calculated to obfuscate "vital" economic issues is fantastic, but has been broached; Schlesinger, *Age of Jackson*, pp. 424 ff.

Walden, wrote with mild contempt for the Irish, but denounced our factory system "as becoming every day more like that of the English," and meant only "that the corporations may be enriched." Theodore Parker was to turn again and again to society's duties to those in want. And if Emerson's theories of individualism and compensation were not applicable to the destitute or to the slave, they did constitute a barbed criticism of a shoddy civilization which required overhauling.[34]

Lewis Tappan was categorical in his respect for labor, his belief in a reasonable limitation on hours of work, homestead opportunities, and related measures. He would, however, probably have joined Garrison in denouncing George Henry Evans for arguing that "the Wages and Tenant system" was "so much more heinous than the Chattel system of the South, as almost to defy comparison."[35] But if Garrison and other abolitionists did not concern themselves about the sordid conditions of the city paupers and such run-down areas of the city as the Five Points of New York, they were no more remiss than labor itself. Garrison and Birney, among other abolitionists, wrote spirited defenses of labor's rights. Greeley reported labor's needs at length in the pages of the *Tribune.* Wendell Phillips and Parker Pillsbury turned to the labor question after the abolition crusade had been completed.[36] In 1836, William Henry Channing, nephew of Dr. Channing, organized a Unitarian church in a poor section of New York City; and though it was not successful, this was not for lack of effort on Channing's part.[37] Charles Loring Brace, as a young minister in 1853, began a distinguished career in child rehabilitation. There was nothing sanctimonious or abstract in his approach:

Is not this crop of thieves and burglars, of shoulder-hitters and short-boys, of prostitutes and vagrants, of garroters and murderers, the very fruit to be

---

[34] William Charvat, "American Romanticism and the Depression of 1837," *SS,* II (1938), 70–71; Henry D. Thoreau, *Walden* (Boston, 1957 ed.), p. 18; Frank Buckley, "Thoreau and the Irish," *NEQ,* XIII (1940), 401 ff.; Henry S. Commager, *Theodore Parker* (Boston, 1936), *passim.*

[35] Commons *et al., Documentary History,* VII, 351–352.

[36] Garrisons, II, 33; Birney to Ezekiel Webb *et al.,* Dumond (ed.), *Birney,* I, 363; Charles E. Russell, *The Story of Wendell Phillips* (Chicago, 1914), pp. 114 ff.; Samuel Bernstein, "Wendell Phillips, Labor Advocate," *SS,* XX (1956), 344–357; Filler, "Parker Pillsbury: an Anti-Slavery Apostle," *NEQ,* XIX (1946), 315–337.

[37] O. B. Frothingham, *Memoir of William Henry Channing . . .* (Boston, 1886), pp. 129 ff.

expected from this seed so long being sown? What else was to be looked for? Society hurried on selfishly for its wealth, and left this vast class in its misery and temptation. Now these children arise, and wrest back with bloody and criminal hands what the world was too careless or too selfish to give. The worldliness of the rich, the indifference of all classes to the poor, will always be avenged. . . .[38]

The Whigs produced their own quota of proslavery respondents and fence-sitters, including, until their party disintegrated, a solid core of Southerners.[39] Among the Northerners, it should suffice to cite Edward Everett as the very substance of treadmill Whiggery: a monumental "dough-face"—a northern man with southern principles—who premised the defense of slave rights in all his actions. For this he was weighed down with honors which included the governorship of Massachusetts, the presidency of Harvard College, and national recognition as Minister to the Court of St. James's and Secretary of State.[40]

The significance of both major political parties, from the abolitionist viewpoint and that of the reformers generally, lay in their ability to advance or retard their causes. In the 1830's and 1840's the Democrats were, for the most part, in control of the major arms of government and constituted the immediate bar to moral reforms.

Many of the reforms should have met little or no opposition at Mason and Dixon's Line. The arguments against capital punishment were, obviously, weakened in a South which constantly patrolled its streets with armed guards alert to possible insurrectionists and runaways. But augmented educational opportunities could have been useful North and South. Prison reform, care for the blind, for the aged, for the poor, were not problems of any one section. Richard

---

[38] [Emma Brace (ed.)] *The Life of Charles Loring Brace* . . . (New York, 1894), p. 217.

[39] Arthur C. Cole, *The Whig Party in the South* (Washington, 1913); see his maps of presidential election returns in the southern states, 1836 to 1852, following p. 367. For a brief treatment, Ulrich B. Phillips, "The Southern Whigs, 1834–1854," in Guy S. Ford (ed.), *Essays in American History Dedicated to Frederick Jackson Turner* (New York, 1910), pp. 203–229. Their major cause was states' rights.

[40] Paul R. Frothingham, *Edward Everett* (New York, 1925). His collected addresses are instructive; see Edward Everett, *Orations and Speeches on Various Occasions* (Boston, 1865–72 ed.); for his speech at Gettysburg, November 19, 1863, *ibid.*, IV, 622–659. See also Van Deusen, "Some Aspects of Whig Thought and Theory in the Jacksonian Period," *AHR*, LXIII (1957), 305–322.

Henry Dana wrote with disgust of "the wildness and fanaticism" of a reformers' convention, "the bitterness and vulgarity of their attacks upon the church and clergy." But it never occurred to him to despise universal education or many other specific reforms because he resented the activities of some of their supporters. Southern defenders, on the other hand, increasingly lumped reforms with northern reformers, and held both to be symptoms of social decay and a product of abolitionist thought. Yet Southerners graciously received Dorothea Dix in her apolitical role of reformer. At the same time, they made efforts to exploit the "fact," revealed by the Fifth Census of the United States, that in the slave states, one in every 1,558 Negroes was insane or idiotic; in the free states, one in every 144.5.[41] The assumption that they enjoyed better mental health in the slave states was unwarranted. It failed to take important facts into consideration, including drastic instances of deliberate fraud. The census controversy helped demonstrate that reform could only hope to advance by forcing respect from its opponents, not by appealing to their sense of justice. As the philosophic Jay remarked: "I have long noticed that when men assign false reasons for their conduct, their conduct is not changed by the refutation of those reasons."[42]

This fact troubled many antislavery reformers, since their cause so directly affronted southern sentiments. How were they to develop their program beyond mere talk in the face of such antagonism? To their aid came John Quincy Adams, in 1836 a veteran of forty-two years of public service, and as pre-eminent in his training for statesmanship as Jackson had been in the local arts of back-country living and Indian killing. In the course of his unequaled career, Adams had served his country throughout Europe; had been one of the negotiators of the Treaty of Ghent and of the Florida purchase. He had been a United States senator and the Secretary of State, in the latter capacity author of the Monroe Doctrine; and he had been President. His many-sided literary, scientific, and political interests had not prevented him from returning to Washington in old age to serve his state in the House of Representatives.

[41] Albert Deutsch, "The First U.S. Census of the Insane (1840) and Its Use as Pro-Slavery Propaganda," *Bull. of the Hist. of Medicine*, XV (1944), 469 ff.

[42] Jay to Gerrit Smith, September 8, 1843, Gerrit Smith Collection, Syracuse University.

It is a paradox that Jackson should have gained a reputation for democracy and nationalism at the expense of Adams, lampooned by his foes as an aristocrat and New England Federalist. Aristocrat he was, as was Jackson, the latter being a frontier aristocrat, a wealthy cotton planter. Adams was a cold, pious man, entirely dedicated to duty. He had but one romance outside his home: his country. With all her faults, he could not but believe the world must gain by its growth and successes. He would have bought Texas himself, as President, in 1825, and also in 1827; at that time, the problem of slavery had not disturbed him.[43] He put his faith in the Union, and in the freedoms of his white fellow citizens, whom he trusted to maintain and develop the American heritage.

Now in 1836, at the age of sixty-nine, he found himself standing in the breach abolitionists had opened between slavery and antislavery. Abolition had come to Congress. Since Walker's *Appeal,* the South had become sensitive to abolitionist writings. Although fear of their falling into the hands of slaves was emphasized by its politicians, so profound a strategist as Calhoun was even more eager to have the circulation of abolitionist propaganda stopped in the North.[44]

Vehicles for antislavery arguments had multiplied. The American Anti-Slavery Society, in June 1835, projected an elaborate program of publications for free distribution, to include a small folio paper called *Human Rights;* another, "a small magazine with cuts," the *Anti-Slavery Record;* still another, an enlarged sheet of the *Emancipator;* and a juvenile, the *Slave's Friend.* At a meeting which raised $14,500 for the purpose, Isaac Winslow, a Maine abolitionist who had paid for the publication of Garrison's *Thoughts on African Colonization,* contributed a thousand-dollar bill.[45]

On July 30, 1835, Charleston citizens, having learned that the mail steamer had brought to town packages of these propaganda writings, broke into the post office, and took them into the street and burned them. Numerous meetings and resolutions materialized throughout the South. They offered rewards for the apprehension of persons carrying

[43] Samuel F. Bemis, *John Quincy Adams and the Foundations of American Foreign Policy* (New York, 1949), pp. 561 ff.

[44] W. Sherman Savage, *The Controversy over the Distribution of Abolition Literature, 1830–1860* (Washington, 1938), pp. 12 and *passim.* Cf. Nye, *Fettered Freedom* (East Lansing, 1949), pp. 54 ff.; Eaton, "Censorship of the Southern Mails," *AHR,* XLVIII (1943), 266–280.

[45] For Garrison's perceptive analysis of the literary style of Whittier, Phelps, May, Bourne, and other noted abolitionists, see Garrisons, I, 461.

"incendiary" papers, approved the Charleston action, and, in instances, recommended the extension of censorship to all mail, printed or private.

The North was unsympathetic to abolitionist strategy, but alarmed by the implications of censorship. Not so the government in Washington. The Charleston postmaster requested instructions from the Postmaster General, Amos Kendall, a vigorous slaveholder and strong arm of the Jackson "Kitchen Cabinet," who concluded that "we owe an obligation to the laws, but we owe a higher one to the communities in which we live."[46]

On the opening of Congress, Jackson in his Message recommended the "passing of such a law as will prohibit, under severe penalties, the circulation in the southern states, through the mail, of incendiary publications intended to instigate the slaves to insurrection."[47] This recommendation was embodied in a bill which passed a perturbed and divided Senate. Van Buren, in the Vice-President's chair, cast the deciding vote. The bill was finally lost in the fine-spun logic of Calhoun, who wished to stop abolitionist use of the mails, but who also wished to preserve freedom of the press and, incidentally, to avoid sustaining a President with whom he had fallen violently out.[48]

It was in this atmosphere of dissent that the question of the right of petition was raised. That Adams should have suffered so much personal harassment in the course of the controversy helps measure the distance between the abolitionists and their government in 1836. Adams was no abolitionist when he entered upon his congressional career. He was scarcely an abolitionist on the twenty-first of February, 1848, when he collapsed at his seat in the House of Representatives, shortly after to die. His strength lay in his restatement of the Constitution as an instrument of freedom; it lay, also, in his vivid sense of the

[46] Jay, *View of the Action of the General Government*, p. 77. The recurrence of "higher law" doctrines must impress any student of the period; close scholarly study of the concept is long overdue. For basic considerations, Richard B. Morris, "Theologico-Political Concepts: the Law of Nature and the Law of God," in *Studies in the History of American Law, with Special Reference to the Seventeenth and Eighteenth Centuries* (New York, 1930), pp. 21 ff.

[47] Richardson (ed.), *Messages of the Presidents*, III, 176. For response of the Executive Committee of the American Anti-Slavery Society, see *A Collection of Valuable Documents* . . . (Boston, 1836), pp. 41–53.

[48] Margaret L. Coit, *John C. Calhoun: American Portrait* (Boston, 1950), p. 309; readable and unpretentiously pro-Democrat is Claude G. Bowers, *The Party Battles of the Jackson Period* (Boston, 1922), p. 446. Decisions on mail were finally placed in the hands of the local postmasters. Abolitionists gave up their attempt to keep the mails free.

Revolutionary ideals on which he had been all but weaned, and which neither antislavery nor proslavery partisans were willing to gainsay. Joining the House in December 1831, Adams quickly assumed unique status from all parties as its mediating intelligence. The "corrupt bargain" had sunk without a trace.

Petitions came to him (not from his constituents) praying an end of slavery in the District of Columbia. Adams' personal interest in the matter was slight. He was unwilling to have the 6,000 slaves affected passed upon, except with the consent of the District's white population; he was even unwilling to have the District's very active slave trade abruptly disturbed.[49] But the right of petition had been secured in the First Amendment of the Bill of Rights, and Adams felt duty bound to preserve it as a cornerstone of liberty.

Petitions were not new to the House, which received floods of them on every subject. Antislavery men had circulated "memorials" for signature in 1806, soliciting an end to the foreign slave trade when its constitutional protection should expire in 1808. There had been petitions to abolish slavery in the District as early as 1814. Benjamin Lundy was a leader in the notable petition campaign of 1828, and never forgot the issue; a year later, the House had adopted a resolution, under pressure from the honest Pennsylvania Federalist, Charles Miner. This resolution, first offered in 1826, denounced the slave trade in Washington and approved gradual emancipation there.[50]

Petitions were not new to Adams, who had presented fifteen of them soon after his arrival in the House in 1831, with an explanation that he personally hoped "slavery would not become a subject of discussion in that house." But since then, slavery had become an object of universal discussion. When, on December 16, 1835, a petition[51] was presented from 172 Maine ladies through their representative, and,

[49] Bemis, *John Quincy Adams and the Union* (New York, 1956), pp. 326 ff.; Robert P. Ludlum, "The Antislavery 'Gag-Rule': History and Argument," *JNH*, XXVI (1941), 203 ff.; Mary Tremain, *Slavery in the District of Columbia* . . . (New York, 1922).

[50] *Minutes of the Proceedings of the Eleventh American Convention for Promoting the Abolition of Slavery* . . . (Philadelphia, 1806), p. 26; *Genius of Universal Emancipation*, IX (November 8, December 6, 13, 27, 1828); X (January 3, 1829); McMaster, *History*, V, 218 ff.

[51] Woman suffragists later took the ground that petitions were the one right granted them by an unjust government. But these petitions did not begin with the fight against the gag law. As the *National Enquirer* observed in 1830: "More petitions from ladies respecting the Cherokee Indians, have been presented to Congress. They mean to put the gallantry of that body to a severe test." *National Enquirer*, X (February 26, 1830).

several days after, another made its appearance, southern congressmen concluded they had had enough. Several days of quarreling resulted in a resolution reporting Congress's inability to interfere with slavery in the District of Columbia. Adams voted with the majority, hoping for peace.

It was the southern contingent which forced the war upon the North, in May 1836, demanding not merely a pledge of congressional immunity to antislavery action, but that the very petitions challenging it be laid upon the table without receiving notice. Now Adams had come to the end of concessions. At the back of his mind, even when he had endorsed the majority opinion opposing agitation of the District question, had been the thought that Congress had a war power permitting her to deal with slavery as she saw fit. On such grounds, Adams mustered his first eloquence opposing the gag on petitions—grounds which would furnish a precedent for the later Emancipation Proclamation by Abraham Lincoln. The gag passed; and Adams, beginning his eight-year battle on the ruling, turned for support wherever he could. He found it among the abolitionists.

The abolitionists (not Adams) had initiated the effort to create an abolitionist issue, and it was southern action (not Adams) which gave the abolitionists work to do, enabling them to evoke disapproval from hundreds of thousands of northern signers of petitions who might otherwise have been indifferent or inert. Henry Clay in 1839 protested that "The government has remained here [in the District] near forty years without the slightest inconvenience from the presence of domestic slavery."[52] Such were the sentiments of a colonizationist, who had been willing to see Kentucky abolish slavery in 1798, and who admitted that slavery was an evil. Most Northerners were intellectually less sophisticated in their contempt for slavery than was Clay, but their stake in it was less. Adams and his aides undertook to show them that their stake in freedom was threatened.

Small, potbellied, bald, and old, with no graces of voice or manner, Adams displayed extraordinary stamina in standing up session after session to attacks which were all but physical. He seemed to gather strength and conviction from them, from the coarse, threatening missives he received, and from the impossible odds against which he worked his way. His eloquence was not of the ornate and studied type

[52] *Speech of the Hon. Henry Clay . . . on the Subject of Abolition Petitions, February 7, 1839* (Boston, 1839), p. 16.

which made Webster and Clay national attractions. It was plain, impassioned, and drawn from long contemplation of legal and religious principles. It also contained the cultural component of a student of Shakespeare who himself wrote verse and had even written a novel.[53] Gagged by the house rule against slavery petitions—it became a standing rule in 1840—Adams became a master at finding ways to introduce his subjects and his petitions which brought him under constant danger of censure and expulsion. Once he put the House into an uproar which lasted for days by asking whether he might present a petition "purporting" to come from slaves. (His powerful summary included the fact that he had not presented the petition, and that it *opposed* abolition.) Again, he presented piles of petitions against the annexation of Texas—not the same as antislavery petitions, but, in the nature of the case, amounting to the same thing. Still another from among the thousands of petitions he sternly brought to the House was from Haverhill, Massachusetts, and asked that Congress "immediately adopt measures peaceably to dissolve the Union of these States." The storm following moved between efforts to have the petition burned before the House and to censure Adams. With days, and even weeks, being given over to petitions, linked to every permutation of the slavery question, it was clear that the antislavery conflict had come to Washington.

Adams' growth as a symbol of northern independence and loyalty to constitutional privileges is unparalleled in American history. He wrote the introduction to the family memoir of the murdered Lovejoy. He was in touch with all abolitionist elements, though his personal feelings brought him closer to Joshua Leavitt, Lundy, and Channing, whose *Slavery* (1835) was one of the most influential endorsements of antislavery. If Channing did not quite meet the harsh opposition which Adams endured, he had the same qualities of intractable independence and moderation which characterized Adams in his congressional operations.

The battle for petitions brought women to the fore as partners in the work of drawing them up and soliciting signatures. The son of

---

[53] The similarities and differences between Adams and his grandson Henry Adams are arresting and thought-provoking. For contributions to the subject (which do not, however, cover the cultural and historical ground requiring comparison), see James T. Adams, *The Adams Family* (Boston, 1931), and the introduction by Brooks Adams to Henry Adams, *The Degradation of the Democratic Dogma* (New York, 1920), pp. 1–122.

Abigail Adams, though old-fashioned in his view of the female role in society, accepted the antislavery ladies with grace. He confounded his admirers as well as his assailants by expressing his personal unwillingness to see the District of Columbia made free; yet he presented a petition which asked that the Capital be moved north, where the principles of the Declaration of Independence would not be treated as a "mere rhetorical flourish." Adams was less the disinterested proponent of free speech than he made himself out to be. "My opinion upon the subject of slavery differs little if anything from yours," he wrote Lewis Tappan, who was impatient to see him enrolled among the abolitionists. "Upon the means of ridding our country of moral evils inflicted upon us, my opinion differs from yours, but this is a difference of deliberate judgment, and not of principle."[54]

In the beginning, Adams stood alone, simply because those in the House disturbed by the challenge of free speech were unable to separate it from the hue and cry raised against abolition. The proslavery enterprise was organized by Calhoun in the Senate. There Thomas Morris met the proposal of a gag rule triumphantly, out of an experience which went back to 1806, when he had begun his eminent career in the Ohio legislature. Denounced by Calhoun as an abolitionist, Morris retorted: "Sir, if I am an Abolitionist, Jefferson made me so." His great speech of February 9, 1839, was kept green by the abolitionists, and he himself was esteemed as their elder statesman until his death in 1844.

The House of Representatives was more sensitive to the fancied demands of its constituents than was the dignified and longer-lived Senate, and Adams needed all the support he could muster to withstand the concerted abuse of the proslavery forces. Lundy, who had followed Adams' policies without pleasure for many years, now found himself at one with him. In 1838, Weld prepared one of his several powerful pamphlets—an accumulation of data citing innumerable precedents throughout the world for government action against slavery—it went rapidly into a number of editions, and reappeared in Adams' perorations.[55] The fight for petitions became part of William Jay's classic indictment of the government's policies on slavery, and he himself read an "Address to the Friends of Constitutional Liberty"

---

[54] Adams to Tappan, February 7, 1837, Tappan Papers, LC.
[55] "Wythe," *The Power of Congress over the District of Columbia* (New York, 1838).

in 1840 which, sinewy with facts, indicted the government in Federalist prose such as Adams had not been able to afford since his battle had begun.[56] Such writings only preceded a flood of articles in the abolitionist press which brought the issue home to the entire North.

In the House, Adams' cause gained increasing strength, mainly from Whigs, outstanding among whom was William Slade of Vermont, moving steadily toward abolition. In 1840, he was clear on the iniquity of the gag rule, vague on abolition, and emphatic on the country's need for William Henry Harrison, whose views on abolition he candidly confessed he did not know. "I do know, however, that they cannot be worse than those of his competitor [Van Buren]." More vigorous was Joshua R. Giddings, a Whig from Ashtabula County in the Western Reserve of Ohio, a self-made man interested in business and law, who, with his partner, Benjamin F. Wade, in 1835 had been "converted" by Weld to abolition. Once Giddings joined the House, late in 1838, he lent his fearless and powerful personality to the petition controversy, disdaining the parliamentary niceties which gave an aura to Adams' campaign. Giddings was a politician. His radical constituents in what was, perhaps, the most abolitionist county in the land, would have reason to chide him for equivocal actions. But in so adverse a House as he faced, Giddings could only appear in all his strength: the first of the "political abolitionists" who were to inherit the antislavery crusade.[57]

Giddings came to Washington, as he wrote, "determined to soothe & reconcile." He voted for a resolution that the government had no power over slavery in the states. He thought well, at first, of the House leaders of southern militancy. He admired Clay, and persisted in regarding him as an antislavery leader despite discontent in his own party. But he became friendly with William Slade, was revolted by the slave coffles which passed before the Capitol, and voted against the gag rule. In February 1839, he voted against a bill for the improve-

---

[56] Jay, *Miscellaneous Writings,* pp. 397 ff.

[57] Willard D. Loomis, "The Anti-Slavery Movement in Ashtabula County, Ohio, 1834–1854" (M.A., Western Reserve University, 1936); Edward C. Reilly, "Early Slavery Controversy in the Western Reserve" (Ph.D., Western Reserve University, 1940); Karl F. Geiser, "The Western Reserve in the Anti-Slavery Movement," *Proc. MVHA, 1911–1912* (Cedar Rapids, Iowa, 1912), pp. 73–98. For a general study by a political associate, see George W. Julian, *The Life of Joshua R. Giddings* (Chicago, 1892).

ment of the District of Columbia, on the grounds that it would not house the government long. He went on with his tirade in defiance of angry southern representatives, denouncing both the slave trade and the gag on petitions; and though he was ruled out of order, the District Bill did not pass.

Thereafter, Giddings was a conspicuous figure in the campaign to raise the gag, and he broadened his own program to oppose the government's war on Indians and runaway slaves. Here he stood alone, for Adams, as a nationalist and former Secretary of State, had earlier approved Jackson's bold and ruthless policies in what had been Spanish territory.

By 1842, there was a solid core of congressmen concerned for the right of petition and more. As Giddings observed: "There has been a great revolution going on here as to human rights since Mr. Adams' 'flare up,' and many members now wish themselves to be regarded as the advocates of the rights of man who would have been angry at being called an abolitionist six months since."[58]

Events pushed northern politicians further on the stony path of antislavery. The campaign opposing the annexation of Texas fittingly closed Lundy's great services to emancipation. It involved abolitionists in the closest relations with Adams, and permitted a marshaling of antiannexationist, antislavery opinion such as had not been earlier conceived. Compared with the agitation which had attended the Missouri controversy fifteen years before, that against the acquisition of Texas was deep and popular.

The settlement of Texas and its place in the Mexican revolution against Spanish rule are matters of infinite complexity, but the proslavery bias accompanying its beginnings is patent. In justification of the American settlers, historians have cited the weakness of the Mexican government, its corruption, ineptitude, and cruelty, the inevitability of American settlement, and the alleged breaking of contracts by the Mexican leaders.[59] The role of the American government has been held to have been officially neutral, though none would claim it was unsympathetic to Texas revolutionists: "It has never been established that Jackson plotted the Texan Revolution. He did not have to do so."[60]

[58] Giddings to his wife, March 13, 1842, cited in Ludlum, "Joshua R. Giddings, Antislavery Radical (Part I, 1795–1844)" (Ph.D., Cornell University, 1935), pp. 143–144.

[59] Justin H. Smith, *The Annexation of Texas* (New York, 1941 ed.), *passim*.

[60] Bemis, *Adams and the Union*, p. 354. For a view of the operation as

As news came of the Texan victory under General Sam Houston at San Jacinto, in April 1836, and the proclamation of the Republic of Texas, Lundy bestirred himself. His three journeys to Texas in 1830 and after had been unfruitful for Negro emancipation and colonization, but his personal knowledge of the temper of the Texas settlers could serve free soil. He published nine letters in the *National Gazette* on the subject, and sent copies to Adams. Though continuing the *Genius* as a monthly, Lundy then, in August 1836, established the *National Enquirer*, a weekly, largely to press the anti-Texas campaign and alarm the country.[61] Thereafter, he was a major influence in Adams' work. When the gentle Quaker died in 1839, in Illinois where he had gone to join his children and where he engaged in antislavery work to the end, Adams felt a keen personal sense of loss. Lundy's articles, as published in pamphlet form, became among the most effective of the era. *The War in Texas . . . Showing That This Contest Is . . . a . . . Crusade against the Government, Set on Foot by Slaveholders . . .* (1836), with much more in the title, went into several editions, and was a magazine of argument and data to abolitionists.

That Jackson and Van Buren desired the entrance of Texas into the Union there can be no doubt. That, as a result, war with Mexico was possible is also clear. Into the breach stepped Adams, quarreling with Congress and the administration in terms of his perennial, freedom of speech, but also in terms of the government plans. Annexation would be a setback for freedom, he asserted; war would be infamous. Adams painted vivid panoramas of catastrophe, involving Texas, Mexico, Cuba, Great Britain, and other nations and territories. Beside him stood his congressional aides, his abolitionist friends and well-wishers, and, not least, the New York Peace Society, including a highly respectable membership, some with memories of wars and issues that went back to 1812. Their arguments, urging the establishment of an international court of arbitration, would be remembered when the Hague Court was being instituted at the close of the century.[62] Their practical accomplishment during the first Texas crisis

---

proslavery, see Horace Greeley, *The American Conflict* (Hartford, 1864). I, 147 ff.

[61] See Lundy's valedictory, *National Enquirer*, III, March 8, 1838. The paper thereafter became the *Pennsylvania Freeman*, and was first edited by Whittier.

[62] Curti, *The American Peace Crusade, 1815–1860* (Durham, 1929), pp. 57 ff.

was that they exposed the fact that Mexico had offered to arbitrate her differences with the United States. By so doing, they forced a compromise which helped stave off war.

There were not only the usual petitions to give Adams his occasions for speech, but resolutions against annexation from the legislatures of eight northern states, all of which were tabled as though they had been abolitionist petitions. Adams' arguments were given additional support by the materials which David Lee Child had developed. Child, who had contemplated joining Lundy in his Texas venture, had studied its possibilities, and incorporated his findings in a memoir to the Société pour l'Abolition d'Esclavage.[63]

Without Adams—without the support he had drawn upon—annexation might well have followed upon the recognition of Texas in 1836 or 1837, and war might conceivably have broken out against Mexico. Thanks to the antislavery front, annexation was resisted until the high public enthusiasm for conquest had temporarily subsided. By 1842, the campaign for annexation had to be undertaken anew. The attitude of the Democrats was clear. Jackson reproved Houston, not for imperialism, but for poor strategy. "The first step that led to the injury of the fame of Texas," he wrote, "was that foolish campaign to Santa Fé [an attempt to incorporate further Mexican territory beyond the acknowledged Texas border]; the next the foolish attempt to invade Mexico, without means and men sufficient for the occasion."[64]

However, Mexico was not swallowed up, and Texas did not become the six to eight slave states Northerners were haunted into anticipating. "It is rather curious to note that the denunciations of the annexation project uttered by eloquent men like Channing and Adams continued to exert their influence, both directly and by reflection in the works of other writers, although time has shown how far astray were the apprehensions upon which they were based."[65] But the fact that the evils foreseen did not materialize does not necessarily mean that they were not forestalled. The sentiments nurtured by Adams, Weld, Leavitt, Lundy, and their familiars were to have a future flowering in the anti-imperialist tradition.

   [63] Correspondence, between the Hon. F. H. Elmore . . . [and] Birney . . . (New York, 1838), pp. 61 ff.; Bemis, Adams and the Union, p. 365; Letters of L. Marie Child, p. viii.

   [64] Andrew Jackson to Sam Houston, August 31, 1843; cited in Smith, The Annexation of Texas, p. 72.

   [65] Ibid., p. 5.

Adams went on to disappoint the abolitionists. He stated flatly that he opposed emancipation in the District of Columbia, and would vote against it: the country opposed the project, which no more than impeded the anti-Texas campaign. In addition, Adams would not oppose the entrance of Florida into the Union as a slave state; this would be a breach of faith. Birney wrote bitterly of his "apostacy." Adams, he believed, "owes much of his present popularity—may I not say, nearly all—to his connexion with the Anti-slavery agitation. Abolitionists have contributed more than any other class of persons to swell the tide of his influence." This was no more real than the view that "Mr. Adams never identified himself with the antislavery men and associations of his day."[66] There was no clear line between those who gathered the petitions, who formulated arguments in their behalf, who stirred up sentiments against a slavery Texas and a gagged Congress, and Adams and others who were gathering about him, in and out of Congress.

Abolitionists in the late 1830's were heady with their dearly bought success. It appeared to them that they were about to supersede the opportunists and sweep the field. Although they failed to do so, it is inaccurate to imagine that national politics swallowed up abolition. Antislavery broadened into a northern cause and, as such, inevitably called into action every manner of practical man and opportunist. But even opportunists found themselves linked, despite themselves, to the plans of the most dedicated fanatics, and familiar with them. The tradition developed, during this period, of putting questions to political candidates, and demanding answers kept the most wily and self-seeking politicians alert to reform slogans and respectful of reformers' wishes.[67] If they were often poor and inconsiderate servants, they were, at least, prevented from becoming masters. They were more or less held to account, and their failures supplemented with private action.

---

[66] Birney to Leicester King, January 1, 1844, Dumond (ed.), *Birney*, II, 772; Wilson, *Rise and Fall of the Slave Power*, I, 433.

[67] See, for example, *An Examination of Mr. Bradish's Answer to the Interrogatories Presented to Him by a Committee of the State Anti-Slavery Society, October 1, 1838* (Albany, 1838).

CHAPTER 6

Schisms and Debates

A young man, named Ralph Waldo Emerson . . . after failing in the every-day avocations of a Unitarian preacher and schoolmaster, starts a new doctrine of Transcendentalism, declares all the old revelations superannuated and worn out, and announces the approach of new revelations and prophecies. Garrison and the non-resistant abolitionists, Brownson and the Marat Democrats, phrenology and animal magnetism, all come in, furnishing each some plausible rascality as an ingredient for the bubbling cauldron of religion and politics.[1]

INNUMERABLE plans and projects characterized the age of reform, and earned an enduring fame or notoriety. It is impossible to chart fully the ramifications of social and spiritual experimentation in this age. Moreover, the projects of the theorists cannot be separated from those of the Free-Soilers and antislavery crusaders. There was no dividing line between the two types of social effort, and reformers moved freely from idealism to free soil and other more "practical" undertakings. Both efforts left themselves open to charges of fanaticism and incompetence.

Abolition was no mere political slogan. Certainly, economic and political motives for abolition had operated largely to free the North of slavery, and they would continue to affect northern opinion. Economic and political motives to continue slavery were also strong. But divorced from moral considerations, they tended to become impotent. Daniel R. Goodloe was a North Carolinian who in 1841 appealed to

[1] Adams (ed.), *Memoirs of John Quincy Adams*, X, 345.

the material interests of the non-slaveholders of the South in his *Inquiry into the Causes which Have Retarded the Accumulation of Wealth and Increase of Population in the Southern States.* His plea had no effect. He went north to become an abolitionist and associate of Dr. Gamaliel Bailey on the *National Era* in Washington.[2] Western Virginia was both antislavery and antiabolitionist. Its most respectable opinion, like that of Dr. Henry Ruffner, president of Washington College at Lexington, Virginia, favored gradual emancipation and denounced the "moral insanity" of abolitionists.[3] Yet it took the Civil War to overthrow the system in that region.

In the 1830's, the union of politics and morality was still to be forged. It required, among other catalysts, the reformer. The process of clarifying aims and differences can be observed in the conversation of two "moral reformers," one a Garrisonian, the Reverend Henry C. Wright, the other the Reverend Francis Wayland, who, in addition to other honors, was a leading Baptist and believed himself to be against slavery. As Wright related:

The conversation turned on the question—*Can a slaveholder be a Christian?* . . . I asked him—"Can a man be a Christian and claim a right to sunder husbands and wives, parents and children—to compel men to work without wages—to forbid them to read the Bible, and buy and sell them—and who habitually does these things?" "Yes," answered the Rev. Dr. and President [of Brown University], "provided he has the spirit of Christ." "Is it possible for [a man] to be governed by the spirit of Christ and claim a right to commit these atrocious deeds, and habitually commit them?" After some turning, he answered, "Yes, I believe he can." "Is there, then, one crime in all the catalogue of crimes which, of itself, would be evidence to you that a man has not the spirit of Christ?" I asked. "Yes, thousands," said the Dr. "What?" I asked. *"Stealing,"* said he. "Stealing what, a *sheep* or a MAN?" I asked. The Doctor took his hat and left the room, and appeared no more.[4]

Thus enthusiasms were more than indications of unrest; they offered keys to social needs; they suggested means for action. They ranged

[2] No more successful was Goodloe's *The Southern Platform* . . . (Boston, 1858), another of the compilations of the opinions of "the most eminent Southern Revolutionary characters" and other distinguished, but deceased, dignitaries.

[3] [Henry Ruffner] *An Address to the People of West Virginia . . . by a Slaveholder* (Lexington, 1847).

[4] Garrisons, III, 12–13.

from manifestly unbalanced nostrums to serious and substantial proposals. The age produced scores of fanatics, who premised their careers —sometimes with remarkable success—on illusory experiences and anticipations, and whose work bore no relation to reality. Such was the career of Robert Matthews, one of Finney's less happy converts, who, in the early 1830's, as the self-appointed "Matthias, the Jew," consummated a weird religious adventure involving rites, prophecies, and sexual orgies with what was almost certainly the murder of one of his disciples, and who swayed numerous lives in the process.[5]

There were even communities which survive as episodes in significant lives, rather than as important social experiments. This would be true of Fruitlands, in Massachusetts, which in 1843 housed the famous family of A. Bronson Alcott and a few others. Fruitlands sought to recapture the primitive simplicity of Paradise. Though its ideas were beneficently intended, including vegetarianism and unwillingness to use animals as beasts of burden, its practice suggests too little that might be used by society to command much attention. Alcott was a utopian who became interested in antislavery. John A. Collins was a competent abolitionist who turned to Owenism and atheism, and whose Skaneateles community, during 1843–46, was one of the interesting co-operative experiments of the time.[6] On a more serious level was Hopedale, Adin Ballou's effort in "practical Christianity," which at its height was composed of some two hundred men, women, and children. It was organized for permanent social living in 1840. When the community had, for all practical purposes, come abruptly to an end in 1856, it had passed through a series of experiences in social and economic living which could be pondered with profit by would-be experimenters.[7]

Such ventures as Hopedale also suggested that life could be an

[5] Gilbert Seldes, "A Messianic Murderer," *The Stammering Century* (New York, 1928), pp. 117 ff.; cf. William L. Stone, *Matthias and His Impostures: or, The Progress of Fanaticism. Illustrated in the Extraordinary Case of Robert Matthews, and Some of His Forerunners and Disciples* (New York, 1835).

[6] Clara E. Sears (comp.), *Bronson Alcott's Fruitlands* (Boston, 1915); Garrisons, III, 95 and *passim*. Collins ended up a gold prospector and, later, a California businessman, "brazen-faced" in his "denial of his earlier & better life"; Samuel J. May, Jr. (cousin of Samuel J. May) to Richard D. Webb, July 12, 1864, May Papers, BPL.

[7] William S. Haywood (ed.), *History of the Hopedale Community . . .* by Adin Ballou (Lowell, Mass., 1897); Noyes, *History of American Socialisms*, pp. 119 ff. and *passim*.

adventure. This was especially true of the renowned Brook Farm community. Like most of the experimental colonies of the reform era, this one was in its inception religiously motivated. The Reverend George Ripley, father of Brook Farm, was a Boston Unitarian minister and one of the Transcendental Club, an exclusive democracy which mixed inchoate idealism with hard Yankee individuality. Its most distinguished figure was Emerson, but it received Alcott with no concern for his worldly failures.[8]

Ripley initiated Brook Farm in 1841, and quickly had an exciting community dedicated to an assault on drudgery and convention. It sought co-operative sharing of necessary labors, a free relationship between men and women within the confines of accepted morality, exploratory education for the children, and an intellectual atmosphere. To Brook Farm, as tenants or guests, came many of the New England cultural notables of the age. Here Margaret Fuller held forth, on her road from child prodigy to editor of the *Dial* and, later, literary critic of the New York *Tribune*. Most complex in his reactions to Brook Farm was Nathaniel Hawthorne. His haunted and lonely youth should have warmed and expanded in its delightful atmosphere; he evidently expected that it would. But he found farm work irritating, and the optimism of the reformers offensive. Hawthorne, in his historical fiction, was a critic of Puritan bigotry and intolerance. In his own day, he found the Democratic party more attractive than Brook Farm, and this was the party in its least attractive guise: that of his doughface friend, Franklin Pierce, whose biography he wrote. Hawthorne, who was upset by Puritan treatment of Quakers in the seventeenth century, was not disturbed by slavery in his own time.[9]

In 1844, Brook Farm ceased to be the Institute of Agriculture and Education and became a Fourierite Phalanx, modeled after the grandiose and nonreligious plans of the great French theoretician Charles Fourier. Now social life, industry, housing, and responsibilities were to be economically organized. "The joyous spirit of youth was

---

[8] Perry Miller (ed.), *The Transcendentalists* (Boston, 1950), pp. 59 and *passim*.

[9] Hawthorne's *The Blithedale Romance* (1852) satirized Brook Farm and generalized about reformers as autocratic and cruel, hypocritical and vain. His story, "The Celestial Railroad," satirized Transcendentalism. Yet, oddly enough, Brook Farm was a romantic memory to a man whose children were scarcely aware, during their youth, that their father was a famous writer; Julian Hawthorne, *Nathaniel Hawthorne and His Wife* (Boston, 1884), I, 244–245.

sobered."[10] The new emphasis was upon techniques, rather than spiritual satisfactions; the individual took second place to the Phalanx. Horace Greeley threw himself into the Fourierite movement, won over by its American exponent, Albert Brisbane, and became president of the American Union of Associationists.[11]

At Brook Farm, a great "phalanstery" was built which was to have housed its expanded enterprises and ensured its material success. In March 1846, it burned to the ground, and its devotees scattered in many directions. Only one of the central Brook Farm figures added marked distinction to his career after the community's disruption. Charles A. Dana moved on to the New York *Tribune,* where he still conceived himself as "more resolute in the cause of reform, but freed from all exclusive devotion to any special method of helping."[12] He became the bitter and cynical editor of the New York *Sun* and an enemy of all experiment.

It is evident that the fire was no more than the occasion for Brook Farm's failure. There is too marked a discrepancy between its rapid disintegration and the courage with which other groups endured persecution and worse to maintain their convictions. There is too striking a contrast between the failure of the socialist experiments and the vitality of those which were based on religious principles. Reform, during the era of reform, certainly, was in large measure a function of religious inquiry, as well as of practical dissatisfaction. This fact assured the development of the antislavery crusade as, in part, a product of developments among religious explorers, as well as religious groups and institutions.

Orestes A. Brownson survives as a classic example of New England religious unrest. Brownson in childhood was exposed to Congregationalism, Methodism, and Presbyterianism; and in 1826, at the age of

[10] Octavius B. Frothingham, *George Ripley* (Boston, 1882), pp. 188–189.

[11] Brisbane's famous book was *Social Destiny of Man, or Association and Reorganization of Industry* (Philadelphia, 1840). Its essentially dogmatic view of human relations may be judged by the categories it finds for "Servitudes to be Abolished" (p. 101): "1. Native Slavery. 2. Slavery of prisoners taken in war. . . . 3. Slave trade, and exploitation of slaves. 4. Sale and Seclusion of women in seraglios. 5. Servitude of the soil or feudal bondage. 6. Military conscriptions. 7. Perpetual monastic vows. X INDIGENCE OR PASSIVE AND INDIRECT SERVITUDE." The abolition of the final category was deemed sufficient to overthrow the others.

[12] Charles A. Dana to Elizur Wright, February 15, 1849, Samuel J. May Collection, Cornell University.

twenty-three, self-taught and self-made, he was ordained a Universalist preacher. In 1829, he was converted to Fanny Wright and rationalism, and to a theoretic approval of the Workingmen's movement, for which he later substituted the Democratic party. In 1831, he was back in the pulpit, a Unitarian and a disciple of Dr. Channing. In 1836, he became associated with the Transcendental Club, and its most muscular element.[13]

So bare an account of Brownson's quick changes gives no sense of the thought which went into his decisions. He was essentially a philosopher, whose efforts to unite meaning and action caused him to tire quickly of all his intellectual conclusions. The workingmen, he observed, were principally interested in higher wages and the ten-hour day. The religious sects he briefly patronized were insufficiently fortified by deeds. In 1836, Brownson became editor of the Boston *Reformer*, but failed to involve himself in any particular reforms. The economic crash of 1837 galvanized him to new concern for the poor and desperate. But· his determination to be "practical" in reform no more than persuaded him to co-operate with George Bancroft, schoolmaster to the elite, historian of Manifest Destiny, and a professional Democratic politician: a truly distinguished Jacksonian, who believed, though abstractly, that "the day for the multitudes has now arrived."[14] Brownson hoped for a political party which would fulfill his search for divinity in the affairs of men. Unlike the abolitionists, who threw themselves into reform and so built meaning into their religious convictions, Brownson could only act from a priori conviction.

Ripley credited Brownson with having inspired Brook Farm,[15] and Transcendentalists contributed to his Boston *Quarterly Review*, which had soon succeeded the *Reformer*. Brownson, however, tired the Brook Farm colony with his religious argumentativeness, while rapidly accepting the party clichés of the Democrats: a policy which blamed all temporal troubles on the vagaries of public finance, and saw the Whigs as sold to "the Money Power." The logic of Brownson's position

[13] Most thoughtful is Theodore Maynard, *Orestes Brownson, Yankee, Radical, Catholic* (New York, 1943). Schlesinger, *Brownson,* is a *tour de force* which argues that Brownson's "iron logic" brought him inevitably to the support of the Democratic party, but that his unwillingness to compromise led to his isolation. See also Henry Brownson, *Orestes A. Brownson* (3 vols., Detroit, 1898–1900), for details helpful to interpretation.

[14] Nye, *George Bancroft, Brahmin Rebel* (New York, 1945), p. 112.

[15] Brownson, *Brownson,* I, 311 ff.

lay in his hope that a triumphant Democratic party would institute philanthropic legislation and so give life to his millennial hopes. In July and October 1840, he published in the Boston *Quarterly Review* his extraordinary essays on "The Laboring Classes," which embodied his passionate hope for action to "emancipate the proletaries, as the past has emancipated the slaves."[16]

The essential weakness of Brownson's outlook may be seen in the immoderate anxiety he entertained for the success of Van Buren and the Democratic party in the November presidential elections, and the immoderate disillusionment he felt with a people who could prefer William Henry Harrison under Whig auspices. Brownson had evidently dreamed, momentarily, that the votes of the people would be the voice of God, though why they should have chosen the year 1840 for expression was not explained. Brownson's essays were a *tour de force,* a product of verbal comprehension rather than of a serious commitment to the poor. It was this rational irrationality which enabled Brownson to disparage the abolitionists with the conventional phrases of southern apologists and the more demagogic labor spokesmen, who argued that the reformers preferred to deal with problems which were "remote" like slavery and "speculative" like sex equality, while *they* "realistically" grappled with—Van Buren's subtreasury plan.[17] Brownson's frantic efforts to reorganize while holding on to his Democratic party allegiance suggested nothing more practical to him than the nation's need for Calhoun and his meteoric swing to Catholicism in 1844 reflected his need for a more substantial authority than Calhoun or his party. As Brownson phrased it, in his role of philosopher, "The human soul [Brownson's name can here be substituted], being dependent, cannot think in or by itself alone; but alike in ideal intuition and in empirical, there must be presented the object, or there is no thought."[18]

The Church, thereafter, would present the objects which Brownson could think about, though he never ceased to worry other Catholic philosophers with rugged intellectual challenges. A curious phrase of his became, "I am now nobody"—a sidelight, if nothing else, upon the role to which he was consigned in public affairs.

[16] Brownson, "The Laboring Classes," *Boston Qu. Rev.,* III (1840), 358 ff., 420 ff.

[17] Schlesinger, *Brownson,* p. 294.

[18] Quoted in Sidney A. Raemers, *America's Foremost Philosopher* (Washington, 1931), p. 62.

Spiritualism was conceived in fraud: a phenomenon of religious unrest and exploration. In a little town near the ever-stirring Rochester, New York, two young girls, the Fox sisters, discovered that they could make rapping sounds by slightly dislocating the bones of their feet.[19] The present manifestations established contact with helpful spirits and beloved dead. Friedrich Mesmer's relatively recent experiments with "animal magnetism" had been identified with disturbances of the individual's own spirit. Emanuel Swedenborg's vivid communications with the other world were also assumed to offer proof of a spirit world; indeed, John Humphrey Noyes's brilliant analysis of spiritualism saw it as "Swedenborg Americanized."

One of the more notable individuals associated with it was La Roy Sunderland, a small, vibrant figure in the Methodist fold, who could claim memorable revivals, and had seemed on the way to becoming one of the most distinguished of the antislavery ministers.[20] His "magnetism" was soon to give him a role in the new "science" of what was essentially faith healing. It combined aspects of mesmerism, spiritualism, phrenology, and (Sunderland's own contribution) pathetism, which pretended to nothing less than mind control and mind reading. But before this had come to pass Sunderland had in 1834 published his "Appeal on the Subject of Slavery" and, along with the Reverend Orange Scott, begun to give form to the antislavery forces within the Methodist Episcopal Church. In 1836, Sunderland, defying his conservative elders, initiated *Zion's Watchman* in New York, an antislavery journal. In 1842, he helped organize the battle which split the church into northern and southern branches; but he himself left it for a public career in popular science. The Garrisonian, Henry C. Wright, tried Sunderland's powers personally in a public demonstration and endorsed his extrasensory abilities. "Mr. Sunderland's lectures," he declared, "are deserving the attention of all those who believe there is a God, who is a SPIRIT, and who believe that man has a soul." Yet in the long course of his labors, Sunderland himself lost his own faith and died a cheerful atheist.[21]

---

[19] Eliab W. Capron and Henry D. Barron, *Singular Revelations. Explanation and History of the Mysterious Communion with Spirits, Comprehending the Rise and Progress of the Mysterious Noises in Western New-York, Generally Received as Spiritual Communications* (Auburn, N.Y., 1850 ed.).

[20] Sunderland (1802–85) merits further exposition; available at present is a sketch by Barnes, *DAB*, XVIII, 222.

[21] His writings include *Anti-Slavery Manual* (New York, 1837); *The Tes-

Reformers deserted old-line churches for Transcendentalism, spiritualism, atheism, and other isms. William Jay foresaw such individual odysseys: "It often happens when an abolitionist abandons an alleged pro-slavery church he finds no other that suits him. Hence the public worship of God and the Sacraments are neglected. Gradually he and his family learn to live without God in the world, and finally enter upon that broad road which leads to destruction."[22]

Yet Jay himself was finally critical of a church which "has been with few exceptions cold, secular and devoted to the sum of all villainies." It is difficult to determine where church reform ended and radicalism began. Lewis Tappan in setting up his "free" churches in the 1830's, though they were conservative in other respects, challenged the unity of worship. His reputation was such that the American Bible Society refused his offer of $5,000, it being suspected that he intended to press for the distribution of Bibles to Negroes. William Goodell, after he had become a stern critic of Garrison, was not a "Come-Outer" as were Stephen S. Foster and Parker Pillsbury, who entered churches systematically and exhorted worshipers to join them in coming out of proslavery churches. Yet Goodell approved "secessions from *all* corrupt churches . . . with a view of organizing Christian churches in their stead." It helped little for abolitionists, moderate or radical, to argue that compromise or proslavery church policies were examples of "practical atheism," and that abolitionists represented true Christianity. "That *screech* of infidelity is a desperate power against us," Pillsbury noted.[23]

Religious unrest aided church reorganization more than organization. In the 1830's, religious zeal helped sweep reforms high into public consciousness. In the period following, major controversies developed

timony of God against Slavery (New York, 1839 ed.); History of the United States (New York, 1834); Book of Human Nature (New York, 1853); Theory of Nutrition (Boston, 1855); Ideology (Boston, 1885-87); Pathetism (Boston, 1848 ed.), the latter including an appendix by Wright which describes the demonstration.

[22] Tuckerman, *Jay,* p. 148; cf. Jay, *Short Discourses to Be Read in Families* (Philadelphia, 1831).

[23] Jay to Tappan, March 31, 1858, Tappan Papers, LC; Tappan, *Letter to the Convention of Ministers and Representatives of the Evangelical Branches in the Church of Brooklyn* (New York, 1866); Clarence W. Bowen, *Arthur and Lewis Tappan* (New York, 1883), p. 10; Goodell, *Come-Outerism. The Duty of Secession from a Corrupt Church* (New York, 1845); Garrison, *The "infidelity" of Abolitionism* (New York, 1860); Pillsbury to May, September 12, 1853, Garrison Papers, BPL.

based on how abolition might best be achieved, rather than whether or not it ought to be; but religion never ceased to be a factor. The militantly irreligious, whose cause was atheism, had little status in the development of reforms. At best they were no more than a special group of reformers with perhaps a limited grasp of human needs.

Phrenology was supposed to be a science, not a religion. Yet it also represented a hunger for understanding and control, and it broke ground for new approaches to both science and religion. Its late-eighteenth-century founder, Dr. Franz Joseph Gall, and his disciple, Dr. Johann Kasper Spurzheim, believed they were recording the facts of experience in locating the sources of various human abilities and feelings in various parts of the skull: the famous "bumps."[24] Despite its pseudo-scientific bases phrenology promised insight into individual capabilities, and also ways and means for increasing those capabilities by the "exercize of the faculties."

Phrenologists mixed incredible generalizations about races, person-alities, sexual manners, and other matters of popular interest with phrenological lore, on the one hand, and hard common sense, on the other. All this they wove into a pattern to please various conventional schools of thought. As such, for better or worse, they constituted one arena in which social and scientific problems could be debated. Even more impressive was their influence on reform and reformers. Had Horace Greeley's suggestion been taken and trainmen selected by the shape of their heads, more harm than good might have resulted. But phrenology's findings about his "amativeness," "ideality," and other qualities may have helped Walt Whitman drop his conventional per-sonality as good fellow and Democratic party hack and assume his fateful role as poet and seer. Horace Mann assured the famous phre-nologist, Dr. George Combe, that the latter's work had advanced his own by years; and Mann's official reports actually reflected tenets of education of the most successful of all popular phrenologists, Orson S. Fowler, including, for example, the view that whipping was no aid in learning. Phrenology focused Dr. Samuel Gridley Howe's attention on the "faculties," and turned his attention to ways for aiding the blind.[25]

[24] John D. Davies, *Phrenology, Fad and Science: a 19th Century American Crusade* (New Haven, 1955), 142–143.
[25] Gay W. Allen, *The Solitary Singer* (New York, 1955), pp. 81, 103 and *passim;* Esther Shephard, *Walt Whitman's Pose* (New York, 1938), pp. 112 ff.;

The basic service of phrenology to reformers was its premise that life could be improved. Howe's vague assertion that even oysters were capable of improvement epitomizes the optimism which phrenology imparted. Although religious conservatives feared that work with the blind and insane questioned God's will—the atheist and civil libertarian Abner Kneeland sold phrenological books from this perspective —there was a religious aspect to phrenology. "Oh, ye Christians, and Christian ministers of every name and denomination!" cried Fowler editorially. ". . . Look well to the welfare of your *bodies*, if you would improve the welfare of your minds." Sylvester Graham's notions of "symmetry," involving, simply, the view that excess fat was not desirable to the physique, along with his famous wheat bread and other aids to health, were naturally aligned with phrenological tenets and, incidentally, appealed to Garrisonians almost as a sect.[26]

It would be difficult to exaggerate the will of the reformers to find physical and spiritual improvement in this world as well as the next. The boldest and most successful of all such attempts was the Oneida Community, from 1846 to 1879 a spot of self-proclaimed perfectionism in the midst of the commonplace and corrupt. John Humphrey Noyes survives in cynical tags of "free love" masking as religion which do not take into acount his frankness and fortitude as well as his intelligence, and in the enormous and distinctive home in Oneida, New York, the center for close to two hundred men, women, and children who lived and worked in all but unbelievable harmony.

Noyes was slow to arrive at his program. He was born in Vermont in 1814; in 1834, a Congregationalist minister for only a short time, he was expelled by the Association at New Haven and forbidden access to any orthodox pulpit. He had proclaimed himself perfect in a fashion which affronted tenets of original sin and grace. He took a longer step in 1846, when at his small community, then working and living in his own home at Putney, Vermont, he instituted his most challenging doctrine: that of complex marriage. He affirmed that the

---

Harold Schwartz, "Samuel Gridley Howe as Phrenologist," *AHR*, LVII (1952), 644–651.

[26] William S. Tyler, "Grahamites and Garrisonians," ed. Thomas LeDuc, *New York Hist.*, XX (1939), 189–191. See also Dr. William A. Alcott, *Vegetable Diet: as Sanctioned by Medical Men, and by Experience in All Ages* (New York, 1853), a Fowler and Wells publication; and Richard H. Shryock, "Sylvester Graham and the Popular Health Movement, 1830–1870," *MVHR*, XVIII (1931), 172–183.

Kingdom of God had come to him and his coworkers. In simpler terms, this meant that they were no longer separated by artificial and man-made laws, no longer even in the transitional state of "spiritual puberty," but that they all belonged to one another. From this point of view, marriage as commonly understood was mean and exclusive. Men and women could approach each other freely, so long as desire was mutual. Thus, sex was an adjunct of community, of interdependence. It was a doctrine which Noyes carried to his flock with startling success.

It was startling doctrine for neighbors, too, and though the Perfectionists did not at any time flout public opinion, it soon appeared desirable for Noyes to accept an invitation and to move his sect to western New York, near Oneida Lake: a new accession to the Burned-Over District. Noyes and his people set up their log cabins, their barn, their farms; and painfully, bravely, and not without having to overcome opposition, set up their heaven. A steel trap which was better than all other steel traps gave the Perfectionists economic security; but this was little beside the inner security which permitted them to publish their views, to receive guests freely, to live simply, raise children, criticize each other, and all under a set of mores that outraged every Puritan tradition. Here, too, Noyes refined his tenets into a system of life.

As Asa Mahan of Oberlin, who preached a mild form of perfectionism of his own, observed, following an admirably restrained consideration of Noyes's scheme of existence, "Perfectionism in its fundamental principles, is the abrogation of all law."[27] Since Noyes's religion told him he was without blemish, and therefore able to do anything which seemed to him right, chaos should have resulted. The marvel is not that Noyes persuaded his followers of the righteousness of complex marriage, but that they escaped riot, not to say lynch law. This miracle can only have resulted from the palpable decorum with which they lived. Noyes made the details public for all to read who so desired.[28]

[27] For a study of Mahan's "perfectionism," Fletcher, *Oberlin*, I, 207 ff.; Eunice M. Schuster, *Native American Anarchism* (Northampton, 1932), pp. 51 ff.

[28] Noyes, *Home-Talks*, ed., Alfred Barron and George N. Miller (Oneida, 1875), I; Noyes, *Male Continence* (Oneida, 1872); Dr. John B. Ellis, *Free Love and Its Votaries: or American Socialism Unmasked* (New York, 1870), an informed, if antipathetic, study of the Noyes communities. For a general

From Noyes to Garrison would seem an astronomical distance; yet Garrison had also been accused of holding irresponsible views. He had also begun with a program of universal reform, and only afterward settled upon abolition as a major crusade. As early as 1834, he had received Noyes's Putney publication, *The Perfectionist,* and joined in denouncing the "Judaism" and "Popery" of the Protestant churches. Noyes's letter to him in 1837, "renouncing all allegiance to the government of the United States, and asserting the title of Jesus Christ to the throne of the world," impressed him. Noyes's sexual theories did not frighten him. They did not interest him; but Garrison was singularly dispassionate about the peculiar hypotheses of his coadjutors in the search for salvation. To this extent, he was indeed "a shining example of moderate and calculated utterance, while little disturbed by the want of it in others whose anti-slavery sincerity . . . he felt to be equal to his own."[29]

Garrison sought perfectionists, and gained support and stimulation not only from Noyes but from Nathaniel Peabody Rogers of New Hampshire, a poet and abolitionist whom Thoreau admired, and Henry C. Wright whom Thoreau did not. Wright was in some ways a central figure of Garrisonianism. Thoreau misunderstood him: he thought Wright too familiar, too persistently benign. He did not understand that Wright had made up his mind that his life on earth was no more than part of the life he would have beyond death. He believed any religion was absurd "which sends me away from the earth, and all human relations and obligations, into unknown regions of space. . . ."[30] One who felt himself in eternity had no need for anger, though Wright was capable of the most deliberate denunciations of "man-stealers" and "man-stealing churches."

Thoreau was misled by appearances, for Wright and he had much in common. Thoreau, as a young schoolteacher, had been ordered to employ punishment; he had feruled a number of children without

---

account, Robert A. Parker, *A Yankee Saint* . . . (New York, 1935).

[29] Garrisons, II, 114, 145; III, 28. For qualifying considerations, see "Perfectionism Not Pro-Slavery," *The Perfectionist,* III (October 1, 1843), p. 16.

[30] *Autobiography of Henry C. Wright. Human Life: Illustrated in My Individual Experience as a Child, a Youth, and a Man* (Boston, 1849), p. 9. One aspect of Wright is noted in Curti, "Non-Resistance in New England," *NEQ,* II (1929), 34–57. Thoreau, *Miscellanies* (Boston, n.d.), pp. 70 ff., is in praise of Rogers and "the unpledged poetry of his prose." For Wright, see Bradford Torrey (ed.), *Writings of Thoreau* (Boston, 1906), XI, 263–264.

cause or discrimination, thrown down his ruler, and left the classroom.[31] Wright was notorious among abolitionists for his opposition to child punishment, yet he was no mere theoretician. He entered imaginatively into the life of the child. He attempted stories from the point of view of the child in the womb, and from a girl's standpoint. He later wrote of maternity and the destiny of the race, and was, like Noyes, a pioneer in eugenics.[32]

Wright was raised as a farmer and laborer in the Burned-Over District, but had developed such an orthodox character that Channing's 1819 Baltimore sermon at the ordination ceremonies of a Unitarian minister, declaring the principles of their sect, shocked him. A skilled hatmaker who pondered eternity and had broadened his mind and sympathies by reading novels, he turned to the ministry, was graduated from Andover, and was licensed to preach in 1823. His work took him among children; the turn of his mind drew him toward the peace movement. Moral reform had turned him into a rigid teetotaler and independent abolitionist. He met Garrison for the first time in November 1835, and introduced him to the idea of nonresistance in all its implications. Thereafter they were one in their ideas though Garrison's central position in abolition gave him a wider range of associations, and a simpler frame of reference.

Garrison's contemporary opponents were convinced that his program was fantastic. Their habit of judging him as irrational prevented them from determining why he was able to beat them so decisively in the battle within the American Anti-Slavery Society which reached its climax in 1840. The colonizationists went off on another direction, crediting Garrison not only with disruptive and immoral principles, but (not intending a compliment) with responsibility for a mighty organization of free-state forces: "By 1840 Garrison had accomplished very well one thing—the consolidation of New England and the then Northwest in an aggressive sectionalism."[33]

Garrison had done neither. The confusion lay in identifying antislavery sentiment only with the American Anti-Slavery Society. (A later confusion would assume that only the Republican party was an

---

[31] Henry S. Canby, *Thoreau* (New York, 1939), p. 67.

[32] "Part I Antenatal History—a History and Education before My Birth," MS., WRHS; Wright, *The Unwelcome Child* . . . (Boston, 1858), and *The Empire of the Mother over the Character and Destiny of the Race* (Boston, 1863).

[33] Fox, *The American Colonization Society, 1817–1840,* pp. 90–91.

important antislavery agency.) The 1830's were a period in which antislavery and related alliances were being tested. Northerners were not agreed that slavery was evil; they were composed of a congeries of interests, some of which were proslavery. National churches, other national institutions, and the national antislavery society were required to clarify their views. Garrison and his cohorts were largely confined to New England: the area farthest removed from any real stake in slavery.

Garrison's intellectual assault on slavery gave him both strength and weakness—strength in that he could build a cohesive body of workers, armed with the moral arguments of antislavery, who could exercise moral influence throughout the North with minimum organization and expense; weakness in that his program took him farther and farther from the day-to-day building of antislavery forces among ordinary people. Thus his place in antislavery was real, but limited. This was also true of other antislavery leaders, especially so of the free-soil partisans.

Those partisans were many and varied, and largely concerned with church policies on slavery. It was evident to them that the future of their antislavery enterprises depended on their ability to force their churches to repudiate slavery. William Goodell's magazine, *The Christian Investigator,* was given over to probing the possibilities of church schisms and unity, in the interest of abolition.[34]

The Quakers, because their problem was less with slavery, of which they were rid, than abolition, had their crisis earlier. Hopper, Buffum, Lundy, James and Lucretia Mott, Whittier, and many others were actively engaged in abolition, but theirs were individual testimonies favoring social action. The aged Elias Hicks, a Long Island Quaker notable for his extended travels and ministerial services among Quakers, was less concerned for antislavery than they were. His emphasis was on the basic principles of their faith. But his challenge to the more conservative groups within his sect precipitated a struggle within the church which, between 1827 and 1829, led to separations within their meetings.[35] Hicks's major contribution to antislavery was his influential pamphlet *Observations on the Slavery of the Africans and Their De-*

---

[34] See his lecture on "Church Unity and Sectarian Schism," *Christian Investigator, New Ser.,* I (1843), 49 ff.

[35] Bliss Forbush, *Elias Hicks, Quaker Liberal* (New York, 1956), pp. 148–149, 241 ff.

scendents . . . (1810), and his plea that Friends abstain from using rice, cotton, and sugar when they were products of slave labor. Yet Hicksites were not necessarily antislavery. Friends of New York, a Hicksite stronghold, disowned Hopper and Charles Marriott for aggressive abolitionist activities, including the "support and publication of a paper, which tends to excite disunity and discord among us."[36] A later development in the 1840's and after was the "Progressive Friends," a radical permutation which included such worthies, at least as associates, as Lucretia Mott; Oliver Johnson; Thomas Garrett, the Delaware friend of fugitive slaves; and Castner Hanway, who later figured in the famous "Christiana riot."[37]

More momentous were rifts in other denominations. Most important were those which disturbed the Methodists and Baptists, both especially strong in the vast rural stretches from the Burned-Over District into the border states and beyond. It is significant that the leader of the antislavery movement within the Methodist Episcopal Church should have been a New Englander influenced by Garrison and the *Liberator*. Orange Scott, son of a Vermont laborer and himself a laborer, was converted at the age of twenty, became a circuit preacher the next year, and advanced rapidly in his church because of his earnest and successful work. In 1831 he was a delegate to the General Conference of the church. In 1833, however, he became an abolitionist and, appointed presiding elder of the Providence District, led the movement to turn the Methodist organ, *Zion's Herald*, published in Boston, to antislavery. Aggressively abolitionist at the General Conference of 1836, he was not reappointed. He was one of the "Seventy" who, in 1837, carried the message of the American Anti-Slavery Society to the North. His "Appeal to the Methodist Episcopal Church," printed in 1838 in the only number issued of the *Wesleyan Anti-Slavery Review*, officially opened the struggle within the church for a change in its stern antiabolitionist policy.[38] With La Roy Sunderland and Luther

---

[36] *National Anti-Slavery Standard*, II (April 28, 1842); *Narrative of the Proceedings of the Monthly Meeting of New-York . . . in the Case of Isaac T. Hopper* (New York, 1843). For the disowning of another antislavery Quaker, by members of a Meeting who feared for their southern business relations, see *Two Quaker Sisters: from the Original Diaries of Elizabeth Buffum Chace and Lucy Buffum Chace* (New York, 1937), p. xxiii.

[37] Albert J. Wahl, "The Progressive Friends of Longwood," *BFHA*, XXLII (1953), 13–32.

[38] John N. Norwood, *The Schism in the Methodist Episcopal Church 1844* (Alfred, N.Y., 1923); Charles B. Swaney, *Episcopal Methodism and Slavery*

Lee, the latter a powerful revivalist from that hot-bed of religious zeal, the Burned-Over District of western New York, Scott persisted in his campaign despite efforts of New England Methodist leaders to seal him off from his communicants. Scott was kept on as pastor of the St. Paul Church in Lowell, Massachusetts, by its belligerent congregation. A meeting of the rebels at Utica in 1843 created the Wesleyan Methodist Connection of America: a body which had no more than about 15,000 members, but which forced action upon other dissatisfied Methodists who were unwilling to leave the church.[39] The General Conference of the main body in 1844 was driven by the northern Methodists to take a stand which would prevent further secessions. A compromise point was provided by Bishop Andrews, a slaveholder, whom it deposed. A meeting the following year at Louisville, Kentucky, formally established the Methodist Episcopal Church, South. The northern branch never became as committed to antislavery as did the Wesleyan Connection. But it condemned the later Compromise of 1850 and asserted its loyalty to the Union, while its southern brethren joined the forces of separation.

Much the same course of events separated Baptists in 1845. The antislavery leader was Elon Galusha, son of a Connecticut legislator, who preached his gospel with notable success in western New York. Antislavery was no new issue in Baptist territory, where there was the same appeal as that of the Methodists to the humble, the rural, and the enthusiastic. Antislavery was generally aided by the loose organization of the church. Thus in 1806 a Kentucky preacher had been expelled from the Association for preaching abolition. With others of similar persuasion, the Reverend David Barrow had founded the Baptist Licking Locust Association, Friends of Humanity.[40]

As antislavery Baptist bodies multiplied, so did the proslavery ones in the South and antiabolitionist ones in the North. A peculiar ele-

---

(Boston, 1926); Lucius C. Matlack (comp.), *The Life of Rev. Orange Scott* . . . (New York, 1847–48); Matlack, *History of American Slavery and Methodism* . . . (New York, 1849); Rev. Daniel Devinné, *The Church and Slavery* . . . (Boston, 1844); and, on a note of triumph, Matlack, *The Anti-Slavery Struggle . . . in the Methodist Episcopal Church* (New York, 1881). See also Donald G. Mathews, *Slavery and Methodism* (Princeton, 1965).

[39] Luther Lee, *Wesleyan Manual: a Defense of the . . . Wesleyan Methodist Connection* (Syracuse, 1862); see also Lee's *Autobiography* (New York, 1882).

[40] Asa E. Martin, *The Anti-Slavery Movement in Kentucky* (Louisville, 1918), pp. 18 ff.; Sweet, *The Baptists*, esp. Chap. XIV, 564 ff.; Mary B. Putnam, *The Baptists and Slavery, 1840–1845* (Ann Arbor, 1913).

ment was the Free-Will Baptist sect, organized in 1780 and scattered throughout the North to the numbers of some fifty thousand.[41] They were strongly antislavery and in 1839 refused fellowship to slaveholders. Most Baptists were engaged in a more complex clarification of their affairs. In 1840 the antislavery party met in New York, organized the National Baptist Anti-Slavery Convention, and addressed other Baptist churches on the issue. A storm of controversy preceded their next Triennial Convention and was a full victory for the southern wing. Their Bible society, home missionary society, and foreign missionary society accepted "compromise" measures which repudiated "new tests" of fellowship, that is, challenges to slaveholders. Elon Galusha was not returned as a delegate. Nevertheless, the Anti-Slavery Convention continued to meet, and in 1843 formed as a permanent organization the American Baptist Free Missionary Society. Dissolution of the Baptist Church into northern and southern branches was all but accomplished.

As with the Wesleyan Connection, the Baptist missionary societies felt the pressures of northern opinion within their church. Their officers struggled to maintain a middle ground which in 1844 resulted in a lame but sufficient resolution. It protested that the status of the slaveholder had never been questioned; however: "If . . . anyone should offer himself as a missionary, having slaves, and should insist on retaining them as his property, we could not appoint him."[42] In May of 1845 the Southern Baptist Convention met and formed a missionary body with the same name. The Northerners responded with the American Baptist Missionary Union, while protesting that Baptists were still united and brethren. The Reverend Francis Wayland had commiserated with the southern Baptists, who, he thought, were abused; but he served as president of the Baptist General Convention which announced the dissolution of the Triennial Convention. In effect, the Baptists had become Southerners and Northerners.

The split which unevenly divided the Presbyterians in 1837 and beyond was presumably based upon doctrinal differences, rather than the right and wrong of slavery. Presbyterian similarities to Congregationalism were sharp enough to permit controversialists to emphasize the role of their governing bodies. Congregationalists being largely

[41] David Benedict, *A General History of the Baptist Denomination in America and Other Parts of the World* (New York, 1850), I, 906–909.
[42] Goodell, *Slavery and Anti-Slavery*, p. 501.

confined to New England, the only problem they posed for abolitionists was whether or not they would co-operate.[43] It was otherwise with Presbyterians, who extended into the South and could claim vigorous adherents on both sides of the slavery question. Antislavery memorials presented to the General Assembly of 1837 were laid upon the table much as though that body were the House of Representatives. The same Assembly expelled four Synods representing the so-called "New School," or liberal views. They were supported by some 60,000 Presbyterians, all in the North. The next year the schism became general, and though both "New" and "Old" schools held to theology and resisted clarification of the antislavery issue, it appeared at every turn. Ministers like the Reverend Albert Barnes of Morristown, New Jersey, who were accused of "heresy," were antislavery in sentiment. Barnes himself would be better known popularly for his *Inquiry into the Scriptural View of Slavery* (1846) than for his Biblical commentaries.

The American Home Missionary Society was an inevitable point of contention. The Lane Seminary crisis had stirred "Old" and "New" School ministers. As late as 1857, there would be national membership for both factions.[44]

The Unitarians, like the Congregationalists, were largely centered in New England, and no friends of slavery. Such controversy as was precipitated in their midst divided those who were, like Emerson, determined to make contact with the human as well as the cosmic. His Divinity School Address in 1838 made him notorious at Harvard College, since it appeared to question the divine nature of Christ. The heated denunciations of Transcendentalism, infidelity, and pantheism which conservative Unitarians heaped upon rebels brought Theodore Parker into the debate. He was ardent and a phenomenon of learning; his knowledge of twenty languages gave him broad avenues to world thought and experience.

[43] See, for example, Calvin M. Clark, *American Slavery and Maine Congregationalists* . . . (Bangor, Me., 1940).

[44] In that year, however, the New School Assembly condemned the holding of slaves by church members. Secession followed by some twenty-one presbyteries in Missouri, Virginia, Kentucky, Tennessee, and Mississippi, which remained suspended organizationally until 1861, when they joined the newly created southern Presbyterian Church. Rev. John Robinson, *The Testimony and Practice of the Presbyterian Church in Reference to American Slavery: with an Appendix* . . . (Cincinnati, 1852); Sweet, *Presbyterians* (New York, 1936); C. Brúce Staiger, "Abolitionism and the Presbyterian Schism of 1837–1838," *MVHR*, XXXVI (1949), 391–414; Irving S. Kull, "Presbyterian Attitudes toward Slavery," *Church Hist.*, VII (1938), 101–114.

Parker had qualities which seemed to make him kin to Orestes Brownson. Like him, he had been a poor country boy, and could now consort with the intellectual elite of New England. Like Brownson, he was an equalitarian, and for Margaret Fuller's *Dial* in 1841 had set down his "Thoughts on Labor." But unlike Brownson his life was his creed, rather than the reverse. The Bible was a precious book, and Parker never doubted the reality of God. But he saw in man an infinite potential for growth which he characterized as "Absolute Religion," and he had a reverence for people which he found in many religions, and often not among professing Christians.[45] Such naturalistic thought turned conservatives against him. As he spelled out his skepticism respecting the authority of the Bible, the reality of miracles, and the authority of Christ, Parker's Unitarian status became problematic.

He was not alone,[46] his congregation was firm in its support; Antislavery Unitarians like Samuel J. May appreciated his humanitarian eloquence. The narrowness of an *ad hoc* Unitarian Council of Boston, which condemned the Reverend John Pierpont for vigorous antislavery and temperance views, helped Parker's cause, as did Pierpont's persecution by members of his church for "too busy interference" with public questions.[47] In 1843 the Boston Association of Ministers questioned Parker, to no purpose. Channing had died the year before; Parker was his energetic successor and had established his creed and his audience:

It was a queer congregation that met to hear him each Sunday morning: men and women from all classes, but mostly the humblest, men and women who had never gone to church before, or who had drifted away from their orthodox moorings and hoped to find refuge here, reformers, zealots, and fanatics, strangers curious to hear the notorious heretic, critics solicitous for new blasphemies, here and there a reporter from the newspapers, in the galleries a liberal sprinkling of Negroes. . . .[48]

It was in this pattern of schisms and debates, which divided the

[45] *Theodore Parker's Experience as a Minister, with Some Account of His Early Life, and Education for the Ministry* (Boston, 1859), published after his death, an autobiographical letter to his congregation, amply expresses his viewpoint.

[46] For example, *A Protest against American Slavery by One Hundred and Seventy-Three Unitarian Ministers* (Boston, 1845), reflected the liberal and reformistic inclinations of its subscribers.

[47] There is a considerable pamphlet literature on and by Pierpont; see Abbie A. Ford, *John Pierpont: a Biographical Sketch* (Boston, 1909).

[48] Commager, *Parker*, p. 115.

churches of North and South, that the antislavery forces went their separate ways. Lundy had watched the schisms develop among his fellow abolitionists with apprehension: "We wish to raise our voice against the spirit of intolerance which has . . . intruded upon the threshold, and even invaded the sanctuary of the Anti-Slavery Cause in this country. . . . *The* ENEMY *is not yet conquered.*"[49] Yet a clarification of aims and a proof of programs had somehow to be developed. The wonder was that so many dedicated partisans, harboring different theories, continued to hold together till 1840. "He that is not with us," Garrison had written in 1836, "is against us." Quoting St. Luke, though perhaps by way of Denmark Vesey, whose motto it had been, Garrison was reprobating none other than Dr. Channing himself; and not for inaction, but for having finally committed himself, in his *Slavery,* to the view that slavery was morally wrong and ought to be ended. Garrison made various points about Channing's book, in print and in private, but none more revealingly than in his letter to Lewis Tappan:

At last, the great little Dr. Channing has condescended to enlighten the world with a little book on slavery—and all the world is agog! Why, one copy of bro. [Amos A.] Phelps's book is worth a hundred of Channing's—and yet what a deference is paid to the latter! O, this cringing man-worship! It sickens me. Portions of the Dr's marvellous production, I grant are sound, excellent, and clearly expressed; but all these have been taken from the writings of the despised abolitionists, without the slightest credit, and are thus grand moral plagiarisms: the rest of it is made up of contradictions, defamation, and servility to popular opinion. Can any thing be more impertinent or more unmerited than his proscription of those who have digged and McAdamised the road, at great cost and labor, upon which he is now so grandly riding his Coach? . . .[50]

Birney was wiser when in 1836 he welcomed a letter from Channing to the *Philanthropist* which dealt positively with antislavery: "It will do us great good here."[51] Birney was thinking of widening public regard for antislavery issues and ideas; Garrison feared for the purity of abolitionism and, to no small degree, identified it with petty questions of personality. But those who held Garrison to be a brake on the

[49] *National Enquirer,* III (October 12, 1837).

[50] Garrison to Tappan, December 17, 1835. Tappan Papers, LC; cf. Garrisons, II, 54 ff.

[51] Birney to Tappan, December 7, 1836, Dumond (ed.), *Birney,* I, 372; *Letter of William E. Channing to James G. Birney* (Boston, 1836).

development of the antislavery movement missed his real significance. He was a barometer of free speech. His insistence upon open debate and individual expression guaranteed the free forum without which abolition could be suppressed by its influential foes. Moreover, Garrison's eccentric individualism brought out aspects of antislavery which he himself had not anticipated.

He became involuntarily the pioneer of woman's rights. His first view of their role in the antislavery crusade had been conventional: his female coworkers had organized in auxiliaries; had knitted, prayed, signed petitions, held Liberty Fairs and Bazaars for raising money. Even such distinct personalities as Lydia Maria Child and Maria Weston Chapman avoided exposing themselves to competition with males and, in their appeals to other women, advocated the moral pressures available to daughters, wives, mothers, and sisters, rather than a battle for the vote. Garrison's own wife kept house, and without notable co-operation from him.

Garrison's radicalism was a product of his will toward perfectionism, rather than his views of human organization. He made no effort to force his opinions on others; on the contrary, he adored controversy. His societies were loose federations of individuals who accepted the *Liberator* as their mouthpiece, but had no control (and do not appear to have sought it) over its highly personalized editing. Garrison matured a number of related ideas which had been latent in his program of universal reform, and, thanks especially to Henry C. Wright, which were brought out by contemporary events.

Lyman Beecher's energetic interest in enforcing Sabbath observance reminded Garrison that it infringed upon personal rights and was controversial on other counts. In 1836, too, Garrison lent his authority to Wright's principle that nonresistance was the only guide to immediatist pacifism. Garrison also repudiated the national government when it compromised freedom and abetted slavery, though not yet in the drastic "no-government" terms Wright preferred. Garrison's disunion conclusions were still in the future. Such views, which, in varying degrees, stirred numerous reformers, took on particular weight when identified with antislavery. Even the Garrisonians never agreed upon responsible limits to their freedom of speech. As late as 1853, Wendell Phillips, though more uncompromising than Garrison on some points, would question the right of associates to challenge the churches on sectarian questions from an antislavery platform. Was it the understanding of Orthodox friends in Massacheetts, he asked, when they contributed funds to pay the salary of Parker Pillsbury, that he would denounce the Bible and total depravity as blocks to abolition? Phillips contended that it was not.[52] In assessing the harm Garrison and his associates may or may not have done the antislavery movement, it must be recalled that their opponents in the antislavery societies also offended elements of the public with irrelevant opinions. The Tappans, for example, with their rigid sabbatarian principles and anti-Catholic bias, outraged as many citizens as did Garrison—in some cases, many more.

Such opinions were peripheral to antislavery and did not breach abolitionist unity. It was otherwise with the question of female participation in antislavery actions, which, while personally offending many of the abolitionists, especially in strategic New York, also seemed to them basic to a practical campaign for northern support. It is incorrect to say that the "woman question" helped or hindered abolition, since after 1836 women were strategic in every phase of the antislavery fight. There was prejudice against them, as there was prejudice against other antislavery spokesmen. But their cause demanded women simply because it required more hands, minds, and creativity. It had actively solicited them from the days of Benjamin Lundy and gradualist abolition.[53] The sole question was the proper role of women in the work, and here two opinions were possible, both bearing a quantity of truth. Thus a division between those who opposed "unseemly" behavior in women and those who approved it was inevitable.

The agents of separation were two young ladies of the distinguished Grimké family of Charleston, South Carolina, both converts to Quakerism. They concluded that slavery was intolerable to them, and went North to give their testimony against it. They were well received by Philadelphia Quakers and, late in 1836, went on to New York to meet the abolitionists there and to attend meetings of the Female Anti-Slavery Society. Angelina's *Appeal to the Christian Women of the South,* issued that year, asked no more than that the ladies seek guidance in the Bible and influence those who made the laws, that is,

---

[52] *Proceedings of the American Anti-Slavery Society* . . . (New York, 1854), pp. 142–143.

[53] See, for example, "An Appeal to the Ladies of the United States," *Genius of Universal Emancipation,* X (September 16, 1829). Lundy's "Ladies' Repository," conducted by young Elizabeth Chandler, contained numerous items soliciting the activity of women.

the men. The talks which she and her sister, Sarah Moore Grimké, gave in the parlors of abolitionists on their experiences passed without comment. It was when talks in the parlor of a church were announced that a sense of shock was felt: "Even Gerrit Smith . . . advised against the meeting, fearing it would be pronounced a Fanny Wright affair, and do more harm than good."[54]

Soon the Grimkés were touring New England, encouraged by Garrison, given comfort and suggestions by Henry C. Wright, whose views on children, the duties of women, and perfectionist tenets attracted them. As late as August 1837, Angelina would be writing him: "What would'st thou think of the *Liberator* abandoning abolitionism as a *primary* object, and becoming the vehicle of *all* these grand principles?"

Conservative abolitionists were quick to fear the influence of those they held responsible for the turn their work had taken. Birney, exasperated, felt that it would be necessary to repudiate Wright's "multiplied writing and his violent spirit." A man, Birney thought, might be a good man and a pernicious antislavery agent: "Can he not be stopped from writing the Misses Grimké's bulletins? What a blunder and that of a most ridiculous kind he has fallen into—the 'LABORS'? of the Miss Grimkés!!"[55]

A preliminary challenge to the Garrisonians was embodied in the Pastoral Letter of the General Association of Massachusetts to the Orthodox Congregational Churches issued in July. The Grimkés had been speaking in the churches of eastern Massachusetts and had created something of a stir. One of the purposes of the Pastoral Letter was to close the churches to them in terms of "the appropriate duties and influence of women." More serious was an "Appeal of Clerical Abolitionists on Anti-Slavery Measures" which soon followed. Its most formidable signatory was the Reverend Charles Fitch of the First Free Congregational Church of Boston. The "Appeal" condemned the *Liberator* for rudeness harmful to abolition. A second appeal, by

---

[54] Catherine H. Birney, *The Grimké Sisters* (Boston, 1885), p. 162.

[55] Dumond (ed.), *Birney*, I, 418. Yet Birney's chivalrous—and, perhaps, southern—nature caused him to take affront when he learned that Reverend Leonard Bacon had compared the Grimkés with the fanatical Quaker woman who had walked the Salem streets naked in Puritan times, "but that Miss Grimké had not yet made such an exhibition of herself." Meeting him on a boat, he demanded to know whether Bacon had made such a statement. Bacon followed, "I did," with a pause; then, "And should I have said that she *did?*" Birney rejoined, "I wish no further intercourse with you " *Ibid.*, I, 478–481.

abolitionists of Andover Theological Seminary, was broader in its charges, itemizing "speculations which lead inevitably to disorganization and anarchy," the teachings of Henry C. Wright, and "public lectures by females, albeit Quakers." Numerous anti-Garrisonians were now encouraged to believe that a movement to overthrow the New England firebrand and his followers was in the making.[56]

Unlike other sections of the country, however, New England had no immediate function for calm, judicious antislavery men. It could use evangelists, and it could employ practical politicians; together these would ultimately create free-soil leaders wielding national influence. Meanwhile, only evangelists could be heard above the hum of New England's machinery, its bustle of industry. This was true even in the panic year of 1837, which saw "flush times" succeeded by crashing banks and personal fortunes, stark poverty in the cities and defaulting debtors throughout the states.[57]

Lewis Tappan looked forward to a moral and conventionally organized antislavery alliance. Elizur Wright, Leavitt of the *Emancipator,* and others in New York dreamed of a national antislavery movement to which Garrison, with his ultra notions, would be no more than an impediment. Their efforts to bring him to reason, when he demanded their support, their live-and-let-live preachments, were not sincere. They wished to bury his point of view. They felt that he was giving abolition a bad name. In their eyes he was driving away, with his extreme views and invective, a large body of Northerners who opposed

---

[56] Garrisons, II, 133 ff. A more polemical account is embodied in John A. Collins' *Right and Wrong Amongst Abolitionists in the United States* (Glasgow, 1841), intended to influence British opinion.

[57] The panic destroyed the promising trade-union movement and encouraged labor to look west for opportunities. It affected antislavery developments by sharpening northern sensitivity to the desirability of free soil. It stimulated interest in the co-operative movements (Zoltán Haraszti, *The Idyll of Brook Farm* (Boston, n.d.), pp. 9 ff.). Its effect on antislavery reformers is more debatable. It destroyed the Tappans' "free church" movement; but this had not persuaded whites to mix with Negroes, in any event. Arthur Tappan's business failed, and his philanthropies suffered. Gamaliel Bailey reported from Cincinnati that he was not aware "that a single pledge made at the anniversary has been redeemed; and subscribers seem to forget that printers have to eat" (Bailey to Birney, Dumond [ed.], *Birney,* I, 385). There is, however, little evidence that during that panic year societies or even individuals gained or lost antislavery ardor as a result of their economic fortunes. See Quarles, "Sources of Abolitionist Income," *MVHR*, XXXII (1945), 63–76. Reginald C. McGrane, *The Panic of 1837* (Chicago, 1924), gives a financial, McMaster, *History,* VI, 389 ff., a social, view of the crisis.

slavery and who would be glad to oppose it, but who feared to be associated with men accused of atheism and social irresponsibility. Garrison, of course, disagreed with this account of his public influence. In his own eyes, he was maintaining abolitionist faith, preventing the sullying of abolitionist principles by false friends and shortsighted politicians. Moreover, he was exercising his right of free speech, so essential to a struggle in which slavery proponents were attempting to stifle discussion about the right and wrong of their operations.

Considering what the intentions of his foes in the antislavery society were, it was no more than self-preservation for Garrison to have determined to fight them. He marshaled his Board of Managers of the Massachusetts Anti-Slavery Society to approve his policies and reprove the authors of the Clerical Appeal, and organized his State Convention to endorse their action.

In the following months he clarified his program, putting at its base woman's rights. When the New England Anti-Slavery Convention met in May 1838, Oliver Johnson was ready with a motion that women be received into their organization on equal terms. Their move cost the Garrisonians their much admired Reverend Amos A. Phelps: he resigned, along with several others who included Fitch and the Reverend Charles T. Torrey, then of Salem. Whittier, now editor of the *Pennsylvania Freeman,* wrote Garrison, gently indicating the "irrelevance" of the "woman question" to abolition, though he had earlier denounced the Pastoral Letter for having closed the churches to "the thrilling tale/Of Carolina's high soul'd daughters."[58]

Garrison, far from retreating, now committed himself to Henry C. Wright's program on the inviolability of life. Although this seemed extreme to conservative leaders of the American Peace Society, it is evident that they in turn outraged others who made much of patriotism and national pride. Differences over peace programs, then, were comparable to those which were breaking down the antislavery confederation. When a peace convention to form a more active society met in September 1838, the Garrisonians were in eager attendance and pressed the woman question upon it. Women were received without enthusiasm and added to committees. Most notable was Abby Kelley,

[58] Whittier, *Poems* (Philadelphia, 1838 ed.), p. 76. For Whittier's antislavery activities, see Albert Mordell, *Quaker Militant: John Greenleaf Whittier* (Boston, 1933), pp. 92 ff., 149 ff.; Roland H. Woodwell, "Whittier on Abolition —a Letter to Emerson," *Essex Institute Hist. Coll.,* XCIII (1957), 254–259.

an eloquent Massachusetts Quaker, an early anti-slavery lecturer, later the wife of Stephen S. Foster. She was about to become the flying wedge of Garrisonian policy. Weld had inspired her to leave teaching for antislavery, though she was to remain a Garrisonian long after Weld had, as some of his associates felt, deserted abolition. She not only served on the business committee of the convention, but undertook to play an active role in its work. At one point she even called a minister to order. As Garrison noted with satisfaction, "Endurance now passed its bounds on the part of the woman contemners, and accordingly several persons (clergymen and laymen) requested their names to be erased from the roll of the Convention. . . ." With the moderates gone, the Garrisonians proceeded to form the Non-Resistance Society, to adopt an extreme statement of principles as well as a program which quickly reduced itself to the speeches of its one agent, Wright, and its organ, *The Non-Resistant:* adjuncts of Garrisonian abolitionism.

Its leader now correctly discerned a gathering of forces to undermine him at the next convention of the state antislavery society. Henry B. Stanton was central to the plan. A curiosity of abolitionist organization was that no hard and fast bylaws separated state and national organization, so that Stanton, as a national representative, could operate freely in Garrison territory. Involved, too, in the deepening crisis were financial differences between the New York office (which was also, essentially, the New York city and state office) and the Boston directors.[59] The "plot," as Garrison persisted in thinking it, moved away from the woman question to stress the duty of abolitionists at the polls and the need for a more responsible newspaper than the *Liberator.* Phelps and Torrey stated their positions. Stanton supported them, charging that Garrison had "lowered the standard of abolition." Garrison appealed successfully to the Negroes present to say that he had not been recreant in his duty. The enthusiasm favoring him was heightened by the speeches of Wendell Phillips, Maria Weston Chapman, and others among the faithful. The "conspirators" were routed, but prepared to issue another publication, the *Massachusetts Abolitionist,* and, with the unofficial sanction of the New Yorkers, to launch the Massachu-

---

[59] See, for example, Birney, Leavitt, and Tappan (for the national society) to the Massachusetts Anti-Slavery Society, February 4, 1839, dissolving financial arrangements based on amounts agreed upon as due both offices from fund collectors, Tappan Papers, LC.

setts Abolition Society. Elizur Wright, Phelps, Torrey, and Orange
Scott were to be mainstays of the organization.

Although they complained that the Garrisonians misrepresented
their views and employed cunning political stratagems against them,
the political and anti-feminist abolitionists made every effort of their
own to dominate proceedings. The 1839 national meeting was strenu-
ously organized. As Stanton wrote Birney:

> It must be a *strong* one—even tho' not a *large* one. Will not the West be
> represented? It should be borne in mind that it is not for members of the
> A. S. Soc's exclusively but for those who "believe in our principles but don't
> like our measures" if they please to come. We are anxious that Senator
> Morris should be present. Can't you see him and persuade him to attend?
> We shall try to get Slade, [Rev. John W.] Alvord, [Governor Joseph] Ritner
> [of Pennsylvania, an outspoken antislavery politician], etc. etc. to be pres-
> ent.[60]

The political abolitionists had their way at this convention, intro-
ducing their political doctrine and refusing Garrison's resolution that
it would imperil "the integrity and success of the anti-slavery enterprise." Although its sponsors were not advocating it as the only
legitimate antislavery tactic, the idea of political action did signal a
new departure and prepare the way for the final rupture.

Elizur Wright,[61] when later in 1839 he expressed his fears for "new
organization" in Massachusetts and condemned what he saw as its
shocking mismanagement, thought the cause was the woman question.
Stanton would later blame the political question. Both were correct, so
far as Massachusetts was concerned. However, on a national scale, the
fate of a no-woman, political approach was more problematic. The
New York abolitionists were, in varying degrees, determined to put
their program to the test, and set the annual meeting of 1840 in which
to establish their authority. They, as well as the Garrisonians, worked
feverishly to acquire sufficient delegates to capture control of the
convention. The New Englanders were the more resourceful. It was
John A. Collins' thought to hire a boat—which could thus carry Negro
delegates—and all the Garrisonian leaders stirred up their followers to

---

[60] Dumond (ed.), *Birney*, I, 490–491.

[61] Wright still later, in his agnostic phase, wrote generously of Garrison and
admiringly of his stand on the woman question; see Wright's *Myron Holley:
and What He Did for Liberty and True Religion* (Boston, 1882), pp. 230,
253.

come in numbers to New York to save their Society. That they might well have a majority was apparently realized by the National Office, since before the meeting it took steps to turn over the Society's newspaper, the *Emancipator,* to the New York Anti-Slavery Society and the Society's books to Lewis Tappan and S. W. Benedict, to secure its indebtedness, they alleged.[62] So it was dead in all save name before the meeting convened.

The crisis was not long in coming. With practiced readiness, Abby Kelley's name was proposed for the business committee, and sustained by a vote of some 560 to 450. Lewis Tappan and Phelps led the withdrawal from the organization. Still earnest for the moral crusade, they refused to join their anti-Garrison brethren in pressing for a political party of abolition. They were soon before the public again as the American and Foreign Anti-Slavery Society, and issuing the *Emancipator.* Garrison, denouncing them for fraud, set up in New York the rival *National Anti-Slavery Standard* with Nathaniel P. Rogers, and then Lydia Maria Child, at its helm. With the principle of woman's participation in public functions established, it was but a matter of time before the woman's suffrage movement would be initiated.[63]

[62] For Tappan's defense of his course, in newspaper extracts, see notebook, "Relating to the division of the abolition body," volume of "Arranged Chronology," etc., Tappan Papers, LC.

[63] The schism created no revolution in female antislavery deportment. It did end the annual meetings of the Anti-Slavery Convention of Women; see *Proceedings,* published in New York in 1837, in Philadelphia in 1838 and 1839. A few more individual women became antislavery lecturers. Lucy Stone, after she was engaged to lecture regularly for the American Anti-Slavery Society in 1848, pioneered the delivery of woman's-rights lectures, and other woman speakers followed her lead. But more preferred to confine their anti-slavery activities to ladies' societies, and to help fill audiences, rather than platforms. For a delightful product of the Rochester Ladies' Anti-Slavery Society, see Julia Griffiths (ed.), *Autographs for Freedom* (Auburn, N.Y., 1854). For a general study of an important aspect of their work, see Bertha-Monica Stearns, "Reform Periodicals and Female Reformers, 1830–60," *AHR,* XXXVII (1932), 678–699. See also Mary Grew, "Annals of Women's Anti-Slavery Societies," in *Proceedings of the American Anti-Slavery Society at Its Third Decade . . .* (New York, 1864), 1 ff.; and Alma Lutz, *Crusade for Freedom: Women in the Antislavery Movement* (Boston, 1968).

CHAPTER 7

The Rise of Political Abolitionism

IT IS only in retrospect that the development of an antislavery movement in politics seems inevitable. Abolitionists who put their trust in conventional attitudes and political parties deemed Garrison fantastic; but they themselves had no clear or single program leading to abolition. Their actual campaigns in the 1840's gave blurred results: doubtful triumphs and manifest defeats. It is only while estimating the latter—from the Mexican War to the shoddier aspects of Reconstruction—that one can appreciate why Garrison's persistent idealism shone with increasing brightness, and made him a legend, at the expense of earnest and apparently more competent abolitionists. Their movement needed realism, but it could not live without the working idealism of the extremists.

The year 1840 was a busy one for Garrison, with its own triumphs at home and abroad. This was the year of the World Anti-Slavery Convention, intended to marshal the sentiment of all mankind against systems of bondage, but having American slavery specifically in mind. It was largely dominated, in self-appointed fashion, by the British and Foreign Anti-Slavery Society. From the United States came Garrisonians, panoplied with the woman's rights issue, and their opponents. Some of the latter were "New Organization" men like Birney, who favored excluding women. Relatively few of them were like Henry B. Stanton, traveling with his new wife, Elizabeth Cady Stanton, warm for political action, but at that time willing to receive women in the Convention. Though there were brilliant, indeed elite, ladies in plenty among the British, including Lady Byron, the Duchess of Sutherland, and, of wealth if not title, the prison reformer Elizabeth Fry, opinion held firm against admitting them to equal status. Joseph Sturge, though "radical" on many counts, "begged submission of us to the London Committee," Lucretia Mott recorded; but, unreconciled, she, Ann Green Phillips, wife of Wendell, and many others were relegated to the gallery. There they were joined by Garrison and his other male sympathizers and became the center of all eyes and discussion.[1] Wendell Phillips had been under the impression that the American Anti-Slavery Society had split on the desirability of entering or discountenancing politics.[2] He found himself on the floor offering motions for the recognition of the full American delegation, including women. The historic Woman's Rights Convention was still eight years away, but it had its beginnings there on the floor of Freemason's Hall, in London.

This was the Convention's major achievement. American abolitionists continued to be anxious over foreign opinion, especially that in Great Britain. They made individual tours of the British Isles which excited audiences about antislavery affairs in America. Philanthropic money came from the British Isles, which, for example, in 1847 provided the runaway slave and abolitionist, Frederick Douglass, with a press for publishing his valuable *North Star*. "English gold" embittered Southerners and provided both political parties with a nationalistic argument against abolitionists. They, on their side, did not hesitate to obtrude upon British affairs, as when Henry C. Wright denounced the Free Churches of Scotland for accepting money from slaveholders, and demanded that it be returned.[3] Lewis Tappan was a one-man agency for influencing English opinion respecting slavery and, at the least, helped keep English abolitionists informed about American issues. Whether, in the last analysis, English abolitionist sympathy was substantial enough to influence the antislavery movement in the United

[1] Frederick B. Tolles (ed.), "Slavery and 'The Woman Question,'" *Lucretia Mott's Diary of Her Visit to Great Britain to Attend the World's Anti-Slavery Convention of 1840* (Haverford, 1952), pp. 27 ff.; see also James Mott, *Three Months in Great Britain* (Philadelphia, 1841).

[2] *Proceedings of the General Anti-Slavery Convention* . . . (London, 1841), p. 45.

[3] George Shepperson, "The Free Church and American Slavery," *Scottish Hist. Rev.*, XXX (1951), 126–143, and "Thomas Chalmers, the Free Church of Scotland and the South," *JSH*, XVII (1951), 517–537.

States, there can be no doubt that the major American battles only incidentally involved English abolitionists.[4]

More important, in many ways, than British sympathy continued to be the British example of emancipation, even though it disturbed the consciences of slaveholders much less than Northerners liked to think. As the fiery James Henry Hammond put it:

> I know of no *slaveholder* who has visited the West Indies since Slavery was abolished, and published *his* views of it. All our facts and opinions come through the friends of the experiment, or at least those not opposed to it. Taking these, even without allowance, to be true as stated, I do not see where the abolitionists find cause for exultation. The tables of export, which are the best evidence of the condition of a people, exhibit a woful falling off. . . . Such are the *real fruits* of your never-to-be-too-much glorified abolition, and the valuable dividend of your twenty millions of pounds sterling invested therein.[5]

Hammond went on to upbraid England for her hypocrisy: for operating a navy for the suppression of the slave trade which actually abetted it—a charge which was less than just, since the squadron assigned labored at great expense and against enormous difficulties, many of them created by American slavers.[6] He was on better ground

---

[4] The subject is shrouded with difficulties. Thus, abolition following West Indies emancipation was largely maintained by some wealthy Quakers and others of a benevolent turn. Yet the most famous English pronouncement on slavery came from a meeting of Manchester workingmen, December 31, 1862, expressing solidarity with the northern cause and hailing the Emancipation Proclamation, and the most famous meeting in support of the North was by workingmen in London, March 26, 1863; E. D. Adams, *Great Britain and the American Civil War* (London, 1925), II, 109–112. On the other hand, it is far from certain that the British workingmen (any more than the American) were united in admiration of the federal cause; Royden Harrison, "British Labour and the Confederacy: a Note on the Southern Sympathies of Some British Working Class Journals and Leaders during the American Civil War," *International Rev. of Soc. Hist.*, II (1957), Pt. I, 78–105. For a discussion of the scholarly status of the subject, George Shepperson, "Confederate Sympathizers in the British Working Class," *British Assoc. of Amer. Studies Bull., No. 5* (1957), 11–14. Klingberg, "Harriet Beecher Stowe and Social Reform in England," *AHR*, XLIII (1938), 542–552, professes to relate the excitement produced by *Uncle Tom's Cabin* in England to the effort of its workers to better their lot, but produces no tangible evidence to support this claim.

[5] *The Pro-Slavery Argument . . .* (Philadelphia, 1853), p. 145.

[6] Christopher Lloyd, *The Navy and the Slave Trade* (London, 1949); *Six Months' Service in the African Blockade from April to October 1848 . . . by Lieutenant Forbes, R.N.* (London, 1849).

when he questioned the realities of emancipation proper and the liberties of unrewarded toil and discrimination which the Negroes endured. That emancipation was not all its sponsors had hoped it would be was attested by numerous visitors.

However, the free Caribbean islands were a banner and slogan for the American abolitionists. They lauded them in prose and verse. One of Wendell Phillips' most admired orations, endured by numerous antipathetic auditors for the sake of its splendor of cadences and imagery, celebrated Toussaint L'Ouverture, the liberator of Haiti. August 1 was set aside every year to remember British emancipation. It attracted not only abolitionists, but such figures as Ralph Waldo Emerson.[7] Many abolitionists reported favorably on free labor and its fruits in the British West Indies. Most influential of such accounts was that by the young abolitionists J. Horace Kimball, who died soon after, and James A. Thome, which served their friends as a source book of data and arguments. Numerous quarrels could be found with their alleged facts, which unsympathetic investigators subsequently attempted to refute. That the latter failed to make an impression equal to that of the liberation tracts was patent and the despair of sincere conservatives, who could not understand why accounts of the West Indies which expressed hope for Negro advancement should be preferred.[8]

Garrison discerned no problem in foreign or domestic relations. As for his own role, he insisted that his critics distinguish between his reform and his antislavery services. In the first capacity, he approved, since he could not join, the Groton convention which in August, while he was en route to England, drew Alcott, Parker, and George Ripley, among others, to discuss whether "the outward organization of the Church [was] a human or a divine institution." Garrison did not call, though he was roundly denounced for having called, the most famous of all conventions on Universal Reform, that at Chardon Street

[7] Emerson, *An Address Delivered in the Court-House in Concord, Massachussetts, on 1st August, 1844, on the Anniversary of the Emancipation of the Negroes in the British West Indies* (Boston, 1844).

[8] Jas. A. Thome and J. Horace Kimball, *Emancipation in the West Indies. A Six Months Tour in Antigua, Barbadoes, and Jamaica in the Year 1837* (New York, 1838). Also effective was Richard Hildreth, *The "Ruin" of Jamaica* (n.d., n.p.). Cf. S. D. Carpenter [editor of the *Wisconsin Patriot*], *Logic of History. Five Hundred Political Texts: Being Concentrated Extracts of Abolitionism; also, Results of Slavery Agitation and Emancipation . . .* (Madison, Wis., 1864 ed.), pp. 14 ff.

Chapel, in November of 1840. Here gathered the eccentrics and the extremists, the sectarians and those in the middle ground of emancipated religious thought; and here also were Pierpont, Parker, and Ripley once more, as well as, in more spectatorial capacities, Channing, Emerson, and Lowell.[9] Precipitated out of the discussion was the anti-Sabbatarian viewpoint, which for Garrison began as a simple question of Bible reading. It multiplied aspects until it became a question of liberty of conscience and civil rights, for there were laws restraining free choices of observance in various states. The most signal victory of the Sabbath-observance party was the stopping of the Sunday mails. The controversy arraigned reformers on both sides, some concerned for the principle involved, others for the good or ill Garrisonians were believed to be doing to reform.[10]

There were those to whom moral reform in any guise offered frustrating limitations, despite the fact that Garrison had great allies in his resistance to political involvement. Dr. Channing, after the launching of the Liberty party, viewed its possibilities with fear: "Any act of the free States, when assembled in Congress, for the abolition of slavery in other States, would be a violation of the national compact, and would be a just cause of complaint. On this account I cannot but regret the disposition of a part of the abolitionists to organize themselves into a political party."[11] Birney himself, soon to be a leading hope of political abolitionism, in 1837 had no vision of abolitionism but as a moral force; as he then wrote Salmon P. Chase:

The abolitionists in Massachusetts believe, they have the balance of political power, as between the two parties here. They will, I doubt not, be disposed to use it, as effectively as possible for the advancement of our free principles. They will not, of course, rear up a party of their own, but they will endeavor to purify both the present parties.[12]

[9] Emerson, "The Chardon Street Convention," in *Lectures and Biographical Sketches* (Boston, 1893 ed.), pp. 351–354.

[10] The literature on Sunday observance and nonobservance is extensive and covers such fields as travel, play, visits to botanical gardens, and various classes of labor. A typical survey is included in *Sixteenth Annual Report of the Philadelphia Sabbath Association* (Philadelphia, 1857). See also Henry M. Parkhurst (reporter), *Proceedings of the Anti-Sabbath Convention, Held in the Melodeon, March 23rd and 24th* (Boston, 1848).

[11] Quoted in the *National Anti-Slavery Standard*, II (February 1842).

[12] Birney to Salmon P. Chase, June 5, 1837, Chase Papers, LC; cf. *Fourth Annual Report of the American Anti-Slavery Society* . . . (New York, 1837), and *Fifth Annual Report* . . . (New York, 1838) of the same society, in which essentially the same position is held.

It was not accidental that he should have addressed these remarks to Chase, who, then twenty-nine years old, occupied a curious position on the social and political and even geographic scene. Born in New Hampshire, he had been raised in Ohio, had attended Dartmouth College, and had become a lawyer in Washington under the tutelage of William Wirt of Maryland, littérateur and late Attorney General of the United States. Chase began as an admirer of Calhoun and Clay, and rose rapidly as a lawyer in Cincinnati. In 1836, he helped defend Birney during a riot, and early the next year became an antislavery hero. His efforts, unsuccessful though they were, to prevent the remanding to slavery of a fugitive, Matilda, gave him status among the crusaders. Matilda had been a servant in Birney's home, and Chase was also called upon to defend Birney's action in harboring her. Chase made ingenious efforts to prove that slavery was a local institution and thus not tenable outside slave territory. Although identified with antislavery, Chase resisted, until the word became respectable, being termed an abolitionist. Leavitt took credit for having instructed him and taught him his mode of antislavery reasoning.[13]

Chase was typical of many northern men who were beginning to reconsider their views of slavery. They varied from ardent abolitionists, dissatisfied with the progress of merely moral reform, to politicians who actively disliked Negroes but feared slavery as an economic or social threat. The pioneer group of political abolitionists were abolitionists pure and simple. Behind them stood an uncounted and amorphous legion, capable of taking any shape which their conflicting interests might devise.

The abolitionists themselves were often less than the unyielding absolutists their principles suggested. Garrison and Weld, Lewis Tappan, and later the Virginian turned emancipationist, young Moncure D. Conway, were inflexible in their regard for Negro rights, the latter, for example, arguing that intermarriage strengthened the white race. But the abolitionists of Massachusetts had to fight a major battle before an antimarriage law of their state was repealed, against resistance from legislators elected as "abolitionists." William G. Allen, a graduate

---

[13] Robert B. Warden, *An Account of . . . Salmon P. Chase* (Cincinnati, 1872), pp. 282–285; Hart, *Salmon Portland Chase* (Boston, 1899), pp. 46 ff.; *Address and Reply on Presentation of a Testimonial . . .* (Cincinnati, 1845), pp. 7–8; Leavitt to his brother, April 4, 1851, Leavitt Papers, LC; *Speech of Salmon P. Chase, in the Case of the Colored Woman, Matilda* (Cincinnati, 1837).

I live in the Faith and Hope of the progressive advancement of Christian Liberty and expect to abide by the same in death

J. Q. Adams

1. JOHN QUINCY ADAMS

2. An illustration for Cheever's *The True History of Deacon Giles' Distillery*

3. Lane Theological Seminary, Cincinnati, in 1841

(The Ohio Historical Society)

4. Flogging the Negro: The view of slavery which the North accepted

5. The rendition of Anthony Burns: Marshal's posse moving down
State Street, Boston

6. THEODORE D. WELD

7. ANGELINA EMILY GRIMKÉ,
wife of Theodore Weld

8. Building in Lexington, Kentucky, where Cassius M. Clay published the *True American*

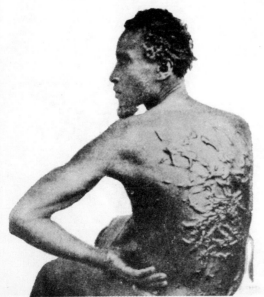

9. A slave with back scarred by whipping

10. MARIA W. CHAPMAN

11. HARRIET BEECHER STOWE

(The New York Public Library)

12. HARRIET TUBMAN

(New England Magazine)

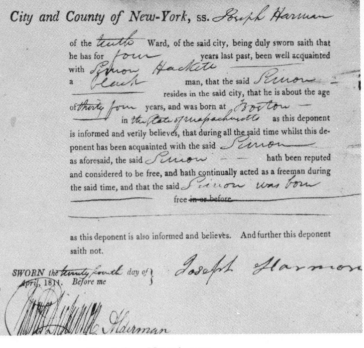

City and County of New-York, ss. *Joseph Harman*
of the *tenth* Ward, of the said city, being duly sworn saith that he has for *four* years last past, been well acquainted with *Simon Hackett* a *Black* man, that the said *Simon* resides in the said city, that he is about the age of *thirty four* years, and was born at *Boston* in *the State of Massachusetts* as this deponent is informed and verily believes, that during all the said time whilst this deponent has been acquainted with the said *Simon* as aforesaid, the said *Simon* — — hath been reputed and considered to be free, and hath continually acted as a freeman during the said time, and that the said *Simon was born* free ~~in or before~~

as this deponent is also informed and believes. And further this deponent saith not.

SWORN the *twenty fourth* day of *April*, 1811. *Before me* *Joseph Harman*

Harman

13. A free Negro's pass
(Western Reserve Historical Society)

14. "Southern chivalry: Argument versus clubs"
The attack on Charles Sumner in the Senate, as seen by Northerners.
(The New York Public Library)

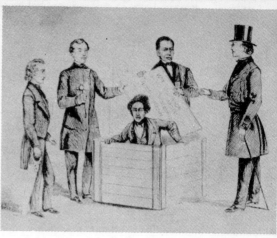

15. Levi Coffin
(New England Magazine)

16. Resurrection of Henry Box Brown

(From *The Underground Railroad* by William Still)

17. "The Big Tent" on Tappan Square, Oberlin College, which later became the property of the Anti-Slavery Society

(Oberlin College Library)

> My Dear Sir
> there are three men now
> at my house. who are in great peril
> — I am un well, I need your advice
> Please come at once
> D. F.

18. Frederick Douglass as an underground railroad agent: A message to Samuel D. Porter, a Rochester, New York, abolitionist.

(University of Rochester Library)

19. An orator denouncing the union at an abolitionist convention

(*Harper's Weekly*, May 28, 1859)

20. LEWIS TAPPAN

21. JOSHUA R. GIDDINGS

(Portrait by Chester Harding,
The Ohio Historical Society)

22. BENJAMIN LUNDY

23. WENDELL PHILLIPS and
WILLIAM LLOYD GARRISON

LET THE NORTH AWAKE!

T. B. M'CORMICK

Will Discuss the Immorality, Illegality and Unconstitutionality of

AMERICAN SLAVERY,

And the Duty and Power of the General Government to Abolish it.

IN _Brown Mills_ _____

AT _7 O'clk P.M. April 30th_ _____

Mr. M'CORMICK is the Clergyman for whom the Governor of Kentucky made a Requisition upon the Governor of Indiana, charging him with aiding in the escape of Fugitive Slaves. The Warrant was issued and Mr. M'Cormick is thereby exiled from his home. All are respectfully invited to attend.

24. Handbill for an abolitionist meeting

25. Ruins of the Free State Hotel, Lawrence, Kansas, during border warfare

26. Mob attacking the Alton, Illinois, warehouse, on November 7, 1837, at time Elijah Lovejoy was murdered. Drawn from an eyewitness account.

27. John Brown and his men en route from Harpers Ferry to the jail at Charles Town. Brown and Aaron D. Stevens, both wounded, in wagon; Shields Green, left, and John Copeland, both colored, following on foot. The prisoners were escorted by a Marine guard detailed by Colonel Robert E. Lee.

(Sketch by Alfred Berghaus, eyewitness, in *Leslie's Illustrated Newspaper*, November 12, 1859)

28. JOHN BROWN

29. "John Brown ascending the scaffold preparatory to being hanged"

(*Frank Leslie's Illustrated Weekly*, December 2, 1859)

30. "The Republican party going to the right house." A cartoon identifying
Lincoln with the reformers during the elections of 1860

of Oneida Institute, known as the only colored man till then called to a professorship in an American college, had a bitter story to tell of his own marriage to the daughter of a minister and supposed abolitionist. Marriage was only achieved over the difficulties set up by her own family, mob action, and all but Allen's own murder. He and his wife emigrated to England, where they could show, one western New York paper sardonically commented, "admiring foreigners the beauties of American abolitionism."[14]

A female antislavery society was agitated by the suggestion that Negroes be invited to join. Leading members thought it reasonable for them to attend, but not to be put on an "equality with ourselves." Although the equalitarians won, this was not always the case. Troy, New York, was said to contain a number of individuals who claimed to be antislavery, and even abolitionist, who kept shy of Negroes, set aside a Negro pew in church, and were ignorant of antislavery publications and affairs. Edward Beecher, Elijah P. Lovejoy's old associate, thought there was "some truth" in the southern theory that "slavery is a necessary & desirable step in the process of civilization & christianization." As arresting was the attitude of Maria Weston Chapman, a very flame of Garrisonian intransigence, who thought Frederick Douglass was being "insubordinate" when he resisted John A. Collins' confusion of Fourierism and abolitionism. Garrison himself, for inadequate reasons, attempted to dissuade Douglass from beginning the *North Star.* Memorable was the Reverend Henry Highland Garnet's retort after he had joined the Liberty party, and was accused by Mrs. Chapman of having received "bad counsel" in preparing his address to the political convention, even though she had not herself seen the speech. His eloquent denunciation of her for seeking to sink him "again in the condition of a *slave,* by forcing me to think just as you do," had chastening effects.[15] It could not, however, expunge the anti-Negro impulses with which abolitionists struggled.

The Negro was different from his white associates and coworkers:

[14] Louis Ruchames, "Race, Marriage, and Abolition in Massachusetts," *JNH,* XL (1955), 250–273; William G. Allen, *The American Prejudice against Color* (London, 1853), p. 88. Allen had been a professor at New York Central College.

[15] *Liberator,* XIII (December 8, 1843); E. C. Chace, *Anti-Slavery Reminiscences* (Central Falls, R.I., 1891), pp. 16–17; "Spurious Abolition," *Emancipator,* IV (April 11, 1839); Edward Beecher to Chase, December 21, 1854, Chase Papers, LC; Douglass, *Life and Times,* p. 255; Foner (ed.), *Douglass,* I, 59, 78; II, 48 ff.

in traditions, in outlook, and relationships. These were, to a degree, similar to those which kept white laborers, Irish, women, country bumpkins, witless or uneducated children, and eccentrics in distinct and often limited circumstances.[16] The stigma of color and slavery vastly increased the distance between Negroes and white people. Lewis Tappan was realistic in attempting to see the problem of proper relations from the point of view of the Negroes: "As Xians—and xian abolitionists—will not tolerate my associating with my colored brethren in a white man's chh it seems my duty to unite with a colored chh. But will it not invite insult to my colored brethren?"[17] Proslavery advocates and dedicated abolitionists took unequivocal stands on the relations with Negroes they would tolerate. Negroes were themselves implicated in the status to which they could aspire, to the extent that their human nature limited the possibilities open to the idealists among them. As one of them pointed out:

Colored mechanics complain and are broken down for the want of patronage—colored Clergymen are embarrassed *all the while* and their efforts paralized for the want of a comfortable support—colored teachers are not half paid and colored youth are not half educated, because of the scarcity of money, and the poverty of their brethren; and yet, thirty thousand dollars or more, in this city, are annually worse than thrown away in porter and gambling houses, and in theatres, by our brethren—a sum sufficient to support three or four manual-labor colleges, where two or three hundred of our youth might be educated and get useful trades; or ten or twelve libraries, reading and lecture rooms, where they might acquire useful, scientific and practical knowledge, such as would qualify them to be respectable, efficient freemen and citizens. Brethren, when shall the state of things be changed —if you say never, we answer then *we never* shall be a respected or happy people.[18]

Between Negroes and white people in the North could be found every grade of individual, from one to whom hatred of Negroes gave a sense of superiority and an outlet for frustrations to another who cared nothing one way or the other about Negroes, and demanded only that Negroes be kept separate. Such people constituted a majority

[16] Thus Delaware kept its subordinate classes of white people under legal conditions which differed little from those controlling Negroes; see Morris, "Peonage in a Slave State," *PSQ*, LXV (1950), 238–263.

[17] Tappan diary, February 26, 1836, Tappan Papers, LC.

[18] "Prostitution of Our Means," *Colored American*, III (May 18, 1839).

of Northerners; abolitionists would have to make them antagonistic to slavery if it was to be curbed or overthrown.

The *content*, too, of emancipation had to be determined. Not until Reconstruction days would the vote for Negroes become a popular political measure. At that time, Radical Republicans would insist that the Negro receive the vote in the southern states—where it was basic to Radical Republican control—while being willing to tolerate his being deprived of it in states above Mason and Dixon's line. In the pre-Civil War period, the matter did not come to a crisis among political abolitionists. No one exceeded Joshua Giddings in his blunt attacks on the slaveholders. He also spoke out clearly in defense of the Negro's qualities. Yet as late as 1858 he had the tables turned on him by a conservative he was attempting to bait in Congress, and who wished to know whether Giddings would commit himself to Negroes voting in his own Ohio.[19] Giddings had no answer.

The exigencies which enforced silence upon Giddings were not all political. Tappan, in 1843, was to express to Gamaliel Bailey his astonishment "to learn that Mr. Morris is opposed to the colored man's voting. Why has his opinion not been announced to those who sit under the 'Cedar Tree' before? It would astound Eastern Liberty Men." It did not prevent them from nominating Morris as vice-presidential candidate of the Liberty party, the next year. Political abolitionists learned compromise fast, though many compromises they supported in 1860 would have been unacceptable to them twenty years before. Tappan was one of those who resisted to the end the dilution of principles, though never with the harsh antagonism which Garrisonians displayed toward compromisers.

Political abolitionism was part of a large, almost august, change which was taking place in the American political constellation. Involved were changes calculated to hold together the Union, or separate it into states. Leading political figures, however, did not see the issue so narrowly. They sought national programs. That Freemasonry

[19] Giddings, *Speeches in Congress* (Boston, 1853), p. 450. Not until 1870 would Ohio give the vote to Negroes; Quillin, *The Color Line in Ohio,* p. 102; *Ohio Politics. Cox after Giddings. "Father Giddings" Dodges under the Bush with His Colored Friend* (n.p., n.d.). For a defense of the Black Codes, see James J. McLoughlin, "The Black Code," *MVHA Proc. . . . 1914–1915* (1916), 210–216.

should earlier have given rise to the first major third party in the country's history—and, in the process, helped precipitate major anti-slavery figures—underscores the complex fashion in which political elements were clarifying their interests. That they had hit upon Free-masonry as an issue was the result of accident and manipulation. It is sentimental to conceive of the struggle which had ensued as one for or against democracy,[20] especially since Antimasons had themselves developed every technique of demagoguery and undemocratic action.

True, the Masons indulged in secret rituals and used fraternal re-lations for personal advancement. But they could claim responsible Americans as brothers, from George Washington to Henry Clay, and a respect for law and order, piety and good fellowship.[21] The murder in 1826 of William Morgan, a stonemason of Batavia, who had be-come disillusioned with Masons and decided to expose their "secrets," had been a local affair with no profound implications.

It had, however, called attention to the Masons at a time which witnessed the congealing of the Jacksonian coalition. By and large, eastern workingmen had tended to be sympathetic to Masonry and suspicious of the "church and state" proclivities of Antimasons.[22] In short order, Masons and Antimasons had been making common politi-cal deals having no connection with Morgan or his fate. The major achievement of the Antimasonic party which arose had been to open the way for the organization of the Whig party. It had enabled Thur-low Weed, as shrewd a Whig political tactician as his Democratic op-ponent, Van Buren, to build a political machine which could oppose his. With Weed on his rise to power had gone Millard Fillmore, destined to be the Chief Executive who signed the Compromise meas-ures of 1850; and also William Henry Seward, who would thrill the country with his denunciation of its Fugitive Slave provisions. Seward had made his reputation as a brilliant lawyer, sympathetic to the underdog. He had also made demagogic use of Antimasonry during his rise to the governorship of New York.[23]

[20] Alice F. Tyler, *Freedom's Ferment* (Minneapolis, 1944), pp. 351 ff.

[21] John Kewley, *Masonry on Christian Principles. A Discourse* . . . (Hart-ford, 1812).

[22] *New York Sentinel*, II (October 29, 1830).

[23] Earl Conrad, *Mr. Seward for the Defense* (New York, 1956); Van Deusen, *Thurlow Weed*, pp. 70 ff.; W. L. Barre, *The Life and Public Services of Millard Fillmore* (Buffalo, 1856), pp. 321 ff. Seward was a felicitous and intelligent commentator; Frederick W. Seward (ed.), *William H. Seward: an Autobi-ography* (New York, 1891), is filled with valuable passages of conscious or unintentional quality.

In Pennsylvania, Anti-Masonry had brought out Thaddeus Stevens, whose career in Harrisburg was a first draft of his later career as leader of the House of Representatives and unofficial ruler of the United States. As during Reconstruction, his early work was a bold mixture of equalitarian aims and ruthless political maneuvers. He had succeeded in massing an Antimasonic union of political forces and uniting it with the Whigs. He had also fought for public education with a brilliance and courage which friend and foe conceded. Stevens was genuinely antislavery, even though he clung to conventional party alliances and had once, in 1821, appeared against a colored woman, claiming freedom for herself, her husband, and two children. He refused to sign a state constitutional provision, adopted in 1837, which limited the suffrage to white citizens. About the same time, he attended a proslavery convention of self-styled "friends of the integrity of the Union," and singlehandedly broke it up with barbed questions and ridicule. He was later a forthright antislavery representative in Congress and a lawyer in fugitive-slave cases.[24]

A third stalwart of quasi-political reform was William Slade of Vermont, who continued sincerely to believe the Masons constituted a national danger. In 1836 a fellow Antimason sharply suggested that, politically speaking, the subject was no longer important: the sole question was whether the Whigs had, in Hugh L. White, a better candidate for the Presidency than Van Buren.[25] Like Giddings, Slade deplored political abolitionism as a separate cause, and pleaded for a united Whig party which could repel what he deemed to be southern aggressions upon northern liberties. In his viewpoint, however, were the seeds of one aspect of political abolitionism.

A movement of somewhat more serious moment to reform was nativism, which had long operated in the thinking of antipopery partisans, but which mounted as Irish immigration brought more and more Catholics into the eastern cities and the Democratic machines. It created strong and organized anti-Catholics in the West and South, disturbed by what seemed to them a flood of immigrants who were

[24] Ralph Korngold, *Thaddeus Stevens* (New York, 1955), does its best to present its subject as "darkly wise and rudely great," and Thomas F. Woodley, *Great Leveler* (New York, 1937), attempts the same task with more scholarly competence. Neither fully overcomes the strictures in Richard N. Current, *Old Thad Stevens: a Story of Ambition* (Madison, Wis., 1942).

[25] [William Slade] *Masonic Penalties* (Castleton, Vt., 1830); *Letters of Mr. Slade to Mr. Hallett, February, 1836* (n.p., n.d.); *Reply to Letters of Hon. William Slade, Member of Congress from Vermont on Anti-VanBurenism, by a Massachusetts Anti-Mason* (Boston, 1836).

inundating the river towns of New Orleans, St. Louis, and Louisville.[26] During the 1820's and 1830's, nativist feeling built up to create a strong anti-Catholicism; but despite riots and prejudice, much of it continued on the level of mere propaganda.

Abolitionists were divided in their attitudes toward Catholics. Many of them resented the Catholic position—from which no notable priest or layman deviated—which opposed immediate emancipation of slaves, and deemed slavery not necessarily a sin.[27] Yet Whittier (to be sure, a Quaker) wrote with tolerance and good will of the Catholic Church and its conduct. Weld's antislavery motivations impelled him to "give a testimony to the world that in Christ Jesus there is neither Jew nor Greek." James G. Birney, during his colonization phase, asked for "the names of . . . distinguished *Catholics* who are friendly to the Society," and Parker Pillsbury, later Garrison's lieutenant, came to respect the Catholics. This burly ex-blacksmith and farmer, a disillusioned cleric whose *The Church as It Is; or, the Forlorn Hope of Slavery* (1847) became a classic of abolitionist polemics, appreciated the antislavery actions of Catholics—the latest being Pope Gregory XVI's bull against the slave trade—and he thought well of their cult of the Virgin: a profeminist view in his interpretation.[28]

[26] Gerald M. Capers, *The Biography of a River Town* (Chapel Hill, 1939), p. 115. Southern plantation owners had no more regard for immigrants than for free Negroes, and seem to have been willing to discourage immigration as bringing no more than a horde of irresponsible riffraff and foreigners who might accumulate strength at the polls and threaten their political power.

[27] Madeleine H. Rice, *American Catholic Opinion in the Slavery Controversy* (New York, 1944), pp. 86 ff. Most vigorously antislavery—though in the context of acceptance—was the great North Carolina jurist, William Gaston. Robert Walsh, Jr.'s *Appeal from the Judgments of Great Britain* . . . (Philadelphia, 1819) is erroneously listed as proslavery in Geraldine H. Hubbard (comp.), *A Classified Catalogue . . . Anti-Slavery Propaganda in the Oberlin College Library* (n.p., 1932), p. 71. Walsh's book apologized for slavery, rather than defended it. This pioneer literary figure performed antislavery services in his later *National Gazette and Literary Register;* see also Sr. M. Frederick Lochemes, *Robert Walsh: His Story* (New York, 1941), pp. 107 ff. For a general study of the Catholic position in the field, see Paul Allard, "Slavery," and James J. Fox, "Ethical Aspects of Slavery," in Charles G. Herbermann *et al.* (eds.), *The Catholic Encyclopedia* (New York, 1912), XIV, 36 ff.; Joseph Butsch, "Catholics and the Negro," *JNH,* II (1917), 393–410, and Rev. Benjamin J. Blied, *Catholics and the Civil War* (Milwaukee, 1945), pp. 19 ff.

[28] Whittier, *Prose Works* (Boston, 1866), II, 138 ff.; Barnes and Dumond, *Weld-Grimké Letters,* II, 603; Dumond (ed.), *Birney,* I, 22–23; Filler, "Parker

However, Lyman Beecher had made a career of anti-Catholicism, and the excellent Reverend Samuel Crothers thought "the whole defense of African Slavery is Popish, both in its origin and spirit." The Reverend George Bourne edited, with W. C. Brownlee, Maria Monk's *Awful* [and thoroughly false] *Disclosures of the Hotel Dieu Nunnery of Montreal* (1836). Bourne had already committed himself, out of a three-year Presbyterian pastorate in Quebec (1825–28), to the equally false *Lorette, the History of Louise, Daughter of a Canadian Nun, Exhibiting the Interior of Female Convents* (1834). The Reverend George B. Cheever, too, lost no opportunity to loose his rhetoric against popery and its alleged works, and maintained his crusade after others were chastened by revelations of fraud or unwanted associates.' The vindictiveness of these enthusiasts cannot be overdrawn. The invective they and others of the abolitionist fraternity applied to slaveholders was not stinted when directed at Catholics.[29] In this they were at one with the political nativists of later vintage, though often opposed to them on other issues, slavery being the most important.

Nativists entered into politics in the 1840's, and, needing to distinguish themselves from rioters who burned convents and attacked defenseless individuals, hit upon inadequate naturalization proceedings as a unifying program. Major successes at the polls enabled nativists to bring their issue to Congress and sponsor bills to establish a twenty-one-year probationary period for immigrants before they could become citizens. The year 1845 was the high point of nativism in its first phase. The Congressional campaign revealed real abuses in naturalization proceedings, from New York to New Orleans. Unfortunately for nativism, it followed after a shocking series of riots in Philadelphia which cost lives, churches, and entire blocks of houses. In addition, it cut across too many political alliances. As a result, nativism declined, emphatically to emerge in the 1850's as a major political force.[30]

Pillsbury: an Anti-Slavery Apostle," *NEQ*, XIX (1946), 315–337; Pillsbury, *The Morality of Nations* (New York, 1867), p. 11.

[29] Samuel Crothers, *Strictures on African Slavery* (Roseville, Ohio, 1833), p. 8; York, *Cheever*, pp. 101 ff., 121 ff.; Ray A. Billington, *The Protestant Crusade: 1800–1860* (New York, 1938). For an example of sectarian polemic, Cheever, *The Right of the Bible in Our Public Schools* (New York, 1854). A systematic attack on Catholicism is Rev. William Nevins, *Thoughts on Popery* (Baltimore, 1836).

[30] *A Brief Review of the Origin and Object of the Native American Party. By a Native American* (Philadelphia, 1844) protests that it is not anti-Catholic,

Such were some of the unorthodox features on the political scene in 1839, when a fragment of the dispersed abolitionists undertook to launch a new political party. Impetus was given to their decision by what seemed a species of apostasy by Henry Clay.[31] Proslavery Northerners also considered it a turning point. Clay had for years remembered his willingness, in 1798, to see slavery end in Kentucky. He had deplored slavery as an institution, supported colonization, and otherwise given hope to his antislavery followers that he would help engineer the close of slavery. But in February 1839, with the elections of 1840 ahead, he decided to appease southern voters. He presented to the Senate a petition of inhabitants of the District of Columbia opposing the abolition of slavery in the Capital—rumor said he had drawn up the petition himself—and followed it with a carefully prepared speech which summed up the proslavery argument against gradual or immediate emancipation. "I am no friend of slavery . . ." he declared, almost in parody of his better efforts. "But I prefer the liberty of my own country to that of any other people, and the liberty of my own race to that of any other race."[32]

It was shortly following this effort that Clay voiced the celebrated thought that he "had rather be right than be President." Yet it was common knowledge that he earnestly desired to be President; and to a few abolitionists, at least, the time had come for action to hold politicians to the mark.[33]

The pioneers of political action were few but select. Most significant, in the long run, was Joshua Leavitt, as morally keen as his associate Lewis Tappan but ruggedly determined to bring their issue before the voters. Elizur Wright and Henry B. Stanton were also moving toward politics, though more fearful of premature decisions. Gamaliel Bailey seemed also reluctant, but because of his relative conservatism: he

---

but simply for freedom. A strong Catholic argument is contained in John N. Pumroy, *A Defence of Our Naturalization Laws, with a Friendly Warning to Members of the Native American Party* (Norristown, 1845).

[31] [Francis Philpot] *Facts for White Americans* . . . (Philadelphia, 1839) is a potpourri of antiabolitionism, reflecting opinions of the time. It took Clay's speech as having been the "funeral sermon" of "White Nigger Demagogues and Amalgamation Abolitionists."

[32] Carl Schurz, *Life of Henry Clay* (Boston, 1892), II, 166; *Speech of the Hon. Henry Clay in the Senate of the United States on the Subject of Abolition Petitions, February 7, 1839* (Boston, 1839).

[33] Theodore C. Smith, *The Liberty and Free Soil Parties in the Northwest* (New York, 1897), pp. 33 ff.; Harlow, *Gerrit Smith*, pp. 136 ff.

sought an inclusive "liberal" party—one which would draw in persons like Charles Hammond of the *Cincinnati Gazette* and William Leggett: men who opposed slavery, certainly, but who worked freely with politicians not in the orbit of antislavery. Whittier was to give strength and moral force to the political abolitionists. Alvan Stewart, a distinguished lawyer and leader of the New York State Anti-Slavery Society, had been one of the earliest distinct advocates of political action. No one better answered Henry Clay's 1839 effort than Stewart: he withered it with heat and learned allusion. His graceful eloquence charged with excitement the argument which made the Constitution a document of freedom. In 1845 he would give the leading argument intended to overthrow the remnants of slavery in New Jersey, on the grounds that the new state constitution abolished it in its bill of rights.[34]

In 1840, however, the man of the hour was Myron Holley, whose abolitionist ardor matched that of his associates, and who had, in addition, a tempered career in public affairs. He had been one of the organizers of the Erie Canal and a leader in Antimasonry. Dignified and eloquent, he took the reins of their enterprise.[35]

In October 1839 an antislavery convention assembled in Cleveland: the first ambitious convention held in the West and a possible prelude to larger abolitionist campaigns. It failed to attract sufficient delegates from outside the state to give it substance; but Birney and Arnold Buffum were there, and Holley, presiding, pleaded for a political party. He was opposed by Mahan of Oberlin, who favored moral action, and Ben Wade, Giddings's partner, who adhered to the Whig party. The *Liberator* exulted in the defeat of the political "plotters." But a few days before, Holley had passed a resolution at the Monroe County Anti-Slavery Convention calling for a party, and he continued

[34] Marsh (ed.), *Writings and Speeches of Alvan Stewart*, pp. 195 ff.; [Alvan Stewart] *A Legal Argument before the Supreme Court of the State of New Jersey, at the May Term, 1845, at Trenton, for the Deliverance of 4000 Persons from Bondage* . . . (New York, 1845). Although Stewart's argument was not accepted, the law of 1846 did abolish the name of slave and make all children born after that year free. See also Simeon F. Foss, "The Persistence of Slavery and Involuntary Servitude in a Free State (1685–1866)," *JNH*, XXXV (1950), 289–314, and Marion T. Wright, "New Jersey Laws and the Negro," *JNH*, XXVIII (1943), 185–186.

[35] Margaret L. Plunkett, "A History of the Liberty Party with Emphasis upon Its Activities in the Northeastern States" (Ph.D., Cornell University, 1930), pp. 56 ff.

to labor in its behalf. "Great efforts are making to form an abolition party in this country," Tappan observed. "The number of abolitionists is now so large here, and their voices on many points so various, that it will be impossible, I think, to have them united long. In fact they are disunited already. There will probably be an abolition political party—a religious association—a Garrison party, &c. &c."[36]

In November a larger meeting at Warsaw, New York, endorsed the idea of political action. Accordingly, Holley, as head of a committee, drafted a letter to Birney and to Dr. Francis Julius LeMoyne, inviting them to accept a nomination for the presidency and the vice-presidency of a not clearly designated party.

Birney valued the nomination, but required a stronger endorsement than that of the Warsaw meeting. Dr. LeMoyne, a gentle, attractive figure, notable among abolitionists of western Pennsylvania, was sincerely modest as well as fearful that a party would detract from the religious crusade.[37] Both, therefore, declined the nomination. The president-makers were not daunted. In the face of ridicule, they called for a national convention, to meet in Albany on April 1, 1840. A self-appointed group chose Alvan Stewart president of the convention, and, as vice-presidents, Ichabod Codding, later prominent in Illinois and Wisconsin abolitionist affairs, and the Reverend Charles T. Torrey. Leavitt was one of the two secretaries. A committee of correspondence included Stewart, Gerrit Smith, and William Goodell. The convention, consisting (after defections) of seventy-six members, chose Birney once more and, for second place, Thomas Earle. The latter was a Philadelphia Friend, long active in antislavery affairs, as well as in Democratic politics.[38]

"So they have done the deed? I am sorry—deeply sorry," wrote Bailey. At this point his concern was for the timing of the nominations, which he feared played into the hands of Garrison. Later, Bailey and

[36] Tappan to John Scoble, December 10, 1839, Tappan Papers, LC.

[37] Margaret C. McCullough, *Fearless Advocate of the Right* . . . (Boston, 1941), pp. 129 ff., 224 ff.; see also "Letters of Dr. F. J. LeMoyne, an Abolitionist of Western Pennsylvania," *JNH,* XVIII (1933), 451–474.

[38] Edwin B. Bronner, *Thomas Earle as a Reformer* (Philadelphia, 1948), pp. 26 ff. Earle had supported Jackson as early as 1824, and he continued sympathetic to the Democrats. Thanks to local conditions, he co-operated with Philadelphia Garrisonians. As a lawyer, he was active in antislavery cases till 1840. After 1845, he disassociated himself from active abolitionism. He later adopted even more conservative views, if, as alleged by Mary Grew, he was indeed the author of *The Law of the Territories* (Philadelphia, 1859).

his supporters would join other political abolitionists in striving to build a program which would reassure ordinary, undedicated Americans. As one of them saw it, the Liberty-party type of abolitionist was charitable, philanthropic, but more selfish than the moral reformer, being concerned only for the well-being of the white man:

The baneful influence of slavery upon the currency, upon our commercial interests, upon manufactures, upon the power of the country to defend itself against foreign aggression—its war upon free labor and the respectability of industry—is seizing on the offices and the government of the country—its unequal distribution of the public funds—its gags, mobs, and murders—its robbery of the North by bankruptcy and the tremendous expense of keeping its victims under the yoke by negociations, Indian wars, and threatened wars upon England, Mexico, &c. These and a thousand like topics are the proper subjects for the consideration of the Liberty Party, but they all centre in the welfare of the white man. The negro's pick of corn a week, his stripes and the sundering his family are legitimate subjects for the discussion of the Liberty Party man, only in so far as they may be prejudicial to the interests of the white man.[39]

Such were the awkward steps taken by abolitionists to secularize their cause. Their hope was that they would gain adherents without losing moral purpose.

There were many other abolitionists, not Garrisonians, who felt that an abolition party would do no more than expose their principles to contempt. Certainly, the election of 1840, one of the most extraordinary of elections, paid the political abolitionists small heed, and Birney himself was abroad, attending the World's Anti-Slavery Convention in London. In the somewhat neutral political figure of William Henry Harrison, once of Virginia's aristocracy, made gaudy by military victories and a homespun character, the Whigs had discovered a hero who might gain the northern vote without losing the southern. They therefore thrust Clay abruptly aside. The "log cabin" fantasy, inadvertently created by the Democrats, gave the Whigs all the theme they needed for a campaign which, in its broad strategy, lacked rationality. John Tyler, a states' rights Southerner of rigid cast, nominally

[39] *Philanthropist*, VI (May 11, 1842); the purpose of the passage is misconstrued in Julian P. Bretz, "The Economic Background of the Liberty Party," *AHR*, XXXIV (1929), 263. Bailey dissented from this view, believing that "Equal and Exact Justice to all" was the object of the Liberty party.

a Whig, was hitched to Harrison for no other purpose than to obtain votes. The Whigs joined the Jacksonians in producing demagogues to entertain or confuse the populace. Harrison himself was no figure of innocence. He had long been in politics, and had to overcome past embarrassments. As a youth, he had briefly associated with a group of Virginia abolitionists. Many years later, as an Ohio legislator, he had voted that persons convicted of petty larceny be sold by the sheriff till they could pay their debts.[40]

Harrison's manner of meeting the issues of the time was exemplified by a speech which the Whigs circulated with great industry:

I rise, fellow citizens, (the multitude was here agitated as the sea, when the wild wind blows upon it, and it was full five minutes before the tumult of joy, at seeing and hearing the next President of the United States, could be calmed). . . .

Fellow citizens, it was about this time of the day, 27 years ago, this very hour, this very minute, that your speaker, as commander-in-chief of the north-western army, was plunged into an agony of feeling when the cannonading of our gallant fleet announced an action with the enemy. . . . With the eagle of triumph perched upon our banners on the lake, I moved on to complete the overthrow of the foreign foe. . . . [Great sensation for several seconds.] . . .

I go farther, I here declare, before this vast assembly of the Miami Tribe [great laughter], that if I am elected, no human being shall ever know upon whom I would prefer to see the people's mantle fall; but I shall surrender this glorious badge of their authority into their own hands, to bestow it as they please! [Nine cheers.] Is this federalism? [No, no, no.] . . .[41]

The Democrats did their best. Amos Kendall sought to awake his fellow slaveholders to Harrison's dangerous potentialities. He cited the *Liberator*. He charged that a Virginia Whig was associating with "abolitionist" Whigs. "People of the South," he appealed, "choose which you will have for President, Mr. Van Buren, who is publicly pledged to *veto any bill to abolish slavery in the District of Columbia*, or General Harrison, who is publicly pledged *to veto no bill which Congress may pass*."[42] The electorate, North and South, had, however,

---

[40] Reinhard H. Luthin, "Some Demagogues in American History," *AHR*, LVII (1951), 22 ff.; Dorothy B. Goebel, *William Henry Harrison: a Political Biography* (Indianapolis, 1926), pp. 356 ff.

[41] *Speech of General William H. Harrison, Delivered at the Dayton Convention, on the 10th of September 1840* (n.p., n.d.), pp. 1, 4.

[42] [Amos Kendall] *Abolition!! Infatuation of Federal Whig Leaders of the*

temporarily tired of peremptory government of the Jackson stamp. The Democratic machine held together, but Van Buren was buried in the Electoral College. Buried, too, it appeared, was a Liberty-party ticket which had received 7,053 votes nationally.

It was not clear which political element had cause to exult. Whigs with abolitionist sentiments gained nothing by the victory. Thaddeus Stevens, for example, had hoped for an office in government, but was ignored by the Whig strategists. A month following inauguration, Harrison was dead. The Whig program, which was to have been administered by Secretary of State Webster and Clay as congressional leader, lay in ruins. The nation once more had a slaveholding President, John Tyler of Virginia—abolitionists had flattered themselves this would not happen again—and one with a stubborn and personal view of affairs. Cabinet changes surrounded Tyler with a guard of Southerners. Only Webster remained to represent the shadow of northern interests.

It has been too patly theorized that the moral crusade had done its work by 1839, and that the antislavery impulse had passed to a junta of organizers and propagandists, whose center was in Washington.[43] The first concept is patently inadequate, and appears to have had no purpose but to exaggerate Weld's monopoly over moral influences and permit him to depart with them early in the 1840's. The moral suasion wielded by Henry Ward Beecher, George B. Cheever, Lewis Tappan, Leonard Bacon, Wendell Phillips, Emerson, May, Hopper, and numerous others in antislavery affairs in the 1840's and 1850's, to say nothing of the revivalist spirit which never entirely flagged in those years,[44] is too manifest to give any meaning to the theory.

Nor is it more meaningful to conceive Adams, Giddings, and William Slade as magisterial among antislavery partisans. Adams saw the matter in better light when he refused to address the antislavery societies in Pennsylvania on July 4 "while my voice is stifled by the will of their Representatives in the Legislative Hall of the Nation."[45] The center of antislavery gravity lay in the states; its density would be

South (n.p., n.d.); cf. *Speech of Edw. Stanly, Establishing Proofs that the Abolitionists Are Opposed to Gen. Harrison, and that Gen. Harrison is Opposed to Their "Unconstitutional Efforts." Delivered in the House of Representatives, April 13, 1840* (n.p., n.d.).

[43] Barnes, *The Anti-Slavery Impulse,* pp. 161, 177.

[44] Smith, *Revivalism and Social Reform,* esp. pp. 45 ff.

[45] Adams to E. P. Atlee, June 25, 1836, HSP.

determined by the antislavery advocates, acting upon state interests. The unprincipled exigencies of northern politics demanded a leaven of moral principles which abolitionists of every stripe could help supply. There was no evidence that Birney or Giddings or Leavitt, or even Adams, could necessarily accomplish more than anyone else. Garrison had a certain justice in his criticism of his critics. Calling the roll of some of his former associates in 1842, he noted:

> The time *was* when Arthur Tappan stood deservedly conspicuous before the nation as an abolitionist, and when he was intensely hated by a pro-slavery church and priesthood; but where is he now? . . . Once a year, he makes his appearance as chairman of that shadow of a shadow, the American and Foreign A. S. Society, and straightway disappears. . . . I do not say this in a reproachful spirit—for my obligations to him are truly onerous [*sic*]; but everybody knows that it is a true statement. . . .
>
> Let us trace this affair a little further. . . .
>
> 1. Where is James G. Birney? In western retiracy, waiting to be elected President of the United States, that he may have an opportunity to do something for the abolition of slavery!
>
> 2. Where is Henry B. Stanton? Studying law, (which crushes humanity, and is hostile to the gospel of Christ,) and indulging the hope of one day or other, by the aid of the "Liberty party," occupying a seat in Congress, in which body he means to do something signal as an abolitionist.
>
> 3. Where is Theodore D. Weld and his wife, and Sarah M. Grimke? All "in the quiet," and far removed from all strife! . . . Once, the land was shaken by their free spirits, but now they are neither seen nor felt.
>
> 4. Where is Amos A. Phelps! . . . He is a petty priest, of a petty parish, located in East Boston. What a fall!
>
> 5. Where is Elizur Wright, Jr.,—once a flame of fire, whose light was distinctly visible across the Atlantic? Absorbed in selling some French fables which he has translated into English! *"Et tu, Brute!"*
>
> 6. Where is John G. Whittier? . . .
>
> 8. Where is Orange Scott, who once shook the Methodist hierarchy to its foundation with his anti-slavery thunder? Morally defunct. . . .
>
> 9. Where is La Roy Sunderland? . . .
>
> 10. Where is Wm. Goodell? Still deeply interested in the anti-slavery enterprise, I admit, but no longer connected with it as formerly. . . .
>
> Behold the catalogue! It might be extended, but let this suffice. . . .[46]

It is evident that part of the decay of antislavery personalities lay

---

[46] *Liberator*, XII (August 12, 1842).

in Garrison's view of affairs. Goodell, for example, had been doing worthy work in Utica as editor of the *Friend of Man* and associate of the New York State abolitionists; he was excellently engaged as editor of the *Christian Examiner*. Whittier, Orange Scott, and others mentioned were also very much alive and responsibly employed. Yet Garrison's indictment contained elements of truth. If the changing scene demanded new versions of antislavery activity, it was unable to do without much that had been embodied in older permutations of abolitionist thought.

The abolitionists became, from one point of view, mere sects. Though Garrison took satisfaction in the Liberty party's debacle and the limited influence of Tappan's group, his own dwindled. In addition, it split disastrously. One of Garrison's best-admired figures, N. P. Rogers, editing the *Herald of Freedom* in New Hampshire, not only opposed the government but also domination by committees. Here were Garrison's chickens come home to roost. An unpleasant battle in New Hampshire left Garrison master of the field, but it was a small field, indeed.[47]

Garrisonian influence thereafter became a quantity separate from mere numbers. That such influence was widespread could be traced in the deliberations in town and state antislavery groups from Boston to the northwest territories. One of the most remarkable islands of interest was Salem, Ohio, developed by antislavery Friends who, aided by such Garrisonian elements as Oliver Johnson, Abby Kelley Foster, and her husband, maintained an active abolitionist testimony in the face of a growing political abolitionism of Whig or Democratic allegiance.[48] The *Anti-Slavery Bugle*, founded in 1845, was one of the few abolitionist papers in the land and, under Marius R. Robinson, was a species of *Liberator* for the Midwest.

[47] Filler, "Parker Pillsbury," *passim;* Pierpont (ed.), *A Collection from the Newspaper Writings of Nathaniel P. Rogers* (Concord, N.H., 1847), is valuable for various abolition and related purposes. See also Whittier, *Prose Works,* I, 426 ff.

[48] George D. Hunt, *History of Salem and the Immediate Vicinity . . .* (Salem, 1898), pp. 137 ff.; William B. McCord, *A Souvenir History of Ye Old Town of Salem . . .* (Salem, Ohio, 1906), pp. 47 ff.; Lewis E. Atherton, "Daniel Howell Hise, Abolitionist and Reformer," *MVHR,* XXVI (1939), 343–358; C. B. Galbreath, "Anti-Slavery Movement in Columbiana County," *OAHQ,* XXX (1921), 355–395; *Proceedings of the Ohio Yearly Meeting of Progressive Friends . . .* (Salem, Ohio, 1852).

Lydia Maria Child, who had given her name and energy to the *National Anti-Slavery Standard* in New York, tired of what seemed to her petty factionalism. By the middle of 1843, she was disillusioned and ready to break all official antislavery relations:

> The ruling idea of my life [she announced bitterly] is to earn money, and I want to do nothing that will obstruct my purpose.
>
> I wish you would likewise caution the Liberator folks against implying, in *any way*, that I shall have anything to do with the Standard. I shall never write another column for it under any circumstances, but I do not want to be driven to announce that publicly.[49]

Although she returned to some of her more superficial literary operations, she did not lose contact with antislavery developments. So it was with many partisans whose views changed under the pressure of affairs. Several factors gave vitality to abolitionists in the years which saw the rise of Free Soilism, and first of all a milieu of free speech which they shared with non-abolitionists. Thoreau, to be sure, was in 1851 to denounce the corruptness of the press, which, he believed, exercised "a greater and more pernicious influence than the church. We are not a religious people, but we are a nation of politicians. . . . Almost without exception the tone of the press is mercenary and servile. The *Commonwealth,* and the *Liberator,* are the only papers, as far as I know, which make themselves heard in condemnation of the cowardice and meanness of the authorities of Boston. . . ."[50] Although Thoreau's judgments had moral weight, they failed to distinguish between the mere desire of journalists for "approbation" and their virtues of forthrightness and representativeness.

The abolitionists did not seal themselves off from each other, nor did their foes pretend they did not exist. They noted each other's arguments, publicly, and attempted to build their own by rebuttals rather than by fostering secretive cliques. Their self-confidence was shown by Garrison's policy of printing proslavery selections at length, and without comment, certain that they carried their own antidote with them. Lewis Tappan, as secretary of the American and Foreign Anti-Slavery Society, published communications in the Garrison press. Abolitionist faith in candor was exemplified in the so-called "Martyr Fund" controversy. The Fund was intended to raise money for the

---

[49] Child to Ellis Gray Loring, June 26, 1843, NYPL.
[50] Torrey (ed.), *Writings . . . of Thoreau,* II, 178–179.

needy families of imprisoned abolitionists. Liberty-party advocates suggested co-operation to the Garrisonians, and were repulsed on grounds that they wished to redeem their "waning reputations" by associating with the Garrisonians. "Leavitt & Co." evidently considered this amusing: a fact Garrisonians imparted to their readers.[51]

---

[51] *National Anti-Slavery Standard,* III (May 25, 1843); V (April 17, 1845).

CHAPTER 8

Fugitive Slaves and Politicians

WHAT gave power and consequence to the abolitionists, and forced respect and attention from the most opportunistic politicians, was the persistence of the Negro problem and the dilemmas posed by slaves and slave catchers. As Edward Bates, a conservative Missouri statesman, later Lincoln's Attorney General, observed in 1859: "Only forbid Cuffie to be a politician, and the Abolitionists will sink out of sight."[1] The Negro's politics, however, were peculiar. Northern politicians were in conventional situations which limited their course of speech and action. Only proslavery and abolitionist workers could act as conscience demanded. An illiterate Negro fleeing slavery could embarrass a presidential candidate as much as foreign emissaries and congressional majorities. An abolitionist aiding such a Negro took on status which fines, prison sentences, and adverse publicity no more than increased as events gave him added glamor and respectability.[2]

[1] Howard K. Beale (ed.), *The Diary of Edward Bates, 1859–1866* (Washington, 1933), p. 101. "Cuffie" was a contemptuous term for Negro.

[2] Wilbur H. Siebert, *The Underground Railroad from Slavery to Freedom* (New York, 1899 ed.), is a compendium of routes and incidents, but lacks unifying analysis and critical insight. William Still, *Underground Rail Road Records, Revised Edition. With a Life of the Author . . .* (Philadelphia, 1883), has similar strengths and weaknesses. Marion G. McDougall, *Fugitive Slaves (1619–1865)* (Boston, 1891), is competent, though with great lacks and an inadequate sense of the magnitude of the subject. Larry Gara, *The Liberty Line: The Legend of the Underground Railroad* (Lexington, Ky., 1961) is an anti-abolitionist account, examined by Filler, *MVHR*, XLVIII (1961), 523. The subject requires further consideration. For a pioneer piece of Negro

Negroes were, of course, persons of varied qualities and abilities. Outstanding among them was Frederick Douglass, a Maryland-born mulatto of fine frame and intelligence who, as a slave, had suffered cruelty and wounds to his spirit because of his independent air and sense of worth. He escaped to New York by a desperate ruse in 1838 at about the age of twenty, there to be befriended by Dr. David Ruggles. Douglass married a free Maryland Negress who had come north to join him. He settled down to a quiet life in New Bedford, Massachusetts, always aware that he was a fugitive from slavery and liable to be recognized at any time by white or Negro informers.[3]

When, in August 1841, he stood up at a Garrison meeting—having long been a reader of the *Liberator*—and made an awkward speech, a career began which was not to end until more than half a century of labors had been fulfilled. Charles Lenox Remond, a free-born Negro, had preceded Douglass on the antislavery platform and been popular and effective at home and abroad.[4] But Douglass grew so fast in strength and expressiveness that he soon had to prove that he had indeed been a slave so recently. His increasing fame, coupled with the fact that he was outside the law, were vivid arguments against slavery. Though he was humiliated and abused, it was difficult for antiabolitionists to distinguish their contempt for Douglass from that accorded white abolitionists.

The Negro thus was, and would continue to be, at the base of the abolitionist crusade. Free Negroes increased in number in conspicuous abolitionist ranks; they entered into and developed along with political abolitionism.[5] "Slave narratives" multiplied as testimonials against

---

enterprise in freeing a fugitive slave in the northwest, see Arthur R. Kooker, "The Antislavery Movement in Michigan, 1796–1840" (Ph.D., University of Michigan, 1941), pp. 63 ff. The incident occurred in Detroit in 1833.

[3] His classic *Life and Times of Frederick Douglass, Written by Himself* was first published in 1845. It was revised and supplemented a number of times, and issued in many editions. Most satisfying is the Centenary Memorial Subscribers' Edition (New York, 1941), though with curious notes. Philip S. Foner, *The Life and Writings of Frederick Douglass* (4 vols., New York, 1950–55), is invaluable as the only and standard edition of his writings. Benjamin Quarles, *Frederick Douglass* (Washington, 1948), is a better-balanced portrait, also employing original sources.

[4] Quarles (ed.), "Letters from Negro Leaders to Gerrit Smith," *JNH*, XXVII (1942), 432–453; an important collection is "Letters to Antislavery Workers and Agencies," *JNH*, X (1925), 343–567, 648–774. *JNH* has a number of studies of individual Negro abolitionists.

[5] Charles H. Wesley, "The Participation of Negroes in Anti-Slavery Political Parties," *JNH*, XXIX (1944), 32–74.

slavery. One by James Williams, edited by Whittier, roused unusual controversy about its authenticity. Another was by William Wells Brown, once, as a slave, hired to Elijah P. Lovejoy in St. Louis. Brown became an early Negro literary figure. The Reverend Jermain W. Loguen was notable for his campaign activities in behalf of the Liberty party.[6] Fugitive escapes and slave narratives, Negro propaganda and co-operation, all did their part in the abolitionist and political abolitionist campaigns. They became more significant as they could be identified with the needs of white Northerners.

As early as 1829, Benjamin Lundy had attempted, without success, to encourage fears that the Fugitive Slave Law of 1793, which permitted the return of Negroes to slavery, could be used to kidnap non-Negroes. A quarter-century later, the political abolitionist John Gorham Palfrey would direct the same argument, not at an abolitionist, but at a conservative:

The simple truth is, at this moment, that if an affidavit comes from Georgia that A. B. has escaped from service there, and somebody can be found to testify that I am A. B., and an irresponsible *Commissioner* . . . chooses to say, for the fee of ten dollars, that he believes his testimony, I must go to Georgia . . . and there is no remedy for me whatever in the laws of my country, unless the Personal Liberty Bill of Massachusetts is good law, and competent to my protection.[7]

The possibility that white individuals might suffer under laws intended for Negroes was early recognized, and laws were passed for

---

[6] [Whittier] *Narrative of James Williams, an American Slave* . . . (Boston, 1838); *Narrative of William Wells Brown, a Fugitive Slave* . . . (Boston, 1848 ed.), p. 26; W. Edward Farrison, "Phylon Profile; XV: William Wells Brown," *Phylon*, IX (1948), 13–23. *The Rev. J. W. Loguen, as a Slave and As a Freeman* . . . (Syracuse, 1859). Ulrich B. Phillips, *Life and Labor in the Old South* (Boston, 1931), p. 219, wrote off all the slave narratives as doctored and unreliable. Although many of them were, many of them were not, including Douglass' classic autobiography. Even the less adequate tales contain qualities worthy of discrimination. See Charles H. Nichols, Jr., "A Study of the Slave Narrative" (Ph.D., Brown University, 1948), a survey and analysis; Margaret Y. Jackson, "An Investigation of Biographies and Autobiographies of American Slaves Published between 1840 and 1860 . . ." (Ph.D., Cornell University, 1954); Marion W. Starling, "The Slave Narrative: Its Place in American Literary History" (Ph.D., New York University, 1946).

[7] John G. Palfrey, *Letter to a Whig Neighbor on the Approaching State Election, by an Old Conservative* (Boston, 1855), p. 10; *Genius of Universal· Emancipation*, X (November 27, 1829).

their protection. The needs of Negroes themselves were largely ignored; Greeley chided them for assisting fugitives. Thus friends of fugitives faced the task of turning law and conscience to the Negro's side. The range of personalities among Negro helpers was remarkable. Distinguished among them was Thomas Garrett, a Delaware Friend, who was said to have aided more than 2,700 fugitive slaves. Delaware and Maryland were the most active areas for them, being slave states in northern territory, though there were many dramatic escapes from Kentucky to Ohio. Garrett (the original for Simeon Halliday in *Uncle Tom's Cabin*) was fearless in his work, and accepted without regret a fine which was understood to have temporarily ruined him financially when he was apprehended in 1848.[8]

As distinguished was Levi Coffin, one of the North Carolina Quakers who had found their state uncomfortable, following its defection from antislavery, and settled in Indiana, where they helped temper its deep conservatism. Here Coffin built up underground-railroad techniques with great effect. He also made elaborate efforts to develop the production and sale of free produce into a system which would attract northern and also southern labor and capital. During his business travels in the southern states, he did not hesitate to express his antislavery views.[9]

The martyr of the fugitive-slave movement was the Reverend Charles T. Torrey, "father of the underground railroad," who crowned an eccentric career among abolitionists by joining his name, also at an early age, with Lovejoy's in their chronicles. He had resisted Garrison in Massachusetts—an action which, in his later soul searchings, he regretted. He had stood with the political abolitionists, and had

---

[8] R. C. Smedley, *History of the Underground Railroad in Chester and the Neighboring Counties of Pennsylvania*, ed. Robert Purvis and Marianna Gibbons (Lancaster, Pa., 1853), pp. 237 ff.; John A. Munroe, "The Negro in Delaware," *South Atlantic Qu.*, LVI (1957), 431, compares the state's policy toward Negroes in pre-Civil War decades with that of the present. It holds Delaware's moderate policy to be a model for national policy. See also Morris, "Labor Controls in Maryland in the Nineteenth Century," pp. 385–387.

[9] Levi Coffin, *Reminiscences of Levi Coffin, the Reputed President of the Underground Railway* (Cincinnati, 1876). A by-product of the antislavery work of Coffin and his friends was a deep schism in the Indiana Quaker fold, which brought delegates from London in an attempt to heal it; Walter Edgerton, *A History of the Separation in Indiana Yearly Meeting of Friends* . . . (Cincinnati, 1856); cf. Marion C. Miller, "The Antislavery Movement in Indiana" (Ph.D., University of Michigan, 1941), pp. 28 ff., 117 ff., 184 ff.

edited the Albany *Patriot*. Lewis Tappan held him to be improvident and undependable, and later wondered that Torrey had not given more thought to providing for his wife and children; presumably, from Tappan's standpoint, Torrey should have avoided dangerous missions. Torrey was in Annapolis in 1842, attending a meeting of slaveholders which he planned to report in abolitionist newspapers. He was recognized, arrested, and in prison first conceived the idea of a prearranged route for underground railroad activities. This differed from the improvised schemes ordinarily followed. Weld did not like Torrey. "He is an exceeding vain, trifling man with no wisdom or stability. . . . He has uncommonly fine natural powers, but will probably do quite as much hurt as good where ever he goes."[10] In the following two years, Torrey was credited with having helped some four hundred Negroes to freedom along his line before he was caught and put on trial. The expectations of abolitionists in 1844 may be judged by John Quincy Adams' belief that Torrey would be best served if tried before Chief Justice Taney. Torrey attempted unsuccessfully to escape prison. Tappan did what he could for Torrey's family, and was paid with abuse and repudiation; his and Torrey's temperaments were poles apart. Shortly after, Torrey died in prison, and settled all accounts by leaving his memory to the abolitionist cause.[11]

Sectional feeling gained by all fugitive-slave actions and decisions. Jonathan Walker, a sea captain, was caught aiding slaves to escape to the Bahamas in his vessel, and was branded upon the hand with the letters "S.S.," for slave stealer, and lodged in prison. Several years later, in 1848, Captain Daniel Drayton and Captain Edward Sayres, who operated a small coastal vessel, attempted to help seventy-three Negro men, women, and children to escape. Seized in Washington, they were held under old Maryland laws, and brought to trial. Horace Mann, increasingly concerned with slavery and its workings, defended the seamen in the face of local excitement and some danger. Although

[10] Weld to A. Grimké, January 18, 1842, Barnes and Dumond, *Weld-Grimké Letters*, II, 896.

[11] J. C. Lovejoy, *Memoir of Rev. Charles T. Torrey, Who Died in the Penitentiary of Maryland, Where He was Confined for Showing Mercy to the Poor* (Boston, 1847); *A Sermon in Commemoration of the Death of Rev. Charles T. Torrey* (Fisherville, Md., 1846); L. A. Chamerovzow, *Slave Life in Georgia* . . . (London, 1855), pp. 215–220. For an example of Torrey's canonization by abolitionists, Goodell, "Martyrs and Their Persecutors," *Christian Investigator*, IV, new ser. (1846), 345 ff.

Mann could not save them from prison, he was able to curb some of the more vengeful punishments planned.[12]

In 1844, Calvin Fairbank, an Oberlin graduate, went to Kentucky to aid a fugitive's wife to escape. Fairbank had been in the work since 1837. In Kentucky, he enlisted the help of Delia Webster, a schoolmistress from Vermont. He was captured, and she was betrayed. Following sentence, she was released and permitted to return to Vermont. Fairbank served five years of his sentence, was pardoned in 1849, but once again left Ohio on an antislavery mission in Kentucky which he accomplished successfully.[13]

Fairbank was, however, seized in Indiana, where he had brought off his fugitive. He was transported to Kentucky and remanded to prison, not to be released until 1864. This was the fate of a number of Northerners, and left uncomfortable their fellows otherwise uninterested in Negroes, since the kidnaping procedure transgressed legal state processes.[14] Southerners, for their part, saw no difference between abolitionists and slave stealers. There was even such an adventurer as John Fairfield, a Virginian who somewhere picked up abolitionist sentiments and over a period of twelve years helped numerous slaves to escape. He used weapons, and was willing to receive money, though he helped without. "He was a wicked man," Coffin concluded, "daring and reckless in his actions, yet faithful . . . and benevolent to the poor."[15] Such sentiments did not endear the interlopers to Southerners. It appeared to them that Northerners inadequately respected the law.

[12] *Trial and Imprisonment of Jonathan Walker, of Pensacola, Florida* . . . (Boston, 1845); *The Man with the Branded Hand, or a Short Sketch of the Life and Services of Jonathan Walker* (Muskegon, Mich., 1879); Louise H. Tharp, *Until Victory: Horace Mann and Mary Peabody* (Boston, 1953), pp. 224 ff.

[13] *Rev. Calvin Fairbank During Slavery Times. How He "Fought the Good Fight" to Prepare "The Way." Edited from His Manuscript* (Chicago, 1890); *Kentucky Jurisprudence. A History of the Trial of Miss Delia A. Webster. At Lexington, Kentucky, Dec'r 17-21, 1844* . . . (Vergennes, Vt., 1845).

[14] See, for example, *Trial of Rev. John B. Mahan* . . . (Cincinnati, 1838). Mahan had been kidnaped on the charge, probably misdirected, that he had helped a slave escape. The Kentucky jury believed—the judge dissented—that he could be tried, even though he had not been in the state. However, they concluded that he was not guilty as charged.

[15] Coffin, *Reminiscences*, p. 432; H. R. Howard (comp.), *The History of Virgil A. Stewart, and His Adventure in Capturing and Exposing the Great "Western Land Pirate"* . . . (New York, 1836); Phillips, *Plantation and Frontier*, II, 75 ff.

They more than suspected the existence of such arrangements as Gerrit Smith and Lewis Tappan made, subsidizing an abolitionist's forays into southern territory.[16] They thus felt justified in fending for themselves in the protection of their slave property.

However, their actions created abolitionist sentiment as fast as did the fact that actual law enforcement tended to restrict northern liberties by augmenting the power of federal agents at the expense of state agencies. The 1840's saw a wave of actions in the courts which taught this fact to a displeased North.

Antislavery partisans had great need for keeping alert to the state of the Union. Not only were rank-and-file Northerners apt to forget matters of conscience; the abolitionists themselves could be duped to believe that all was well in some such areas. Thus the foreign slave trade maintained a hardy strength in the Americas, and American slave ships became central to its operations. The United States consul at Havana, Nicholas P. Trist, who had been Andrew Jackson's "intelligent"[17] young secretary, connived at the use of the American flag for this purpose.[18] It was not possible to dramatize this issue; Americans were not interested in the foreign slave trade. What was impressive was that such seasoned veterans of antislavery as Lewis Tappan and Judge Jay persuaded themselves that the foreign slave trade to America had been ended. Parker Pillsbury, orating in the British Isles in 1855, asserted that 19,000—or 9,000; his figure was obscurely reported—slaves were introduced from Africa every year in the United States. This was an extraordinary statement, Tappan thought; he could not believe that domestic slave dealers would countenance such competition, and he hastened to Jay for an authoritative comment. Jay, too, denied absolutely that "one single slave had been landed in the United States from Africa" in the last twenty years.[19]

---

[16] Dr. Alexander M. Ross, *Recollections and Experiences of an Abolitionist; from 1855 to 1865* (Toronto, 1867 ed.), pp. 32 and *passim.*

[17] Schlesinger, *Age of Jackson,* p. 102.

[18] R. R. Madden, *A Letter to W. E. Channing, D.D., on the Subject of the Abuse of the Flag of the United States* . . . (Boston, 1839). Another *Letter to Wm. E. Channing* . . . (Boston, 1840) by a "Calm Observer" is an obviously face-saving production, but is persuasive neither in detail nor in presentation. Cf. Hubert H. A. Aimes, *A History of Slavery in Cuba, 1511 to 1868* (New York, 1907), p. 131.

[19] L. Tappan to L. A. Chamerovzow, February 22, April 3, 1855, Tappan Papers, LC. In fact, the slave trade had moved from New England to New York; Du Bois, *The Suppression of the African Slave-Trade to the United States of America, 1638–1870* (Boston, 1896), pp. 178 ff.; "The Slave-Trade

Yet Pillsbury, suspicious and alert to rumors, was more nearly correct than Jay, for all Jay's knowledge of the ways in which government agents had co-operated with southern interests, most notoriously in refusing Great Britain's fleet the right to search American vessels for possible slaves. That Great Britain may have mixed national interest with her antislave-trade zeal is possible.[20] In addition, there were American naval officers who sincerely despised the slave trade. In any event, the realities of Anglo-American policy and practice permitted a quiet, busy traffic in slaves, introduced from outside the country, which domestic dealers expediently ignored.[21]

The *Amistad* defendants were another matter. In June of 1839, this vessel had left Havana bearing some fifty-odd Negro slaves, including the soon to be famous Cinqué. An African headman, he led the other slaves in an uprising, killing the captain and three of his crew, and saving two for navigating them back to Africa. These seamen began a strange journey, sailing east in daylight or moonlight, but west when darkness obscured their purpose. Finally, the *Amistad* landed in Long Island waters, where it was boarded by Lieutenant Commander Thomas R. Gedney of the United States Navy. The ship was taken into New London. There, Cinqué and thirty-eight of his followers were charged with piracy, and committed to prison for trial.[22]

The greatest danger was that the defendants would be rushed back into Spanish hands before any action could be taken to protect them. This the Secretary of State, John Forsyth, a stanch Georgian slave-

---

in New York," *Littell's Living Age,* VIII (1855), 32–34; Foner, *Business and Slavery,* pp. 164 ff.

[20] As one American commander put it: "Under the pretence of suppressing the slave-trade, I have not a doubt that it is the intention of both England and France to make as many settlements on the [African] coast as they can, for the purpose of monopolizing the trade of the continent"; H. G. Soulsby, *The Right of Search and the Slave Trade in Anglo-American Relations, 1814–1862* (Baltimore, 1933), p. 119.

[21] Du Bois, *Suppression of the African Slave-Trade,* pp. 143 ff.; see also Commander Andrew H. Foote, *Africa and the American Flag* (New York, 1854), and Basil Burwell, *Slave Cargo* (Prairie City, 1948), pp. 7 ff., a modern poem of high relevance and validity. For a detailed examination, Warren S. Howard, *American Slavers and the Federal Law, 1837–1862* (Berkeley, 1963).

[22] John W. Barber, *A History of the Amistad Captives . . .* (New Haven, 1840); Simeon E. Baldwin, *The Captives of the Amistad* (New Haven, 1886); *Africans Taken in the Amistad. Congressional Document Containing the Correspondence, &c. . . .* (New York, 1839); Bemis, *Adams and the Union,* pp. 384 ff., the latter for an excellent brief account. William A. Owens, *Slave Mutiny* (New York, 1953), is a novel, written with delicacy and grasp.

holder, was eager to do. The slaves, including three children and a cabin boy, might have been hurried out of the country as mere murderers requested by a friendly power, but for the decisive action of the abolitionists, headed by Lewis Tappan. They obtained counsel, including Theodore Sedgwick, Jr., an antislavery Democrat. An interpreter brought to light the circumstances attending the enslavement of the *Amistad* victims, which abrogated the treaties into which Spain had entered with Great Britain and the United States. Leavitt and S. S. Jocelyn organized and publicized the defense. Missionaries concerned themselves for the religious state of the Negroes.

A quiet settling of the case became infeasible; but the government, in effect, sued to obtain the persons of the Negroes, who were to be tried by the Federal District Court. With Andrew J. Judson as its judge, there was cause for uneasiness among the antislavery party; Judson had been their antagonist during the Prudence Crandall persecution. The intentions of the government were no secret. The Spanish Minister had applied for a ship in which the Negroes could be immediately removed if the court should find for the United States District Attorney, an administration appointee. Secretary of the Navy Paulding, at Forsyth's request, promptly sent the United States schooner *Grampus* to anchor off New Haven. An Executive Order from Van Buren ordered the United States Marshal to deliver the Negroes to the *Grampus*. Forsyth's own instructions to the District Attorney were memorable: "Unless an appeal shall actually have been interposed, you are not to take it for granted that it will be interposed."[23]

Judson, however, ruled in favor of the Africans: they had been illegally kidnaped from Africa, and were by Spain's own laws free and to be sent home. It was a conscientious decision; Judson found the cabin boy, Antonio, a bona fide slave, and ordered him returned to his owners. (The boy decided otherwise, and simply escaped, with the aid of abolitionists.) But it was the government which needed the support of law, now, to attain its ends. The Circuit Court passed the case on to the Supreme Court, and John Quincy Adams was brought in for the final defense.

The glare of publicity, the humanizing of the captives in American

---

[23] *20th Congress. 1st Session. Doc. No. 185. Africans Taken in the Amistad. Congressional Document Containing the Correspondence, &c. . . .* (New York, 1840), pp. 36, 48.

eyes, and the careful work of the legal staff which had exposed the illegality of the Spanish claims had impressed Judson sufficiently to prevent him from ruling in terms of his natural inclinations. Whether these factors were strong enough to affect a largely proslavery Supreme Court was problematic. It was just as well that Adams was present to add his varied and passionate argument to that of the other defense counsel. He exposed the bias of the government, and its compliance with illegal demands and tainted causes.[24] Soon he was able to write Tappan:

The captives are free!
The part of the Decree of the District Court, which placed them at the disposal of the President of the United States to be sent to Africa is *reversed.* They are to be discharged from the custody of the marshal—*free.* . . . But Thanks—Thanks! in the name of humanity and of Justice, to *you.*[25].

The abolitionists were triumphant. A new edition of Jay's *View of the Action of the Federal Government, in Behalf of Slavery,* first issued in 1839, contained an appendix by Leavitt detailing the case, and noting particularly the role of Martin Van Buren, whose Executive Order striving to hasten the Negroes back to slavery ought, Leavitt gravely stated, "to be engraved on his tomb, to rot only with his memory."

It was, above all, concern for personal liberties which alerted the northern states to dangers inherent in the administration of slave cases. Massachusetts had been particularly receptive to interpretations which advanced freedom. In the Med case, in 1836, Chief Justice Lemuel Shaw of its supreme court had for the first time applied the common law of England to slaves taken to a free state voluntarily by their master, and declared the slave free.[26] That year also had seen the first slave rescue in Boston. Two hunted women had been held by the captain of the brig in which they had escaped till they were seized. It was Justice Shaw again who ruled that the captain had no right to turn the brig into a prison. Before a fresh arrest could be made, the

---

[24] *Argument of John Quincy Adams, before the Supreme Court of the United States, in the Case of the United States, Appelants, vs. Cinque, and Others* . . . (New York, 1841).

[25] Adams to Tappan, March 9, 1841, Tappan Papers, LC.

[26] *Right and Wrong in Boston in 1836: Annual Report of the Boston Female Anti-Slavery Society* . . . (Boston, 1836), pp. 64 ff.

Negroes had been hurried by Garrisonians into a carriage and disappeared. A later case involved a Massachusetts woman whom living in New Orleans had turned "southern" in sentiment. Her attempt to reclaim a slave in Massachusetts took the ground that "the girl Anne's" services were "voluntary." Abolitionists, she complained, had engaged in a conspiracy to defraud her by drawing up a writ for freeing the girl without her consent. The argument failed before the court.[27]

The State of Pennsylvania, with little regard for fugitive slaves and some public interest in disenfranchising her own Negro citizens, had chosen, like Massachusetts, to control her own affairs by means of a law which gave her courts authority to rule in matters rising out of the Fugitive Slave Act of 1793.[28] Now, in 1842, Pennsylvania found her authority challenged: the Supreme Court attempted to reassert beyond equivocation the primacy of federal authority by denying states the right to legislate on the subject of fugitive slaves at all. As a measure for easing tensions between North and South, the decision of *Prigg v. Pennsylvania* accomplished the opposite. Southerners saw this building up of government prerogatives as being at the expense of their treasured states' rights, for all that the decision protested that it did not intend to infringe on the "general sovereignty" of states. Nor were Southerners pleased by the Supreme Court's view that state authorities were not responsible for enforcing the federal law; in other words, that slave catchers need expect no co-operation from the northern states. Northerners, on the other hand, resented this taking away of their authority to administer the fugitive-slave problem within their own borders as they pleased; *Prigg v. Pennsylvania* they saw as a capitulation to southern sentiments.[29] But more important, they were

[27] Leonard W. Levy, "The 'Abolition Riot': Boston's First Slave Rescue," *NEQ*, XXV (1952), 84 ff.; *Report of the Holden Slave Case . . .* (Worcester, 1839).

[28] *An Act to Give Effect to the Provisions of the Constitution of the United States. Relative to Fugitives from Labor, for the Protection of Free People of Color and to Prevent Kidnaping* (n.p., 1826). Other states did likewise. Connecticut prescribed a trial by jury. New York and Vermont, in 1840, provided the first true personal liberty law by ensuring attorneys for alleged fugitives. Salmon P. Chase tried to persuade the state courts that the Act of 1793 was unconstitutional. See Joseph Nogee, "The Prigg Case and Fugitive Slavery, 1842–1850," *JNH*, XXXIX (1954), 198; *Address and Reply on the Presentation of a Testimonial . . .* , p. 5; Leslie, "The Fugitive Slave Clause, 1787–1842," pp. 192 ff., 326 ff.

[29] *Report of the Case of Edward Prigg against the Commonwealth of Pennsylvania . . .* (Philadelphia, 1842); Charles Warren, *The Supreme Court in*

roused to a defense of their privileges. If they might not administer the Fugitive Slave Law, they could refuse to co-operate with federal officials who did. Personal-liberty laws broke out in the North, which, in their clear intention to frustrate slave catchers and in their assumption that federal officers did not merit co-operation, helped close the gap at several points between abolitionists and conservatives.

Merely wishful thinking enabled Garrison to imagine that the personal-liberty laws were "tantamount to disunion." Associate Justice Joseph Story himself felt that the Prigg decision had localized slavery.[30] Many abolitionists were to follow Story's reasoning, at least to the extent of agitating for a diminished sphere of influence for the institution. Others developed constitutional arguments, while resisting the federal law, which helped support their contention that the Constitution abhorred slavery.

The Latimer case of 1842, first fruit of the Prigg decision, showed that Massachusetts, at least, opposed slave catching. George Latimer was seized in Boston at the behest of James B. Grey, of Norfolk, Virginia, who asserted that Latimer was his property. Grey began proceedings which ultimately cost him more than the market value of Latimer. Excitement in the North was fed by the *North Star and Latimer's Journal,* which Dr. Henry I. Bowditch edited. A monster Latimer Petition went to Adams in the House of Representatives and was ignored in standard fashion, despite Adams' efforts to present it. It served its purpose in linking the cause of the fugitives with the right of petition.

Quick abolitionist action made it certain that Latimer would evade re-enslavement, and his sponsors demanded that his owner sign a deed of emancipation in exchange for $400. Faced with the possibility of losing all, including his court costs, Grey acceded. In effect, in this first duel, the Fugitive Law had been publicly flouted.[31]

In this atmosphere of sharpening northern sentiments, the fight for

United States History (Boston, 1924), II, 357; Commager, *Documents of American History,* I, 292–294.

[30] Leslie, "Fugitive Slave Clause," p. 335.

[31] *Proceedings of the Citizens of the Borough of Norfolk, on the Boston Outrage in the Case of the Runaway Slave George Latimer* (Norfolk, Va., 1843). For an example of the work done to discourage slave catchers, *Fifth Annual Report of the New-York Committee of Vigilance, for the Year 1842* . . . (n.p., n.d.). See also Whittier's poem, "Massachusetts to Virginia," which bitterly accuses the Old Dominion of having betrayed their common Revolutionary heritage; *The Poetical Works* (Boston, n.d.), pp. 62–63.

the right of petition came to a close, and the Liberty party was suddenly thrust upon national attention. Seen from hindsight, the party's
role in the election of 1844, coupled with the antislavery victory over
the gag rule at the opening of the Twenty-eighth Congress, can appear
to be milestones on the road to freedom. Seen more closely, the "victories" become more questionable.

True, northern antislavery feeling was receiving increased room for
self-expression. By 1844, the spirit had subsided which had permitted
the harsh treatment of Reuben Crandall and the danger to Ransom
G. Williams in the nation's capital. Lewis Tappan was able to report:

A friend of mine, now on a visit to Washington, writes that when he was
there a few years since most Northern men hesitated about even speaking
to a man of color, lest he should be taken for an abolitionist and be
"lynched," but now abolition is the topic of conversation in all the board-
inghouses, hotels, parties, &c., and that [sic] the House of Representatives
appears to him like an Anti-Slavery Convention.[32]

Tappan was, as usual, oversanguine, but there was, indeed, augmented freedom for Southerners to resent. They resisted, as long as
they could, Adams' demand, supported by Giddings and Slade, for a
raising of the gag rule. Helping Adams, too, was Leavitt, who came
to Washington, late in 1841, mainly because the *Emancipator,* which
he still edited, was not providing a living wage. He was soon, after
twenty years, again to be a resident of Massachusetts and editing
Liberty-party papers: first the *Free American,* later the *Emancipator,*
in several permutations of names. Meanwhile, he acted as an antislavery reporter; consorted with Bailey, Adams, and their familiars;
and corresponded on possibilities for Liberty-party action. Also in
Washington, for his last contribution to the abolitionist movement,
was Weld, as a researcher: "[The anti-slavery congressmen] have little
leisure for gathering materials," he explained, "[and] request me to
spend the winter here and aid them in the matter."[33]

[32] Tappan to John Beaumont, January 30, 1844, Abel and Klingberg (eds.),
A Side-light on Anglo-American Relations, 1839–1858 (Lancaster, Pa., 1927),
p. 172. See, however, *The Case of William L. Chaplin, being an Appeal to All
Respecters of Law and Justice against the Cruel and Oppressive Treatment to
which, under Color of Legal Proceedings, He Has Been Subjected, in the
District of Columbia and the State of Maryland* (Boston, 1851), a circum-
stantial account of the persecution in 1850 which followed alleged assistance to
two slaves. It took $31,000 of forfeited bail to free Chaplin.
[33] Weld to Tappan, December 14, 1841, Barnes and Dumond (eds.), *Weld-*

At the beginning of each session of Congress, Adams presented his usual demands for the right of petition. In 1842, the gag rule was passed with but four votes to spare, in 1843 with but three. On December 3, 1844, Adams's motion to strike it out was carried by a vote of 108 to 80, and the triumph was received with joy and congratulations in the North, with resentment in the South.[34]

The joy and anger were but surface responses; the question of power and national perspectives continued to be more consequential. Many Southerners had fought for the gag rule who favored the right of petition. They had been defending slavery, rather than opposing freedom of speech. As one Georgia planter wrote to a southern statesman:

If the agitation on the subject is continued for three months longer we will be compelled to arm our Militia and shoot down our property in the field. If the thing is not already incurable, tell the agitators we had rather fight them than our own negroes, and that we will do it too. . . . I have expressed myself as I feel, and it is the feeling of the whole South.[35]

Numerous Northerners who finally concluded to grant the right of

---

Grimké Letters, II, 880. An ill-advised effort to make Weld central to Adams' campaign and the development of antislavery sentiment in Congress is contained in Barnes, *Anti-Slavery Impulse,* pp. 177 ff. It is not substantiated by published or unpublished sources. Among its more extraordinary statements is one that Giddings was returned to Congress, following his censure and resignation, because Weld had made the Western Reserve antislavery, years before; *ibid.,* p. 188. Another undocumented impression sees Weld as "so clearly the spokesman for the interest centering" in an alleged "headquarters of abolitionism" in Washington "that some of the abolitionists urged him to attempt a union of the anti-slavery factions throughout the north"; *ibid.,* p. 194. Adams' diary offers only three passages respecting Weld, of which the following is representative: "Mr. Weld came, with a kind offer of assistance in the search for documents, books or papers. Mr. Weld spoke of the temper of the people here . . . but he said he thought the tide was turning in my favor"; Adams (ed.), *Memoirs of John Quincy Adams,* xi, 75. Leavitt was an admirer of Weld, but his Washington correspondence offers no aid to the Barnes conjectures. For Weld's own statement on why he withdrew from reform in favor of what he called a "higher sphere of experience"—that is, private life—see his interview with Henry B. Blackwell; Alice S. Blackwell, *Lucy Stone: Pioneer of Woman's Rights* (Boston, 1930), pp. 126 ff.

[34] For a brief but valuable chronicle and analysis, see Alexander Johnston, in *Cyclopaedia of Political Science* . . . , ed. John J. Lalor (New York, 1890), III, 167–169.

[35] Ulrich B. Phillips (ed.), "Correspondence of Robert Toombs, Alexander H. Stephens, and Howell Cobb," *AHA Annual Report, 1911* (Washington, 1913), II, 55.

petition to antislavery advocates had no interest in disturbing or even containing slavery. Although southern resentment against petitions continued, erupting as late as 1850,[36] southern statesmen were too realistic to lay all hopes on the issue. With elections to win, and concrete problems of domestic and foreign policy to master, they could afford to concede to the North its relatively minor victories.

The immediate prize was Texas. The great slogan, which might win a northern majority from its concern for free labor, was nationalism. Thus the South, despite its "peculiar institution," might be the banner bearer for the nation. Since Northerners in large measure shared their pride in "manifest destiny," the hunger for free land, the cry for western expansion, might well drown out the antislavery concert. The South had been the active and self-sacrificing element in support of the Texas insurrection.[37] It might well lead Texas into the Union to northern plaudits.

Lewis Tappan was signally active, at this time, in plans for keeping a slave Texas out of the Union. He mixed fantastic hopes that southern states might still be persuaded voluntarily to abandon slavery with hopes that Texas might do so. In the spring of 1843, he suddenly concluded to go to England to attend the second world antislavery convention in London and attempt to influence British statesmen in his cause. With him went Stephen Pearl Andrews, a Texan highly esteemed at the bar, who had undertaken with considerable success, the southern press warned, to persuade his fellow countrymen to emancipate the Negroes.[38] Leavitt was also in England, as aid and propagandist for their cause.

British and American antislavery had deep economic roots which affected their course at every turn.[39] Thus Granville Sharp's project

---

[36] *The Right of Petitions. Remarks of Messers. Seward, Hale, and Chase, with a Sketch of the Debate in the Senate on Various Petitions and Other Matters Connected with the Subject of Slavery* (Washington, 1850).

[37] John H. Franklin, *The Militant South* (Cambridge, Mass., 1956), p. 102.

[38] Smith, *Annexation of Texas*, pp. 112–114. Andrews was a remarkable figure who requires full-scale treatment; see Wish, "Stephen Pearl Andrews, Pioneer American Sociologist," *Social Forces,* XIX (1941), 477–482, and Rocker, *Pioneers of American Freedom*, pp. 70 ff. See also Madeleine B. Stern, *The Pantarch: a Biography of Stephen Pearl Andrews* (Austin, Tex., 1968).

[39] The American historian of antislavery and economics is Thomas P. Martin; immediately relevant is his article, "Come International Aspects of the Anti-Slavery Movement, 1818–1823," *Jour. of Econ. and Business Hist.*, I (1928), 137 ff. See also Henry H. Simms, *A Decade of Sectional Controversy, 1851–1861* (Chapel Hill, 1942), pp. 169 ff., and Caroline Lewis, "The Antislavery

for making Sierra Leone an African haven for free Negroes was a speculative and colonial, as well as humanitarian, venture. The early promotion of cotton growing in Africa by abolitionists, it was hoped, would increase British independence of southern cotton. Government protection of British West Indies sugar was gall to East India traders —including John Gladstone, father of the future Prime Minister, and Zachary Macaulay, one of the great abolitionists.

British antislavery men had a stake in seeking to end the Corn Laws, raising as they did protection barriers to the wheat grown by western farmers in the American North. Many of these were emigrated Englishmen, with bitter memories of old landlords and high-priced bread. Their free-trade sentiments gave them a link with the South which Calhoun hoped to rivet. As Richard Cobden, English anti-Corn Law reformer, put it to Joseph Sturge, the Corn Laws had thrown "the entire power over the legislature into the hands of the *slave owners.*" Leavitt was outstanding in America in his perception of the harm which the Corn Laws did to Anglo-American antislavery relations. In 1841, Leavitt was able to persuade the Committee on Agriculture in Congress to order printed his "Memorial . . . Praying the Adoption of Measures to Secure an Equitable and Adequate Market for American Wheat." His memorial was echoed not only in the American press but in Great Britain as well.[40]

Official British interest in Texas coincided with that of the abolitionists. Great Britain had every reason to wish a separate Texas Republic, without slavery. It would be a basin for surplus British population, a market for their manufactured goods, a competitor with southern cotton, a means for undermining the American tariff and for stabilizing peaceful relations with Mexico.[41] Tappan's visit abroad included intimate interviews with the Prime Minister and his Foreign Secretary, in the course of which he urged them to grant a loan to

---

Argument as Developed in the Literature 1830–1840" (Ph.D., Cornell University, 1916), pp. 145 ff.

[40] Martin, "The Upper Mississippi Valley in Anglo-American Anti-Slavery and Free Trade Relations: 1837–1842," *MVHR*, XV (1928), 204–220, and "Free Trade and the Oregon Question, 1842–1846," in *Facts and Factors in Economic History: Articles by Former Students of Edwin Francis Gay*, ed., N. S. B. Gras *et al.* (Cambridge, Mass., 1932), p. 471; Jesse S. Reeves, *American Diplomacy under Tyler and Polk* (Baltimore, 1907), p. 139.

[41] Smith, *Annexation of Texas*, pp. 79–80; Ephraim D. Adams, *British Interests and Activities in Texas, 1838–1846* (Baltimore, 1910), pp. 53–54 and *passim.*

Texas to enable that Republic to put its finances on an independent basis. The British statesmen were interested and friendly; Tappan optimistically believed that "our impulse has been given to the anti s. cause." The great probability was that his visit accomplished little more than to give the South an added patriotic, anti-British argument.

Whether abolitionists were helping or harming antislavery was the chief question which emerged from the election of 1844. Liberty Men were sanguine. They had received some 65,000 votes in the free states in the 1843 elections, and some of the more optimistic of them predicted increases of votes which ranged as high as two million by 1848. There was even a Liberty party in Virginia which dared believe it had a future. Chase had broken loose from the Whigs, and was to be an intimate correspondent of Leavitt, who was then still determined to see Birney the President of the United States. Tappan "stood aloof" from the movement, but could not resist being concerned for its politics and hoping the party would be worthy of its principles. He himself arranged a "Cabinet dinner" for Birney: "He sat at the head of the table with six men around & opposite T. D. Weld at his right, Sec. of State! Poor S. S. J[ocelyn] blushed when I called him P. M. General."[42]

Birney averred he would readily concede his place as presidential candidate to a better choice. But Adams, for all his fine qualities, was inadequately abolitionist in sentiment. So was Governor Seward, for all that he had been gaining a national reputation by his firm antislavery rejoinders to official demands put upon him by Virginia and Georgia leaders. William Jay was Tappan's own choice, but had too little faith in political abolitionism to run in its name.

The year 1844 appeared to be Clay's. Respectful of the South's interests, regardful of the North's prejudices, loved and distinguished everywhere, his goal seemed at hand. The Democrats were broken into at least two huge fragments, headed by the rivals Calhoun and Van Buren. Moreover, they were embarrassed by revelations of Democratic thievery in official capacities. Most notorious had been the stealing of nearly a million and a quarter dollars by Samuel Swartwout, over a period of years, since his appointment by Jackson as Collector of the Port of New York.[43] Nevertheless, Texas loomed too large and

[42] Tappan to Whittier, December 9, 1843, Tappan Papers, LC.
[43] *25th Congress, 3d Session. Rep. No. 313 Ho. of Reps. Defalcations. Reports of Majority and Minority . . . On the Subject of the Defalcations of*

decisive for Whigs to disdain Liberty-party influence, once the Democrats had defeated Van Buren's presidential hopes and closed ranks behind the little-known James K. Polk. Whig strategy was to frighten Northerners with the expectation of inevitable annexation should Polk be elected, but also to emphasize to Southerners Clay's mildness of purpose, his willingness to receive Texas into the Union under honorable circumstances. A combination of factors defeated Clay in that tense election, but it was the Liberty party which created the sensation. As the New York *Express* analyzed it:

> It is clearly ascertained by the official returns of the State of New York, that the abolition vote amounts to 15,812.—The "liberty party," as they style themselves, caused the defeat of the Whig presidential electoral ticket, the governor and lieutenant governor, six members of congress, four canal commissioners, four senators, viz[.]: in the fourth, fifth, sixth, and seventh districts, and twenty-six members of assembly. The result is most disastrous. . . . There has never been a vote of any fragment of a party so extensively disastrous in its consequences, or so pernicious to the ostensible objects of its authors.[44]

Leavitt took the defeat of Clay to heart. Though unbending in his abolitionist faith, he believed the people must be reached on their own terms. Accordingly, he expected, as he wrote Chase, to "die under the odium of having caused the defeat of Henry Clay, and therefore [to merit] few tokens of respect except from those who are in a like condemnation." Some of Leavitt's coworkers were unrepentant. Even before the election, Tappan had suggested that Polk's election might do less damage than Clay's, for the latter "will carry nearly all the north with him & all the South. The man who made the Compromise for Missouri will attempt it for Texas. I prefer an out & out friend & advocate of slavery to an intriguer." Alvan Stewart roundly scored the two major parties as dominated by mean programs. The Liberty

Samuel Swartwout and Others . . . (Washington, 1839); *Speech of Mr. Wise, of Virginia, on the Subject of the Late Defalcations, Delivered in the House of Representatives, December 21, 1838* (n.p., n.d.). For a spirited but unpersuasive defense of the Democratic party, see *Speech of Mr. Duncan, of Ohio* (n.p., n.d.).

[44] Quoted in *Niles' Weekly Register*, LXVII (December 21, 1844), 244. Michigan, too, turned out a Liberty-party vote which, under other circumstances, might have given Clay the state. Michigan had, in 1841, offered the first Liberty-party ticket in the Northwest. It was still led by Birney, soon, tragically, to be invalided; Floyd B. Streeter, *Political Parties in Michigan, 1837–1860* (Lansing, 1918), pp. 62 ff.

party, he declared, had refused homage and empire in the interests of honor.[45]

If Liberty Men had become a force to conjure with, the moral reformers had not dwindled in significance. Little distinguished the assertions of the two groups at points of crisis. Thus, Garrison stood foursquare on the need for dissolving the Union. But John Quincy Adams, if against disunion, believed the annexation of Texas would be the equivalent of dissolution. Lewis Tappan, in one of his moments of alarm for annexation, urged William Slade to "blow the trumpet" for disunion in Vermont in such an eventuality.

Moral and political reformers, they were all unable to prevent the accession of Texas. The appeal of Robert J. Walker of Mississippi to northern fears of being inundated by "blacks"—an argument he had borrowed from northern congressmen—became the "textbook" of annexationists.[46] In their last desperate efforts, the abolitionists achieved a united front which involved Daniel Webster himself briefly and even furtively. They held monster rallies, embracing Garrison as well as the most calculating politicians, and executed a petition campaign protesting the admission of Texas "for various reasons, but this especially, because its constitution, as far as it can, supports and perpetuates slavery." The Liberty party held the balance for its "great and governing object" between anti-Texas conservatives and those who wished to "embrace other objects," that is, Garrisonians. But in their appeal, the Liberty Men sounded themselves like Garrisonians: "Turn not away from us—but hear us. If, as a representative of the Liberty Party, a little and hated party—we have but small claim on your attention; nevertheless, as your countrymen, we are to be respected and listened to."[47]

[45] Leavitt to Chase, July 4, 1856, HSP; Tappan to Benjamin Tappan, October 14, 1844, Tappan Papers, LC; Greeley, *American Conflict*, I, 167; Marsh (ed.), *Writings and Speeches of Alvan Stewart*, pp. 410–411.

[46] *Letter of Mr. Walker, of Mississippi, Relative to the Annexation of Texas* . . . (Washington, 1844); George M. Weston, *Progress of Slavery* (Washington, 1827), p. 295.

[47] *Proceedings of the Great Convention of the Friends of Freedom in the Eastern and Middle States. Held in Boston, Oct. 1, 2, & 3, 1845* (Lowell, 1845), pp. 13 ff.; *Proceedings of a Convention of Delegates Chosen by the People of Massachusetts, without Distinction of Party . . . to Take Into Consideration the Proposed Annexation of Texas, to the United States* (Boston, 1845), a more respectable assembly, but at one in their objects. *How to Settle the Texas Question* (n.p., n.d.), a petition pamphlet, contains the "Report on

The forces which they were not yet able to convert were well symbolized by Benjamin Tappan, senator from Ohio, and a brother of Arthur and Lewis: a nonreligious Democratic politician who had refused to offer antislavery petitions for the consideration of Congress on the grounds that they infringed upon the South's particular institutions, and because they had been drawn up by women, "whom nature has not given rights in governing."[48] He had been repelled by President Tyler's complicated intrigues for drawing up a secret treaty with Texas and having it passed by the Senate without public discussion. Tappan took it upon himself to expose in the New York *Post* the secret documents presented to the senators. He and his brother Lewis maintained contact for many years, on Lewis's part because of his warm feelings for old family ties, on Benjamin's at least partly because of Lewis's proved financial abilities. Texas entered into their correspondence in terms of Texas debt certificates or bonds, originally issued to finance the revolution of 1835 or to sustain the Texas Republic thereafter. Benjamin later gained $50,000 when the United States redeemed Texas paper which he had acquired as a speculation. The financier Jay Cooke believed that possession of such paper helped overcome the scruples of northern legislators against admitting Texas over northern disapproval, though such Democratic stalwarts as Duff Green and Robert J. Walker, Samuel Swartwout and William C. Preston, sought it freely without scruples to overcome.[49] As for Benjamin's role in the situation, his brother Lewis' view of his business ventures and related politics summarized the differences between them:

---

the Annexation of Texas" adopted by the Liberty Convention in Boston, October 1, 1845.

[48] *Remarks of Mr. Tappan, of Ohio, on Abolition Petitions, Delivered in Senate, February 4, 1840* (n.p., n.d.).

[49] Ellis P. Oberholtzer, *Jay Cooke: Financier of the Civil War* (Philadelphia, 1907), I, 73–74; cf. David L. Child, *The Taking of Naboth's Vineyard, or History of the Texas Conspiracy, and an Examination of the Reasons Given by the Hon. J. C. Calhoun, Hon. R. J. Walker, and Others, for the Dismemberment of the Republic of Mexico* (New York, 1845), pp. 30 ff., for a list of some of the "Texas scrip-holders and land-jobbers." James Hamilton of South Carolina, one of those named, was the late Texas Minister to Great Britain, accused of having embezzled Virginia Canal funds and of having offered a bribe of $200,000 to the Mexican chief, Santa Anna, for the recognition of Texas. Elgin Williams, *The Animating Pursuits of Speculation: Land Traffic in the Annexation of Texas* (New York, 1949), is a valuable study of the subject.

I absolutely decline making any investment for you in *Texas* stock, and my advice to you is—as you regard your reputation—to have nothing to do with that Stock. Be above suspicion. . . . That you should vote for the admission of Texas, with slavery, after the professions of your whole life, after your indignant exposure of the Tyler treaty, after the instructions from your Legislature, is, I conceive dishonorable to you as a man & as a Senator. By your single vote you could have stopt the nefarious project. What honor you would have gained if you had had the consistency & patriotism to have done it![50]

Benjamin Tappan later found himself unable to accept Lewis Cass as Democratic standard-bearer, and became a Free-Soiler.[51] Thus, from widely different standpoints, the brothers approached areas where they agreed, but not where either could afford to relax his vigilance.

The United States, in 1840, extended no farther than the borders of Missouri. The nation was about to make a stunning advance which would carry its territorial holdings to the Pacific Ocean. The West was a giant prize; why could South and North not share alike? So the South's representatives asked with mounting anger. Was not equal treatment the very least they deserved under the federal compact? The question failed to probe the differences in the two societies. Northerners were not antislavery; they were, with minor variations, nonslavery, and in constant competition with their opposite numbers farther south. Vast stretches of territory did not end this competition. Free land was not money; it was an arena in which differences could be debated.

The North was unwilling to allocate further lands for the spreading of a slave society. Its social and economic predilections, in prosperity or depression, left it open to arguments which were narrowing the distance between abolitionists and neutrals. As the Garrisonian Edmund Quincy unconsciously revealed, in 1847, in his effort to denigrate Liberty Men:

There are many more A. S. Whigs and Democrats than Third Party men, and many more Whig papers, especially, which are more thoroughly antislavery than any of the Third Party ones. There is not a Third Party paper

[50] L. Tappan to B. Tappan, March 13, 1845, Tappan Papers, LC. Tappan was mistaken; his brother had, in fact, followed the instructions of his legislature.

[51] Weisenburger, *Passing of the Frontier*, pp. 443, 463, 465.

that compares in thoroughness and usefulness with the Boston *Whig*, or even the N. Y. *Tribune*. And they have not a man who comes near Charles F. Adams (son of J. Q. A.), editor of the *Whig*, Charles Sumner, J. G. Palfrey, S. G. Howe, Stephen C. Phillips, or other of the A. S. Whigs. . . .[52]

Nevertheless, Liberty Men gave a type of thought to antislavery problems such as neither the Garrisonians nor the anti-cotton Whigs could match. Their role was well illustrated in the Oregon crisis, and in their search for a policy toward Great Britain.[53] Liberty Men could not, at first, decide whether advocating free trade or protection would best serve an Anglo-northern alliance. Free trade would please the British, and give them equal status with the free-trade South. But western farmers might prefer a policy that retaliated against the British Corn Laws, which kept American wheat out of the British market. The "Hungry Forties" were depression years in the United States, as well as in England, before the Mexican War brought prosperity. A protection policy, on the other hand, might antagonize Great Britain, and strengthen nationalistic feeling between North and South. In general, Liberty Men moved toward free trade; almost unique was the publication which Arnold Buffum issued in Indiana in 1841, *The Protectionist*, which not only demanded "protection" from slavery aggressions, but from the products of European pauper labor as well—a forerunner of later Republican protectionism.

Duff Green, a proslavery journalist, was in England in 1843, urging its statesmen to devise a better wheat tariff as a means for cooling off American interest in Oregon, which was a way out to ruined eastern merchants and unhappy eastern farmers. The Anti-Slavery Convention in London, in 1843, was a forum for free-trade antislavery Americans, a goad to proslavery lobbyists. In March 1845, the new President Polk announced United States title to Oregon, which the new Secretary of State, Buchanan, pressed upon the Minister Plenipotentiary of Great Britain. Polk's administration organ, the *Daily Union*, as well as Bailey's *Philanthropist*, both urged a free-trade tariff. It was the opinion of Sir Robert Peel, the Prime Minister, that "the admission of Maize [Indian corn] will . . . go far to promote a settlement of

[52] Garrisons, III, 185–186.
[53] A definitive statement of economic factors in this crisis is in Martin, "Free Trade and the Oregon Question," pp. 470 ff. See also Frederick Merk, "The British Corn Crisis of 1845–46 and the Oregon Treaty," *Agricultural Hist.*, VIII (1934), 95–123.

Oregon."[54] Southern senators mixed nationalism with sectionalism in helping to arrive at a settlement of the Oregon boundary, which, at latitude 49° was considerably less than their party had promised during the 1844 elections. The Walker Tariff of 1846—year of the repeal of the British Corn Laws—was a free-trade tariff, for revenue only. If the South lost little by these negotiations, the North had, at least, avoided catastrophe: war with antislavery Great Britain and Canada. It had maintained its standing in British eyes, and gained what would ultimately be the three free states or territories of Washington, Oregon, and Idaho. None were concerned for Negro rights; their official antislavery sentiments were but gambits in close political contests and national relations. Thus in 1857, two years before statehood was achieved, Oregon overwhelmingly adopted a constitution excluding free Negroes and mulattoes, having earlier driven out settlers of their race under threat of periodic flogging.[55]

The crisis of crises for the antislavery North was the Mexican War. The year 1846 was, indeed, a "Year of Decision" in that, thanks to Mormons, adventurers, and military men, it gave the United States title to the Great Plains and all the land between to the Pacific Ocean. But whether or not "[at] some time between August and December, 1846, the Civil War had begun," must always be conjectural.[56] Daniel Webster was to plead that nature itself had decreed that New Mexico could not sustain slavery, and that it was unnecessary as well as insulting to bind down that territory to nonslavery. Others would simply observe that southern generals had helped win that area for the United States; that southern soldiers had laid down their lives for it.

Which factors decisively made northern sentiment intransigently Free Soil can never be determined; but in the crisis created by the Mexican War, the political abolitionists were at the center of decisive events, and the moral reformers contributed the moral arguments they needed. There was a difference between the war with Mexico and the war "Mr. Madison" had waged in 1812 against the popular will of New

---

[54] Merk, "British Corn Crisis," pp. 479–480, 490; *Last Letter of Mr. Buchanan to Mr. Pakenham, on the American Title to Oregon* (Baltimore, 1845); cf. Thomas Falconer, *The Oregon Question; or, a Statement of the British Claims to the Oregon Territory, in Opposition to the Pretensions of the Government of the United States of America* (London, 1845).

[55] Robert W. Johannsen, *Frontier Politics and the Sectional Conflict* (Seattle, 1955), pp. 20, 44–46.

[56] Bernard DeVoto, *The Year of Decision* (Boston, 1943), p. 496.

England. The earlier crisis had also precipitated a peace movement, but the movement had been small and esoteric when compared with that which the Mexican adventure brought out.[57]

It may well be that the international character of the peace movement made it seem deceptively strong and widespread. For it was on the national scene that the issue between pacifists and those who welcomed war had to be joined. With proslavery and nationalist forces contemplating nothing less than the total acquisition of Mexico,[58] and the movement for war irresistible, the Garrisonians and the dedicated pacifists were neither more nor less impotent than their more conventional fellow Northerners. In fighting a rear-guard action to ensure that free-state partisans were not thrown into confusion, both made their contributions.

The achievement of the Garrisonians needs precise statement to be appreciated. As Wendell Phillips explained:

I remember being one of the committee which waited on Abbott Lawrence [Massachusetts merchant and politician], a year or so only before annexation, to ask his countenance to some general movement, without distinction of party, against the Texas scheme. He smiled at our fears, begged us to have no apprehensions; stating that his correspondence with leading men at Washington enabled him to assure us annexation was impossible, and that the South itself was determined to defeat the project. A short time after, Senators and Representatives from Texas took their seats in Congress![59]

It was in their influence upon others that the radicals exerted their moral force. There would be relatively few—though there would be a few—who would be so blunted to distinctions as to decry Thoreau's nonresistant pacifism, when he expressed it in such an essay as "Civil Disobedience," as though it had been mere eccentricity and noncooperativeness. They would sometimes seek to pass it off as mere "literature." But most readers would, more or less clearly, perceive that

[57] In Elihu Burritt pacifism produced a major figure whose efforts would influence pacifist thought throughout the western world, but his work relates too little to abolitionism to be treated here; see Curti, *The Learned Blacksmith* . . . (New York, 1937), and Elihu Burritt, *Voice from the Forge* (London, 1848?).

[58] Edward G. Bourne, "The Proposed Absorption of Mexico—1847–48," *AHA Annual Report, 1899* (Washington, 1900), I, 155–169; John D. P. Fuller, "The Slavery Question and the Movement to Acquire Mexico, 1846–8," *MVHR*, XXI (1934), 31–48.

[59] Phillips, "The Philosophy of the Abolition Movement," in *Speeches and Lectures,* p. 125.

Thoreau's writings were deeds and, as such, part of the tissue of contemporary reality.

Channing's famous "Remarks on National Literature"[60] had protested against mere imitation of European writings in America. By 1846, New England literature bristled with individualism and experimentalism. As the *Emancipator* could observe, apropos Sydney Smith's famous question, "Who reads an American book?" it had become almost obsolete.[61] The challenge of vital prose—and, inevitably, of antislavery prose—was as unmistakable as the challenge of vital politics.

Whittier, Emerson, Richard Hildreth as author of the pioneer antislavery novel, *The Slave: or Memoirs of Archy Moore* (1836), John Pierpont and Theodore Parker among the many literary preachers, made their powerful contributions to the literature of antislavery protest. Although Whittier was the poetic star of antislavery, there were many others; and the antislavery partisans utilized all available prestige for their cause. They issued Longfellow's felicitous if not profound rhymes on the subject, and reprinted Phillis Wheatley's verses to remind readers that she had earned appreciation in Revolutionary times, though a woman and a Negro.

Like many reform movements, antislavery also produced song—not always good song, and too often derivative and pedestrian. It was felt that one could not have a good crusade without singing; hence Negroes, abolitionists, and others with humanitarian impulses expressed themselves in verse and in song. Garrison published a volume of sonnets, Maria Weston Chapman a volume of songs and hymns. She also edited many volumes of *The Liberty Bell,* to which better versifiers and poets than herself contributed. George W. Clark's compilation, *The Liberty Minstrel* (1844), offered musical notations as well as words, and included not only those of Longfellow and Whittier, but even Elizur Wright, Jr., and Oliver Johnson in unwonted roles. William Wells Brown's *The Anti-Slavery Harp* (1848) ranged farther afield for tunes and verses.

The crusade produced not only songs but singers. Most famous was the Hutchinson Family of New Hampshire, whom northern neutrals patronized for their talents, if not their antislavery principles. Lucretia Mott primly regretted that they were to sing at an antislavery meet-

---

[60] *Complete Works of W. E. Channing* (London, n.d.), pp. 103 ff.
[61] *Emancipator and Weekly Chronicle,* X (August 6, 1845).

ing. They did, however, carry to massed popular audiences their message that:

> We're the friends of emancipation,
> And we'll sing the proclamation
> Till it echoes through the nation
> From the Old Granite State—
> That the tribe of Jesse
> Are the friends of equal rights.

They sang for temperance. They sang sentimental, religious, and patriotic songs. But, increasingly, their voices would mount for the Liberty party:

> Ho, the car emancipation
> Rides majestic through the nation,
> Bearing on its train the story,
> Liberty, our nation's glory.
> Roll it along, roll it along
> Through the nation,
> Freedom's car, Emancipation.[62]

But the genius-critic of the Mexican War, who summed up northern impulses toward personal expression, as well as political views, was James Russell Lowell. He was twenty-seven years old when the conflict opened, and at the height of his wit, versatility, and sensitivity to social issues. An admirer and friend of the radical abolitionists, receptive to their arguments, and at one with their spirit of protest against imperialist purpose and fear of southern and Democratic leadership, he poured out memorable verses which challenged the nation.[63] His immortal *Biglow Papers* were bluntly pacifistic, antislavery, antiadministration, and defiantly disunionist. War he called murder, the hunger for "Californy" no more than hunger for more slave states. He appealed to Yankee pride and fears:

> Wy, it's jest ez clear ez figgers,
>   Clear ez one an' one make two,
> Chaps thet make black slaves o' niggers
>   Want to make wite slaves o' you. . . .

[62] Charles E. Mann (ed. and comp.), *Story of the Hutchinsons (Tribe of Jesse), by John Wallace Hutchinson* (Boston, 1896), pp. 70, 115.
[63] Arthur Voss, "Backgrounds of Lowell's Satire in 'The Biglow Papers,'" *NEQ,* XXIII (1950), 47–64, and "The Evolution of Lowell's 'The Courtin,'" *Amer. Literature,* XV (1943), 42–50.

Ef I'd *my* way I hed ruther
We should go to work an' part,—
They take one way, we take t'other,—
Guess it wouldn't break my heart;
Man hed ough' to put asunder
Them that God has noways jined;
An' I shouldn't gretly wonder
Ef there's thousands o' my mind.[64]

Such sentiments tallied with those which many northern politicians felt free to voice. Most famous were those enunciated in the Senate on February 11, 1847, by former Governor of Ohio Thomas Corwin, who had earlier accepted the budget for war:

Sir, look at this pretence of want of room. With twenty millions of people, you have about one thousand millions of acres of land, inviting settlement by every conceivable argument—bringing them down to a quarter of a dollar an acre, and allowing every man to squat where he pleases. But the Senator from Michigan [Cass] says we will be two hundred millions in a few years, and we want room. If I were a Mexican I would tell you, "Have you not room in your own country to bury your dead men? If you come into mine we will greet you with bloody hands, and welcome you to hospitable graves."

Wrote Giddings to Henry Wilson, the "Natick shoemaker" (actually manufacturer), a Massachusetts Free-Soiler and legislator long kept firm in his antislavery opinions by defeats for national office: "The question asked in the cars, streets, houses, and everywhere men assemble is: 'Have you read Tom Corwin's speech?' Its boldness and high moral tone meet the feeling here, and the people of New England will respond to it, and tens of thousands want to hear more from him. . . . How I should like to vote for him and some good nonslaveholder for vice-president in 1848. . . ."[65]

Corwin had expressed a feeling, rather than a program. It was otherwise with David Wilmot, Pennsylvania Democrat, who, on August 8, 1846, offered his celebrated Proviso to a bill which would have given President Polk two million dollars with which to make peace with Mexico and acquire parts of its domain. Wilmot was a party man of

[64] *The Poetical Works of James Russell Lowell* (Boston, 1885 ed.); see also his *Antislavery Papers* (2 vols., Boston, 1902).
[65] Josiah Morrow, *Life and Speeches of Thomas Corwin, Orator, Lawyer, Statesman* (Cincinnati, 1896), pp. 50, 305.

long standing, who admired Van Buren, and had voted in 1845 to restore the gag rule. He had voted against receiving petitions protesting the admission of Texas as a slave state, and others praying the abolition of slavery and the slave trade in the District of Columbia. He had helped exclude a proviso prohibiting slavery in Texas.[66] That his Proviso reflected free state sentiment there can be no doubt; on its very first appearance in the House, it was adopted by a vote of 83 to 64. The reason could be found in the disappointment of northern Democrats who had tied the question of Texas to that of Oregon, only to find their administration unexpectedly generous at their expense, and willing to settle the Oregon claims at far below the touted 54° 40′ line. The sense of outrage which Wilmot expressed scarcely rated as political abolitionism: its Free-Soilism comprehended little more than "repugnance to the presence of the Negro."[67]

Yet the northern politicians needed political abolitionism if they were to stand before the country in more than the tawdry clothes of self-interest. In 1846, there were still deep differences between the mere politicians and Salmon P. Chase, even though he still dreamed of bringing abolitionists of all descriptions together into one single party. He had been the organizer of the great Southern and Western Liberty Convention, which had brought together some two thousand delegates from everywhere in the North. It had included the Honorable Samuel Fessenden of Massachusetts, as well as Elihu Burritt and Lewis Tappan. Chase had written its thoroughly abolitionist Address.[68]

A significant phenomenon of 1845, too, had been the emergence of John P. Hale of New Hampshire, as an abolitionist and politician. Hale had joined Adams and Slade in the House of Representatives in 1843. (Slade, the next year, was elected governor of Vermont, for the first of two separate terms.) Two years after, Hale made his great effort against the intrenched state Democratic machine of Charles G. Atherton (author of the gag rule) and Franklin Pierce. Pierce's efforts,

---

[66] Charles B. Going, *David Wilmot: Free-Soiler* (New York, 1924), pp. 49–51. See also Chaplain W. Morrison, *Democratic Politics and Sectionalism: the Wilmot Proviso Controversy* (Chapel Hill, 1967).

[67] Clark E. Persinger, "The Bargain of 1844 as the Origin of the Wilmot Proviso," *AHA Annual Report, 1911* (Washington, 1913), I, 189–195; cf. Richard R. Stenberg, "The Motivation of the Wilmot Proviso," *MVHR,* XVIII (1932), 535–541.

[68] *The Address of the Southern and Western Liberty Convention, Held in Cincinnati, June 11 & 12, 1845* (n.p., n.d.).

that year, to stave off the free-soil challenge in New Hampshire made him President in due course; but the victory of Hale and his associates stirred Liberty Men everywhere; as Whittier wrote, in his "New Hampshire 1845":

> Courage, then, Northern hearts!—be firm, be true:
> What one brave State hath done, can ye not also do?[69]

Hale would have been the choice of Liberty-party men in 1848, had not the phenomenon of Van Buren's candidacy occurred. Hale was now a United States senator, though read out of the Democratic party. Opposed to the Mexican War and to a "dough-faced constituency,"[70] Hale was prepared to advance a temperate abolitionism beyond where the ailing and largely retired Birney, or the deceased Adams, had been able to carry it.

Van Buren had been everything he thought a loyal Democrat should be. He had accepted graciously his defeat for the Democratic nomination of 1844. He had been patient with the Polk administration, which had not adequately given him what he thought of as his political rights. He had first raised, for party purposes, and then willingly tabled the slavery issues arising out of the Mexican War, and restrained his party's "radical" wing in New York, the "Barnburners," from antiparty action.[71] A militant southern wing, however, had again deprived him of the Democratic nomination at a time which made more feasible the idea of an antislavery party; as one of the Liberty Men wrote: "What, then, is the difference on this great question between the two candidates? . . . None whatever! If one is a Northern man with Southern principles, the other is a Southern Man with Southern principles. Both candidates are utterly unworthy the suffrages of a free people."[72]

Unreconciled Barnburners and other Democrats, with Liberty Men

[69] John L. Hayes, *A Reminiscence of the Free-Soil Movement in New Hampshire, 1845* (Cambridge, Mass., 1885); Whittier, *Anti-Slavery Poems: Songs of Labor and Reform* (Boston, 1888 ed.), p. 102.

[70] *Massachusetts Liberty Convention and Speech of Hon. John P. Hale, Together with His Letter Accepting His Nomination for the Presidency* (n.p., 1847).

[71] Alto L. Whitehurst, "Martin Van Buren and the Free Soil Movement" (Ph.D., University of Chicago, 1932), pp. 57 ff., 129 ff., esp. 136; Herbert D. A. Donovan, *The Barnburners* . . . (New York, 1925), pp. 52 ff., 84 ff.

[72] [William I. Bowditch] *Cass and Taylor on the Slavery Question* (Boston, 1848), p. 23.

and disaffected Whigs who saw opportunities to develop at the expense of major parties committed to slavery principles, held numerous meetings throughout the North. These culminated in a convention at Buffalo.[73] There Chase was large and significant, eager to create a major party. Leavitt had written him that the Liberty party was "the last hope of the country ridding itself of slavery peacefully."[74] Leavitt was present at Buffalo, active but conflicted, desiring a mass party but unable to forget Van Buren's erstwhile proslavery roles. Most striking was Henry B. Stanton, who had become a lawyer, a journalist, and a New York politician, and had dropped all of his old moral attitudes. Lewis Tappan later wrote him with dismay of his actions at the convention. Stanton had been cold to his old associates, the complete politician in Van Buren's behalf. His most remarkable act had been to use, without permission, a private letter from Hale to undermine Hale's candidacy: "[Hale] was written to at length by some influential person from Buffalo informing him of your . . . electioneering for Mr. Van Buren from the moment you arrived there, and of your course of proceedings. That he was greatly hurt at such a course, and of the use you made of the letter he wrote to you, I have reason to believe."[75]

The election put Tappan himself into a quandary. Though he kept himself separate from the political abolitionists, he had always voted Liberty party. Martin Van Buren was the bitterest pill he had yet been asked to take, and he sought, vainly, to have that politician dissociate himself from the worst aspects of his administration's *Amistad* actions.[76]

[73] *Oliver Dyer's Phonographic Report of the Proceedings of the National Free Soil Convention at Buffalo, N.Y., August 9th and 10th, 1848* (Buffalo, 1848); Whitehurst, "Van Buren," pp. 132 ff.; Donovan, *Barnburners,* pp. 98 ff.; Joseph G. Rayback, "The Liberty Party Leaders of Ohio . . ." *OAHQ,* LVII (1948), sees the convention as climaxing "an eight year struggle by Ohioans to broaden the abolition movement," and, controversially, that it marked "the end of old-fashioned political abolitionism" (p. 178); cf., Smith, *Liberty and Free Soil Parties in the Northwest,* pp. 121 ff., 138 ff.

[74] Leavitt to Chase, March 1, 1848, HSP.

[75] Tappan to Stanton, September 28, 1848, Tappan Papers, LC.

[76] Van Buren, who had already accepted the Free-Soil nomination with habitual equivocations, was, for once, relatively firm: "Conscious that I did no more in the matter than I sincerely believed to be my official & imperative duty, I am willing to be judged by the record as it stands. . . ." Van Buren averred that he could not recall the details of the transaction, and he neither offered nor solicited information; however: "I would be unwilling under any circumstances, & particularly in my present position to transfer any portion of

The convention proceeded on the purest lines of expediency. It sought Edward Everett as a vice-presidential associate for Van Buren. It ended by accepting Charles Francis Adams, whose anti-Texas pamphlet of 1844 had held Van Buren up to scorn and would hold Adams himself up to ridicule in the coming election.[77] Leavitt himself rose to offer Van Buren to the Liberty Party, with the words "Mr. Chairman, this is the most solemn experience of my life. I feel as if in the immediate presence of the Divine Spirit." Later he would write with deep emotion of his experiences and decision, and plead with his political friends to close ranks behind the cause rather than behind men:

The Liberty Party of 1840 is not dead. It has expanded into the great Union party, or Free Democracy of 1848. What have we lost? Not one of our principles—not one of our aims—not one of our men. Let John P. Hale stand as he stood, in the Senate of the United States; he is young enough to bide his time, and we could not spare him to be elected to the Presidency now. We have gained everything, lost nothing. . . .[78]

It was one of the new type of elections to which the country, fearing civil war, was striving to accustom itself. The Whigs (including Corwin and Seward) had found another Harrison, Zachary Taylor, only one with more than a hundred slaves, who professed himself willing to abide by the will of Congress. Lewis Cass, for the Democrats, offered "popular sovereignty," or the will of the people in the territories. Only Martin Van Buren's anomalous position between the parties offered instructive lessons to the electorate.[79]

His 291,678 votes were a fraction over 10 per cent of the total vote, but they were votes for free soil, not for abolition. Van Buren could be remotely conceived of as an early harbinger of the later Republicanism, but he himself voted for Franklin Pierce in 1852. Leavitt to the contrary, the Liberty party was dead; Gerrit Smith and a persistent

---

the responsibility incurred by the transactions referred to, from my own shoulder to those of a subordinate & deceased associate [Forsyth] in the Government"; Martin Van Buren to Tappan, October 2, 1848, Tappan Papers, LC.

[77] George Julian, *Political Recollections* (Chicago, 1884), pp. 60–61; cf. Grace J. Clarke, *George W. Julian* (Indianapolis, 1923); Charles F. Adams, *Texas and the Massachusetts Resolutions* (Boston, 1844).

[78] *Speech of Hon. Horace Mann . . . To Which Is Added, a Letter from Hon. Martin Van Buren and Rev. Joshua Leavitt* (Boston, 1848), pp. 47–48.

[79] *Inconsistency and Hypocrisy of Martin Van Buren on the Question of Slavery* (n.p., 1848); a feeble defense of Van Buren's slavery positions is contained in the broadside *Both Sides; or, a Short Chapter of Facts* (n.p., n.d.).

fragment would maintain its principles with no more or less significance than the Garrisonians.[80] Leavitt's own *Emancipator* had become *The Emancipator and Free Soil Press,* "A Family Paper—Devoted to Politics, News, Morality, Literature, Agriculture, Markets, Etc." The Free-Soil party was not an expansion of Liberty-party principles, but a catch-all political platform for abolitionists and antiabolitionists.

There continued to be an urgent role for moral reformers. Yet there was also logic to the decision of Henry B. Stanton—tarnished warrior though he was—to continue in Democratic politics: "In my sober judgment, the day for 'third parties' on the slavery question is gone. I am a thorough radical; & I think I can do more good by acting in & trying to impress my principles upon the great ruling party of the country, than by any other mode of actions."[81]

---

[80] *Proceedings of the National Liberty Convention Held in Buffalo, N.Y., June 14th & 15th, 1848; including the Resolutions and Addresses Adopted by That Body, and Speeches of Beriah Green and Gerrit Smith on That Occasion* (Utica, 1848).

[81] Stanton to Chase, September 23, 1850, Chase Papers, LC. His strategy, however, showed how far it was possible for former abolitionists to fall from earlier positions: "Our true mode of operation is, both from stern principle & wise policy, to go strait [sic] forward as we did last year; but making a broad distinction between the Hunkers who really agree with us, & those who have not a drop of real democracy in their blood. We must & can win the former"; Stanton to Samuel D. Porter, August 20, 1849, Porter Papers, University of Rochester.

CHAPTER 9

The Compromise of 1850

THE YEAR 1848 was marked by new emphases upon moral reform and the rights of man. A combination of politics and humanitarianism permitted Great Britain to take the edge off her human suffering without the worst excesses of catastrophe. The Continental governments chose to police their troubled classes, rather than propitiate them. The result was a series of uprisings which overthrew cabinets and ruling houses. Events in France, Italy, Germany, Austria, Hungary, and elsewhere were reported to an American public which, North and South, sympathized with republican aspirations.[1]

European reformers who avoided the issue of slavery met increasing embarrassment when exposed to American conditions. Father Theobald Mathew was world famous as "The Apostle of Temperance." He had signed the "Address" deprecating slavery which 70,000 other Irishmen, including Daniel O'Connell, had in 1842 sent to their countrymen in the United States. In 1849, Father Mathew visited the United States in behalf of his crusade. He was welcomed by temperance advocates, Whigs in search of Irish votes, and the many curious people who enjoyed foreign dignitaries.[2]

Courtesies and crusade were soon disturbed by Garrison, who invited Father Mathew to address the Massachusetts Anti-Slavery So-

[1] Raymond Postgate, *Story of a Year: 1848* (New York, 1956); see also Arnold Whitridge, *Men in Crisis: the Revolutions of 1848* (New York, 1949), esp. Chap. V, "Repercussions in America," pp. 283 ff.

[2] See Garrisons, III, 244 ff., for a vivid account of the controversy precipitated.

ciety on the anniversary of British West Indies emancipation. This Mathew could not do without destroying his usefulness in the southern states. Garrisonian pertinacity soon drove the Irish ecclesiastic to repudiate abolitionism, on the grounds that the Scriptures did not forbid slavery. He received sympathy and support, including that of Elizur Wright, then editor of the Boston *Chronotype* and violent in his hatred of Garrison. Nevertheless, Mathew's prestige suffered. Southern leaders demanded a categorical repudiation of the 1842 address which he could not supply. *Punch* satirized him in the person of a correspondent named "Sambo," who cited Scripture and asked: "How fader Mathew him like to be slabe? Whose nigger, tink you, him wish to be?"

Louis Kossuth fared little better. The hero of the defeated Hungarian Revolution arrived in England late in 1851, bound for the United States. He had been brought to England by special presidential direction and the joint resolution of Congress. He was warned by abolitionists of Mathew's fate. They placed in his hands copies of the Fugitive Slave Law and Weld's *American Slavery as It Is,* but he refused to be warned.[3] His mission to America was only partially a failure. He attempted to avoid the question of slavery, but he spoke necessarily of freedom, and his distinguished bearing and double-edged speeches offended sensitive slavery advocates, who had orginally applauded what could be interpreted as Kossuth's secessionist efforts in Hungary. The United States government cooled to his presence, partly at the urgings of Austrian and Russian representatives. The English contributed their usual mead of relevant irony.[4] But "Anti-Kossuth" dinners only called to public attention the Kossuth dinners with which admirers regaled him. And though his popularity declined to commonplace proportions by the spring of 1852, when he left the United States, the more substantial regard which he had won entered into the American liberal tradition.

[3] Luthin, "A Visitor from Hungary," *South Atlantic Qu.,* XLVIII (1948), 29–34; John B. Moore, "Kossuth: a Sketch of a Revolutionist. II," *PSQ,* X (1895), 257–291.

[4] "Ran away from the subscriber, on the 18th August, 1849, a likely Magyar fellow, named Louis Kossuth. He is about 45 years old, 5 feet 6 inches high, dark complexion, marked eyebrows, and grey eyes. He pretends to be free, but says he was robbed of his freedom. . . . Captains and masters of vessels are particularly cautioned against harboring or concealing the said fugitive on board their ships, as the full penalty of the law will be vigorously enforced." London *Morning Advertiser,* quoted in *Letter to Louis Kossuth, Concerning Freedom and Slavery in the United States* (Boston, 1852), pp. 108–109.

Thus reform continued active and energetic in America. The cause of woman's rights advanced with antislavery. Like it, woman's rights inspired the Bible argument, which favored or opposed them. Antislavery produced fewer adventuresses of the type of Adah Isaacs Menken, but woman's rights did produce successors to Frances Wright who helped pioneer aspects of their cause.[5]

There were, however, numerous persons, women as well as men, who sought a middle ground between radical reform and realistic social needs. It is noteworthy that by 1850, utopian experimentation was in decline. The merry days of Brook Farm were far in the past. Even Noyes's Oneida Community would soon settle into a relatively routine way of life, unrelated to national interests.

In 1847 and 1848, two journals were begun which would help the North tide itself over into a firm antislavery position. Lewis Tappan was important to the establishment of both. He had got over an earlier resentment at what had seemed to him Leavitt's amoral approach in 1840 to the problem of political abolitionism. However, he turned down Leavitt for a favorite project: the founding of a newspaper in the Capital which would help unify antislavery opinion among the legislators there. Tappan had developed criteria for a proper editor, and he believed Leavitt wanting in meekness and nonsectarian persuasiveness. He found those qualities in Gamaliel Bailey. Leavitt's professional antagonism toward Bailey did not prevent his appointment to the strategic post, and the *National Era* got under way in January 1847.

It was to have been edited by Bailey, Whittier, and Amos A. Phelps, but Phelps was seriously ill and died not long after the founding. Whittier's articles were a staple of the *National Era* through much of its career. Popular writers and serious ones were found for every taste. The journal became one which, though "tainted with the spirit of compromise," in Garrison's words, offered valuable information and an essentially antislavery position. Southern partisans paid it the com-

---

[5] Rev. Luther Lee, *Woman's Right to Preach the Gospel. A Sermon Preached at the Ordination of the Rev. Miss Antoinette L. Brown* . . . (Syracuse, 1853); Alonzo J. Grover, *The Bible Argument Against Women Stated and Answered* . . . (Earlville, Ill., 1870); Allen Lesser, *Enchanting Rebel* (New York, 1947); D. C. Bloomer, *Life and Writings of Amelia Bloomer* (Boston, 1895); E. Douglas Branch, "The Lily & the Bloomer," *Colophon*, XII (1932), unpaged [1–12]; Yuri Suhl, *Ernestine Rose and the Battle for Human Rights* (New York, 1959).

pliment of launching *The Southern Press,* in Washington, to combat its point of view. Bailey's subscription list rose to 15,000 weekly copies by 1850, and by 1853—with *Uncle Tom's Cabin* completed in its pages—to 25,000. Bailey estimated that each copy had five readers. He was also successful in bringing together the antislavery forces in the Capital; "they found solace for their social ostracism in delightful gatherings which assembled weekly at [Bailey's] residence . . . where they met philanthropists, reformers, and literary notables."[6]

The *Independent* was born in part of Joshua Leavitt's need for employment, partly from the weakness of the old *Emancipator;* but largely because active and energetic Congregationalists, including Tappan, wanted an organ which would combat Presbyterianism. As Tappan wrote, in discussing Leavitt's situation with him: "Perhaps, if your feelings are right, a religious newspaper would be the most useful thing you could attend to. Such a paper, advocating Congregationalism, Bible Missions, Temperance, the Sabbath, might also advocate anti-Slavery principles. . . ."[7]

Two of the editors eventually chosen, Joseph P. Thompson and Richard Salter Storrs, were influential and industrial New York ministers, orthodox in their religious principles and conservative in their antislavery feelings. The other pillars of the journal were Leavitt and the Reverend Leonard Bacon, the latter still respectful of colonization, still opposed not only to Garrison but even to Weld's *American Slavery as It Is,* which he thought harmed the public relations of antislavery men. Bacon's own *Slavery Discussed in Occasional Essays from 1833 to 1846* categorically condemned slavery in a phrase which later found its way into Lincoln's thoughts, as well as in a notable passage in his letters.[8] Bacon's program was not intended to smooth over differences between proslavery and antislavery people. It sought a sound approach to ending slavery.

Important to the *Independent* was Henry C. Bowen, son-in-law of Lewis Tappan, formerly one of his clerks, now a well-to-do drygoods merchant in his own right, and one of the supporters of the *Independent.* He was later to become its sole and governing owner. But

[6] Julian, *Political Recollections,* p. 112; Grace Greenwood, "An American Salon," *Cosmopolitan,* VIII (1890), 437–447.

[7] Tappan to Leavitt, December 9, 1846, Tappan Papers, LC.

[8] "I am naturally anti-slavery. If slavery is not wrong, nothing is wrong"; Lincoln to Albert G. Hodges, April 4, 1864, Roy P. Basler (ed.), *Collected Works of Abraham Lincoln* (New Brunswick, 1953–55), VII, 281–282.

most striking of the *Independent* associates were Henry Ward Beecher and George Barrell Cheever. The latter developed slowly as an antislavery evangelist. He was a weathervane of antislavery. He had once enjoyed a visit to the South, and would not resent its policies till after the passage of the Compromise of 1850. Not till the Dred Scott decision would he help disperse, in rotund, apocalyptical prose, "the fog of pious compromise which between periods of excitement settled inexorably upon New York."[9] Beecher, on the other hand, from the *Independent's* beginning in 1848 developed his curiously ingratiating prose, which charmed northern readers at uncritical levels of their thought. He had come East as the son of his famous father and as the author of *Seven Lectures to Young Men* (1844), a book on temperance. His pulpit presence soon made his Plymouth Church in Brooklyn a show place, as his "slave auction," which raised money to purchase the freedom of two mulatto girls, gave his sentimental auditors a new view of the slavery controversy. "A sale by a human flesh dealer of Christian girls!" he had cried. "Suppose them so comely that no price less than $3,000 would purchase them. Suppose this, and act as you would act then!"[10] Beecher wisely varied such appeals with less exciting ones, in and out of the *Independent,* but he emphasized an emotionalism which attracted attention.

The *Independent* was neither liberal nor receptive on many issues. It viewed unsympathetically the famous United States Patent Report of 1850, terming "novel and peculiar" Thomas Ewbank's effort to relate inventions to human progress. Ewbank hoped inventions would help also to undermine slavery, but the *Independent* preferred to concentrate upon what it termed (with some justice) his bad theology, "private and paltry speculations," and what would later be called Darwinism. The paper published a review of Melville's *Moby-Dick* by one "familiar with the scenes described in the volume," who recognized Melville's "possession of powers," which, however, made the reviewer "ashamed of him that he does not write something better and freer of blemishes." Yet the *Independent* could surprise: a minister who visited Albert Brisbane's Fourierite colony in New Jersey, the North American Phalanx, enjoyed "a delightful excursion" among its emancipated tenants, whose principles he did not approve.

[9] Smith, *Revivalism and Social Reform,* p. 209, places Cheever's awakening earlier; cf. York, *Cheever,* pp. 135 ff.

[10] Paxton Hibben, *Henry Ward Beecher: an American Portrait* (New York, 1942 ed.), p. 111.

The *Independent* began with a notable list of Congregationalist ministers among its subscribers—who could carry its message to tens of thousands of their congregations—but with little else. It struggled for financial stability through much of the 1850's. By the end of 1854, however, it claimed not only 3,000 clergymen as subscribers, but 6,000 professional men and approximately 15,000 other readers, with circulation increasing at the rate of 350 to 400 weekly. Its rise, thereafter, was almost barometric, and reached the self-sustaining basis of close to 50,000 in 1860. Its original program avoided political commentary, but its influence upon free-soil thought in the North began with the first issue.

Indicative of the role the *Independent* was to play through the 1850's was one it assumed in a controversy over the American Board for Foreign Missions. During three decades missionaries had established themselves among the Choctaw Indians of Arkansas. In 1849, nine hundred of the Indians were in communion, but one hundred of them were slaves and thirty-eight masters. The abolitionist problem was how best to attack the system. There were numerous arguments favoring American Board policy. Slavery was deplorable, but the task of the missionaries was to stay at their posts. Their first concern was spiritual salvation, rather than freedom. The confidence of the slaveholders had to be gained.[11]

The *Independent* reported the matter with marked disapproval, but it published lengthy epistles defending or denouncing the American Board. Its own conclusions, following three months of controversy, was that the American Board was proslavery. But the *Independent* did not repudiate this national body in the interests of its antislavery competitor, the American Missionary Association.[12] The Choctaw mission was thereafter a staple of reference in the *Independent*, a factor in its growing antislavery platform.

The election of 1848 had brought Chase to the United States Senate, and introduced into that body a number of others about whose

[11] "Report of the Committee on Antislavery Memorials," MS., 1845, WRHS.

[12] Founded in 1846, the American Missionary Association was a flourishing organization dedicated to abolition and the education of the Negro. Among its achievements were the founding of Berea College, Hampton Institute, and Fisk University; Lewis Tappan, *History of the American Missionary Association* (New York, 1855); Frederick L. Brownlee, *New Day Ascending* (Boston, 1946), *passim*.

antislavery progress Leavitt was his usual optimistic self.[13] Chase was little more discriminating. Hannibal Hamlin was a Maine Democrat who had also just been sent to the Senate; wrote Chase:

> I do not regard Mr. Hamlin as occupying the same position as I do. He is a democrat, acting within the old line democracy. I am a democrat acting with the free democracy, though ready at any time to act with the old line democracy, whenever they take a decided ground against slavery as they do against other institutions inconsistent with democratic principles. I regard Mr. Hamlin, however, as a sincere and consistent opponent of Slavery extension and of the aggressions of the Slave Power. . . .[14]

Hamlin had voted to overthrow the gag rule, and he was opposed to slavery. But he had supported the candidacy of Cass, and he would support similar old-line measures down to 1856.[15] It was among such individuals that political abolitionists had to find their way. Proslavery elements were also perplexed by the line-up of forces in the nation. A Pennsylvania representative reproved another from Indiana who had once voted for the censure of Giddings and now supported him; supported, too, the Wilmot Proviso; and though Indiana—like Connecticut and Illinois and recently Pennsylvania—gave Negroes no political rights, he now favored freeing the Negroes of the District of Columbia:

> There seems to be an inexplicable mystery hanging over all of these doings. The gentleman from Indiana tells us he and his people are conservative on this question [of slavery]; that they do not . . . want to commit any wrong upon the rights, or feelings, or interests of the people of the south. . . . How is it, then, and why is it, their votes here, and their conventions at home, are all with those they denounce as fanatical abolitionists?[16]

[13] Leavitt to Chase, March 2, 1849, Chase Papers, LC; Smith, *Liberty and Free Soil Parties in the Northwest,* pp. 160 ff. Giddings had failed to attend Chase's Free Territory Convention, June 20, 1848, in Columbus which had recommended the convention at Buffalo of August 9. He thus probably deprived himself of the Free Soil leadership of Ohio which brought Chase his Senate seat; Richard W. Solberg, "Joshua Giddings, Politician and Idealist" (Ph.D., University of Chicago, 1952), p. 300.

[14] Chase to———, June 15, 1850, Chase Papers, LC.

[15] Charles E. Hamlin, *The Life and Times of Hannibal Hamlin* (Cambridge, Mass., 1899), pp. 59 ff.

[16] *Abolition and Slavery. Speech of Charles Brown, of Pennsylvania, in the House of Representatives, February 3, 1849. In Reply to Hon. Richard W. Thompson, of Indiana, on Abolition and Slavery* (n.p., n.d.), pp. 2, *passim.*

In this atmosphere of increased northern resistance to proslavery measures, an angry South determined to demand respect and an equitable division of the West. The South had reason for alarm. The new Whig President, Zachary Taylor, startled Polk, on Inauguration Day, by suggesting that California and Oregon were too far away to be administered, and ought to be organized as an independent country. Taylor had fallen under the influence of Seward, now senator from New York, and turned much of the Whig party patronage in the North over to him, thus aiding the distinctly antislavery wing of the party. Taylor expressed his willingness to accept California into the Union with an antislavery constitution. Above all, he was a unionist as Jackson had been, and his respect for congressional rights conceivably jeopardized southern interests.[17]

Oddly opposed to Taylor in his greater willingness to propitiate the South was Henry Clay, for the last time the center of all eyes. Thirty years after his Missouri Compromise, he was working to satisfy all interests. He was willing to admit California as a free state, but also to organize New Mexico with or without slavery. He planned to abolish the slave trade in the District of Columbia, but also to strengthen the Fugitive Slave Act so that it would end, once and for all, disturbing Negro cases. Clay's Compromise took in numerous details aimed at settling all territorial problems. To the great debate came Calhoun and Webster, Calhoun, with his dying breath, demanding what amounted to an autonomous South. Webster came to Clay's support. Beneath the pyrotechnics of their oratory, much practical political wire pulling ensued.[18]

Taylor was suspicious of the men and the measures involved in the Compromise, but it is difficult to believe that he would have stood out against them. Suddenly, he was dead. Wrote Chase to his wife: "Well, it is all over. The funeral pageant has passed by. The Old General sleeps the last sleep. Multitudes mourn sincerely—other multitudes secretly rejoice."[19]

Taylor served antislavery better than had been expected, certainly

---

[17] Brainerd Dyer, *Zachary Taylor* (Baton Rouge, 1946), pp. 318–319, 370. For general analysis, see Joel H. Sibley, *The Shrine of Party, Congressional Voting Behavior 1841–1852* (Pittsburgh, 1967), pp. 98 ff., and *passim*.

[18] George R. Poage, *Henry Clay and the Whig Party* (Chapel Hill, 1936), pp. 197 ff. A vigorous claim for Stephen A. Douglas of Illinois as "author" of the Compromise is in George D. Harmon, *Political Aspects of Slavery and the Civil War* (Bethlehem, Pa., 1952), "Douglas and the Compromise of 1850."

[19] Chase to S[arah] B. Chase, July 13, 1850, Chase Papers, LC.

by the moral reformers. He had resisted southern efforts to promote filibusters to overthrow the Spanish regime in Cuba. He had even heard with equanimity the speech of March 11 with which Seward had electrified the country—a speech denouncing compromise and appealing to a "higher law" than the Constitution.[20] The press rang with what appeared Seward's invitation to lawlessness. Yet the concept of a "higher law" had circulated freely for many years. Seward himself had used it on a number of occasions.[21] Now, however, it had struck a psychological moment and released varying political compulsions. Though Seward deprecated the phrase, and sought to emphasize the more conservative aspects of his thought, it clung to him and stigmatized him, inaccurately, as a radical.

With Taylor dead, the movement for passage of the Compromise measures moved rapidly. They were approved by the new President, Fillmore (whom Chase hastened to send "a part of the Wine received by you from your friend S. H. Yeatman, Esq.").[22] Early in September, the Compromise rode triumphantly through Senate and House, with the approval of such politicians as Corwin, Fillmore's new Secretary of the Treasury.[23] Remarkably, though free soil, rather than antislavery, was at the base of popular unrest, the western territories were too far away seriously to affect popular political attitudes. Antislavery, not free soil, divided the country. The South was affronted by the expunging of the slave trade from the District of Columbia, even though the slave traders simply moved their establishments across the river to Alexandria, Virginia. The newly implemented Fugitive Slave Act set up commissioners to administer the law, and offered them fees to do so in the interests of the slave catchers. It implicated northern citizens in their activities and provided drastic penalties for obstructors of the law. It touched off an unprecedented excitement throughout the North.

Webster's March 7 speech in defense of the Compromise was widely received as that of a traitor to northern interests. Many respectable

[20] George E. Baker (ed.), *The Works of William H. Seward* (Boston, 1884), I, 74–75.

[21] John P. Lynch, "The Higher Law Argument in American History, 1850–1852" (M.A., Columbia University, 1947); see also Frederic Bancroft, *The Life of William H. Seward* (New York, 1900), I, 242 ff.

[22] Millard Fillmore to Chase, July 23, 1850, Chase Papers, LC.

[23] Norman A. Graebner, "Thomas Corwin and the Election of 1848," *JSH*, XVII (1951), 162.

business elements did their best to oppose the trend. They appealed successfully to the clergy to preach against the higher law. In New York, businessmen circulated a call for a monster meeting at Castle Garden, endorsing the Compromise. Bowen's firm was one of those which were attacked in the *Journal of Commerce* for refusing to cooperate, whereupon he published in the New York *Herald* his memorable "card," stating that he wished it "distinctly understood that our goods, and not our principles are on the market." Though Bowen's stand lost the *Independent* half of its six thousand subscriptions, it gained five thousand new ones. Leonard Bacon himself spoke out in support of the higher-law doctrine as it was being interpreted by the northern populace.[24]

The moral revolution which the North was experiencing was not apparent to everyone. Even though the Compromise precipitated a political revolution in Massachusetts which put Charles Sumner in the Senate, even though it had been resisted by Thomas H. Benton of Missouri, southern in feeling but free soil in preference, Benton felt able to advise Sumner that the latter had "come up on the stage too late, sir. Not only have our great men passed away, but the great issues have been settled also. The last of these was the National Bank, and that has been overthrown forever. Nothing is left you, sir, but puny sectional questions and petty strifes about slavery and fugitive slave-laws, invoking no national interests."[25]

Benton's sights were too high to enable him to see the Negroes, but it was their stirrings which distracted the North and aggravated the South. As a result of the passage of the Fugitive Slave Law, there was a rapid exodus of fugitives into Canada. Canadian prejudice increased toward Negroes, but also inspired the formation of an antislavery society. Many Negroes in the northern states remained in jeopardy, and their numbers were augmented by new fugitive slaves in need of succor.[26]

---

[24] *The Proceedings of the Union Meeting Held at Castle Garden, October 30, 1850* . . . (New York, 1850); Bacon, *The Higher Law. A Sermon* . . . (New Haven, 1851). Lewis Tappan proudly reproduced Bowen's "card" in his *Annual Report of the American and Foreign Anti-Slavery Society* . . . (New York, 1851), p. 32.

[25] Ben: P. Poore, *Perley's Reminiscences of Sixty Years in the National Metropolis* (Philadelphia, 1886), I, 409–410.

[26] Fred Landon, "Negro Migration to Canada after the Passing of the Fugitive Slave Act," *JNH*, V (1920), 22–36. The Premier of Canada later estimated

They found it not only in abolitionists, but in aroused elements in the North to whom personal liberties had become a shibboleth. In the Western Reserve, the effect of the Compromise was catastrophic: the Fugitive Slave Law was unenforceable.[27] Elsewhere, responsible Northerners were willing to assert, with a thoroughly angry Horace Mann, speaking on the floor of Congress, that "this doctrine—which is one of the off-shoots of slavery—that there is no higher law than the law of the state is palpable and practical atheism." Their ill opinion of the Fugitive Slave Law shamed New York merchants who had helped return to slavery James Hamlet, probably a free Negro.[28] They helped purchase him out of captivity. In Boston, Shadrach, alleged to be a fugitive, received prompt aid. In the course of legal proceedings, he was rescued—by Negroes, his respectable counsel insisted—and whisked away to Canada. Richard Henry Dana, in behalf of a violator of the Fugitive Slave Law, fought to maintain the latter's status within the law:

When I said resistance to the law [is not permissible], I did not mean to include resistance for the purpose of raising a constitutional issue. If an unconstitutional tax is levied, you refuse to pay it and raise the constitutional question. The right seems to be lost sight of. Persons seem to think we are to obey statutes and not the constitution. I understand that the duty to the constitution is above the duty to the statutes.[29]

Fugitive-slave cases and rescues multiplied. They ranged from Solomon Northrup, kidnaped in Washington City in 1841 and not rescued till 1853, to a rescue in Christiana, Pennsylvania, during which the slave catcher died and his son was seriously wounded. Friends of fugitives in Indiana were made aggressive by the strong proslavery sentiment in that state, and did not scruple to kidnap slave hunters, to poison their bloodhounds, and sometimes, under provocation, to com-

---

that some 40,000 of his countrymen had joined the Union Army; Landon, "The Anti-Slavery Society of Canada," *ibid.*, IV (1919), 40.

[27] William C. Cochrane, *The Western Reserve and the Fugitive Slave Law* (Cleveland, 1920).

[28] *The Institution of Slavery. Speech of Hon. Horace Mann . . . August 17, 1852* (Boston, 1852), p. 11; cf. his *New Dangers to Freedom, and New Duties for Its Defenders . . .* (Boston, 1850); *The Fugitive Slave Bill . . . with an Account of the Seizure and Enslavement of James Hamlet, and His Subsequent Restoration to Liberty* (New York, 1850).

[29] *U.S. v. Charles G. Dawes, Report of the Proceedings at the Examination of Charles G. Dawes, Esq., on a Charge of Aiding and Abetting in the Rescue of a Fugitive Slave . . .* (Boston, 1851), pp. 23 ff.

mit murder. In Ohio, a fugitive slave, given no redress in the law, killed her own daughter to keep her from being re-enslaved.[30]

Such disturbances made lurid impressions, but were the surface features of a deep unrest among Negroes, and of their own day-to-day efforts. The phenomenon of the decade was Harriet Tubman, whose life was obscured, first by her insignificance under slavery, next by the ceaseless plottings of her later free existence. "This most wonderful woman,"[31] as Susan B. Anthony called her, had been born, probably in 1820, in Maryland, that best of all thoroughfares to freedom. A powerful, unco-operative slave, she was almost killed by a plantation overseer who struck her on the head with a two-pound weight: a wound which probably caused the somnolent spells from which she suffered all her life. Nat Turner's rebellion in 1831 inspired her, but many years had to pass before she formulated a plan of escape. Meanwhile she labored, using a strength which could draw a loaded stone boat.

In 1849, she fled to Pennsylvania. In Philadelphia she met William Still, a Negro who had been a clerk since 1847 in the office of the Pennsylvania Anti-Slavery Society and an agent of the underground railroad. In 1850, year of the Fugitive Slave Act, Harriet began a career which took her nineteen times into the South, including the Deep South. Her underground stations extended, for the most part, from Maryland through New York, Albany, Troy, and Schenectady into Canada. Her work was carefully planned, involving rendezvous, the singing of spirituals, and other elements of conspiracy. John Brown called her "General Tubman," and "the most man, naturally, that I ever met with." She was active in the North, bringing off one fugitive captured in Troy, New York, with the help of a mob she had raised: all this despite the fact that she was herself liable to capture and dire penalties.

Harriet Tubman and the merest fugitive, aided by northern sympathizers, were bringing the law into contempt. Also, as William Jay

[30] Solomon Northrup, *Twelve Years a Slave* . . . (Auburn, 1853); *Report of Trial of Castner Hanway for Treason in Resisting the Fugitive Slave Law* (Philadelphia, 1852); Julius Yanuck, "The Garner Fugitive Slave Case," *MVHR*, XL (1953), 47–66; William S. Cockrum, *History of the Underground Railroad as It Was Conducted by the Anti-Slavery League* . . . (Oakland City, Ind., 1915); Miller, "Anti-Slavery in Indiana," pp. 150 ff.

[31] Written on flyleaf of Sarah H. Bradford, *Harriet, the Moses of Her People* (New York, 1901 ed.), in LC.

noted with satisfaction, in two years and nine months, not fifty slaves of the thousands who had fled had been discovered—not an average of eighteen in a year.[32] Nowhere was the hunt for Negro fugitives made more infamous than in Massachusetts, despite conservative efforts to hold the line for law and order. The conscience of Boston had come alive.[33] It defied Cotton Whigs, machine Democrats, and, more painfully, the law itself.

Theodore Parker now rose to the stormy heights of his career, putting at his city's disposal his conscience and learning. Thereafter, Boston, and the nation to a degree, would have no rest from his appeals to resistance. "Minister at large" to all the fugitive slaves in the city, he took the Fugitive Slave Law as a personal challenge. Through his Illinois admirer, William H. Herndon, he would help instruct Abraham Lincoln in moral principles. He headed a Boston Committee of Vigilance which included among its members Samuel G. Howe, Wendell Phillips, Lewis Hayden—whom Calvin Fairbank had freed, and who had since become one of the most active underground agents —and Dana as counsel. The Committee, in April 1851, made desperate efforts to prevent the rendition of Thomas Sims, a Negro boy. That time the law had its way. Chains were strung before the court house doors; the pleas of counsel were ignored. Horace Mann spoke at Tremont Temple, and Parker shook his thunder at the federal agents. Wrote Sumner, "You have placed the Commissioner in an immortal pillory to receive the hootings and rotten eggs of the advancing generation."

It was all in vain. At three o'clock in the morning of April 13, members of the Vigilante Committee were present to see the United States Marshal walk Sims "down State Street, past the spot where Crispus Attucks fell, and to the Long Wharf where the *Acorn* was moored." It took Sims to Savannah, where, on April 19, he was publicly whipped: "the first slave Massachusetts had returned since she had made that date memorable."[34]

[32] Julia Griffiths (ed.), *Autographs for Freedom* (Auburn, 1854), p. 89.
[33] David Van Tassel, "Gentlemen of Property and Standing. Compromise Sentiment in Boston in 1850," *NEQ*, XXIII (1950), 307–319; Harold Schwartz, "Fugitive Slave Days in Boston," *NEQ*, XXVIII (1954), 191–212.
[34] Commager, *Parker*, pp. 221 ff.; Leonard W. Levy, "Sims' Case: the Fugitive Slave Case in Boston in 1851," *JNH*, XXXV (1950), 39–74; *Trial of Thomas Sims, an Issue of Personal Liberty . . . Arguments of Robert Rantoul, Jr., and Charles G. Loring, with the Decision of George T. Curtis. Boston, April 7–11, 1851* (Boston, 1851).

Although there were those whom the Fugitive Slave Law discouraged—Birney shocked his associates by despairing for abolition
and urging Negroes to go to Africa[35]—it put new firmness into some
who had previously avoided antislavery fighters. The Sims affair was a
costly victory for Boston conservatives. They were, indeed, in the
position of the British at Lexington and Concord. Their own hearts
were not in their work: the United States Marshal who returned
Sims, Charles Devens, himself would in 1860, with civil war in the
immediate offing, pay the entire $1,800 necessary to purchase Sims out
of slavery.[36] The entire defense of the Fugitive Slave Law was quixotic
in its inception. It had begun as a regard for states' rights; it was
concluding as an effort to foist southern standards of civil justice upon
Northerners. Nonabolitionist free-soilers had no alternative but to
defend themselves with constitutional arguments which Alvan Stewart,
William Jay, Chase, Goodell, and others had been urging for more
than a decade.

It was a complex argument which increasingly divided into two:
either the disunionist pleas of the Garrisonians or the argument of the
Free-Soilers, intended to shield them from appearing to be anti-
Unionist law violators. Distinguished opponents of the Fugitive Slave
Law were much concerned to avoid such appearances. Richard Henry
Dana was only one of many Northerners who insisted that they were
conservatives, and that they were interested in nothing more than
preserving the Constitution. Dana denounced "a compound of selfish-
ness and cowardice which often takes to itself the honored name of
Conservatism. That false conservatism I call *Hunkerism*"—the name
reserved for the diehard supporters of political-machine Democracy.
In the name of his "true" conservatism, which included a blunt contempt for the woman's rights movement, Dana criticized radicalism,
which seemed to him less reliable than his own principles of justice.

Certainly, he could expect small support from the Garrisonians, who
never ceased to argue that the Constitution affirmed the rights of
slavery, and was therefore—in the phrase from Isaiah which they had
borrowed from Ann Lee, the Shaker—"a covenant with death and an
agreement with hell." Garrisonians had delved deep into American

---

[35] *Examination of the Decision of the Supreme Court of the United States,
in the Case of Strader, Gorman and Armstrong vs. Christopher Graham . . .
Concluding with an Address to the Free Colored People Advising Them to Remove to Liberia* (Cincinnati, 1852).

[36] *Letters of L. Maria Child,* pp. 144–145, 189.

law. Wendell Phillips was their spokesman. He observed that the Constitution discriminated between free people and others; that the Federalist debates and subsequent interpretations premised acceptance of slavery; that "until 1819 the laws of Congress authorized the States to sell into slavery, for their own benefit, negroes imported contrary to the laws of the United States."[37]

Whether this approach of the Garrisonians did more harm than good to the antislavery enterprise is difficult to judge. It did provide a constant reminder of the role of the federal government in perpetuating slavery. William Jay was even complacent about disunionist arguments. As late as 1857, he received a circular which included the signatures of Higginson, Garrison, and Wendell Phillips, calling for a National Disunion Convention. It did not disturb him: "I . . . rejoice in every exposure of the demoralizing influence of the Union. I rejoice in such exposure, not as tending to bring about dissolution, but to render it unnecessary."[38]

Perhaps the least defensible act of the Garrisonians was their proscription of Frederick Douglass because he had, in 1851, become a constitutionalist. Garrison's remark, "There is roguery somewhere," was unjustified, and the subsequent insults and imputations to which he and his associates subjected Douglass and the *North Star* lacked any shred of substance or charity. The oddity about their attacks was that Douglass' conversion to the use of the ballot box and his new regard for the Constitution did not change his views or actions. He continued his editorial labors in behalf of the Negro cause; continued to help maintain the underground railroad and such contacts as those with John Brown, whom he had known since 1847. He had not shifted his orbit; he had enlarged it.

Gathering resistance to the Fugitive Slave Law called up every species of debater. Jay had long held, not only that the Constitution did not sanction slavery, but that the government had fallen from its high estate to do so. Weld had emphasized that the government was free to legislate *against* slavery. Goodell elaborated on what he termed the spirit of the Constitution, and on natural law, to arrive at the same result. Fugitive-slave lawyers, and editors commenting upon higher-court decisions, made attempts to win judges and public

[37] Phillips (comp.), *The Constitution a Pro-Slavery Compact: or, Extracts from the Madison Papers, Etc.* (New York, 1856 ed.), *passim.*
[38] Tuckerman, *Jay,* p. 154.

opinion to antislavery views. The Supreme Court they stigmatized as prejudiced and even corrupt.[39]

Most remarkable of the constitutionalists who protested the Fugitive Slave Law was Lysander Spooner, whose theories and enterprises illustrated the strength of the individual to affect events in that generation. Spooner was a libertarian of resolute qualities.[40] He fought state statutes in Massachusetts that required three years of study before admission to the bar, and had them removed. Dissatisfied with the federal postal service from Boston to New York, he successfully opened his own in competition with the "monopoly," and though prosecutions forced him to suspend operations he persuaded Congress twice to reduce postage rates in the following years. He was an inexorable theorist, whose views, though extreme enough in later years to challenge all government, did probe the meaning of laws and their justification.

Spooner's pamphlets on the unconstitutionality of slavery, published in 1845 and 1847, though conceding, "for the sake of argument," the legitimacy of law, maintained that the law of the land required interpretation in the light of natural law. *A Defence for Fugitive Slaves* (1850) pushed this argument farther. It offered an arsenal of ingenious constructions to fugitive-slave counselors, encouragement to citizens unwilling to accept the challenge of federal law to personal liberties. Wendell Phillips, believing that the Constitution needed to be condemned, rather than salvaged, attacked Spooner's argument in a major effort to demolish its logic. In this instance, however, northern interests found more use in what Phillips called "hair-splitters and cobweb spinners" than in his own robust assertion that abolitionists would be better advised to "take the Constitution to be what the Courts and Nation allow that it is."[41]

[39] Jay's constitutional program is implicit in all his writings, for example, "Hancock," *A Letter to the Honorable Samuel A. Eliot, in Reply to His Apology for Voting for the Fugitive Slave Law* (Boston, 1851); "Wythe" [Weld], *The Power of Congress over the District of Columbia, passim,* cf. Goodell, *Views of American Constitutional Law, in Its Bearing Upon American Slavery* (Utica, 1845); Warren, *Supreme Court,* II, 156; cf. Leslie, *The Fugitive Slave Clause, 1787–1842,* pp. 231 ff.

[40] Rocker, *Pioneers of American Freedom,* pp. 86 ff.; A. John Alexander, "The Ideas of Lysander Spooner," *NEQ,* XXIII (1950), 200 ff.

[41] Phillips, *Review of Lysander Spooner's Essay on the Unconstitutionality of Slavery* (Boston, 1847); see also his *Can Abolitionists Vote or Take Office under the United States Constitution?* (New York, 1845), which profited from

The year 1852 was notable for the publication of what should have been a mere firecracker—a woman's fictional attack on slavery. It detonated, instead, as a major explosion, rocking the North and shattering much of neutral opinion in Great Britain and Europe.

Harriet Beecher Stowe lacked the disinterestedness of a great artist, the simple trust of a Johnny Appleseed, or the mental fight of a Theodore Parker. Her need for reassurance that the universe was benign and working in her interest she shared with numerous Northerners. Others besides herself had experienced a Calvinist upbringing and had, perhaps, like her, had a child die in infancy, or, again like her, suffered for a sister whose fiancé had died without conversion. Mrs. Stowe's sense of the physical realities of New England she shared with far greater writers, though with a housewife's interest in details for which they had little space.

Her powerful sense of popular feelings she shared with the other Beechers who were writing their names into the nineteenth century, if not into the twentieth. She was steeped in religion, challenged no contemporary mores, especially as they related to what she termed "the dominant sex," and she experienced fully the cycle of marriage and the joys and tragedies of motherhood. Thus she was a barometer rather than a pilot, and her colossal success was a measure of northern unrest. She was closer to the "mob of scribbling women" whom Hawthorne denounced than she would ever be to the Stantons and Stones and Chapmans of her time. Yet Mrs. Stowe, who favored neither abolitionism nor feminism, was recognized as having aided and advanced both by her epochal achievement.[42]

The best of Mrs. Stowe was the New England observer and reporter who, as she confessed in her later *Oldtown Folks,* was "seeing much, doubting much, questioning much, and believing with all my heart only a very few things." Her powers of observation were, however, at a minimum in *Uncle Tom's Cabin.* A few hours spent on a plantation in Kentucky, and the dark pages of Weld's *American Slavery as It Is,* had told her all she knew about servitude, except through fancy. The

---

John Quincy Adams' assertion that "the preservation, propagation, and perpetuation of slavery is the vital and animating spirit of the National Government." The pamphlet also denied that "because a person thinks the Federal Government bad, he necessarily believes in no-government"—a favorite accusation of anti-Garrisonians.

[42] S. P. C. Duvall, "W. G. Simms's Review of Mrs. Stowe," *American Lit.,* XXX (1958), 112 ff., brings out these aspects of the author's career.

"original" Uncle Tom she probably did not meet until *Uncle Tom's Cabin* was completed, though her imagination persuaded her that she had living characters in mind. Thus Negroes were not real to her in themselves, but (as with her fellow Northerners) were made to serve such purposes as fitted her view of attitudes and relations proper to deserving freemen.

It was a stroke of genius for the book to make Tom's first masters, Shelby and St. Clare, well-meaning if improvident Southerners, and to make the cruel Simon Legree a New Englander-born. It was somewhat less than durable psychology for Mrs. Stowe to provide a cast of Negroes whose spirit and intelligence varied inversely with the darkness of their skins; but it served a mighty contemporary purpose. Harriet disarmed her northern readers by confiding that she had long "avoided all reading upon or allusion to the subject of slavery considering it too painful to be inquired into, and one which advancing light and civilization would certainly live down." She set herself down as a conservative by advocating colonization as late as 1852. It seemed to her natural and desirable to impute a desire for emigration to Africa to her almost-white hero, George Harris, even though he had escaped with Eliza and their child to Canada, where they were happily settled.

Mrs. Stowe and her Negro spokesman went on to argue that although the Negro deserved equal status in America, he preferred not to avail himself of it. The novel sent on to Africa not only Harris and his family, but his reunited sister and her reunited mother, and even Topsy, with more immigrants promised. All this tended to reassure the novelist's white readers. Emancipation need not, in her cosmos, make Negroes offensively familiar, embarrassingly near, dangerously competitive to white people in social and economic pursuits.

It was not lack of careful reading which enabled Harriet's major work to escape careful dissection. Its phrases and characters were assimilated in every detail. Its religious banalities were as earnestly regarded as the noblest passages of the Bible she utilized. "Woe unto the world because of offenses, but woe unto them through whom the offense cometh" was one of them which Lincoln later gave a more stately setting. Mrs. Stowe's northern readers were not disturbed at seeing slavery as through a glass darkly, for it helped obscure the fact that they viewed the Negro little differently from the Southerner. It was the politics of slavery which were in controversy. The Southerner, on

that level, scorned *Uncle Tom's Cabin,* reviled its author, and wrote
countless refutations of it. He, often more readily than the sentimental
northern reader, penetrated its crude, fictional mechanics, its fantastic
coincidences and limited understanding. The Northerner had no need
to think critically. Conservative opinion in the North did its best to
harm the novel's reputation and was strong enough to frighten the
Reverend Joel Parker, Tappan's old associate, whom Mrs. Stowe had
cited in proof of some of her statements. Parker had since accepted
the Mexican War, and all compromises, and now threatened to sue
her for false quotation.[43] Aside from such responses, there was little
antiabolitionists could do to combat interest in *Uncle Tom's Cabin.*

Generally, the abolitionists viewed the sensation it created with deep
satisfaction. Lewis Tappan was disturbed by its enthusiasm for colonization, and Garrison pondered the meaning of Harriet's fear that he
would take "from poor Uncle Tom his Bible, and give him nothing
in its place." Garrison observed that slaves in the South were denied
possession of the Bible under severe penalties. But such qualms over
the novel disturbed relatively few abolitionists. Mrs. Stowe had helped
to create an emotional bond between Northerners, not an antislavery
program. By means of stage presentations, the novel began the second
of its unprecedented careers; and though abolitionists dared hope it
was giving moral tone even to the theater, the liberties taken with it
there further frayed its scant intellectual content. It was not surprising
that there could even be southern versions of *Uncle Tom's Cabin,* and
points at which they met with northern versions in distortions of Negro character.[44]

Almost as extraordinary was the triumph of *Uncle Tom's Cabin* in
Europe, where editions and dramatizations of it multiplied. In Great
Britain alone, it sold perhaps a million copies. In 1853, *A Key to
Uncle Tom's Cabin* and Mrs. Stowe's own celebrated visit to the
island stoked fires of interest. The result of all this excitement is more
difficult to gauge. Fashionable proslavery attitudes persisted in Great
Britain, their most distinguished exponent being Thomas Carlyle,

---

[43] *The Discussion between Rev. Joel Parker, and Rev. A. Rood, on the
Question "What Are the Evils Inseparable from Slavery," Which Was Referred
to by Mrs. Stowe* . . . (New York, 1852).
[44] *First Annual Report Presented to the New York Anti-Slavery Society,
May 12, 1854, by Its Executive Committee* (New York, 1854), p. 21; Joseph
P. Roppolo, "Uncle Tom in New Orleans: Three Lost Plays," *NEQ,* XXVIII
(1954), 213–226.

whose thoughts on "The Nigger Question" offended his antislavery admirers. Their effect on northern attitudes was small, thanks to fashionable anti-British prejudice.[45]

Popular British antislavery, on the other hand, linked itself emotionally with that created in the North by *Uncle Tom's Cabin*. Its most impressive result was the "Stafford House Address," sponsored by Lord Shaftesbury, which was signed by about half a million Englishwomen, who begged their American sisters to do something for the slave. Shaftesbury had no great background in antislavery, but he turned to it with enthusiasm: "My campaign for the niggers," he noted, "is both laborious and expensive. We want more shoulders and more purses to the work." There was little Southerners could do besides renew their charges of British hypocrisy and fraud.[46]

Certainly, 1852 gave no evidence that the moral revolution in the North had crystallized a national program. The combination of *Uncle Tom's Cabin* and Louis Kossuth did not prevent the Democrats from convening in Baltimore in June to consider whether they would again prefer as their Presidential candidate Lewis Cass, or the ambitious Stephen A. Douglas, or perhaps one of the party wheelhorses like William L. Marcy of New York or James Buchanan of Pennsylvania. Heavy political trading canceled out the major candidates and gave the nomination to the tractable Franklin Pierce of New Hampshire. William R. King of Alabama was added to the ticket to counterstamp its basic character; the Democracy had closed ranks on a southern platform. The Whigs met, appropriately, in the same Baltimore hall to offer the more distinguished military man and personality, General Winfield Scott, but no more distinguished program. Disunited and directionless, they pleaded for a cessation of slavery controversy.

Typical of the weaving of principle and politics was Seward's

[45] Elizur Wright, *Perforations in the "Latter-Day Pamphlets," by One of the "Eighteen Millions of Bores"* (Boston, 1850); Whittier, *Prose Works*, III, 133 ff. For a bibliography of the English and foreign editions of the novel, see Harriet B. Stowe, *Uncle Tom's Cabin . . . New Edition, with Illustrations, and a Bibliography of the Work by George Bullen . . .* (Boston, 1883), xxxix–lviii.

[46] Rev. Leander Ker, *Slavery Consistent with Christianity, with an Introduction, Embracing a Notice of the "Uncle Tom's Cabin" Movement in England* (Weston, Mo., 1853 ed.); "British Philanthropy and American Slavery," *De Bow's Review*, n.s., I (1853), 258–280; [Samuel S. F. B. Morse] *The Present Attempt to Dissolve the American Union a British Aristocratic Plot, by B.* (New York, 1862).

strategy: he declared that he would accept no public favors from Scott if the Virginia-bred hero should be elected. The subtlety in Seward's announcement lay in its seeming to express Seward's northern loyalties; yet he had less to fear from Scott than he had had from Taylor. Scott was a Unionist and had opposed (though he had accepted) the Compromise of 1850. Seward's words were intended for the South, not the North: they were intended to help Scott's chances of winning southern votes. Southern Whigs were leaving the party for fear that Scott, like Taylor, might be inclined to give positions to abolitionist-minded Whig politicians.[47]

The Democrats had sharpened their demand for equal treatment in the territories, for a firm control over would-be fugitive slaves, and for expansionism south and in the Caribbean. They had even profited from the 1848 revolutionary wave, which in Cuba produced an abortive movement for freedom, and which they hoped would lead to annexation by the United States. Narciso López, a Spanish-American filibuster who had once been active against the patriots of Venezuela, in 1849 went against the Spanish in Cuba. Enthusiasm for his cause brought volunteers for his army from Cincinnati as well as from New Orleans. The collapse of López' plots, his garroting, and the execution of United States citizens for complicity in his efforts caused riots in New Orleans and anger elsewhere.[48]

The Democrats denounced the "murder" of the American filibusters. They were humiliated because of the "supine" Whig government's apology to Spain for the actions of a New Orleans mob, which burned the Spanish flag in Lafayette Square and sacked the shops of Spanish-speaking citizens. Southern spokesmen felt sincerely that the slogans of "Young America" and "Manifest Destiny" represented progress, and that effete nations had to stand out of the path of American expansionism. Yet they needed northern votes for their program to succeed.[49] In Pierce, in Marcy, in Buchanan, and in similar personages they found Northerners who were willing to further it. As a political slogan, "Pierce and Cuba" rang with strength, at least in its latter half.

[47] Cole, *Whig Party in the South,* p. 259; McMaster, "The Passing of the Whigs," in *History,* VIII, 166 ff.

[48] *Ibid.,* VIII, 133 ff.; Basil Rauch, *American Interest in Cuba: 1848–1855* (New York, 1949), *passim.*

[49] C. Stanley Urban, "The Ideology of Southern Imperialism: New Orleans and the Caribbean, 1845–1860," *Louisiana Hist. Qu.,* XXXIX (1956), 48–73; cf. Rauch, "Economic Considerations," pp. 181 ff.

In the Whig camp Scott was incomparable, but as a soldier rather than politician. He had lost the South, but he could not win the North. The landslide for Pierce was a tribute to expansionism, rather than a repudiation of free soil. The popular vote gave Scott 1,386,578 votes against Pierce's 1,601,474. The four states to prefer Scott were Massachusetts and Vermont, Kentucky and Tennessee.

The fate of the Free-Soilers proper in 1852 was deceptive. They appeared to have come down from their 291,263 votes of 1848; as "Free Democrats," their campaign of 1852 netted them no more than 156,149. But Van Buren had taken his Barnburners back into the Democratic fold. The Free Democrats (including Chase) now gave John P. Hale his chance; with him campaigned George W. Julian of Indiana, later son-in-law of Giddings. Julian had developed militant antislavery opinions since 1840, when he had attended Harrison's Dayton, Ohio, meeting and gazed with awe at the old chieftain. Julian had made efforts to advance inside the Whig party, but was unable to compete with the machine politicians. Elected to Congress as a Free-Soiler, he had made more than a local reputation before his defeat for re-election in 1851.[50]

Thus Free Soil in 1852, despite the demoralization which attended Whiggism, and to a degree because of it, had a more upright banner than before and was attended by a splintered Liberty party, which nominated William Goodell. Julian, as vice-presidential candidate for the Free-Soilers, even addressed a meeting at Maysville, Kentucky, seconded by John G. Fee and Cassius M. Clay, which was somewhat disturbed by rowdies but concluded in good order.[51] In sum, the North had shown itself unwilling to support the Whigs and unable to accept unequivocal antislavery. Tappan's dream of a party which would oppose not only the extension of slavery, but the existence of slavery, was dead.

Pierce was determined, more forcefully than Fillmore had been, that the Fugitive Slave Law must operate. His spirit he imparted to the stipendiaries of his administration. On May 24, 1854, a Negro named Anthony Burns was arrested in Boston under circumstances

[50] Patrick W. Riddleberger, "The Making of a Political Abolitionist: George W. Julian and the Free Soilers, 1848," *Indiana Mag. of Hist.*, LI (1955), 222–236; Miller, "Anti-Slavery in Indiana," pp. 146 ff., 175–176, 192 ff.; Smith, *Liberty and Free Soil Parties in the Northwest*, pp. 245 ff.

[51] Julian, *Political Recollections*, p. 126.

which indicated careful planning. Burns was twenty-four years old, had taught himself to read and write, and had been well treated by his master. His freedom of movement had permitted him, that February, to escape by boat to Boston.[52]

The warrant for his arrest had been issued by Edward G. Loring, not only a commissioner but a judge of probate for the County of Suffolk, Horace Mann's old college chum and former law partner, who had since become a judicious but no less dedicated servant of the Fugitive Slave Law. Dana, Wendell Phillips, and others gathered to see what could be done. The remarkable fact of the day was the state of public opinion. "Whigs, the Hunker Whigs, the Compromise men of 1850," Dana observed, ". . . who would not speak to me in 1850 and 1851, and who enrolled themselves as special policemen in the Sims affair, stop me in the street and talk treason."

Massachusetts was far from having been won over to radicalism. The direct reason for Dana's new respectability was the Nebraska Bill, which was about to be made law. But in addition, the bold government effort to give slavery status in the North was too much for northern sensibilities. A great meeting at Faneuil Hall heard Wendell Phillips and Theodore Parker all but urge violence to prevent the rendition of Anthony Burns. At the same time, Thomas W. Higginson led an attempt on the Court House to free him which was repulsed for lack of numbers; in the course of the action, a volunteer deputy was shot and killed. Dr. Samuel G. Howe, who had become a fiery opponent of the Fugitive Slave Law, was not daunted by the tragedy. He would probably have led a larger mob to the rescue, had the United States Marshal not proceeded to call to Boston a company of Marines from Charlestown and a company of artillery from Fort Independence. The mayor, too, ordered out several companies of volunteer militia, who were recruited from "the lowest villains in the community, keepers of brothels, blacklegs, convicts, prize-fighters, etc."[53]

Dana and his associates worked desperately to put the evidence in doubt, but to no avail. The commissioner's decision was final and against their client. Sims had been hurried out of Boston while the city slept. The town and federal officials had no intention of hurrying

---

[52] *Boston Slave Riot and Trial of Anthony Burns* . . . (Boston, 1854); Charles E. Stevens, *Anthony Burns, a History* (Boston, 1856).

[53] Adams, *Dana*, I, 273, also 269–270.

again before public opinion. All the armed forces of the city were called out to line the streets from the courthouse to the wharf. A cannon was leveled at the 20,000 spectators in the bright daylight of three o'clock in the afternoon. But Theodore Parker, who was soon to be indicted for conspiracy, though not tried, had already held a court of his own. He called upon his congregation to remember the trial of Sims: "You remember the judges of Massachusetts stooping, crouching, creeping, crawling, under the chain of Slavery, in order to get to their own courts." This, he asserted, was the consequence of nonresistance to the Fugitive Slave Law, of believing that there was no higher law. Boston was a law-abiding community, but now there was in force a law she would not keep. Loring had known this: "He knew the slave-holders had no more right to Anthony Burns than to his own daughter. . . . He knew there would be a meeting at Faneuil Hall—gatherings in the streets. He knew there would be violence." Parker concluded his indictment:

EDWARD GREELEY LORING, Judge of Probate for the County of Suffolk, in the State of Massachusetts, Fugitive Slave Bill Commissioner of the United States, before these citizens of Boston, on Ascension Sunday, assembled to worship God, I charge you with the death of that man who was killed on last Friday night. He was your fellow-servant in kidnapping. He dies at your hand. You fired the shot which makes his wife a widow, his child an orphan. I charge you with the peril of twelve men, arrested for murder, and on trial for their lives. I charge you with filling the Court House with one hundred and eighty-four hired ruffians of the United States, and alarming not only this city for her liberties that are in peril, but stirring up the whole Commonwealth of Massachusetts with indignation, which no man knows how to stop—which no man can stop. You have done it all![54]

On July 4, a meeting convened at Framingham, Massachusetts, to protest the Burns decision. Present as a speaker was Thoreau. He had avoided, heretofore, becoming implicated in the plans of Brook Farm or of the abolitionists. Now he felt stirred to commune with his fellow citizens; his old and worthiest pursuits, he confessed, had lost their attractiveness: "I feel that my investment of life here is worth many

[54] Parker, *Additional Speeches, Addresses, and Occasional Sermons* (Boston, 1855), II, 71 ff. Parker's subsequent sermon on the cause and consequences of the Burns rendition is one of his major efforts. For an adverse view of Parker, see James F. Rhodes, *History of the United States, from the Compromise of 1850* (New York, 1893), I, 288–290. Cf. Commager, *Parker,* pp. 232 ff.

per cent. less since Massachusetts last deliberately and forcibly restored an innocent man, Anthony Burns, to slavery."[55]

Garrison was the sensation of the day. He produced a copy of the Fugitive Slave Law, set fire to it, and permitted it to burn to ashes. "And let all the people say, *Amen,*" he declared. Amen echoed from the large assembly. Garrison burned also the decision of Commissioner Loring and the charge of another judge to the Grand Jury for action on the Court House assault. Amens followed these deeds. Finally, Garrison held up the Constitution of the United States, and denounced it as "a covenant with death and an agreement with hell." Then he burned it, exclaiming, "So perish all compromises with tyranny! And let all the people say, Amen!" The few hisses and protests were drowned by the shout of Amen!

Here was the acme of Garrison's defiance of constituted authority—the evidence his detractors would use to illustrate his irresponsibility and, less clearly, his insignificance. Yet it would seem that Garrison was, if anything, more important than he had ever been. True, the mass of spectators did not rally to his colors; they continued to invest others with authority. But Garrison's antislavery principles they made more and more reputable.

Their problem was how to preserve a Union which incorporated slavery, while turning it to antislavery. Garrison was a pillar of disunion, but he was also a pillar of antislavery: there was inspiration in his work. Northerners retained their votes and negotiated with compromisers. At the same time they gave ear to the suggestion that Loring might be fit to be an agent of the federal government, but not a judge of Massachusetts. Dana was upset by this campaign. Loring, he thought, had been wrongheaded, and the Fugitive Slave Law gave him too much discretionary power. Loring had, however, done his duty as he had seen it.[56]

The abolitionists had no time for courtesy. Wendell Phillips turned his eloquence on Loring and pleaded with the state legislature to petition the governor to remove him from his judgeship. Hand in hand with this effort went one for passing a Personal Liberty Law which would stop further renditions of fugitive slaves. The law passed by

[55] Thoreau, *Writings of Henry David Thoreau* (Boston, 1906), XII, 355.
[56] *Remarks of Richard H. Dana, Jr., Esq., before the Committee on Federal Relations, on the Proposed Removal of Edward G. Loring, Esq., from the Office of Judge of Probate, March 5, 1855* (Boston, 1855).

Massachusetts all but separated that state from the nation on the issue. One of its conspicuous provisions made it illegal for a state judge to be a United States commissioner. Loring was thus outside the law, though he persisted in holding on to his two positions. The petition for his removal was denied in 1855. By 1858 there was a more conciliatory attitude in Massachusetts toward the federal government, infiltrated as it was by political abolitionists. Though the Fugitive Slave Law could not be enforced, the more defiant clauses of the Personal Liberty Law were removed. In exchange, Loring was separated from his judgeship. A combination of abolitionism and political abolitionism had accomplished this result.

CHAPTER 10

Kansas and Abolition: The Irrepressible Conflict

SOUTHERN statesmen had no choice but to press for further assurances from the nonslavery North. The sensitivity of some of their leaders was such that they could even perceive an abolitionist taint in Franklin Pierce.[1] More reasonable Southerners faced their problem realistically. Wrote Robert Toombs, a leading Georgian Whig and earnest Unionist: "The true policy of the South is to unite: to lay aside all party divisions . . . and to uphold and support that noble set of patriots at the North who have stood for the Constitution and the right against the tempest of fanaticism, folly and treason. . . ." But what program would their northern constituents accept? The Whig party, by attempting to separate itself from Free-Soilism, had collapsed. Whig politicians like George Ashmun, who had "shaken [their] skirts clear of the abolitionism which had fouled them too much and too long," found themselves in a dust storm of Free Soil.[2]

Among them, and fearful of innovations which might threaten the Union, was Abraham Lincoln. He was a true son of the State of

[1] Rhodes, *History,* I, 420–421.

[2] Robert Toombs to T. Lomax, June 6, 1855; George Ashmun (Whig Congressman from Massachusetts) to Howell Cobb, October 11, 1851, in Phillips (ed.), "Toombs, Stephens, Cobb Correspondence," *AHA Annual Report, 1911,* pp. 261, 353. Ashmun later presided at the Wigwam Convention of the Republican party in 1860 which nominated Lincoln for President.

Illinois and, like it, conflicted in his feelings about slavery. For Lincoln in the early 1850's, "the race of ambition [had] been a failure—a flat failure," yet he was reluctant to experiment with radical doctrine. That chattel bondage was wrong he would never deny. He had even, in 1849, introduced a bill in the House of Representatives abolishing slavery in the District of Columbia, claiming that it spoke for the will of the District's residents. He had, on an earlier occasion, voted to lay on the table a resolution looking toward the abolition of the slave trade in the District. Beyond such tentative gestures, he had little plan for resolving the country's dilemma. He had "no prejudice against the Southern people. They are just what we would be in their situation." As for the problem of slavery, "I surely will not blame them for not doing what I should not know how to do myself." His instincts opposed treating Negroes as equals, and he knew that in this he was like "the great mass of white people." He believed, too, that "[a] universal feeling . . . can not be safely disregarded." The Missouri Compromise was a pillar of his faith. But in one of his earlier challenges to his younger, yet vastly more famous fellow Illinoisan, Senator Douglas, he accepted the Compromise of 1850. Lincoln's grounds were tenuous: the North had received a free California in exchange for an undefined New Mexico and Utah. The Compromise, Lincoln insisted, had not been overthrown.[3] His position said more for his love of the Union than for his free-soil principles.

His depth of character aside, little distinguished Lincoln's antislavery position from that of Horace Greeley, who was also moving from a total acceptance of slavery in the South to an intransigent stand on free soil.[4] Indeed, Greeley, as a reformer, seemed on the surface the more ardent and idealistic of the two. Neither was, however, so much as a political abolitionist; both sought not to abolish slavery, but only to prevent its extension.[5]

Greeley expressed himself often and freely against such outrages as the murder of Lovejoy; Lincoln had spoken more generally against throwing printing presses into rivers and shooting editors. As fellow congressmen in 1848, neither Greeley nor Lincoln was conspicuous

---

[3] Basler (ed.), *Collected Works of Abraham Lincoln,* II, 247 ff., 382–383.

[4] Harlan H. Horner, *Lincoln and Greeley* (Urbana, 1953), traces their paths and relations.

[5] This view may be compared with that of Dumond, *Anti-Slavery Origins of the Civil War,* p. 100, which sees Lincoln as having been an abolitionist.

for reformist zeal.[6] Greeley's heated opposition to the Mexican War gave him a more radical mien than Lincoln, who struck a strictly political pose in asking whether or not the exact "spot" on which American blood was first shed during border differences was on Mexican soil. Yet Owen Lovejoy, the dead evangelist's brother, a minister in Illinois and an ardent abolitionist, not only supported Lincoln but defended him from more eager spirits who would have had him come out boldly for radical measures.[7]

As practical politicians, Lincoln and Greeley best showed their mettle. Greeley's strength lay not in his personality but in his *Tribune,* for which his fellow Whigs, Weed and Seward, had a due respect. Greeley's frantic efforts to receive their support for the governorship of New York no more than tarnished his verbal salutes to reform. He confided to Theodore Parker that "a large majority of the voters are impelled by interest rather than principle, and . . . any political movement which appeals wholly to mind, ignoring material considerations, is doomed to failure."[8] Lincoln essentially agreed, but was less pretentious in expressing his worldly knowledge, more responsible in weighing the arguments of idealists against those of practical men.

Greeley and Lincoln were typical Northerners, one of the East, the other of the West, who had managed heretofore to think of themselves as nationalists rather than sectionalists. They were being forced by events to give up in their minds the universal appeals which their much-admired Henry Clay had managed so adeptly. In the America which followed the publication of *Uncle Tom's Cabin,* both Lincoln and Greeley had to concentrate upon issues and promises which would persuade a majority of their countrymen east and west, but especially north of Mason and Dixon's line.

Alone, they could have formulated no program leading to abolition. Their respect for constitutional guarantees and limitations was too great, their faith in emancipation too meager. Their lack of regard for Negroes gave them no basis for criticizing or influencing slaveholders

[6] Donald W. Riddle, *Congressman Abraham Lincoln* (Urbana, 1957), esp. pp. 162 ff. See also Benjamin Quarles, *Lincoln and the Negro* (New York, 1962).

[7] Owen Lovejoy was almost a barometer of antislavery tendencies in Illinois, mixing caution with extreme doctrine. See Edward Magdol, *Owen Lovejoy, Abolitionist in Congress* (New Brunswick, N.J., 1967), and *Addresses on the Death of Hon. Owen Lovejoy* . . . (Washington, 1864).

[8] Iseley, *Greeley,* p. 84.

in principle. But the more aggressive Free-Soilers whom they increasingly addressed included elements with every combination of beliefs, conservative as well as abolitionist. At crucial points in their resistance to proslavery demands, Free-Soilers and abolitionists joined forces.

The influence of each varied, and was often deceptive. Thus there was now a formidable contingent of them in Congress. Yet the Capital, for all the attention which had been focused upon it, continued to hold free Negroes and slaves in reins, as well as in contempt.[9] In Tennessee, antislavery was never more than the constitutional, poor-white aspirations toward dignity and property best represented by Andrew Johnson, which, during the Civil War, would save the state for the Union. Antislavery in Missouri was largely antiabolition, as well as antagonistic toward Negroes. It produced such figures as Frank and Montgomery Blair, sons of Andrew Jackson's old comrade, Francis Preston Blair.[10]

Kentucky, even after the expulsion of Birney, appeared to offer a genuine abolitionist movement, and deceived such hopeful seekers after peaceful emancipation as Lewis Tappan. It brought James Freeman Clarke, Unitarian minister and friend of the Transcendentalists there, in 1841, to preach culture and religion as well as Channing's version of antislavery.[11] The most arresting figure in Kentucky antislavery was Cassius M. Clay. As a student at Yale, this son of a wealthy slaveholder had been stirred by Garrison and become acquainted with Whittier, John A. Andrew, later Civil War governor of Massachusetts, and other abolitionists and Free-Soilers. Clay returned to Kentucky an advocate of antislavery, in part because he saw it as the politics of

[9] [Worthington G. Snethen] *Snethen's Black Code of the District of Columbia* (New York, 1848). This was a publication of the American and Foreign Anti-Slavery Society.

[10] Chase C. Mooney, *Slavery in Tennessee* (Bloomington, 1957), pp. 64 ff.; Benjamin Merkel, "The Anti-Slavery Movement in Missouri, 1819–1865" (Ph.D., Washington University, St. Louis, 1939); W. Sherman Savage, "The Contest over Slavery between Illinois and Missouri," *JNH*, XXVIII (1943), 311 ff.

[11] *Annual Report of the American and Foreign Anti-Slavery Society* . . . (New York, 1849), pp. 92–93. For a valuable retrospect concerning abolitionists in Kentucky, as well as Wisconsin, see E. Dyer to Z. Eastman, January 29, 1884, Chicago Hist. Soc.; Edward E. Hale (ed.), *Autobiography, Diary and Correspondence, by James F. Clarke* (Boston, 1891); Arthur S. Bolster, Jr., *James Freeman Clarke: Disciple to Advancing Truth* (Boston, 1954). See also Martin, *Anti-Slavery Movement in Kentucky, passim,* and Ivan E. McDougle, "Slavery in Kentucky," *JNH,* III (1918), 211–328.

the future.[12] In Lexington, his program of gradual emancipation and his stormy temperament inspired the drawing of pistols and bowie knives. In 1845, his great year of defiance of border-state prejudices, Clay published *The True American* in a building protected by sheet iron and an arsenal which included two four-pound brass cannon and kegs of powder for blowing up invaders. His paper was terminated by Kentucky citizens who took pride in the fact that they did it without bloodshed and through relatively peaceful processes.

Clay's desperate courage thrilled northern abolitionists into making exaggerated appraisals of his dedication to the cause of abolitionism, and it was inevitable that they would be disillusioned. Clay was at least as much opposed to the inefficiency of the plantation system as he was to the morality of slavery. In due course, he supported his kinsman, Henry Clay, served in the Mexican War, showed no moral discrimination in his reasons for fighting mortal duels, and expressed sympathy with Kentucky slaveholding interests. He reminded white mechanics that Negro slaves were their economic rivals, and repeatedly expressed aversion for Negroes. Yet he did emancipate his own slaves. The year 1849 was a turning point for him and his program: a number of sturdy and distinguished emancipationists, including Cassius M. Clay, agitated for a constitutional end to slavery in Kentucky, but were overwhelmingly defeated.

More significant of antislavery in a border state than Clay was a combination of circumstances: rugged terrain in the middle of Kentucky—which made the use of slaves impractical—the generosity of Clay himself, and the coming of the Reverend John G. Fee, a Lane convert to abolitionism. These resulted in the founding of what became Berea College. Encouraged by Lewis Tappan's strong American Missionary Association, and aided by the Oberlin graduate Reverend John A. R. Rogers, Berea became an oasis of antislavery and democratic education in a state which was not ardently wedded to slavery.[13]

Abolitionists and moderates helped one another under conditions which made moderates seem like extremists. Lincoln would inherit the labors of both and administer them with an understanding beyond any of them. His Kentucky background and western rearing gave him in-

[12] David L. Smiley, *Lion of Whitehall: The Life of Cassius M. Clay* (Madison, 1962), p. 23.

[13] Elizabeth S. Peck, *Berea's First Century, 1855–1955* (Lexington, 1955); *Autobiography of John G. Fee* (Chicago, 1891), pp. 90 ff.

sights not available to abolitionists. The border states, when civil war broke out, carried the fate of the Union. As Lincoln then observed to his friend, Senator Orville H. Browning of Illinois: "I think to lose Kentucky, is nearly the same as to lose the whole game. Kentucky gone, we cannot hold Missouri, nor, as I think, Maryland."[14]

In 1854, however, the Democratic party was in power and, though heavy with discontented factions, determined that there need be no civil war: policies which appeased the South would prevent its breaking out. Opposing the party Democrats was an increasingly formidable Free-Soil faction, in Congress and out. Typical of the Free-Soilers in many ways was Horace Mann, who had once been so chary of associating his educational enterprises with antislavery. Now he was fully committed to political abolitionism. In 1852, he ran for governor on the Free-Soil ticket of Massachusetts and, defeated, left for southwest Ohio to head what soon became one of the distinguished educational institutions of the period. Antioch College was near Cincinnati and thus at the opposite end of the state from the Western Reserve and Oberlin. It now joined the latter as antislavery, coeducational, and reformist in its concepts of education. Though Antioch was erected by enthusiasts of the Christian Church, Mann supported liberal religious principles against opposition and added a vital, and final, chapter to his career.[15]

Horace Mann brought his Massachusetts idealism to Ohio; Ben Wade came from the Western Reserve to Washington in 1851 to join his rough energies to those of other antislavery senators. Once a common laborer on the Erie Canal, Wade retained a respect for the foreign-born which distinguished him from many other Whigs and political climbers. He had become a lawyer and a religious skeptic, as well as a businessman who refused to accept bankruptcy during the financial panic of 1837 and eventually paid off all his debts. Wade served a hard apprenticeship in the state legislature, joining the move-

---

[14] Basler (ed.), *Collected Works of Abraham Lincoln*, IV, 532; cf. William H. Townsend, *Lincoln and the Bluegrass: Slavery and Civil War in Kentucky* (Lexington, Ky., 1955), pp. 70 *et seq*.

[15] Harvard F. Vallance, "A History of Antioch College" (Ph.D., Ohio State University, 1936), pp. 59 ff. Mann's Inaugural Address won fame as a masterpiece; it condemned the world and circumstances men had made for themselves as contrasted with those with which God had endowed them; *Dedication of Antioch College, and Inaugural Address of Its President, Hon. Horace Mann; with Other Proceedings* (Yellow Springs, Ohio, 1854), pp. 40 and *passim*.

ment to abolish imprisonment for debt and successfully fighting passage of a fugitive-slave law which outlawed evidence by "persons of color."[16]

Despite his bold demeanor, which seemed to make him a senatorial counterpart to Giddings in the House of Representatives, Wade's political abolitionism was of a special stripe. He was ambitious, and ready to deal with slavery politicians when common ground could be found; willing to think of them as his "friends from the South, who with me have fought many a political battle shoulder to shoulder— though far distant from each other." His ambition would ultimately sink his abolitionism into sordid political maneuvers as he rose within the Radical Republican party during the Civil War.[17] What held him to antislavery principles during the 1850's was the obdurate attitude of the southern bloc; as he wrote: "I am Abolitionist at heart while in the slave-cursed atmosphere of this capitol whatever I may be at home. But here pride and self-respect compel a man either to be a dough-face, flunky, or an abolitionist, and I chose the latter. I glory in the name."[18]

The key to Wade's abolitionism—as with many of his companions —was his dislike of the Negroes. Even the Western Reserve Anti-Slavery Convention had once, in 1842, declared that abolition was the one way to keep the North from being flooded by Negroes. Slavery they equated with runaway slaves headed North, and in need of aid and co-operation. Emancipation alone "could relieve them of the presence of a class whose contiguity was so offensive."[19] Wade not only agreed; he was in agreement with Horace Greeley's virulent newspaper correspondent, James Shepherd Pike. At first glance, Pike, a journalist and politician from Maine, was the most extreme of radicals, advocating disunion. But he was less anxious to separate himself from Southerners than from Negroes. A severed Union meant separation from the "great forest of Negro Slavery," and thus progress in avoid-

[16] Mary G. G. Land, "Old Backbone: 'Bluff' Ben Wade" (Ph.D., Western Reserve University, 1957); see also A. G. Riddle, *The Life of Benjamin F. Wade* (Cleveland, 1886), by a participant in free-soil and abolitionist politics.

[17] Wade was within a shadow of becoming President of the United States. As President of the Senate in 1868, he would have succeeded Andrew Johnson, had the latter's impeachment been triumphantly concluded; George F. Milton, *The Age of Hate: Andrew Johnson and the Radicals* (New York, 1930), pp. 515 ff.

[18] Land, "Old Backbone," p. 176.

[19] Reilly, "Early Slavery Controversy in the Western Reserve," p. 186.

ing "Negro equality in its most offensive form." Hence Pike approved Wade's suggestion that the free colored people might be colonized somewhere on the southern border of the United States. The South feared Cuba might be "Africanized" through natural increase and emancipation by the Spanish—thus giving the South a "mongrelized neighbor";[20] Pike feared that the South itself might be Africanized, and thus threaten the purity of the white South.[21]

Emancipation for the purpose of ridding the country of Negroes haunted troubled Northerners and Southerners who wished to avoid a sectional clash, until war actually came and even after. Indeed, Northerners, once they received full federal power, sought to carry out large-scale colonization projects, and the possibility that the government might force the deportation of free Negroes gave a moment· of renewed national significance to the plodding but alive American Colonization Society.[22]

Although Free Soil became the major political slogan of the North, as the sectional crisis deepened, it was accompanied by a division of opinion respecting the Negro, and complicated by the unwillingness of some Negroes to co-operate with plans which would have kept them quiescent as slaves or freemen. How complex these differences were could be seen in the experience of Gerrit Smith, who was elected to Congress in 1855. He grieved abolitionists by addressing his pro-

[20] Urban, "The Africanization of Cuba Scare, 1853–1855," *Hispanic American Hist. Rev.*, XXXVII (1957), 29–45.

[21] Robert F. Durden, *James Shepherd Pike: Republicanism and the American Negro, 1850–1882* (Durham, 1957), pp. 14 ff.

[22] Willis Boyd, "Negro Colonization in the National Crisis, 1860–1870" (Ph.D., University of California, L.A., 1953), *passim*. Curious, too, were the colonization plans of James Redpath, abolitionist and an admirer of John Brown, but whose colonizing schemes were much like those of other colonizationists (*ibid.*, pp. 87 ff.). Lincoln planned ceaselessly to eject the Negro from the country, and his efforts "make a long story and a dismal one"; J. G. Randall, *Lincoln the President* (New York, 1946), II, 139. For a valuable case study of Lincoln's strategy, H. Clay Reed, "Lincoln's Compensated Emancipation Plan and Its Relation to Delaware," *Delaware Notes, Seventh Series* (Newark, Del., 1931), pp. 27–77. Lincoln was said, though on the dubious word of General Benjamin F. Butler, to have worried over the Army's one hundred thousand Negro veterans, who might turn their military training against white Southerners. Butler's suggestion that Lincoln, as Commander in Chief of the Army, send them to dig the proposed Panama Canal was said to have been seriously received by the President; Boyd, "Negro Colonization," pp. 166–167. For a scholarly statement which sums up distaste for slavery and the Negro, James Schouler, *History of the United States* (New York, 1880–1891), II, 233–242.

slavery colleagues with courtesy, and by refusing to join in the free-soil strategy of quashing undesired bills by concerted absence from the House, which prevented the convening of a quorum. This, Smith insisted, was undemocratic. It was revolution. Yet he was for resisting the Fugitive Slave Law. Similarly, abolitionists abused him for favoring the annexation of Cuba, with slavery. Smith believed that Cuban slavery was cruel and that its excesses would be mitigated under American authority; and it might yet be abolished. Such were Smith's dilemmas.[23] They, as well as vanity and personal affairs, inspired his eccentric decision to resign from Congress.

Could such confusions among abolitionists help the proslavery Democratic administration? In 1854, under Pierce, it boldly projected a domestic and foreign policy meant to begin an era of peaceful association between slavery and nonslavery Americans. In the foreign field, 1854 was the year during which Commodore Perry opened Japan to American trade, and in which reciprocity arrangements were made with Canada— arrangements which always disturbed abolitionists, who feared that Canada might weaken in her protection of resident fugitive slaves.[24] Above all, it was the year of the South's major effort to weave the defense of slavery into American foreign policy. The seizure of an American merchant vessel, *Black Warrior,* by Havana administrators for an error in her clearance papers stirred the militant exponents of manifest destiny in Congress to demand war. Their goal was patently Cuban annexation. Negotiations for redress proceeded with more energy between Secretary of State William L. Marcy and his Minister to Spain, Pierre Soulé, a high-spirited Southerner, than with the Spanish government.[25]

The Spaniards apologized and revoked a fine levied on *Black Warrior;* but in the meantime Marcy had instructed Soulé to meet at Ostend, Belgium, with John Y. Mason of Virginia, Minister to France,

[23] *Speeches of Gerrit Smith in Congress* (New York, 1856), pp. 376 ff. and *passim.* For the problem of Cuban slavery, cf. Arthur F. Corwin, *Spain and the Abolition of Slavery in Cuba, 1817–1886* (Austin, Tex., 1967), and Herbert S. Klein, *Slavery in the Americas: a Comparative Study of Cuba and Virginia* (Chicago, 1967).

[24] Roman J. Zorn, "An Arkansas Fugitive Slave Incident and Its International Repercussions," *Arkansas Hist. Qu.,* XVI (1957), 139–149.

[25] John H. Latané, "The Diplomacy of the United States in Regard to Cuba," *AHA Annual Report, 1897* (Washington, 1898), p. 250, argues that the fact that no war occurred shows the relative moderation of the administration. It indicates, rather, the unwillingness of northern politicians to support an adventure which could only have benefited their southern counterparts.

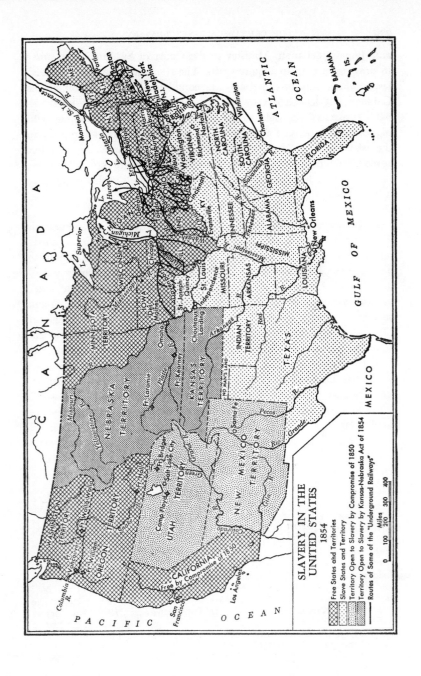

SLAVERY IN THE
UNITED STATES
1854

Free States and Territories
Slave States and Territory
Territory Open to Slavery by Compromise of 1850
Territory Open to Slavery by Kansas-Nebraska Act of 1854
Routes of Some of the "Underground Railways"

Miles
0   100   200   300   400

and James Buchanan, Minister to the Court of St. James's, in order to draw up a plan to acquire Cuba. The result was the Ostend Manifesto, which was intended for the confidential consideration of the Cabinet, but leaked out to become part of the antiexpansionist debate. It asserted the right of the United States to Cuba, and her willingness to compensate Spain with more money (it was alleged) than the island was worth. Every effort ought to be made, the ministers agreed, to purchase Cuba peacefully. Should Spain refuse, however, "then by every law human and divine, we shall be justified in wresting it from Spain, if we possess the power."[26]

In January 1854, Stephen A. Douglas presented to the Senate his first version of his Kansas-Nebraska Bill, an effort to begin organization of that vast territory. It was Seward who took it upon himself to persuade the Kentucky Whig Archibald Dixon to move the repeal of the Missouri Compromise as an amendment to Douglas' bill, in order to force the issue of the future of the West upon the country. There had been threats to abridge the Missouri Compromise throughout 1853, in arguments which involved the Indian problem, the problem of a Pacific railroad, and related questions. Now, incorporating the "squatter" principle of "popular sovereignty" which Lewis Cass had originated, Douglas' purpose was less to carry slavery into the northern territory than to serve a number of economic and political purposes.[27]

Douglas hoped to appease southern representatives and also to satisfy Missouri Democrats, to permit the building of a Pacific railroad using Chicago as its eastern terminus, and to further other special interests, not excluding his own.[28] Douglas was far from being a mere agent of southern ambitions. True, there was no need to repeal the

[26] R. G. Horton, *The Life and Public Services of James Buchanan* . . . (New York, 1856), p. 398; Commager, *Documents of American History*, I, 333–335.

[27] Milo M. Quaife, *The Doctrine of Non-Intervention with Slavery in the Territories* (Chicago, 1910), pp. 98 ff.; *Letters for the People, on the Present Crisis* (n.p., [1853]); Rhodes, *History*, I, 425 ff.; Simms, *Decade of Sectional Controversy*, p. 58.

[28] Douglas' precise intentions are the subject of scholarly debate; Frank H. Hodder, "Genesis of the Kansas-Nebraska Act," *Wisconsin State Hist. Soc. Proc.* (Madison, 1912), pp. 69–86; P. Orman Ray, *The Repeal of the Missouri Compromise: Its Origin and Authorship* (Cleveland, 1909); Ray, "The Genesis of the Kansas-Nebraska Act," *AHA Annual Report, 1914* (Washington, 1916), I, 261 ff. See also Colonel John A. Parker [of Virginia], "What Led to the War; or, the Secret History of the Kansas Nebraska Bill" (1880), typescript of rare pamphlet, WRHS.

Compromise: Missouri was reconciled to it as a political fact. But Douglas' was a national perspective. He could even be seen as a western leader who was "progressive" in wishing to augment his section's economic status and build its industrial potential. His Democracy was typical of his section, as was his indifference to Negroes.[29] The northern response to his bill astounded and angered its astute promoter.

In the January 24 issue of the *National Era* appeared the "Appeal to Independent Democrats" drawn up by Salmon P. Chase and endorsed by his fellow Senator Charles Sumner, as well as by Representatives Giddings, Edward Wade (a more principled abolitionist than his brother Ben), Gerrit Smith, and Alexander DeWitt of Massachusetts. The "Appeal" was widely reprinted, a major achievement of the political abolitionists. It was doubtless unfair to Douglas. The motives of its signatories may be questioned, in their assumption that Douglas headed a plot to overthrow free soil.[30] But Northerners who had heretofore ridiculed the moral approach to politics were confounded. For Douglas had done no more than they had themselves implied was proper. As he cried out indignantly:

They talk about the bill being a violation of the compromise measures of 1850. Who can show me a man in either house of Congress who was in favor of those compromise measures in 1850, and who is not now in favor of leaving the people of Nebraska and Kansas to do as they please upon the subject of slavery, according to the principle of my bill? Is there one? If so, I have not heard of him. The tornado has been raised by abolitionists, and by abolitionists alone.[31]

Nevertheless, it was a tornado. It would cause numerous individuals not only to revise their attitudes toward abolitionists, but even to create antislavery records for themselves which did not, in fact, exist, but which had become the mode.[32] Harriet Beecher Stowe published, in the *Independent,* "An Appeal to the Women of the Free States of

[29] Henry C. Hubbart, *The Older Middle West, 1840–1880* (New York, 1936), pp. 21 ff., 98 ff.

[30] Milton, *The Eve of Conflict* . . . (Boston, 1934), pp. 117 ff.; J. W. Schuckers, *Life and Public Services of Salmon Portland Chase* . . . (New York, 1874), pp. 140 ff.; Solberg, "Joshua Giddings, Politician and Idealist," pp. 390 ff.; Rhodes, *History,* I, 441 ff.; Commager, *Documents of American History,* I, 329–331.

[31] *Speech of Hon. S. A. Douglas, of Illinois, in the Senate, January 30, 1854, on the Nebraska Territory* (Washington, 1854).

[32] Merton L. Dillon, "John Mason Peck: a Study of Historical Rationalization," *Jour. of Ill. State Hist. Soc.,* L (1957), 385–390.

America, on the Present Crisis in Our Country," which, with other features in that increasingly influential organ, offered emotional resistance to Douglas' bill. That many people who criticized Douglas' bill had not seen it, but accepted Chase's interpretation of its provisions, was a fact which earned Douglas' outraged rebuttal—even though he had not himself been objective about the work of the abolitionists.[33] The wide popularity of the "Appeal" as an expression of northern sentiments, however, was the result of choice, not ignorance. Many Northerners preferred free soil to railroads. Ultimately, they demanded both.

The year 1854, therefore, saw deep movements for a reorganization of parties. The temperance crusade had already done its work in a dozen states under the dedicated Neal Dow. The intolerance and fanaticism of some of its leaders would cause the movement to rise and fall in public regard, depending on various social circumstances. But meanwhile, temperance gave antislavery Whigs and Democrats something in common, while they struggled to free themselves of their party obligations.[34]

Temperance, however, soon made way for Know-Nothingism, as well as the more permanent Republican party. The Know-Nothings stemmed from the old nativist alliances of previous decades; but in their new guise, they were a sensational manifestation of political unrest. They still advocated antipathy to Catholics and immigrants in general, but could claim to have publicized the less temperate statements of some Catholic Church officials, as well as to have exposed immigration laws which were kept weak for venal or political purposes. Their mission was only partly antiforeigner. As their official

---

[33] *Letter of Senator Douglas, Vindicating His Character . . . against the Assaults Contained in the Proceedings of a Public Meeting Composed of Twenty-five Clergymen of Chicago* (Washington, 1854), p. 4; *Right of Petition. New England Clergymen. Remarks of Everett . . . Douglas . . . Seward . . .* [etc.] *on the Memorial from Some 3,050 Clergymen of All Denominations and Sects . . . in New England, Remonstrating against the Passage of the Nebraska Bill* [,] *Senate of the United States, March 14, 1854* (Washington, 1854), p. 15.

[34] Frank L. Byrne, "Neal Dow and the Prohibition Movement" (Ph. D., University of Wisconsin, 1957), pp. 93 ff. For an example of antislavery and temperance in politics, see Rev. Austin Willey, *The History of the Antislavery Cause in State and Nation* (Portland, Me., 1886), p. 270; *The Reminiscences of Neal Dow. Recollections of Eighty Years* (Portland, Me., 1898), pp. 181 ff., 334 ff. See also *The Mistakes and Failures of the Temperance Reformation* (New York, 1864).

name, the American party, suggested, they were militantly nationalistic. Theirs was an effort to find a program which could ward off the
sectional conflict and give the demoralized Whigs a home.

In the South, Know-Nothingism grew as a defense against immigrants who might ultimately threaten the value of slave labor and give
the Free-Soilers an irresistible strength in the territories.[35] In the
North, Know-Nothingism was a major opportunity for Free-Soilers;
as Greeley saw: "Know-Nothingism is but the outworking of an idea.
It is but one of the many forms of protest against the corruptions of
party politics, and especially against the deep treachery of the leaders
of the Nebraska party to the vital principles of Democracy."[36]

Most successful in seizing the Know-Nothings for free-soil purposes
was Henry Wilson of Massachusetts, who late in 1854 was sent to the
Senate as its representative. It was indicative of the yeasty nature of
the political scene that Wilson should have hoped that the Know-
Nothing party in the South might help create southern dough-faces,
more strongly attached to the Union than to slavery.[37] Nothing came
of this dream, and in the North nativism succumbed to sectionalism.
In Illinois, Nebraska and anti-Nebraska politicians joined the Know-
Nothings as distinctive elements, and upbraided one another for being
bigots. Both sought support from "loyal" Americans, whether born
abroad or not. In Ohio, Chase won the governorship in a tense race,
during which he represented the Know-Nothings while also appealing
for the votes of the German-Americans.[38] In California, too, the essential infirmity of the American platform was shown in its meteoric
rise in 1856 and its equally meteoric disappearance the following year.
Nativism was impractical, in the long run, in a land where political
parties needed the votes of the foreign-born and the Catholics.[39]

[35] W. Darrell Overdyke, *The Know-Nothing Party in the South* (Baton
Rouge, 1950), pp. 198 ff. Concentrations of Catholics in the South were only
in Maryland and Louisiana, and represented no reasonable threat to southern
ways; for the distribution of Know-Nothing votes in the South, however, see
maps in Billington, *The Protestant Crusade*, pp. 400–401. Moreover, immigrants did threaten Whig home rule in such cities as New Orleans, and as such
excited prejudice and political discrimination.

[36] Iseley, *Horace Greeley and the Republican Party*, pp. 112–113.

[37] Wilson, *Rise and Fall of the Slave Power in America*, II, 420–423.

[38] Arthur C. Cole, *The Era of the Civil War* (Springfield, Illinois, 1919), p.
138.

[39] Peyton Hurt, "The Rise and Fall of the 'Know Nothings' in California,"
Qu. of the California Hist. Soc., IX (1930), 16–49, 99–128.

Henry Wilson forced the slavery issue upon the Know-Nothings. At their June 1855 meeting, he faced a proslavery majority and held his position despite physical threats. Following acceptance of the majority report, he convened the northern faction of the American party, issued an "Appeal to the People," and left the nativist ranks. With him went a majority of the antislavery lodges. An attempt to form a Know-Something party, advocating nativism, temperance, and antislavery, failed. Exulted the Boston *Pilot,* a Catholic publication: "Sam[40] has lived too fast. He has lived a hundred years in one. He is already old, crazy and tottering. He has to lean on a black, wooly headed staff. He is a little, worn-out, weazened, stunted, dried-up, helpless, toothless, brainless, heartless, soulless, miserable, malignant dwarf."[41] Wilson had served sectionalism at least as much as he had antislavery.

The Republican party rested on firmer ground.[42] Significantly, it first flung out its banner in the Northwest, where social roots were less deep, politicians less committed. With a Whig machine disintegrated and a proslavery Democratic machine in operation, the movement toward a new party followed immediately after the passage of the Kansas-Nebraska Act. The Northwest had its quota of proslavery partisans.[43] There were aggressively matched pro- and antislavery forces in Iowa. But economics, as well as sentiment, combined to incapacitate proslavery in Illinois, Michigan, Wisconsin, and Minnesota.[44] Illinois had the most rugged group of abolitionists in such veterans as Ichabod Codding, Zebina Eastman, and Owen Lovejoy,

[40] "Sam" was the original brand of nativism, which was distinguished from "Jonathan," the more distinctly antislavery though not necessarily abolitionist version.

[41] Cited in Billington, *Protestant Crusade,* p. 427. See also Julian, *Political Recollections,* p. 143, which regrets Wilson's efforts, in his *Rise and Fall of the Slave Power,* to "white wash [Know-Nothingism] into respectability."

[42] Henry Wilson, *Rise and Fall of the Slave Power in America,* "Origin of the Republican Party," II, 406 ff.; Hoar, *Autobiography,* I, 131 ff., for a more personal view.

[43] Barnhart, "The Southern Element in the Leadership of the Old Northwest," *JSH,* I (1933), 186–197; W. O. Lynch, "Anti-Slavery Tendencies of the Democratic Party in the Northwest, 1848–50," *MVHR,* XI (1924), 319–331; Louis Pelzer, "The Negro and Slavery in Early Iowa," *Iowa Jour. of Hist. and Pol.,* II (1904), 471–484; J[ohn] E. B[riggs]., "The Convention of 1844," *Palimpsest,* XV (1934), 106–113.

[44] Avery Craven, *The Coming of the Civil War* (New York, 1942), pp. 303 ff.

among others, and such lively organs of abolition as *The Gem of the Prairie, Western Citizen,* and, in the middle 1840's, *The Liberty Tree.* However, the effort of the Illinois abolitionists to organize politically was a failure. The popular free-soil movement of 1848 obscured their movement, and forced them to abandon what an Alton abolitionist called "the *one idea*": to associate themselves, instead, with the dominant (and not wholly friendly) conservative antislavery men. Pierce and Douglas, thought Greeley, had made more "abolitionists" in three months of Kansas politics than Garrison and Phillips would have made in half a century. What the Kansas-Nebraska Bill had made were antislavery men, antisouthern men, not abolitionists. Working from a submerged position, the abolitionists could no more than counsel their betters.[45]

Michigan, a territory until 1837, was in somewhat the same condition, though with fewer proslavery elements or abolitionist "bitter-enders." Two women ranked high in having founded an abolitionist tradition there. Elizabeth Chandler, a Quaker poet and pioneer feminist from Philadelphia, and an associate of Lundy, in a few brief years spread her gospel of abolition among settlers in Michigan. Laura S. Haviland for thirty years served the fugitive slaves, for the most part in Michigan, but also elsewhere.[46]

Nevertheless, river and harbor improvement bills were at least as influential as moral reform in heightening free soil and sectional feeling in Michigan, whose hero was, after all, Lewis Cass. Jackson County became a strong center of political abolitionism. A convention in Jackson, July 6, 1854, first adopted the name Republican: it was called by energetic organizers who included Zachariah Chandler, one of the state's wealthiest men—rich on land speculation and later famous as a manipulator of Republican patronage.[47]

[45] Arthur C. Cole, *Era of the Civil War,* pp. 218 ff.; Dillon, "The Anti-Slavery Movement in Illinois, 1809–1844" (Ph.D., University of Michigan, 1951), pp. 368 ff.; Hannah M. P. Codding, "Ichabod Codding," *Hist. Soc. of Wisconsin Proc.* (Madison, 1898), pp. 171–196; *A Memorial of Zebina Eastman by His Family* (n.p., n.d.); see also Charles W. Hunter to Z. Eastman, June 11, 1847, and Zebina Eastman Scrapbook of Clippings, Chicago Hist. Soc.

[46] Dillon, "Elizabeth Chandler and the Spread of Antislavery Sentiment to Michigan," *Michigan Hist.,* XXXIX (1955), 481–494; Laura S. Haviland, *A Woman's Life Work* (Grand Rapids, 1881).

[47] Streeter, *Political Parties in Michigan,* pp. 43 ff., 230 ff.; Kooker, "Anti-Slavery in Michigan," p. 314; Wilmer C. Harris, *Public Life of Zachariah Chandler 1851–75* (Lansing, 1917). *Zachariah Chandler: an Outline Sketch* . . . (Detroit, 1880), though eulogistic, contains useful details.

Minnesota, organized as a territory since 1849, had its proslavery and antislavery factions. Its abolitionists had been exposed to Garrison, Whittier, and Wendell Phillips in the East, and reflected their views. Conservative free soilism in the Illinois pattern held the ascendency until 1857. In that year, abolitionism in Minnesota received a valuable addition. From western Pennsylvania came Mrs. Jane Grey Swisshelm, famous as a militant abolitionist editor. She had fought a twenty-year battle for self-expression against the hindrances thrown up by a rigid, unsympathetic husband. His quality was shown in his threat to sue her for time spent in nursing her dying mother, whom he had forbidden her to visit on the grounds that it was a wasted trip. Mrs. Swisshelm had written for several antislavery and Whig newspapers in Pittsburgh. Her own family troubles had taught her the need for protecting married women's property. She had studied the law on the subject, written about it, and in the state legislative sessions of 1847 and 1848 secured the legal right of women to their own belongings. She began the Pittsburgh *Saturday Visiter* (spelled so on the authority of Doctor Samuel Johnson). It was a free-soil paper which rapidly acquired thousands of readers and was widely quoted. Mrs. Swisshelm was no idealist. She was indifferent to woman suffrage, contemptuous of drunkards, and uninterested in their reformation.

Now in 1857, legally separated from her husband but exhausted by the marital difficulties she had experienced, she moved to St. Cloud in Minnesota, above St. Paul on the Mississippi River. She there revived her newspaper as the St. Cloud *Visiter,* in the face of outraged anti-feminist, anti-abolitionist opinion. She was contemptuous of Garrisonians, and hated Indians: "red-jawed tigers," whose extermination she preached in print and on the lecture platform. Stormy quarrels culminated in the destruction of her press on March 24, 1858, but a large public meeting pledged funds for the purchase of a new press. It was extraordinary how public opinion, with its keen sense of the value of communication, rose in such crises to ensure that it was not being deprived of its choice of reading matter. On May 13, her paper, renamed the St. Cloud *Democrat,* resumed publication, and in it Mrs. Swisshelm continued her sharp criticism of compromisers and Republicans alike.[48]

[48] Jane G. Swisshelm, *Half a Century* (Chicago, 1880), *passim;* Arthur J. Larsen (ed.), *Crusader and Feminist: Letters of Jane Grey Swisshelm, 1858–1865* (St. Paul, 1934), Introduction, pp. 1–32; Lester B. Shippee, "Jane Grey

Wisconsin, which had entered statehood in 1848, assumed leadership in the movement to link antislavery with political action. The state was less notorious than any other in the Northwest for anti-Negro laws, though a legend that there had been no slavery in the state does not survive examination.[49] In 1849, its legislature passed resolutions opposing the entrance of new slave states into the Union and asked the repeal of slavery in the District of Columbia and elsewhere.[50]

Part of the credit for Wisconsin's record was due to a vibrant group of abolitionists, part to the familiar economic interests which offered no impediment to the most extreme abolitionist attitudes. Part of it was due to free-soil organization and strength which made almost all Wisconsin papers sympathetic to the Wilmot Proviso. The state had been inspired, in 1843, to defy Illinois during a quarrel over landholdings, in her own antislavery version of squatter sovereignty.[51]

There was an abolitionist party in Wisconsin as early as 1840, an antislavery newspaper as early as 1843. Sherman M. Booth ranked above his abolitionist coworkers in energy and persistence. He was author of the Buffalo Platform of 1848, though he had attended that meeting with misgivings. He took the Compromise of 1850 hard, and

---

Swisshelm: Agitator," *MVHR,* VII (1920), 206–227; S. J. Fisher, "Reminiscences of Jane Grey Swisshelm," *Western Pennsylvania Hist. Mag.,* IV (1921), 165–174; Frank Klement, "The Abolition Movement in Minnesota," *Minnesota Hist.,* XXXII (1951), 15–33, and "Jane Grey Swisshelm and Lincoln: a Feminist Fusses and Frets," *Abraham Lincoln Qu.,* VI (1950), 233–234.

[49] John N. Davidson, "Negro Slavery in Wisconsin," *Proc. of the State Hist. Soc. of Wisconsin* (Madison, 1893), pp. 82–86; Raymond V. Phelan, "Slavery in the Old Northwest," *ibid.* (Madison, 1906), pp. 252–264.

[50] C[hauncey] C. Olin, "A History of the Early Anti Slavery Excitement in the State of Wisconsin from 1842 to 1860," WHRS MS.; Olin edited the antislavery *American Freeman.* See also *Resolutions of the Wisconsin Legislature, on the Subject of Slavery; with the Speech of Samuel D. Hastings, in the Assembly, Madison, January 27, 1849* (New York, 1849); Chas. E. Dyer to ?, January 25, 1883, Chicago Hist. Soc. MS.

[51] The Samuel D. Hastings Papers, 1838–1872, Wisconsin Hist. Soc., throw light on a former merchant and secretary of the Union Anti-Slavery Society of Philadelphia, who became a merchant, banker, real-estate dealer in Wisconsin, and ardent abolitionist. See also the papers of Dr. Moses M. Davis, whose business activities also did not interfere with his dedicated antislavery labors. For a general study, Aaron M. Boom, "The Development of Sectional Attitudes in Wisconsin, 1848–1861" (Ph. D., University of Chicago, 1948); cf. Theodore C. Smith, "The Free Soil Party in Wisconsin," *Proc. State Soc. of Wisconsin* (Madison, 1894), pp. 97–162, and Albert H. Sanford, "State Sovereignty in Wisconsin," *AHA Annual Report, 1891* (Washington, 1892), pp. 177 ff.

asked questions of Chase which suggested the need, to his mind, of desperate remedies.[52]

On March 9, 1854, Joshua Glover, a fugitive slave from Missouri who worked at a sawmill four miles from Racine, was seized and jailed in Milwaukee. He had probably been betrayed by another Negro. The news came quickly to Racine, from which a committee raced to Milwaukee. Booth, then editor of the *Free Democrat*, rode a horse through the streets, crying: "Freemen! To the rescue! Slave-catchers are in our midst! Be at the court-house at two o'clock!" Glover was forcibly released and hurried away. Booth was arrested on a United States warrant and applied for a writ of habeas corpus, not from the federal court, but from the state supreme court. Armed with the argument of concurrent rights of states—which, in effect, gave the state equal jurisdiction with the federal government—he sought and received the agreement of the state judiciary.[53]

Booth was fined and imprisoned by Federal authorities, but forcibly delivered. Sympathizers protected him from the pursuing officers. Meanwhile, his case dragged on in the courts. Late in 1858, Taney delivered an opinion overthrowing the Wisconsin decision, which had been obeyed as law for five years. Wisconsin now thrust itself to the forefront as the South Carolina of the North. Indeed, Carl Schurz, leader of the powerful German element in Wisconsin, refugees of 1848 and antislavery in feeling, cited Calhoun in support of nullification.[54] Wisconsin citizens defied government agents who sought to seize Booth, though his arrest on a morals charge dampened some of the enthusiasm for his cause.[55] He was finally imprisoned. In 1861, Booth's

[52] Sherman M. Booth to Chase, July 5, 1850, Chase Papers, LC; Warren, *History of the Supreme Court*, II, 320 ff.; Kate E. Levi, "The Wisconsin Press and Slavery," *Wisconsin Mag. of Hist.*, IX (1926), 423 ff.; Joseph Schaefer, "Stormy Days in Court—the Booth Case," *ibid.*, XX (1936), 89 ff.

[53] Vroman Mason, "The Fugitive Slave Law in Wisconsin, with Reference to Nullification Sentiment," *Proc. State Hist. Soc. of Wisconsin* (Madison, Wis., 1895), pp. 117–144; Sanford, "State Sovereignty in Wisconsin," pp. 177 ff.

[54] Ernest Bruncken, "The Political Activity of Wisconsin Germans, 1854–60," *Proc. State Hist. Soc. of Wisconsin* (Madison, 1902), pp. 190–211; cf. James L. Sellers, "Republicanism and States Rights in Wisconsin," *MVHR*, XVII (1930), 213–229. The conservative side of German-American republicanism is observed in Joseph Schafer, "Who Elected Lincoln?" *AHR*, XLVII (1941), 51–63; the Germans and Irish largely supported Douglas—the votes for Lincoln came from native stock. See also Carl Wittke, *Refugees of Revolution* (Philadelphia, 1952); for a general view, A. E. Zucker (ed.), *The Forty-Eighters . . .* (New York, 1950).

[55] George W. Carter, "The Booth War in Ripon," *Proc. State Hist. Soc. of*

fine was remitted by outgoing President Buchanan, who, in one of the last acts of an administration which had been propitiating southern nullifiers as a whole, dropped all charges against the Wisconsin rebel. The case had done its work in mustering civil defiance of law. The constitutional argument created and refined by abolitionists, that law supporting slavery need not be obeyed, was about to be taken over by the antislavery North. Here were no Garrisonian disunionists but responsible citizens of a northern state, who appealed to every precedent, including the Kentucky and Virginia Resolutions of 1798, Jefferson's war on the Supreme Court, and Virginia's somewhat similar action of 1814, and whose senator, an old Barnburner, cried: "What, sir! hold that an enactment of Congress can confer an authority upon anybody which the Constitution itself, the source of all authority, forbids?"[56]

With free-soil sensibilities rampant, the Kansas struggle came to a head. Kansas was a practical problem in national politics, as well as in homesteading and real-estate opportunities. After 1854, Horace Greeley and his *Tribune* would give the subject no rest. Congress would be constantly agitated over developments in the territory. Railroad entrepreneurs and speculators would work ceaselessly to advance their personal and corporative interests.[57] The essential problem was one of settlement and votes. It appeared that proslavery must triumph. As Greeley bitterly charged: "The pretense of Douglas & Co. that not even Kansas is to be made a slave state by his bill is a gag of the first water. Ask any Missourian what he thinks about it. The Kansas Territory . . . is bounded in its entire length by Missouri, with a whole tier of slave counties leaning against it. Won't be a slave state! . . . Gentlemen! Don't lie any more!"[58]

The opening of Kansas to settlement brought to that frontier every type of homesteader and every shade of political opinion. In the last

---

Wisconsin (Madison, 1903), pp. 161–172; Boom, "Development of Sectional Attitudes in Wisconsin," p. 204.

[56] *Speech of Hon. J. R. Doolittle, of Wisconsin. In the United States Senate, February 24, 1860* (Washington, 1860), p. 4.

[57] *34th Congress, 1st Session. House of Representatives. Report No. 200. Report of the Special Committee Appointed to Investigate the Troubles in Kansas; with the Views of the Minority of Said Committee* (Washington, 1856); Paul W. Gates, *Fifty Million Acres: Conflicts over Kansas Land Policy, 1854–1890* (Ithaca, 1954), pp. 3–4 and *passim;* Nevins, *Ordeal of the Union,* II, 301 ff., 412 ff.

[58] Quoted in William H. Hale, *Horace Greeley, Voice of the People* (New York, 1950), p. 160.

analysis, it was the unaffiliated settler who cast the deciding vote. It was indicative of the essential weakness of the southern program that it was unable—despite natural advantages of priority of settlement, sympathetic neighbors, and a unified viewpoint—to deliver Kansas to the southern column.[59]

The Free State settlers were unified by the New England Emigrant Aid Company (or Society, as it was better known). Its major aim was profit. Abolitionists it "shunned as though they had been lepers." As Amos A. Lawrence, its capitalist sponsor, testified:

The money paid in for subscriptions of stock, about $95,000, and the donations, about $4,000 was received by me, as treasurer, and has been disbursed by me, under the direction of the executive committee. No part of it has been expended for sending out emigrants, nor for any purpose except those made known to the public, viz[.]: the establishment of saw mills, taverns, a printing press, for exploring the Territory, &c. No money has been spent for fire arms. The stock of the company has not been an object of speculation, though some persons think it will be profitable. Some prefer to give money without taking stock. The pecuniary advantage derived by the emigrants has been a reduction of fare of about fifteen per cent. . . .[60]

Nevertheless, the Kansas Emigrant Aid Society became a stormy petrel of congressional debate. It did attract such Free-Soilers as Dr. Samuel G. Howe, Thomas W. Higginson, and Edward Everett Hale. It did raise a cry for volunteers to rescue Kansas which brought out many more than the 1,300 it officially claimed. It inspired a National Kansas Committee and a Union Emigrant Society, the latter mainly composed of members of Congress. But its true character was best seen in the work of its chief promoter, Eli Thayer.

He was born the son of a Massachusetts farmer, worked his way through Brown University, and became principal of a school in

---

[59] William O. Lynch, "Population Movements in Relation to the Struggle for Kansas," *Indiana U. Studies,* XII (1925), 381–404; and "Popular Sovereignty and the Colonization of Kansas from 1854 to 1860," *MVHA Proc., 1917–1918,* IX (1919), 380–392. *Report of the Special Committee Appointed to Investigate the Troubles in Kansas . . .* is, among other things, a compendium of pioneer experiences and views.

[60] *Report of the Special Committee . . . ,* p. 874. See also Samuel A. Johnson, *The Battle Cry of Freedom: the New England Emigrant Aid Company in the Kansas Crusade* (Lawrence, 1954), p. 31; Harlow, *Gerrit Smith,* pp. 334 ff.; William H. Carruth, "The New England Emigrant Aid Company as an Investment Society," *Trans. of the Kansas State Hist. Soc., 1897–1900 . . .* (Topeka, 1900), pp. 90 ff.

Worcester. In 1853 and 1854 he served in the state legislature. The idea of a peaceful invasion of freemen to combat slavery inspired him, and he dropped all other work. Thayer favored squatter sovereignty, but intended that it should serve free soil. He became, for a brief period, a symbol of free-soil enterprise, and not only in Kansas but everywhere; and was praised by Amos Lawrence, and also by Theodore Parker, who endorsed Thayer's plans for colonizing Central America:

> We can't prevent the spread of an industrious, thoughtful, and enterprising people into the domains of an idle, heedless, and unprogressive people, but can prevent the fitting out of hordes of pirates [i.e., filibusters].
> Immigration from the Free States to Kansas, to Virginia, to Central America, is a most important thing.[61]

In 1857, Thayer became a representative in Congress, where he continued his campaign for free soil, accepting the "anti-Negro party" as the natural buffer between proslavery and antislavery factions. He himself established a colony of 3,000 acres in Western Virginia, which received the approval of none other than the state's governor, Henry A. Wise.[62]

Thayer later bitterly upbraided the Garrisonians for their role in the antislavery struggle. Logically, he should have had no reason to notice them, since they were supposed to have been inconsequential, and their "impotence," their "blasphemies," their "irresponsibility" should have made it unnecessary for him to give them any attention.[63] Instead, he gave them almost all of it. For he could not but be aware that they were attracting a major part of posterity's regard in the North, and he himself close to none. This paradox, which he sought unsuccessfully to fathom, was even truer of John Brown, who was out of tune with the leading interests of the 1850's, but who survived with Garrison as the most famous of all abolitionist figures.

The case against Brown has been spelled out in detail. He had no extended career in abolition; he was a businessman and a farmer, who was a marked failure in ventures which took him all over the country

---

[61] *Letters from Theodore Parker to Eli Thayer* (broadsides). These were evidently printed by Thayer for promotion purposes.

[62] *Six Speeches with a Sketch of the Life of Eli Thayer* (Boston, 1860); Eaton, *Freedom of Thought in the Old South* (Durham, 1940), pp. 180–181, 239–240.

[63] Eli Thayer, *A History of the Kansas Crusade: Its Friends and Its Foes* (New York, 1889).

and to England. He may have come to Kansas, late in 1855, not primarily to ensure its freedom, but as a homesteader. He was in no way central to the transactions of that disturbed territory. Part of his fame derived from the confusion of eastern correspondents, among others, who identified him with other Browns, including Orville E. Brown, the original "Ossawatomie" Brown.[64] John Brown's most notable action in Kansas was the brutal one at Pottawatomie, in May 1856: the apparently senseless murder of five proslavery men by his small band, one of the victims twenty years old. The repeated and embroidered justifications for the wanton deed—Brown's anger over Border Ruffian outrages, his grief over the derangement of a son, allegedly because he had been abused by proslavery partisans, among more fanciful conjectures—appear to have no foundation. Brown's victims were connected with the district court, which might have been about to try him and his few followers as outlaws for their Border War activities.

Brown may have been made famous by eastern newspapers; yet, by common standards, his ceaseless movements and plans for freeing slaves were neither effective nor carefully worked out. Responsible society should logically have repudiated his dangerous activities, if only because there was woven into them evidence of temper and impetuosity which could be ascribed to the strain of insanity in his family.

Brown was not only a poor businessman; he was not too scrupulous a businessman. Nor was he too scrupulous an abolitionist. In June 1855, while on his way to Kansas, he appeared at the Radical Abolitionist Convention, in Syracuse, which represented the fragmented hopes of Lewis Tappan, Gerrit Smith, Goodell, Frederick Douglass, and a few others.[65] Brown asked money of them for what could be rationalized as defensive measures in Kansas, but which could readily spill over into civil war—an activity some of the Radical Abolitionists theoretically opposed. Brown received $60 from them. Thereafter, he received numerous sums for expenses in defending the free-soil cause in Kansas, and for services to Negroes. He never presented an accounting for contributions received, and much of them he obviously used for personal living and other expenses.

Responsible society had aims in common with Brown which it was

---

[64] James C. Malin, *John Brown and the Legend of Fifty-Six* (Philadelphia, 1942), pp. 307–308.

[65] Harlow, *Gerrit Smith*, 340–341; Quarles, *Douglass*, 154 ff.; *Proceedings of Convention of Radical Political Abolitionists* (Syracuse, 1855).

impotent to advance. It was limited by its own caution and entangled in webs of self-interest. It lacked daring and inspiration. All the criticisms of Brown were true, but they were irrelevant to the purposes he served. Thus Brown was no major factor in Kansas hostilities, but he was peculiarly pertinent to them. Kansas was a pawn in the battle being waged between North and South, and the triumph of the John Brown legend was a victory of the North over the South. Free Soil needed a hero, and Brown provided it with one.

There were numerous others willing to symbolize the Kansas struggle, including Thayer. There were courageous men who carried the Sharps rifles, or "Beecher's Bibles"—a term which was itself a milestone in the lengthening, and not well-earned, reputation for radicalism of that pampered preacher. None offered so rounded a variety of Brown's indubitable qualities: harshness, Puritan simplicity, genuine devoutness, dedication to the abolitionist creed, and, in addition, a will toward deeds. As Brown later wrote, with his remarkable sense for words: "It has been my deliberate judgment since 1855 that the most ready and effectual way to retrieve Kansas would be to meddle with the peculiar institution."[66] However obscurely Brown may have viewed tanning, farming, land speculations, surveying, sheep-raising, cattle, and even breeding race horses, there can be no doubt of the white light through which he viewed slavery, with the resourcefulness of the rebellious slave himself. In offering advice to Negroes engaged in outwitting slave catchers, following the passage of the Fugitive Slave Act, Brown wrote:

After effecting a rescue, if you are assailed go into the houses of your most prominent and influential white friends with your wives; and that will effectually fasten upon them the suspicion of being connected with you, and will compel them to make common cause with you, whether they would otherwise live up to their professions or not. This would leave them no choice in the matter.[67]

He utilized this strategy in his own work. His thinking was that of a desperate man, rather than the mere lawbreaker he seemed to his foes. His qualities won him the regard and admiration of Emerson and Thoreau, Theodore Parker and Gerrit Smith, Dr. Howe, Frederick

[66] Oswald G. Villard, *John Brown, 1800–1859: a Biography Fifty Years After* (London, 1910), p. 93.
[67] Franklin B. Sanborn, *The Life and Letters of John Brown* (Boston, 1885), p. 125.

Douglass, and numerous others.[68] That his plans were arbitrary and impractical was beside the point; what Brown was working toward was outside the law. He had gone far beyond the most drastic fugitive-slave rescuers. He meant to carry the war to the South.

There was no justification for the Pottawatomie atrocity which could be defended in candid debate. Brown's sympathizers could extricate him from it only by distorting the facts, and sentimentalizing the circumstances:

> Then he grasped his trusty rifle and boldly fought for freedom;
>   Smote from border unto border the fierce, invading band;
> And he and his brave boys vowed—so might Heaven help and
>   speed 'em!—
>   They would save these grand old prairies from the curse
>   that blights the land;
>   And Old Brown
>   Ossawatomie Brown,
> Said, "Boys, the Lord will aid us!" and he shoved his ramrod down.[69]

Brown himself was of easy conscience. His ultimate perception—that slavery was itself murder—took him out of the category of those who continued to appeal to northern conscience and to urge a moral revolution. Brown represented revolution itself. Yet he could walk the northern streets boldly and solicit aid for purposes which were recognizably subversive, but which he was not called upon explicitly to declare. His success was a measure of how much social radicalism responsible groups in the North were willing to condone after 1854, though not yet to countenance. Kansas gave Brown his career. In the following years, the North permitted him to further his aims and to vie for support with such others in abolition and free soil as Garrison, Wade, and Lincoln.

If the gathering crisis shook the supports of society, it also created

[68] Particularly instructive is Quarles, *Douglass*, pp. 169 ff. Brown attracted the respect of Richard Henry Dana in 1849, when Brown was relatively unknown and living in the wild Adirondacks on part of the land donated by Gerrit Smith, primarily to white settlers. North Elba struck Dana as being a Negro community; Brown had chosen it as a homestead because of its hospitality to Negroes. Dana, on vacation, came upon his "humble, hospitable door," learned that he was "a strong abolitionist and a kind of king" among the Negroes, and was struck by his "grave, serious . . . countenance and . . . dignity which is unconscious, and comes from a superior habit of mind"; Adams, *Dana*, I, 155 ff.

[69] *The Poems of Edmund Clarence Stedman* (Boston, 1908 ed.), p. 3.

opportunities for essential conservatives. Anti-Nebraska parties had, indeed, swept the North in the fall elections of 1854, and had a majority in the House of Representatives: a fact which, among other things, ended hopes for implementing the Ostend Manifesto. Douglas defied them: "The allied forces of abolitionism, Whiggism, and Know-Nothingism have by stratagem attained a partial victory over the Democratic party," he conceded. "Responsibilities and spoils," however, he believed, must soon force them to fall to pieces.[70] For nine weeks, from December 1855 to February 1856, the House of Representatives in the Capital was unable to elect a Speaker. Anti-Nebraska men were in the majority, but included so many variations of politician that they could not agree on a candidate. For a while, the House resembled an armed camp, in which southern patriots, Know-Nothings, and several species of Free-Soiler milled about in vengeful confusion. When, finally, the northern representatives obtained their Speaker, they were hailed and denounced for their achievement. Alexander H. Stephens of Georgia condemned it as a sectional victory—the first where the Speakership was at stake. But victory salutes were fired from Maine to Illinois, and organization of the Republican party hastened. Even the *Liberator* marked the occasion as a triumph for freedom.

Yet the quality of the new Speaker, Nathaniel P. Banks, was inadequately probed. He helped indicate how deep the chasm between North and South had become. The South had nothing to fear from him. This Massachusetts politician had opposed the Wilmot Proviso, and favored the Compromise of 1850. He had declared for Pierce as a "New England President, who was a true exponent of New England principles." True, he had also declared against the Kansas-Nebraska Bill, but this was only thanks to the unequivocal views of his constituency, and he had labored for moderation on the issue in practice. His most famous pronouncement, that he made no fetish of the Union but was willing to "let it slide" under certain circumstances, had been a meaningless concession to local feeling. Banks as Speaker labored to persuade Southerners and northern conservatives that he had meant nothing at all by his celebrated phrase.[71]

Banks reflected northern uncertainty, its unwillingness to force crises

[70] Andrew W. Crandall, *The Early History of the Republican Party, 1854–1856* (Boston, 1930), p. 25.

[71] Fred H. Harrington, *Fighting Politician: Major General N. P. Banks* (Philadelphia, 1948), *passim*.

upon the country. Charles Sumner seemed cut out of Massachusetts rock: a living immortal who, as late as 1877, three years following his death, would be hailed as having lived a great life, whose works, in nine volumes, left the "moral impression of a most unique character."[72] The contrast between Sumner and Banks was presumably complete. It pitted a reformer against a trimmer, a scholar and idealist against a political opportunist. Sumner had learned his abolitionism from the *Liberator,* his social goals from the Boston reformers and literary figures. Travel had broadened him, and intensive reading evidently deepened him. Yet Sumner had already passed his prime as a figure capable of growth and maturity when, in 1851, the coalition put him in the Senate. His Boston Independence Day oration of 1845 had developed, in ornate and glittering phrases, his view of peace as representing "The True Grandeur of Nations." His denunciation, in 1848, of the "lords of the lash and the lords of the loom" had given the country a phrase. His most disinterested act had been his defense, in 1849, of the right of a Negro to attend a school for white children: a case which foreshadowed the outlawry, six years later, of segregated schools in Massachusetts.[73]

The famous Massachusetts Coalition of 1849–53, which united Democrats and Free-Soilers, put Sumner in the Senate and removed him from the byways of reformers. It put him out of touch with Negroes, whose innate inferiority he assumed. It placed him on a pedestal from which he never, in his mind, descended, but from which he commanded dubious forces. Increasingly, he represented political party relations and sectional feeling, rather than abolition. When, in 1852, he delivered his first ambitious oration in the Senate, demanding the repeal of the Compromise of 1850, he thought himself the voice of protest and action, and, in fact, was so regarded North and South. Yet it was his friends, not he, who were at that moment fighting to prevent the rendition of Thomas Sims. Giddings had fought for the right of petition and the slave trade in the District of Columbia. Hale and Slade had also acted in behalf of abolition. Sumner's contribution, in this first and highly touted phase of his political career, was the figure of speech and learned reference.

---

[72] *Atlas Essays, No. 2. Biographical and Critical* (New York, 1877), p. 202.
[73] *The Works of Charles Sumner* (Boston, 1874), I, 5 ff., II, 81, 327 ff.; for an exploration into his status, Louis Ruchames, "Charles Sumner and American Historiography," *JNH,* XXXVIII (1953), 139 ff.

When, on May 19, 1856, he rose in the Senate to discourse on "The Crime against Kansas," it appeared to his admirers that he had accomplished an imperishable work. His tirade continued for two days, involving in its aspersions the character of Stephen A. Douglas and the absent senator from South Carolina, Andrew P. Butler. On May 22, while Sumner sat at his desk in the Senate Chamber, he was approached by Butler's nephew, Representative Preston S. Brooks and, in the presence of some fifteen or eighteen persons, violently assaulted with a cane until he collapsed. Public response was entirely sectional. The southern press praised Brooks. The North was roused to horror. Echoes of the assault were heard as far as Kansas, now linked to the East by telegraph, where they may have encouraged John Brown's decision to deal as he did with his Pottawatomie foes.

In the midst of such events, the Republican party was formed and made its first campaign for the Presidency. As typical a personal decision as any that was reached was that of Hannibal Hamlin, who now left the Democratic party. He had "harmonized" with it for nine years, he observed, and been a "working" member, rather than a talking member—though he was one of the best-known campaign orators of his day. He had avoided questions which "agitated" the country. He considered the repeal of the Missouri Compromise an immoral act; hence (almost two years following passage of the bill accomplishing the act), he resigned from a position he considered he owed to the party in power.[74] It was a decision which would bring Hamlin the Republican Vice-Presidency four years after. Political figures in every section of the North were multiplying who, like Hamlin, would give the gathering Republican forces all the qualities of conservatism. In Indiana, its more fluid political elements, though opposed to the extension of slavery into the territories, were reluctant to accept the name of Republicans. One of the state's leaders, Schuyler Colfax, who was to be Grant's first Vice-President, was one among many who even conceived of Stephen A. Douglas as the proper leader of antislavery.[75]

[74] *Remarks of Mr. Hamlin, of Maine, on Resigning His Position as Chairman of the Committee on Commerce* . . . (n.p., 1856); cf. Hamlin, *Life and Times of Hannibal Hamlin*, pp. 218 ff.

[75] Willard H. Smith, *Schuyler Colfax: the Changing Fortunes of a Political Idol* (Indianapolis, 1952), pp. 91 ff.; Ovando J. Hollister, *Life of Schuyler Colfax* (New York, 1887), pp. 119 ff.; Miller, "Anti-Slavery in Indiana," p.

The need for abolitionist criticism of doubtful antislavery adherents —if the antislavery enterprise was not to sink under their weight— was evidenced by fears for the Union which inspired frantic appeals for concessions to southern demands. Most pathetic was the appeal of Charles Miner, who dedicated a pamphlet "with profound veneration and respect" to Taney and his associate justices, and pleaded for peace. The thought of a dissolution of the Union filled him with horror. The Fugitive Slave Act, and the fact that it could not be enforced, troubled him. He suffered nightmare visions of an invading foreign army, perhaps Negro regiments from the West Indies who could profit from domestic dissension and unite with disaffected Negro hordes. Miner urged the appropriation of a $100 million for "gradual but certain extinction of slavery in the Border States," and for other measures which would make for peace and the reign of law.[76]

Hence, it was anything but confused thinking for abolitionists to have kept a critical watch over the organization of the Republican party in 1856. It was too popular a movement to be guided by abolitionists; but they were able to aid in launching it, and it profited from their many criticisms and reminders of abolitionist experiences.

Gamaliel Bailey had met, on Christmas Day of 1855, with Sumner, Chase, Banks, and Preston King, a radical New York Democrat, at the Silver Spring, Maryland, estate of Francis Preston Blair in order to plan organization of the anti-Nebraska Democrats. This was among the last of Bailey's significant appearances as an abolitionist spokesman. Thereafter, although he graced high political councils, it was more as window dressing for practical-minded Republicans than as a true political force. It was the tragedy of the political abolitionists that they should have been absorbed by the antislavery extensionists,

---

260; Thornborough, *The Negro in Indiana* (Indianapolis, 1957), pp. 92 ff., 119 ff.

[76] Charles Miner, *The Olive Branch; or, the Evil and the Remedy* (Philadelphia, 1856), pp. 5 ff. An even more remarkable response to crisis was that of Joseph C. Lovejoy, brother of Elijah, and formerly an active member of the Maine Anti-Slavery Society, who had offered the funeral sermon for Torrey at Tremont Temple in Boston and memorialized him in a book. In 1859, he became fearful of Republicanism and of the harm his brother Owen might be doing in Congress by denouncing slavery. He pressed upon him all the arguments respecting the virtues of slavery, the need of Negroes for masters, and the South's rights under the Constitution; *The North and the South! Letter from J. C. Lovejoy, Esq., to His Brother, Hon. Owen Lovejoy, M. C., with Remarks by the Editor of the Washington Union* (n.p., 1859); Willey, *History of the Antislavery Cause in State and Nation, passim.*

whereas the allegedly impractical Garrisonians and other moral reformers survived as independent voices and factors in the antislavery crusade.

The first Republican organization with a national perspective was formed in Washington in January 1856, and included Daniel R. Goodloe, Bailey's assistant editor, among its members. It circularized political groups throughout the nation in behalf of a national convention. The subsequent meeting in Pittsburgh, on February 22 and 23, and the choice of Francis P. Blair as chairman, stirred Lewis Tappan to apprehension. "Think of an anti Slavery Convention being presided over by a slaveholder!" he wrote. Moreover, its platform was weaker than had been the old Buffalo Platform of 1848 or the Pittsburgh Platform of 1852. Tappan observed that it made no mention of the Fugitive Slave Act, slavery in the District of Columbia, the slave trade, or the inclusion of new slave states.[77]

It also made no mention of the belief that all men were created equal, though it was recognized as "a self-evident truth, that all men are endowed with the inalienable right of life, liberty, and the pursuit of happiness"—a distinction which raised a quarrel and caused Giddings to stride out of the assembly. "I see that I am out of place here," he remarked in passing to George William Curtis of the New York delegation.[78] Nevertheless he returned, to join a variety of others, ranging from abolitionists to fearful conservatives, for the campaign of 1856. These included Seward, who had gracefully avoided the Silver Spring meeting as being composed of Democrats; Hale, who had hoped to be the President of an abolitionized party; the Reverend John G. Fee of Kentucky, Wilmot, Banks, Colfax, among many others.

The caution of Lincoln was beyond that of the most conservative of these Republican figures. His friends and associates, Herndon and Codding, were in the Republican party at its inception in 1854; but Lincoln himself preferred merely to voice his disapproval of the repeal of the Compromise. By the end of 1854, he was still a Whig, and regarded with suspicion by the builders of the Republican alliance in Illinois. Neither Lincoln nor his associates were at Pittsburgh, nor,

---

[77] Tappan to Rev. John G. Fee, February 29, 1856, Tappan Papers, LC; see also Julian, "The First Republican National Convention," *AHR*, IV (1899), 313–322; Lewis Clephane, *Birth of the Republican Party . . . An Address . . .* (Washington, 1889), pp. 10–12.

[78] Solberg, "Joshua Giddings, Politician and Idealist," p. 4; Kirk H. Porter (comp.), *National Party Platforms* (New York, 1924), p. 48.

as late as May 24, 1856, would he attend an anti-Nebraska convention. Five days later, he had crossed the line into Republicanism and dominated a convention at Bloomington, where he delivered his famous "Lost Speech," in which he declared that Kansas must be free and endorsed a "reasonable" fugitive-slave law.[79]

Chase hoped, futilely, that he would be given the Republican nomination. As he wrote longingly to Sumner, as late as June 1856, "What about Presidential matters? Before we departed a year ago, you expressed a preference for me. . . . Our people here in Ohio appear at present to be in my favor." Cassius M. Clay was also among those who thought they had qualities which would attract nomination votes.[80] But both Republicans and Democrats were seeking a compromise candidate with minimum antislavery associations. As the greatest of the explorers of the West, the man who had done most to bring California into the Union, and a major promoter of railroad and land developments, John Charles Frémont might help turn Americans from their dangerous preoccupation with slavery. Like his father-in-law, Thomas Hart Benton, he favored slavery restriction and therefore rejected Democratic overtures. Nathaniel P. Banks was his intermediary with Republicans; and soon a variety of political figures —none of them connected with abolitionists—were furthering his candidacy.[81]

Most significant in the final result was the dying Know-Nothing party, too weak to elect their candidate Millard Fillmore, but still able to influence a substantial portion of the vote. They doubtless helped Republicans as much as they harmed them by exposing their operations in Congress, which had included the passage of a fugitive-slave law for Kansas.[82] Their contribution to the ruthlessly exploited, if false charges that Frémont was "secretly" a Catholic is more difficult to assay. Committees of churchmen were appointed to look into the charges, though rumor carried them beyond reasonable regard for

[79] Luthin, "Abraham Lincoln Becomes a Republican," *PSQ*, LIX (1944), 420 ff.; see also Anson D. Morse, "Our Two Great Parties—Their Origin and Task. II. The Republican Party," *ibid.*, VII (1892), 322–335, which perceives the genesis of the party in conservatism.

[80] Luthin, "Chase's Political Career before the Civil War," p. 526; Smiley, *Lion of Whitehall*, pp. 149 ff.

[81] Nevins, *Frémont: the West's Greatest Adventurer* (New York, 1928), II, 473 ff.; Iseley, *Horace Greeley and the Republican Party*, pp. 161 ff.

[82] *Is Millard Fillmore an Abolitionist?* (Boston, 1856), pp. 28–29.

facts. The Know-Nothing vote was decisive and defeated Frémont, though less because of his alleged Catholicism—he had himself been somewhat sympathetic to nativist tenets—than because of the sectional quality of the Republican platform. By 1860, Know-Nothingism would have become strictly sectional, and it at least helped elect Lincoln.[83]

I was a looker on during the late election [wrote Tappan]. The Republican "Platform" had no room for the slave or the free man of color; of course I could not stand upon it. It is well the party has not succeeded. It will be stronger as a minority than as a majority, constituted as it was, of recruits from all parties united by only a feeble tie. The leading Republicans begin to think so themselves. Most of the Amer. Abo. Soc. [a feeble projection of Tappan, Gerrit Smith, and their coworkers] voted for Fremont, I suppose. As the Republican party was the first large party in this country that ever arraigned itself directly against Slavery, in any form [,] they could not resist the impulse to "take hold & give a lift." Until their sentiments have pervaded the country it will be [wisest?] I think to nominate separate candidates. Their mission is to elevate the principles of citizens in the free states.[84]

Tappan believed that if the "enemies of Slavery would take higher ground" against its existence, rather than its extension, "the inhabitants of the free states would be unanimous [sic] in resolving that slavery should come to an end."[85] Tappan appears to have considered the Platform of 1856 a low point in Republican history; he was not aware that it was a high one. Five-sixths of the 1856 Platform dealt with slavery; less than one-third of the Platform of 1860 would deal

[83] The Republicans made sturdy efforts to diminish the sectional content of their doctrine, but to no great effect; see Samuel M. Smucker, *The Life of Col. John Charles Fremont and . . . Explorations and Adventures* (New York, 1856), p. 61. See also *The Fearful Issue to Be Decided in November Next . . .* (n.p., n.d.), which sought to link Frémont with Garrison, Giddings, Banks, and other "sectionalists," and George M. Weston, *Who Are Sectional?* (Washington, 1856), which saw Buchanan as the candidate of the South; also Luthin, *First Lincoln Campaign* (Cambridge, 1944), p. 222; Charles G. Hamilton, *Lincoln and the Know-Nothing Movement* (Washington, 1954), p. 20.

[84] Tappan to L. A. Chamerovzow, December 10, 1856; see also Tappan to Douglass, November 27, 1856, Tappan Papers, LC, and H. Warren to Z. Eastman, December 24, 1856, Chicago Hist. Soc.

[85] Tappan to William Slade, December 30, 1856; see also *The Kansas Struggle of 1856, in Congress and in the Presidential Campaign . . .* (New York, 1857), written perhaps by Tappan, which advocated bold abolitionist policy as a means for winning votes.

with that subject.[86] Tappan's view that the American electorate was more radical than its politicians was doubtful. Garrison was, in a sense, more realistic in disdaining politics as a mart for hucksters and maintaining his appeal to the moral sense of the northern community. Abolitionism—to say nothing of equal rights—was still a cause to be fought for and won. To this crusade, Garrison, Tappan, Giddings, and Wade, as well as Chase and Seward, had at least as much of a contribution to make as did Lincoln and the merest politicoes of the Banks stamp.

The nation could still deceive itself concerning the direction the crisis was taking. This was shown by the observations of E. L. Godkin on the election of 1856. Godkin, fresh from Great Britain and the Crimean War, was successful beyond his years, thanks to an unusual sense of order, a limiting set of free-trade principles, and a lucid pen. He had emigrated to America, but was continuing his correspondence for the London *Daily News,* for which he reported a Frémont meeting which had been attended by "excellent citizens with dirty habits." Buchanan, in his view, was unlikely to compromise his fame after having reached the summit of the Presidency. "Parties are broken to pieces, and nobody is going to make war on Mr. Buchanan." Frémont himself had declared his wish that Buchanan might make a better President than he might have done. "These signs indicate the reign of men has gone by, and the era of principles begun."[87]

Despite Buchanan's good will and sincerity (as illustrated by his decision not to run for re-election, his desire only to "serve my country, and to live in the grateful memory of my countrymen"), the actual state of politics made Godkin's comment fatuous. Buchanan was thoroughly bent on satisfying the South, which from his elevated position seemed even more deserving of regard than it had before. He sent to Kansas as governor Robert J. Walker of Mississippi, a loyal member of the Democratic party, who convinced himself that the territory could not be won for slavery; there were too many Free-Soilers, and they continued to flow into Kansas irresistibly. Walker's strategy, therefore, was to ally proslavery Democrats with free-state Democrats, and to work for the creation of slave states as political balance wheels. With the addition of new foreign territory, the pro-slavery cause should more than maintain its position; as he wrote

[86] Porter, *National Party Platforms,* pp. 47–50.
[87] Quoted in Filler, "The Early Godkin," *Historian,* XVII (1954), 56–57.

Buchanan: "Cuba! Cuba! (and Porto Rico, if possible) should be the countersign of your administration, and it will close in a blaze of glory."[88]

Yet Walker was treated as a traitor by southern leadership. Only an active proslavery program, promising an equal division of territory and equal treatment for slaveholders before the law, was acceptable to them. Slave insurrections and rumors of insurrections in 1856 no more than appeared to endorse the wisdom of their plans. It was the duty of the government, they insisted, to protect their private property, at least by repressing inciters of insurrection in the North.[89] Slavery, then, was no longer to be a "peculiar institution," peculiar to the South, but the government was to force respect for slavery in territories above 36° 30′. There were even suggestions approving expansion of slavery as a system into the North.[90] The failure of slavery defenders in Kansas only increased southern demands for redress.

Hence Buchanan struck what was one of two major blows at the unity of his party. A proslavery convention of settlers had met at Lecompton, in Kansas, and, recognizing their weakness in an open election, drawn up a state constitution and set up election procedures which would have at least protected property in slaves. Buchanan, by concluding to support the Lecompton constitution, opened a chasm between himself and Douglas. In effect, he had taken a stand against the free exercise of squatter sovereignty.[91]

It was already dead, so far as law was concerned. On March 4, 1857, the Supreme Court of the United States convened in Washington and delivered a complex set of rulings, the aged Chief Justice Taney himself handing down the majority report. It not only officially struck down the Missouri Compromise, to the dismay of those northern conservatives who had held that the Compromise of 1850 had not done so, but struck down squatter sovereignty as well.[92] The case of *Dred Scott v Sandford* (a misspelling of the name of Dred Scott's

---

[88] Harmon, "President James Buchanan's Betrayal of Governor Robert J. Walker of Kansas," p. 8 [separately paged].

[89] Wish, "The Slave Insurrection Panic of 1856," *JSH*, V (1939), 206 ff., and "American Slave Insurrections before 1861," *JNH*, XXII (1937), 299 ff.

[90] Percy Roberts, "African Slavery Adapted to the North and North-west," *De Bow's Review*, XXV (1858), 378–395.

[91] Roy F. Nichols, *The Disruption of American Democracy* (New York, 1948), pp. 94 ff.; Nevins, *The Emergence of Lincoln* (New York, 1950), I, 133 ff.

[92] Cf. p. 228.

legal master, John F. A. Sanford of New York) had been in the courts for over ten years, and before the Supreme Court since 1854. Gamaliel Bailey had helped to raise the costs of appeal by a levy of $2 from each of the seventy-five Republican congressmen. The case had been ready for a decision since the court term of 1855–56, when it had been deferred in order not to influence the elections of the latter year. It was widely believed that had the anticipated decision been released before the day of election, Frémont would have become President.

It was indicative of Harriet Beecher Stowe's sense of contemporary concerns that she should have named her second antislavery novel, serialized in the *Independent* and issued before the decision was out, *Dred;* it was better than *Uncle Tom's Cabin,* though with its faults. Dred's name she had given to a symbolic figure roughly modeled on Nat Turner. The real Dred Scott was no insurrectionist; but within his civilized campaign for freedom were seeds which had found ruder fruition in Turner's insurrection. Dred Scott had been a slave of a Dr. John Emerson, a surgeon in the United States Army, who had in 1834 been transferred to Rock Island, Illinois, and then to terrain in Minnesota covered by the Missouri Compromise. Dr. Emerson's widow later transferred Dred to her brother Sanford. Dred received advice which caused him to sue for his freedom in a case which the United States Supreme Court was finally asked to pass upon. Taney could have returned Dred to slavery on the sole grounds that he was no citizen and had no standing before the Court. He preferred to go further and to declare the Missouri Compromise unconstitutional: a sweeping decision which, if enforced, would have nationalized slavery. It was a sign of changing times that their dissent from Taney's dicta should have given Associate Justices John McLean of Ohio and Benjamin R. Curtis of Massachusetts temporary status as antislavery defenders. Both had been long-time and consistent conservatives; Curtis had been attorney for the proslavery claimant in the notorious Med case.[93] They were a far cry from Spooner, Wendell Phillips, Jay, and Goodell. But the arguments of the latter were not lost on a North which now needed every argument it could muster. Although James Shepherd Pike, writing in the New York *Tribune,* declared that Taney's views merited no more regard "than any proslavery stump

[93] Weisenburger, *Life of John McLean* (Co'umbus, 1937), *passim; Case of the Slave Child, Med . . .* (Boston, 1836). For the Dred Scott decision, Commager, *Documents of American History,* I, 339–345.

speech made during the late Presidential canvass,"[94] Taney's opinion was circulated as a campaign document by the southern protagonists; Republicans, in retaliation, circulated it too, along with the minority views of McLean and Curtis, and made notorious the less defensible passages in the Chief Justice's decision. The major response in the North was moral, and this the *Independent* best expressed in linking the administration's fight against a free state, Kansas, with the Dred Scott decision. Three columns of burning commentary scarcely sufficed Dr. Cheever with which to inveigh against the government in Washington.

The South had received the legal sanction it required, but its provisions could not be enforced. They were, of course, defied by fugitive slaves and their aides; but in addition the free-soil North as a whole co-operated to turn them into dead letters. The union of abolitionist principles and antislavery politics was complete. An overwhelming preponderance of Northerners and Southerners opposed war and were eager to support compromise measures; but as the free-soil North refused to accept the dictates of the Supreme Court, so the South would refuse to accept the results of a popular election. Defiance of law was no longer the trademark of dissidents.

Many citizens wondered that a nation so amply endowed with wealth and opportunity could find itself in dangerous straits; as President Buchanan himself emphasized:

Our present financial condition is without parallel in history. No nation has ever before been embarrassed from too large a surplus in its treasury. . . . No nation in the tide of time has ever been blessed with so rich and noble an inheritance as we enjoy in the public lands. . . . We at present enjoy a free trade throughout our extensive and expanding country, such as the world has never witnessed. . . .[95]

Although the President's constituents gave more attention to their short-term discomforts than he would have preferred, these also in 1857 redounded to the benefit of the Democratic party. The panic which detonated in the summer of that year capped a period of speculation and prosperity. It created anarchy in the stock market, unem-

[94] James S. Pike, *First Blows of the Civil War* (New York, 1879), p. 370.
[95] *The Messages of President Buchanan, with an Appendix* . . . (New York, 1888), pp. 8–11.

ployment which reached a hundred thousand laborers in New York City alone. The panic appeared to show the South at its best, thanks to its "relative immunity" from the worst effects of industrial disturbance, the contrast between the "security" of the Negro slave and the predicament of the poor northern freeman. The Association for Improving the Condition of the Poor had denounced "pseudo-reformers" for asserting the "universal right to subsistence." Amasa Walker, in his role of economist rather than abolitionist, recognized the propriety of banks fending for themselves first, rather than for their depositors.[96] The Republican party, less adept at dispensing patronage and contracts than the Democrats, and not yet united behind the protective tariff, momentarily lost public confidence and votes. This happened in New York in marked degree; there the Republicans were defeated by a combination of factional differences and disagreement over financial and tariff policy.

"I look now to see matters of finance, the tariff, and so on become the leading topics in Congress," Frank Blair, Jr., concluded. Such was the eager hope of one of the foremost advocates of colonization for the Negro as a means of settling the slavery question.[97] The time had passed, however, when issues could be isolated from slavery. It did not even help men with northern principles to be sympathetic to southern problems and aspirations. Frederick Law Olmsted was not political. He was a traveler. He came of good family, had been broadened, like so many other young men of his generation, by a voyage before the mast, and had been touched by the social sympathies of his friend Charles Loring Brace. Olmsted had an orderly mind, a gift of clear vision and forthright expression. When he made his famous trips through the South, he steeled himself against prejudice and sought to understand the Southerner's point of view. A foe of immediate emancipation, he probed the economic potentialities of the South in order to try to find the equation between its social organization and its productivity.[98]

[96] Samuel Rezneck, "The Influence of Depression upon American Opinion, 1857–1859," *JEH*, II (1942), 4, 18; George W. Van Vleck, *The Panic of 1857: an Analytical Study* (New York, 1943), pp. 33, 81, and *passim*.

[97] For a major speech on this subject by the Missouri statesman in 1858, when a member of the House of Representatives, see James D. McCabe, Jr., *The Life . . . of Horatio Seymour: Together with a . . . Life of Francis P. Blair, Jr.* (New York, 1868), pp. 302 ff.

[98] Arthur M. Schlesinger, "Was Olmsted an Unbiased Critic of the South?" *JNH*, XXXVII (1952), 173–187. Olmsted's books on the subject were *A Jour-*

His desire to be helpful did not lighten his task. To Southerners, his work appeared part of the northern attack more openly maintained by such a critic as George M. Weston, formerly editor of a leading Democratic newspaper in Maine, now an active propagandist for the Republican party. Weston's program reflected the party's increasing confidence that northern industry and physical and population resources were overwhelming, that the Negro was an inconsiderable factor as well as an inferior being, and that the slave states must accept northern leadership. Weston dreamed that poor whites of the South would help him spread his gospel.[99]

Weston's arguments were not appreciated south of Mason and Dixon's line, and their influence was small. It was otherwise with Hinton Rowan Helper's *The Impending Crisis,* which in 1857 delivered a stunning blow to southern prestige among Northerners. The author was a young North Carolinian who had failed as a prospector in California and returned east. He had long brooded over the thought that slavery was the curse of the South. The Negro he despised; his feelings were all for his own people, the poor whites, male and female, who suffered from the competition, as Helper saw it, of the unfruitful slavery system.[100] All this he explained in rousing and unequivocal terms. He contrasted southern agriculture, industry, land values, and other property with those found in the North. He set southern culture and communication against that which he found enviable in the nonslave areas. Helper drew up elaborate systems of statistics to prove slavery wasteful, unprogressive, demoralizing: "Within its pestilential atmosphere, nothing succeeds; progress and

---

ney in the Seaboard Slave States (New York, 1853); A Journey Through Texas (New York, 1857); A Journey in the Back Country (New York, 1860). These were condensed and published as *The Cotton Kingdom* (New York, 1861).

[99] Weston, *Southern Slavery Reduces Northern Wages* (Washington[?] 1856); *Lands for the Landless* (n.p., n.d.); *The Poor Whites of the South* (Washington, n.d.); *The Progress of Slavery in the United States* (Washington, 1857). Cf. [Tappan] *Address to the Non-Slaveholders of the South, on the Social and Political Evils of Slavery* (New York, n.d.).

[100] The collection of Helper's pamphlets in the St. Louis Mercantile Library helps explain his purposes and the influences upon him. His own copy of the 1867 enlarged edition of *The Impending Crisis* includes the inscription "For proof that this work was *not* written in behalf of negroes,—as has been erroneously stated—but in behalf of the *whites* rather see pages [twenty-two citations follow]." See also Hugh T. Lefler, *Hinton Rowan Helper, Advocate of a "White America"* (Charlottesville, 1935), and Hugh C. Bailey, *Hinton Rowan Helper: Abolitionist-Racist* (University, Ala., 1965).

prosperity are unknown; inanition and slothfulness ensue . . . everywhere, and in everything, between Delaware Bay and the Gulf of Mexico, are the multitudinous evils of slavery apparent."[101]

Earnestness and thought had given eloquence to this self-schooled southern abolitionist. He called to his support living distinguished Southerners—among the first, Cassius M. Clay—who had declared themselves against slavery. Nothing served Helper any more than it had Olmsted or Weston. His book was proscribed in the South (it had been printed in Baltimore), and he himself was declared an outlaw. Although he appealed to self-interest and reason, he could not avoid quoting Southerners who had voiced classic condemnations of slavery as a sin. Helper was at one with the great bulk of Northerners who denounced slavery on practical grounds, but found the moral argument necessary to add the force of justice to that of debate.

Helper's program was revolutionary in its implications. In effect, poor whites were to refuse to cooperate with slaveholders; slavery would fall for lack of support. Instead, the Helper analysis failed in the South. It did not rouse the poor whites, bemused as they were with anti-Negro sentiment, and it stirred emotional rebuttal from self-designated intellectual leaders.[102]

In the North, the book began its career slowly, but became a phenomenal success. By the time of John Brown's raid on Harpers Ferry, it was a major document of the national crisis. Millions of copies circulated during the presidential election which followed, especially in the doubtful states. So pedestrian a politician as John Sherman of Ohio, brother of the later famous Civil War general, William T. Sherman, and like him of extreme conservative temper, became the center for harsh debate as candidate for Speaker of the House of Representatives. He was charged with having endorsed Helper's book, though at the time he had not read it.[103]

[101] Hinton R. Helper, *Compendium of the Impending Crisis of the South: How to Meet It* (New York, 1860 ed.), pp. 31.

[102] Saml. M. Wolfe, *Helper's Impending Crisis Dissected* (Philadelphia, 1860); see the more friendly criticisms of *The Union: Being a Condemnation of Mr. Helper's Scheme, with a Plea for the Settlement of the "Irrepressible Conflict." By One Who Has Considered Both Sides of the Question* (New York, n.d.). This work, arguing for compensated emancipation, merely quarreled over Helper's calculations. Louis Schade, *A Book for the "Impending Crisis!"* . . . (Washington, 1860), attacked Helper from a northern perspective, denouncing his interest in building up southern industry at the expense of northern commercial interests. See also Gilbert J. Beebe, *A Review and Refutation of Helper's "Impending Crisis"* (Middleton, N.Y., 1860).

[103] Winfield S. Kerr, *John Sherman: His Life and Public Services* (Boston,

Helper was an abolitionist; Sherman only opposed the extension of slavery. Both sought to abstract the Negro from solutions to northern and southern differences. Both failed to devise a peaceful solution to them, based on a division of national spoils.

1908), I, 94 ff.; cf. *The Republican Party—Its History and Policy. A Speech by Hon. John Sherman, of Ohio, Delivered at the Cooper Institute in the City of New York, April 13, 1860* (n.p., n.d.).

CHAPTER 11

Reform and Revolution

REPUBLICAN politicians were aware of their own increasing strength and eager to repudiate agitators who might frighten away potential voters. With Gamaliel Bailey, who taught them many of their attitudes, they could look forward to inevitable growth in the North.

Meanwhile a series of new free States is in process of rapid formation. MINNESOTA has now population enough for a State, and in due course, her area being 166,000 square miles, will form the basis of three states. A bill passed the House during the last Congress, for the organization of a State Government in OREGON, and will pass both Houses during the next Congress; but Oregon, too, with an area of 185,000 square miles, must hereafter be divided into three states.[1]

Bailey thought there must be eight free states on the Pacific Coast alone, and such advances did not take in Nebraska, "destined to prove the nursery of five or six free states."

While Garrisonians and such neo-Garrisonians as Higginson publicly preached disunion, Henry Wilson vigorously rejected it as a remedy, and Giddings and Charles Francis Adams held to the Union as it stood.[2] After them came a legion of others—former Whigs and Democrats, and even abolitionists—who would not so much as recognize such a gathering of disunionists, large as it was, as respectable.

[1] *Facts for the People*, I (July 1, 1855), 33–34.
[2] *Proceedings of the State Disunion Convention Held at Worcester, Massachusetts, January 15, 1857* (Boston, 1857), pp. 61 ff.

Yet the difference between Garrisonians and anti-Garrisonians was often in tone rather than in program. If the title of one of Stephen S. Foster's Garrisonian pamphlets declared that *Revolution* [was] *the Only Remedy for Slavery,* Foster said what many of his harshest critics were saying in their own fashion. Thus the *Independent,* for all its moderation, considered disunion a topic fit for discussion. In its November 6, 1856, issue it weighed the benefits of disunion and concluded that if Georgia, South Carolina, and Virginia wished to secede, they might be allowed to do so; they were neither economical nor political assets. By February 1858, the *Independent* was asking whether the Union was worth preserving, and warning that it might be better to part. Voluntary dissolution of the Union not only grew in popularity among abolitionists; it would finally become a notorious part of Greeley's program. As late as 1861, with southern secession a fact, Sumner, by then recovered from the Brooks assault, would think it possible to treat secession as inconsequential; he believed the South needed the North and would soon sue for peace and pardon. Giddings favored voluntarily ejecting the border states from the Union.[3]

But even after the Dred Scott decision, war was not clearly envisioned, and most Northerners and Southerners continued to hope it would not materialize. Northern politicians catered to their pacifistic hopes. They sought reasonable issues, minimum programs. They recognized how little separated them from their southern associates in expectations or outlook. Only extremists, they felt, abhorred or adored slavery. There was room for infinite variations in ordinary politics: for compromises on tariff issues, territorial quarrels, and treatment of fugitive slaves.[4]

[3] Thomas N. Bonner, "Horace Greeley and the Secession Movement, 1860–1861," *MVHR,* XXXVIII (1951), 425–444; Laura A. White, "Charles Sumner and the Crisis of 1860–1861," in Craven (ed.), *Essays in Honor of William E. Dodd* (Chicago, 1935), pp. 148 ff., 171. In his collected works, Sumner hid the evidence of his eccentric course, which veered from vague echoes of his old pacifist position to desperately militaristic pronouncements.

[4] As a border-state senator later observed, who opposed secession and was willing to mete out to secessionists "every punishment that can be constitutionally inflicted": "[The South] had some cause to complain of a few old women and fanatical preachers and madmen in the Northern States, who were always agitating this [slavery] question, but nine out of ten of the Northern people were sound upon the subject. . . . They were willing to accord to the slaveholder and the slave States all their constitutional rights"; "The War: Not for Emancipation or Confiscation. A Speech by Hon. Garrett Davis, of Kentucky, delivered in the U.S. Senate, January 23, 1862. Revised by the Author," in *The Pulpit and Rostrum* (New York, 1861), II, 55, 60.

Republican strategists thought they were asking for no more than a bare minimum of constitutional privilege. Yet to southern leaders little separated them from the most abandoned abolitionists. Republicans only wished to question the progress of slavery and to oppose its extension into the West. They respected state sovereignty, but felt free not to co-operate with slave catchers in their own domains. But arrant abolitionists had asked no more in their battles for the right of petition and against the Fugitive Slave Law. The abolitionists had added a moral component to the political debate which Republicans could not expunge. An inflamed southern opinion had been too long exposed to northern arguments to distinguish between Garrisonians and Republicans. The moral component had altered the shape of ordinary political argument: it had turned common differences into antagonism.

Although neutral opinion bulked large, in politics and in society, it lacked a program. The average American went his own "busy way," indeed.[5] Negro unrest and sectional feelings were facts with which the neutral citizen could not cope. Only the extremists, North and South, offered solutions to the problem of slavery.

They furnished emotional content for political expedients which otherwise had little drawing power. Thus, the Tariff of 1857 was intended, among other things, to turn the nation's attention from slavery. The tariff schedule was calculated to give eastern manufacturers and southern low-tariff advocates an economic platform in common. Protection had not yet become a Republican tenet, and the new tariff should have harmed Republican unity. Yet when the tariff issue entered into the critical elections of 1860, even when it was deliberately separated from the antislavery issue, as in Pennsylvania, it took on a sectional quality.[6]

Indicative of the changing temper in the North was the furor which the American Tract Society had to endure throughout the 1850's. In 1848 the American Sunday School Union had been subjected to attack for having dropped from its list of publications the Reverend Thomas H. Gallaudet's little tract *Jacob and His Sons*. (It had briefly deprecated the selling of Joseph into slavery.)[7] Jay, the Tappans,

---

[5] Craven, *The Repressible Conflict, 1830–1861* (Baton Rouge, 1939), p. 91.
[6] Thomas M. Pitkin, "The Tariff and the Early Republican Party" (Ph.D., Western Reserve University, 1935), pp. 14, 51–52, 212.
[7] [Tappan] *Letters respecting a Book "Dropped from the Catalogue" of the*

Bacon, and others of the *Independent* as well as of the not yet entirely defunct American and Foreign Anti-Slavery Society had taken the lead in protesting the stand of the Sunday School organization.[8]

The American Tract Society was a powerful agency which had, since 1826, issued some six hundred tracts and some three hundred books. It opposed profanity, Sabbath breaking, drink, covetousness, gaiety, novel reading, and sleeping in church. Although it strictly cut out any passages opposing slavery in its writings, it was less strict about the printing of proslavery expressions.[9]

Opposition to American Tract Society policy had resulted in the organization of the Western Tract and Book Society in 1851, with headquarters in Cincinnati. This organization, in which the Reverend John Rankin was a leading spirit, issued antislavery tracts and was a testimony against the parent body.[10] With increasing bluntness, the *Independent* assailed the American Tract Society for its sins of omission and commission. Yet the *Independent* seemed, on the other hand, as conservative as it had ever been. "Why must we have this constant agitation about slavery?" it had asked in its November 30, 1854, issue. "When shall we be permitted to enjoy a season of quiet?" However, Leonard Bacon had come a long way since he had sponsored a resolu-

---

American Sunday School Union in Compliance with the Dictates of the Slave Power (New York, 1848).

[8] The American and Foreign Anti-Slavery Society was reconstituted in 1852, its list of innovators including the Tappans, Charles Francis Adams, John Pierpont, Giddings, Fee, among others. However, it was no more than a paper organization; *An Address to the Anti-Slavery Christians of the United States* (Washington, 1852). Remnants of these moderate abolitionists reconvened into the American Abolition Society, which was little more: a small propaganda center maintained by William Goodell, its corresponding secretary, which issued a small monthly sheet. The Letterbooks of the Society are in the Oberlin College Library.

[9] "Suppose you should run away from your master, and never come back till you get old and can't do any work; do you think your master would care for you then? If you was in his place, would you not say, What do you come for now? When you was strong and could do work, you keep out; now you sick and old and can't work, you come home. Begone; I'll have nothing to do with you. Well now, if you serve the devil all the best of your days, and when you can't serve him any longer, then you come and call upon God to take you, may-be God say, Begone. . . ." *Sambo and Toney: a Dialogue Between Two Servants. Originally Published by the Late Rev. Edmund Botsford, Minister in Georgia and South Carolina. Published by the American Tract Society* (n.p., n.d.), p. 2.

[10] *Statement and Catalogue of the Western Tract and Book Society for 1866* (Cincinnati, 1866).

tion of Congregationalist ministers barring antislavery speakers from the use of the churches. A turning point was the *Independent's* article of March 1, 1855, "The Duty in Regard to Slavery," which announced that the time for equivocation had passed. The *Independent* continued to be soft-spoken in its political recommendations, but it spoke out resoundingly on the moral wrong of slavery.

Bailey's *National Era* declined in influence as northern journals assumed, in watered form, his burden of moderate political abolitionism. The *Independent,* on the other hand, attracted more and more readers for whom cautious expediency no longer sufficed. Bacon and the Tappans had once been opposed in their antislavery programs. Into the Civil War, Bacon would protest that he was no more of an abolitionist than Channing, and that he had had no fellowship with abolitionists.[11] In 1857, however, Bacon and the Tappans were at one in their stand on the American Tract Society, with Bacon in the forefront with charge and rebuttal.

Demands for an inquiry into the Society's affairs multiplied and broadened, and included heavy criticisms of the American Board of Commissioners for Foreign Missions. This agency had never given up its policy of condoning slavery among the Indians. Arthur Tappan, though limited in influence by his diminished income, was as evangelical as ever on the need for antislavery churches, and watched events intently. He cautioned against taking on too much, too soon: "I fear that an attack at this time on the Old Board [of Commissioners for Foreign Missions] would have a tendency to cool off the zeal of many against the Tract S[ociet]y. Let us carry the question with the latter first & then we can turn our united artillery against the former."[12]

As the campaign mounted, it drew increasing support. Suppressed pamphlets were published. Contributions were stopped in amounts worrisome to the Tract Society's directors. They felt constrained to reprove Bacon and the *Independent* for their agitation, and to appeal for peace. Pressure forced approval of the publication of a mildly antislavery pamphlet through the Society, "but the notes of victory were sung so loud," protested a pillar of the Society, "and . . . circulated so swiftly by those who had raised this excitement that the south was led to consider it as an Abolitionist triumph." It roused

---

[11] Bacon, *The Jugglers Detected. A Discourse* . . . (New Haven, 1861), p. 38.

[12] A. Tappan to ?, February 2, 1858. Benjamin Tappan Papers, LC.

sharp remonstrances from southern "ministers, colporters, agents, the Press, ecclesiastical bodies, and men of every name."[13] The American Tract Society, which had so long hewn the firmest line of conservatism, could no longer function within its relatively narrow range of interest.

The attack on the Society reached its height in 1858, the greatest year of revivalism since the high days of Finney's crusade. The nation had much to express, but what it wished to say was less clear. William Goodell, out of a long concern for the church as a source of social action, took a moderate view of the meaning of the revival to the antislavery cause:

It is doubtless a *mixed* affair. Some of the smaller sects are anti Slavery, though less thorough than they should be. The "revival" among them must be a revival of anti Slavery, of their type, and perhaps somewhat improved. —In the larger Sects, where there is a general preponderance of pro slavery or professedly neutral influence, the character of the "revival" would be likely to correspond. In the Slave States (except where we have Anti Slavery Missionaries, as in Kentucky & N. Carolina)—I hear of no anti slavery influence from the revivals.[14]

The year 1858 was the year, too, of the Free Convention, which drew every type of reformer who had given color to the past thirty years. Among the many speakers were Henry C. Wright, Ernestine L. Rose the suffragist, Elder Frederick W. Evans of the Shaker persuasion, Parker Pillsbury, and Andrew Jackson Davis, the spiritualist. For three days they discussed government, free trade, slavery, woman's rights, marriage, the Sabbath, land reform, immortality—often without reference to each other's arguments.[15] It was as though these rest-

---

[13] *Speeches of Chief Justice Williams, Judge Parsons and ex-Governor Ellsworth . . . at the Anniversary of the Hartford Branch of the American Tract Society* (Hartford, 1859), pp. 8 ff.; *A Review of the Official Apologies of the American Tract Society for Its Silence on the Subject of Slavery* (New York, 1856); *The Unanimous Remonstrance of the Fourth Congregational Church, Hartford, Conn., against the Policy of the American Tract Society . . .* (Hartford, 1855); *Letters to the Members, Patrons and Friends of the Branch American Tract Society* (Boston, 1858); *American Tract Society. Responsibilities of the Publishing Committee under the Constitution, February 1858* (New York, 1858); *To All Evangelical Christians. The Suppressed Tract! And the Rejected Tract! . . . Shall the Society or the Committee Rule? . . .* (New York, 1858).

[14] Goodell to John Smith, April 18, 1859, Am. Abol. Soc. Letterbooks.

[15] *Proceedings of the Free Convention Held at Rutland, Vt., June 25th, 26th, 27th, 1858* (Boston, 1858).

less perfectionists were convening for all but the last time—at least as a coherent body—before civil war made largely irrelevant their configuration of causes.

If a new radicalism was manifesting itself in church affairs, it was otherwise in politics, where a new conservatism was in the making. The Republican party had seemed to lose ground nationally during 1857. Giddings was defeated for re-election to Congress in 1858. Such signs encouraged politicians to believe that compromisers would inherit the political world. William Goodell deplored growing Republican conservatism, but maintained an unwarranted optimism about its meaning:

Some criticize me for speaking *too favorably* of the Republican Party, or for laboring to bring it to higher ground. They regard the enterprise a hopeless one & think we lose ground by encouraging the friends of liberty to look any longer in that direction. Scores of thousands who voted with that party, hesitantly, in 1856, have come to that conclusion. Hence (in part) the falling off in our N. Y. State election, of about 90 thousand votes: and nearly in the same proportion in Ohio—This last vote of the Republicans in the House for the Crittenden and Lecompton Bill will drive off many more.[16]

The abolitionists for whom Goodell spoke were poor prophets but excellent moralists, who had a capacity for influencing others. A respect for their significance was not shared by all. Stephen A. Douglas was in the van of those who believed they could advance their fortunes by unequivocally repudiating the abolitionists, and by identifying their opponents with them. Douglas believed he had a message for Southerners and for Northerners as well. He had declared himself for squatter sovereignty, but he had also decided to support the Dred Scott decision. If Douglas could persuade his northern countrymen that this did not require them to turn slave catchers, he might win the Presidency.

It was more than coincidental that his major political opponent hailed from his own state. The western states, heavily peopled with Southerners, yet committed to free tenets, held the balance of power. No state had more of a stake than Illinois in the delicate question of how best to maintain white supremacy and also freedom. The result was the Lincoln-Douglas debates, with their closely reasoned argu-

[16] Goodell to John S. Mann, May 31, 1858, Am. Abol. Soc. Letterbooks.

ments; they were regarded with an interest given to no other senatorial race.

Little, on the surface, distinguished Lincoln from his opponent. Questioned at Charleston, Illinois, in the southern part of the state, on his view of Negro-white relations, Lincoln answered:

> I am not, nor ever have been, in favor of bringing about in any way the social and political equality of the white and black races. . . . I am not nor ever have been in favor of making voters or jurors of negroes, nor of qualifying them to hold office, nor to intermarry with white people; and I will say in addition to this that there is a physical difference between the white and black races which I believe will forever forbid the two races living together on terms of social and political equality. And inasmuch as they cannot so live, while they do remain together there must be the position of superior and inferior, and I as much as any other man am in favor of having the superior position assigned to the white race.[17]

Douglas, speaking at Galesburg, was angered that Lincoln should express himself so in the southern part of the state, but in Chicago take the ground of the Declaration of Independence, which saw all men as equal. Douglas was equally annoyed that the pro-Lincoln auditors to whom he cited contradictory passages in his opponent's speeches cheered for Lincoln on both counts. It was a piece of imperception on Douglas' part which won him the senatorial race but would lose him the presidential election of 1860. For if Lincoln and his followers saw but dimly the potentialities of Negroes, they saw clearly where slavery tended. As Lincoln emphasized:

> The Judge [Douglas] tells . . . [us] that he is opposed to making any odious distinctions between free and slave states. I am altogether unaware that the Republicans are in favor of making any odious distinctions between the free and slave states. But there still is a difference, I think, between Judge Douglas and the Republicans in this. I suppose that the real difference between Judge Douglas and his friends, and the Republicans on the contrary, is that the Judge is not in favor of making any difference between slavery and liberty—that he is in favor of eradicating, of pressing out of view, the questions of preference in this country for free over slave institutions; and consequently every sentiment he utters discards the idea that there is any wrong in slavery.[18]

[17] Paul M. Angle (ed.), *Created Equal? The Complete Lincoln-Douglas Debates of 1858* (Chicago, 1958), p. 235.
[18] *Ibid.*, p. 303.

The view that slavery was wrong was the message of the new Lincoln emerging from these debates. True, he qualified it in every way, so that his version appeared to the abolitionist an empty phrase. Nevertheless, he had also taken a public position in declaring that the government could not endure permanently half-slave and half-free—a view he may have abstracted from Theodore Parker.[19] Lincoln repudiated Douglas' accusations that he planned war against the slaveholders. He was predicting, rather than demanding, he affirmed: any changes which might occur would result from democratic decisions and plans. Lincoln was responsible as well as moderate.

It was these qualities which distinguished him from Seward, whose language was more brilliant but whose substance was less sure. Lincoln offered his dictum on the nation becoming slave or free on June 16, 1858. On October 25 of that same year, in a speech at Rochester, Seward expressed himself on "the irrepressible conflict" which existed between North and South.[20] As one who had worked to sustain party harmony, Seward felt himself justified in addressing an antislavery North with a certain freedom of expression. The unexpectedly sensational success of the phrase took him aback: it was the "higher law" phenomenon over again. Seward tried to erase the effect of his argument with qualifying explanations, but managed only to exhibit his vagarious temper under stress. Sounding more radical than Lincoln, he was subject to more fickle changes of policy and dangerous theorizings. The abolitionists—including Leavitt—who preferred him to Lincoln were misled by their preference for strong phrases.

Garrison was said to have "had the gift for making every one mad —including himself."[21] Although the veteran agitator was now in good and almost reputable standing in the North, he was called in on no conferences having any material consequence. Northern leaders avoided his company. Northern capitalists (who would later be accused of having engineered the war in order to crush the South's competing agrarian economy) were frantic in their efforts to combat tendencies toward disunion. This would mean, they felt, the ruin of

[19] John Weiss, *Theodore Parker. A Lecture. Delivered in the Parker Fraternity Course, Nov. 19, 1872* (Boston, 1873), pp. 13–14.

[20] Baker (ed.), *Works of Seward*, IV, 289–302; Bancroft, *Seward*, I, 458 ff.

[21] Craven, *The Repressible Conflict*, p. 79. It also charges Garrison with having "had an unusual capacity for hating" (*idem*), an accusation which accords with no known facts, unless one equates hatred of slavery with hatred of people.

their trade and the defaulting of southern debtors, who owed them two to three hundred million dollars.[22] If abolitionist principles had any influence upon the deepening crisis, it was because they were inadvertently mingled with the purely expeditious statements which Republican spokesmen were forced to make, to distinguish themselves from northern Democrats.

The Republicans also found themselves reluctantly at one with the abolitionists who were protesting a new proslavery aggressiveness. Southern leaders were endorsing a reinforced slavery: the slave trade was not only being more boldly practiced outside the law, but its re-establishment was being demanded within the law.[23] Gamaliel Bailey wrote with moderation, rather than malice, about developments in this field: "There can be no doubt that the idea of reviving the African slave trade is gaining ground in the South. We sincerely regret this, but the fact cannot be disguised. Some two months ago, we could quote strong articles from ultra Southern journals against the traffic; but of late we have been sorry to observe with the same journals an ominous silence upon the subject, while the advocates of 'free trade in slaves' are earnest and active."[24]

Under such conditions of heightened feeling, abolitionism flung a bomb which blew the sections apart and revealed them in their stark antagonism. John Brown was not a member of any abolitionist group, but he had patronized them all. William Lloyd Garrison was saved from being inculpated in Brown's plans by his pacifist convictions; Leonard Bacon's shade of abolitionism removed him from the patterns and deeds of Brown. But Joshua Leavitt understood Brown to have rendered distinguished services in Kansas. Amos A. Lawrence, who had known Brown when the latter was in the wool business, called him the "Miles Standish of Kansas," and collected a thousand dollars for the purchase of improved land which would afford his wife a living if he should die. Thoreau, following Brown's death, wrote an eloquent "Plea for Captain John Brown," who had been his guest in Concord, and remembered him as a "man of rare common-sense and

---

[22] Arthur C. Cole, *The Irrepressible Conflict* (New York, 1934), pp. 278 ff.

[23] Wish, "Revival of the African Slave Trade in the United States, 1856–1860," *MVHR*, XXVII (1941), 569–588; W. J. Carnathan, "The Proposal to Reopen the African Slave Trade in the South, 1854–1860," *South Atlantic Qu.*, XXV (1926), 410–429; *Message on the African Slave Trade*, House Exec. Doc. No. 7, 36th Cong., 2nd Sess.

[24] *National Era*, XIII (March 10, 1859).

directness of speech, as of action; a transcendentalist above all, a man of ideas and principles."

Giddings was only one of scores of responsible abolitionists, political and otherwise, who attended the meetings at which Brown spoke, pleading for aid in prosecuting his war against proslavery Kansans. Following a raid into Missouri in the course of which a slaveholder died and a number of Negroes were freed, and as a result of which Brown was declared an outlaw, he received help in profusion. In Kansas, fleeing with his Negro charges, he was welcomed by Augustus Wattles, a noted abolitionist and writer for the *Herald of Freedom;* in Iowa, he was generously received by the Reverend Josiah Bushnell Grinnell of the famous "Iowa Band" of missionaries. Aid accompanied Brown all the way to Chicago. There Allan Pinkerton, of later·detective fame, helped raise funds and deliver the Negroes to Canada. Between lectures, public appeals for funds ("I will endeavor to make a judicious and faithful application of all such means as I may be supplied with"),[25] and innumerable business trips, Brown crisscrossed the country, receiving hospitality from every type of Northerner within the spectrum of free soil and abolition.

To be sure, there were those who met Brown who mistrusted his spirit, and none of his patrons knew of Pottawatomie, or, having heard it, credited the murders. But an astonishing number knew that he was turning over in his mind more than defensive action in Kansas, more than raids into Missouri. Frederick Douglass was Brown's earliest confidant respecting the Virginia plan, though Brown's mind wandered as far south as Louisiana in search of a suitable base of insurrection.[26] In due course, Brown was to speak freely of his plans to large numbers of Negroes, including, among the leaders, J. W. Loguen and Harriet Tubman. On one level, Brown came to Boston in 1857, introduced as a Kansas militant. There he met a committee of militants, including Theodore Parker; Higginson; Dr. Howe; George Luther Stearns, a businessman; and Frank B. Sanborn, recently out of Harvard College and afire with zeal to serve free soil. But on another level, Brown was recruiting some Negroes and a nondescript, if steadfast, group of white persons unrelated to him except for his own sons. These he intended to lead upon a revolutionary adventure.

[25] *Ibid.,* XI (March 26, 1857).
[26] August Bondi, "With John Brown in Kansas," *Trans. of the Kansas State Hist. Soc., 1903–1904 . . . Vol. VIII* (Topeka, 1904), p. 284.

Brown negotiated with an eccentric soldier of fortune, Hugh Forbes from Great Britain, who was privy to his plans. He convinced himself that Brown had mistreated him, and undertook to inform the world of the fact. Forbes even forced himself upon Senators Seward and Henry Wilson with the news. In the meantime, Brown had himself imparted his plans to Gerrit Smith, and soon the Boston enthusiasts were aware of them and raising money for Brown. A convention at Chatham in Canada, held May 8–10, 1858,· which Brown hoped would bring together his few volunteers and also his respectable sponsors, brought only the former. Implemented with elements of the Canadian Negro colony and others, they proceeded to adopt a fantastic constitution, previously drawn up by Brown, and to set up a provisional government in which they gave themselves titles appropriate to constituted nations and to boys' clubs. If the Boston Free-Soilers and Brown's odd little band had nothing else in common, they shared a mighty earnestness, which would carry the latter up to, and then through, their terrible venture.

A letter from Senator Wilson to Dr. Howe put a momentary damper upon Brown's plans in May of 1858. It underscores how lightly these highly placed citizens, neither of them a moral reformer of the Garrison stamp, lived with plans of the highest desperation:

I write to you to say that you had better talk with some few of our friends who contributed money to aid old Brown to organize and arm some force in Kansas for defense, about the policy of getting those arms out of his hands & putting them in the hands of some reliable men in that Territory. *If they should be used for other purposes, as rumor says they may be, it might be of disadvantage to the men who were induced to contribute to that very foolish movement. . . .* This is in confidence.[27]

Moderate reformers had come a long way since they had feared the "incendiary" views of Garrison. Gerrit Smith, who knew as precisely as one could what Brown planned, put it thus: "You see how it is; our dear old friend has made up his mind to this course, and cannot be turned from it. We cannot give him up to die alone; we must support him." Smith, and others, apparently believed that not having direct knowledge of Brown's movements somehow absolved them of complicity in them. Later, Smith would escape from his responsibility by temporarily losing his mind. Theodore Parker, from

[27] Villard, *John Brown*, p. 339.

Italy, spoke up boldly for Brown and insurrection. Higginson bravely stood his ground in Worcester. But Sanborn, Stearns, and Howe fled, Howe protesting his innocence in terms which were less than courageous. Frederick Douglass had better reasons than Howe for being judicious and leaving the country.[28]

Considering that Brown had been several years developing his plans, and been in touch with numerous persons, white and Negro, and received money from many of them, he had a meager number of volunteers and little to show in the way of a military program. Howe, who had been a soldier, was not asked his opinion and did not offer one. Higginson, who was to lead Negro troops in the Civil War and bear the rank of colonel, evinced no curiosity about coming events—though he committed himself to the thought that he was "always ready to invest in treason." Brown's followers, whose lives were at stake, let him plan for them. Brown's iron will alone held his enterprise together; and it is evident that the actors in it were willing to have him direct its performance. The ultimate revelation of how little resourcefulness he had to draw upon did not disillusion the generality of Northerners.[29] More surprising, it did not disillusion his direct followers, though several were in their death throes because of it, and others had the choice of defending him or repudiating him as the tragedy unfolded before the world. All seem to have appreciated that it was not Brown's military prowess which was at stake, but the validity of his intentions.

On the evening of Sunday, October 16, 1859, John Brown, Commander in Chief of the Provisional Army created by the Chatham Convention, ordered his men to arm themselves. They left a Maryland farmhouse they had inhabited since midsummer, and moved upon Harpers Ferry six miles away. Brown's band of sixteen white men and five Negroes, drawn together by their hatred of slavery, held together by Brown, were for the most part hardy individuals in their own right, and with a sense of the uniqueness of their mission.[30] As Brown's son Owen had observed one day, looking up at their Maryland hideout: "If we suceed, some day there will be a United States

---

[28] For a valuable account of Brown's relations with Smith and the New England Free-Soilers, see Harlow, *Gerrit Smith,* pp. 391 ff.

[29] "Our Kansas Cid is hard bested, but a lion to the last. I keep a hope for him yet. How so wise a soldier got into this corner I know not, but he is a true saint and miracles wait on such," Emerson, *Journals,* IX, 242.

[30] Villard, *John Brown,* 678 ff., provides short descriptions of the conspirators.

flag over this house. If we do not, it will be considered a den of land pirates and thieves."

The key to Brown's thoughts were the slaves, whom he expected to rise to the opportunity of freedom given them and so create a revolutionary situation. Brown took possession of the government arsenal in the hilly, river-bound tip of Harpers Ferry, and brought in a number of prisoners, watchmen, and others in the vicinity, including Colonel Lewis W. Washington, great-grandnephew of George Washington. The first man to die at Harpers Ferry was a free Negro, Hayward Shepherd, baggage handler at the railroad station, who failed to obey an order from one of Brown's men to halt.

In the meantime, the citizens of Harpers Ferry had been roused by the raid; and Brown helped discover its purpose by permitting a train coming through to proceed, carrying the news which ultimately brought state troops, volunteer militia (long alert to the possibilities of Negro uprisings), and government troops headed by Brevet Colonel Robert E. Lee and Lieutenant J. E. B. Stuart. Both were ordered to the scene following a conference in the White House with President Buchanan and Secretary of War John B. Floyd. Brown's raid did not lack for eminent associations.

It is unlikely that Harriet Tubman, had she succeeded in joining the expedition as she had hoped to do, would have willingly stayed hemmed in at Harpers Ferry, as Brown permitted himself to be. She was a person too direct of action, and she had a too practical sense of the need for quick gains and self-preservation. She must have realized immediately (what Brown was reluctant to admit) that the local Negroes were not only few but were unwilling to join in the insurrection. She would have spent fewer of her precious moments in refining protocol with her prisoners, and none on the breakfast which Brown ordered from the nearby hotel for forty-five persons whom he roughly estimated to be in his keep or care. Had the bridge leading to the Maryland side of the Potomac River been closed, as it soon was, she would have made off with the surviving raiders and perhaps a few prisoners for the Virginia wilds, and there lived or died.

Brown just missed death from the wounds inflicted upon him by the brave Lieutenant Israel Green, who led the final assault on the engine-house in which Brown was trapped. By chance, Green was not carrying his regulation saber. The sword he wore struck Brown's metal belt and bent, and was too light to cut Brown's head with decisive effect. Whether in either case of escape or death Brown might have lost the immortality he gained cannot be known.

What was irrevocable was the spilling of blood by insurrectionists from outside the slavery fold. Southerners had long denounced abolitionists for abusing them from the safety of the North. An abolitionist had now been found who did not respect states' rights, and who justified direct war on slaveholders. Was he one or many? Brown, carried wounded into the office of the armory paymaster, was surrounded by an assembly of inquirers. These included Lee and Stuart; Senator J. M. Mason and Governor Henry A. Wise, both of Virginia; and Congressman Clement Vallandigham of Ohio, among others. They sought to learn who it was that had sponsored Brown's foray, and to discredit his aims.

Wise was especially anxious to gain a proper perspective on the affair, and on Brown. By dint of energy, public personality, and political wit, Wise had explored his own possibilities as a national figure as far as he could. He had concluded that his career lay in Virginia. After interviewing Brown, he took the position that the captured chieftain was eminently sane: "He is a man of clear head. . . . He is cool, collected and indomitable. . . . He is a fanatic, vain and garrulous, but firm, truthful and intelligent." He added, gratuitously but significantly, "His men, too, who survive, except the free negroes with him, are like him."

That the mercurial Governor Wise could have changed the course of events in the John Brown case may be granted. He had the power to pardon or commute all sentences except those involving treason to the state: a fact which explains Brown's trial and conviction on this impossible charge—Brown was neither a resident of Virginia nor owed allegiance to it, but the prosecutor did not wholly trust Wise's discretion. But the sentiment in Virginia was not created by Wise. The John Brown raid unleashed a campaign through the South intended to cow Negroes, persuade white dissidents that their liberal aims served no good purpose, and discourage further meddling from the North. The Reverend John G. Fee was only one of many who was made an outcast from the South, and he only in part because of a rumor that he had received a box of Sharps rifles, presumably for insurrectionary purposes. Even Cassius M. Clay, who was wholly opposed to servile insurrections, was under attack in his native Kentucky. Whippings, proscriptions, expulsions, arraignments, and even hangings were the means employed to make slavery's defense the *sine qua non* of southern patriotism.[31]

Here was a political fact which prevented Governor Wise from taking advantage of the major way out of an impasse which threatened the Union: the incarceration of John Brown as a monomaniac who was not representative of public opinion. For Wise to have brought such a conclusion to the Harpers Ferry raid, he would have needed a statesmanship which he sadly lacked. Instead, he retreated to legal technicalities; Brown was sane, therefore he must hang. Above all, as he told his constituents, Brown had posed a dangerous threat to the public peace and safety:

The uppermost theme in this my last regular message must be, that our peace has been disturbed; our citizens have been imprisoned, robbed and murdered; the sanctity of their dwellings has been violated; their persons have been outraged; their property has been seized by force of arms . . . [T]he state and federal troops have been called out and been compelled to fight, at the loss of several killed and wounded, to subdue rebellion and treason, at Harpers Ferry in the county of Jefferson, within our jurisdiction.[32]

Yet Northerners of every persuasion were eager to repudiate Brown's action and to ascribe it to madness. Most judicious of his Republican critics was Abraham Lincoln in his February 27, 1860, Cooper Union Address in New York—the address which put him on the road to the Presidency. In it Lincoln vigorously denied for the Republicans any connection with Brown's thought or intentions. Lincoln had already, in earlier speeches, conceded Brown's courage and unselfishness, though "no man, north or south, can approve of violence or crime." In a speech delivered at Leavenworth on December 3, 1859, the day following Brown's execution, Lincoln acknowledged the justice of Brown's sentence, "even though he agreed with us in thinking slavery wrong," but used Brown's execution to warn that "all violence, bloodshed and treason" would be similarly handled.

Now, at Cooper Union, Lincoln summed up the matter dispassionately:

[31] *The New "Reign of Terror" in the Slaveholding States for 1859–60* (New York, 1860); William Goodell's weekly, *The Principia*, I (November 19, 1859), and following issue, records the difficulties of Clay, and especially Fee, Goodell's abolitionist associate.

[32] *Doc. No. 1. Governor's Message and Reports* . . . (Richmond, 1859), p. 3.

John Brown's effort was peculiar. It was not a slave insurrection. It was an attempt by white men to get up a revolt among slaves, in which the slaves refused to participate. In fact, it was so absurd that the slaves, with all their ignorance, saw plainly enough it could not succeed. That affair, in its philosophy, corresponds with the many attempts, related in history, at the assassination of kings and emperors. An enthusiast broods over the oppression of a people till he fancies himself commissioned by Heaven to liberate them. He ventures the attempt, which ends in little else than his own execution.[33]

But while Lincoln sought to minimize Brown and his effort, others in the North sought to apotheosize Brown as a martyr. True, it was prudent for some first to obliterate the tracks which led from Brown to his respected friends in the North, especially those associated with the Republican party. Since Brown had had free and ready access to members involved in its fortunes, it was impossible to repudiate him. Typical of the tactics employed to rationalize law and lawlessness were those used by John A. Andrew, a key Republican of Boston. Publicly, he praised Brown and his companions as martyrs. He refused to judge their actions as wise or foolish, right or wrong: "I only know that whether the enterprise was one or the other, John Brown himself is right (Applause)."[34]

Privately, Andrew was less disingenuous:

I am confident that there are some half dozen men who ought not to testify *anywhere;* and who never will, with my consent as counsel, or otherwise, do so. Not that they knew, or foreknew Harpers Ferry;—but, that their relations with Brown were such & their knowledge of his movements & intentions, as a "practical abolitionist"; aiding the escape of slaves by force,—even at the risk of armed encounter,—that they could not without personal danger say anything, nor could they be known as having those relations, without giving some color to the charge that Republicans cooperate in such movements.

Otherwise, sympathy for Brown flowed freely in the North. He himself aided it by the dignity and fortitude with which he accepted his fate, his kindly reception of friends and foes, and his succession of letters which moved the North by their eloquence and simplicity. His own contribution to the John Brown legend reached a milestone—for

[33] Basler (ed.), *Collected Works of Lincoln*, III, 502, 541.
[34] *Speeches of John A. Andrew at Hingham and Boston . . . Also the Republican Platform and Other Matters* . . . (n.p., [1860]), p. 8.

it did not end except with his resolute death—in his peroration before being sentenced:

> This Court acknowledges, too, as I suppose, the validity of the law of God. I see a book kissed, which I suppose to be the Bible, or at least the New Testament, which teaches me that all things whatsoever I would that men should do to me, I should do even so to them. It teaches me, further, to remember them that are in bonds as bound with them. I endeavored to act up to that instruction. I say I am yet too young to understand that God is any respecter of persons. I believe that to have interfered as I have done, as I have always freely admitted I have done, in behalf of His despised poor, I did no wrong, but right. Now, if it is deemed necessary that I should forfeit my life for the furtherance of the ends of justice, and mingle my blood further with the blood of my children and with the blood of millions in this slave country whose rights are disregarded by wicked, cruel, and unjust enactments, I say, let it be done. . . .

Emerson wrote of Brown, while his "fate yet hangs in suspense," that his "martyrdom, if it shall be perfected, will make the gallows as glorious as the cross." Leonard Bacon (a schoolmate of Brown's in Ohio) was so far won over as to observe that no such letter as one of Brown's had come from a condemned cell since St. Paul's to Timotheus. Cheever, too, assured his congregation that "John Brown is received of God, though outlawed by those whose very government is itself a piracy against God's government."[35]

Such sweeping endorsements of Brown by the northern intellectual leaders were no more than part of a popular excitement and sympathy which extended over the entire North. As Wendell Phillips observed, above Brown's coffin before its burial at North Elba on December 8: "How vast the change in men's hearts! Insurrection was a harsh, horrid word to millions a month ago." The tolling of bells, the funereal shrouds, the innumerable commemorative meetings added strength to Phillips' belief that history would date Virginia emancipation from Harpers Ferry: "True, the slave is still there. So, when the tempest uproots a pine on your hills, it looks green for months—a year or so. Still, it is timber, not a tree. John Brown has loosened the roots of the slave system; it only breathes,—it does not live,—hereafter."

[35] Ralph L. Rusk, *The Life of Ralph Waldo Emerson* (New York, 1949), p. 402; *The Anti-Slavery History of the John Brown Year . . .* (New York, 1861), p. 121; Cheever, *The Curse of God against Political Atheism . . .* (Boston, 1859), p. 24.

It is doubtless correct that "[a] dozen *obiter dicta* [like the Dred Scott decision] would not have spread slavery over the North, and a hundred John Browns could not have produced a general revolution among the slaves."[36] Southerners were, however, more than a combination of economic integers and political realists; as a society, they acted from spontaneous premises and expectations. Similarly, Northerners accepted shibboleths of freedom which antagonized their southern brethren. Both had been taught too much of a sense of their differences. The reformers irritated and upset what was essentially an unreal and ill-founded North and South alliance. They probed its qualities and challenged its defenders with every ingenuity of argument, on every level of dissatisfaction. Free soil was a very different thing from free speech or free men, but the reformers found common denominators which united these concepts. Southern protagonists also fought for freedom; but so rigidly circumscribed was it by the rules governing slavery as to challenge northern liberties.

The moral factor in North-South relations disrupted peaceful sectional relations. Southern religious leaders assured their fellow citizens that they were more than justified in their ways. Their northern counterparts were, contrariwise, habituated to the thinking, if not the deeds, of abolitionists. One proslavery advocate in the North bitterly summed up the religious element in abolition, though unfairly ascribing it to the established churches alone:

What has been the influence of these clerical fanatics? They have contributed to the formation of revolutionary societies, throughout the length and breadth of the land, and invited all men to join in the holy crusade. Appealing to their congregations, they have worked with honied phrase and flattering carresses [*sic*] upon the tender imaginations of women until they have learned to look upon the slaveholder as a sort of moral monstrosity. Sewing parties have been turned into abolition clubs, while little children in the Sunday schools have been taught that A. B. stands for Abolition, from books illuminated with graphic insignia of terror and oppression; with pictorial chains, handcuffs and whips, in the act of application to naked and crouching slaves. This latter remark is truer of the past than the present generation; but we see the influence around us in the millions of young men that now constitute the bulk of the republican party, who may trace their opinions upon the question of slavery to the early prejudices thus acquired.[37]

[36] Craven, *Repressible Conflict*, p. 95.
[37] E. G. de Fontaine, *American Abolitionism from 1787 to 1861 . . . originally published in the New York Herald* (New York, 1861), p. 52.

Republicans were less consistent in their attitudes than this diatribe assumed. The Republicans had, however, closed their minds to the virtues of slavery, and were willing to draw freely from the arsenal of libertarian and humanitarian thought. Southerners, outraged that Garrison and Brown had been permitted to flourish, lumped all anti-slavery advocates together. The attitude which had once linked Frémont and Garrison would ultimately join Lincoln and Garrison.[38]

Had there been no pressures upon the South, a less martial spirit might have prevailed there: hatred of the foreign slave trade, more generous policy toward slaves, a less repressive body of laws. Such circumstances would not have pointed to antislavery tendencies but to a self-confident slavery system. Abolitionists did not increase repressions in the South; they exposed its tenacious proslavery premises. John Brown represented a militant arm of the crusade Garrison had instituted thirty years before. Brown's demand for action would echo among the soldiery of the Union Army, as Garrison's demand for free speech had finally echoed in Congress.

Whether the moral crusade did more to sever the Union than the sectional issue can never be entirely known. It has been argued that "a study of the slavery controversy finally narrows down to a study of sectionalism," but even such a thesis had to conclude that the slavery issue had contained "an emotional appeal" which stirred action based on moral and social principles. As persuasive was the view that ideals, "the result of a thousand years, it may be," had dominated more practical considerations during the antislavery controversy.[39]

The demand for reforms was, in part, a demand for adjustment of conditions which no longer served their original purposes. Elizabeth Cady Stanton bewildered her father by the bitterness she displayed over her lack of privileges in society. It appeared to him that although she was not expected to compete with males for public places, her position among the rich and well-born entitled her to more privileges

[38] *Anti-Abolition Tracts.—No. 3. The Abolition Conspiracy to Destroy the Union; or, a Ten Years' Record of the "Republican" Party. The Opinions of William Lloyd Garrison . . . Abraham Lincoln . . . Gen. Nathaniel P. Banks . . . James S. Pike . . . also, The Helper Program . . . &c. &c.* (New York, 1866).

[39] Arthur Y. Lloyd, *The Slavery Controversy, 1831–1860* (Chapel Hill, 1939), pp. 268–269; Ephraim D. Adams, *The Power of Ideals in American History* (New Haven, 1913), pp. 33 ff.

than most men could boast. Mrs. Stanton gave up none of her female prerogatives in turning to journalism and public appearances; she expanded her opportunities. Her view that women were "slaves" was bluntly exposed in 1869 by Frederick Douglass, when he deserted the suffragists temporarily in order to endorse the vote for male Negroes during the fight for the Fifteenth Amendment. "When women, because they are women, are dragged from their homes and hung upon lamp-posts," he declared; "when their children are torn from their arms and their brains dashed upon the pavement . . . then they will have an urgency to obtain the ballot." And to the shouted question, "Is that not all true about black women?" Douglass retorted, "Yes, yes, yes, it is true of the black woman, but not because she is a woman but because she is black."[40]

Inasmuch, however, as Constitution, churches, and prejudice were raised to prevent the increase of justice, reformers did not hesitate to use more drastic measures. In the case of the Fugitive Slave Act, they responded either by denouncing the Constitution (which was ultimately corrected to include their point of view) or by denouncing the law as opposed to natural rights. All reformers (and revolutionists) were not equally steady in purpose and argument, and willing to accept the logic of their conclusions. But even the most irresponsible of them, as in the case of John Brown, were sustained by a social tissue of consent which gave dignity to their acts.

Reforms were not necessarily bloodless, and revolutions were not necessarily violent. Free speech in the North was won at the expense of Lovejoy's life, as well as of numerous riots; yet the right of free speech was theoretically conceded in law as in custom. The Industrial Revolution was more momentous in its results than the operation of many fanatics. Indeed, it was a major southern argument that the purpose of abolition was not to free the slaves, but to override the rights of honest agriculture and saddle the nation with industrial masters. To this extent it could be argued that the antislavery crusade was a failure, that Negroes had not attained their goal of freedom, and even that the nation was, as a whole, where it had been before the crusade had been initiated.[41]

Yet it could be held in refutation that, whatever the crusade failed to accomplish, slavery as a social system, with sanctions in law, had

[40] Foner (ed.), *Life and Writings of Frederick Douglass,* IV, 43.
[41] Craven, *Repressible Conflict,* pp. 95 ff.

been overthrown; and that to that extent the abolitionists had succeeded in their goal. True, many of the "ideals" which the reformers
continued to proclaim began to sound fatuous, in view of the patently
self-serving actions of their political friends during the Civil War and
after. But this had also been the case before the abolitionists and reformers began their struggle. Colonization had promised them great
social advances which it could not produce. Orthodox ministers who
urged them to put their faith in conformity had once been energetic
leaders in their own right. The reformers had been unable to accept
their easy rationalizations of social evils. The active and critical approach of the reformers had not brought on the millennium, but it
had changed outmoded circumstances and repressive principles.

Moderates and extremists, it is difficult to see that the abolitionist
campaign—summing up as it did the basic premises of reform—could
have triumphed without all of them. Birney, Leavitt, Douglass, Garrison, Jay, Bacon, Giddings, Sojourner Truth, Adams, Parker, the
Beechers, the Childs, Tubman, the Stantons, Weld, Lovejoy, Lundy,
the Grimkés, Phelps, Stowe, Torrey, Rankin, Swisshelm, Brown—
William Wells Brown as well as John Brown—Sumner, Wright—
Elizur and Henry—Whittier, and their innumerable coworkers and
friends: all were essential to the crusade. Even persons like La Roy
Sunderland, John A. Collins, and Joseph C. Lovejoy, who made contributions to the cause before leaving or deserting it, were necessary
to its development. Above all, it was the people who furnished their
audiences, who purchased their printed materials and signed their
petitions, who joined their societies, contributed to their support, or
helped uphold the underground railroad, who made certain the success of their cause. They wove and interwove grass roots and flower
stems of abolitionist sentiments and deeds until they covered the
northern landscape with patterns of vital design.

The abolitionists finally gave color to the far more numerous people
of the North who had had scarcely antislavery in mind, let alone
emancipation, and who actively disliked Negroes. This was dramat-
ically revealed when, on January 1, 1863, the Emancipation Proclamation went formally into effect. Even though it freed no slaves of
itself,[42] it brought to their feet numerous representatives and senators

---

[42] This famous measure freed slaves *only* where federal troops were not in
control. It specifically ruled out, county by county, those slave-tenanted areas
where federal authority existed; in other words, it failed to free slaves where

in Congress, deploring and denouncing a measure they had not fore-seen, in endorsing military measures for subduing the South.

It is difficult to assign precedence to any of the protagonists of abolition. All had strategic moments of authority. Some functioned for lengthier periods or took on greater symbolic significance. Some contributed to related aspects of reform in ways which gave greater complexity, if not importance, to their careers. What gave all their efforts consequence was their consistency and their dedication. They established standards to which others might repair or which others might seek to tear down. Thus the antislavery concert built up a power which raised it from a reform enterprise to a revolutionary movement which has not yet run its course.

slaves could actually be freed; Commager, *Documents of American History*, I, 420–421. Only the Thirteenth Amendment to the Constitution, passed December 18, 1865, following the Civil War, placed slavery tangibly outside the law. Southern states accepted this measure with relatively good grace and as a proper result of the defeat of the Confederate States of America. It was the Fourteenth and Fifteenth Amendments, protecting the rights of male Negroes as citizens and voters, which were resisted by the South. See, however, John H. Franklin, *The Emancipation Proclamation* (New York, 1963), and also United States Commission on Civil Rights, *Freedom to the Free: Century of Emancipation* (Washington, 1963).

Bibliography

Few fields in American history require more competent and co-operative guides to materials than antislavery and abolition. Studies and listings are required of manuscript and also of printed collections by students aware of unanswered questions concerning personalities and events. The field, in its present state, can be approached in terms of work suitable for general readers or for scholars. The following bibliography offers material for both. It should be noted that, for chapter listings, only *selected works* have been set down, intended to open a view of particular topics. The interested reader should turn back to the pages of the chapter which concerns him for further readings and suggestions.

I. GENERAL CATEGORIES

The following works serve all American historians: James T. Adams (ed.), *Dictionary of American History* (5 vols., New York, 1940), with an index volume; *Index to the Writings on American History, 1902–1940* (Washington, 1956); Henry P. Beers, *Bibliographies in American History. Guide to Materials for Research* (New York, 1942); Ray A. Billington, "Guides to American History Manuscript Collections in Libraries of the United States," *MVHR,* XXXVIII (1951), 467–496; and Christopher Crittenden and Doris Godard (eds., and comps.), *Historical Societies in the United States and Canada, a Handbook* (Washington, 1944). Oscar Handlin *et al., Harvard Guide to American History* (Cambridge, Mass., 1954), pp. 353–354, 361–364, and *passim,* offers one useful springboard into antislavery and abolition, and John R. Bartlett, *The Literature of the Rebellion* (Boston, 1866), though emphasizing the Civil War, includes much pertinent material among its more than six thousand items. Geraldine H. Hubbard (comp.), *A Classified Catalogue of the Collection of Anti-Slavery Propaganda in the Oberlin College Library* (n.p., 1932), though imperfect, and, vastly better, Crawford B. Lindsay, "The Cornell University Special Collection on Slavery. American Publications through 1840" (Ph.D., Cornell University, 1949), are invaluable to the student. There are at present no comparable bibliographies for other collections. The general student can profit by having available Richard B. Morris (ed.), *Encyclopedia of American History* (New York, 1953), and Henry S. Commager (ed.), *Documents of American History* (New York, 1958 ed.). A valuable series of works is *American History Told by Contemporaries,* ed. Albert B. Hart; particularly relevant are the following volumes: *National Expansion, 1783–1845* (New York, 1923) and *Welding of the Nation, 1845–1900* (New York, 1924).

GENERAL ACCOUNTS

A study of the changing prestige of antislavery and abolition movements would be enlightening. Involved in it would be the formal and informal histories of the movements. Among multiple-volumed treatments are George Bancroft, *History of the United States* (New York, 1883 ed.); John B. McMaster, *History of the People of the United States* (New York, 1883–1913); Edward Channing, *History of the United States* (New York, 1905–25); James F. Rhodes, *History of the United States, from the Compromise of 1850* (New York, 1893–1906), esp. Vol. I, and Allan Nevins, *The Ordeal of the Union* (New York, 1947), and *The Emergence of Lincoln* (New York, 1950). These works were useful for varied purposes and have not been repeated in the chapter bibliographies. Notoriously disappointing, though once highly esteemed, is Herman E. von Holst, *Constitutional and Political History of the United States* (Chicago, 1877–92), large with presumptions as well as detail. W. O. Blake, *History of Slavery and the Slave Trade, Ancient and Modern* (Columbus, 1860 ed.); Horace Greeley, *The American Conflict* (New York, 1864–66), and Henry Wilson, *History of the Rise and Fall of the Slave Power in America* (Boston, 1872–77), are all unscholarly in form, but valuable for contemporary insights. E. G. de Fontaine, *American Abolitionism, from 1787 to 1861* (New York, 1861), is a proslavery account, as is Hilary A. Herbert, *The Abolition Crusade and Its Consequences* (New York, 1912). Albert B. Hart, *Slavery and Abolition, 1831–1841* (New York, 1906), and Theodore C. Smith, *Parties and Slavery, 1850–1859* (New York, 1906), suffer from oversimplification as well as from the separation of antislavery from abolition, but still repay examination, especially for their valuable bibliographies. Living, as these authors did, somewhat closer to the events they discussed than did later scholars, they had many natural understandings of those events which were later lost to scholars infatuated with "hypotheses" at the expense of patent facts. Jesse Macy, *The Anti-Slavery Crusade* (New Haven, 1919), is brief and based on obvious sources, but it too warrants attention, thanks to its breadth and disinterestedness.

MANUSCRIPT COLLECTIONS

Materials are widely scattered and must be often traced in more nondescript collections. Thus the great Simon Gratz Collection in the Historical

Society of Pennsylvania emphasizes distinguished personalities, rather than reformers, but serves both categories. The antislavery collections at the Boston Public Library include the basic papers of William Lloyd Garrison, and also letters of the Westons, Amos A. Phelps, Samuel J. May, Jr., cousin of the more famous Samuel J. May but an industrious abolitionist in his own right, and important miscellaneous papers; see Janet Wilson, "The Early Anti-Slavery Propaganda," *More Books,* XIX (1944), 343–360. The Garrison collection was used in [Wendell P. and Francis J. Garrison] *William Lloyd Garrison, the Story of His Life Told by His Children, 1805–1879* (New York, 1885–89). It is debatable whether published or unpublished Garrison materials merit most urgent review; the Garrison *Life* has been inadequately used, in recent decades, and, as one student said of the Garrison papers, "Rarely have papers been so much examined to so little purpose."

Much more can be said of the Weld-Grimké and James G. Birney papers in the Clements Library of the University of Michigan and the Birney Collection in the Library of Congress. Gilbert H. Barnes and Dwight L. Dumond (eds.), *Letters of Theodore Dwight Weld, Angelina Grimké Weld and Sarah Grimké, 1822–1844* (New York, 1934), and Dumond (ed.), *Letters of James Gillespie Birney, 1831–1857* (New York, 1938), exploit them to excellent purpose. See also Betty Fladeland, *James Gillespie Birney . . .* (Ithaca, 1955). Even more important are the inadequately used papers of Lewis Tappan, Salmon P. Chase, and Elizur Wright, Jr., among others, in the Library of Congress. The Gerrit Smith Papers can be invitingly approached through the *Calendar of the Gerrit Smith Papers in the Syracuse University Library . . . Prepared by the Historical Records Survey . . .* (Albany, 1941–42). The two volumes contain errors, and deal with no more than some 2,000 out of 40,000 available items, but almost by themselves overcome many clichés on the subject. Among other repositories, the following offered manuscript materials of direct value: the Western Reserve Historical Society; the Chicago Historical Society; the New York libraries, especially the New York Public Library and the New-York Historical Society Library; the Houghton Library at Harvard University; and the Ohio State Museum. Of special interest was the volume of antislavery papers in the Samuel D. Porter Papers at the University of Rochester, Porter being one of the unassimilated antislavery figures. The entire Porter collection wants intensive study; see University of Rochester Library, *Fortnightly Bulletin,* XXIII (January 27, 1945). The William Henry Seward Papers at the same institution, though one of the great collections in American history, have not been given due attention. Jane H. Pease, "William Henry Seward and Slavery, 1801–1861" (M.A., University of Rochester, 1957), is based on study of the collection. The McKim Papers, Cornell University, have also been brought to bear on aspects of the subject, as have been the Samuel D. Hastings and other papers at the Wisconsin Historical Society.

THE PAMPHLET LITERATURE

As important as manuscript materials is the pamphlet literature on abolition and reform. The present writer made his first large thrust into it by working his way through the Bancroft Collection at Columbia University. Since then, and including the Bancroft materials, he has examined some half a million pamphlets during the nineteen years of his researches. He supplemented his findings through collections at the Library of Congress, Oberlin College, the St. Louis Mercantile Library, the Library Company of Philadelphia, the American Philosophical Society, the Historical Society of Pennsylvania, the Samuel J. May Collection at Cornell University, and many others. Even the smaller, unindexed collection at Swarthmore College contained rare pamphlets which lit up corners of developments remarkable for their strength and continuity. The Seward Collection of pamphlets at the University of Rochester is peculiarly valuable because (like Seward's personal contacts) it is so catholic in its approach, ranging from canal building to abolitionism. Pamphlets were central to the Era of Reform: the "gocarts" of ideas. They were issued by organizations, reprinted by thousands out of the *Congressional Record,* published directly from type used in newspaper columns. Individuals published them at their own expense. Debates were continued from pamphlet to pamphlet. Reformers maintained pamphlet collections for ready reference. Samuel J. May, Jr., *Catalogue of Anti-Slavery Publications in America* (New York, 1864), focuses narrowly on abolitionist literature, but is an introduction to the subject. Why pamphlets were strategic to reform, as compared to magazines for the later muckraking period, deserves separate consideration.

UNPUBLISHED THESES

There is important work to be done in bringing together the findings in masters' and doctoral theses. Too often they suffer from lack of awareness of other dissertations, or from simple incompetence. Taken together, however, they embody much pioneer labor and accomplishment. They need to be supplemented by other theses which bring to light important careers in reform now unfortunately in the shadows. Modern listings are included in *Doctoral Dissertations Accepted by American Universities* (New York, 1934–55). These overlap with the more valuable *Microfilm Abstracts* (Ann Arbor, 1938–51), which became *Dissertation Abstracts* (Ann Arbor, 1952–). Many lesser works repay examination. Hildegarde F. Graf, "Abolition and Anti-Slavery in Buffalo and Erie County" (M.A., University of Buffalo, 1939), says as much as some larger-scaled works.

Among the more strategic unpublished theses—many others are noted in the text—are Lulu M. Johnson, "The Problem of Slavery in the Old Northwest, 1787–1858" (Ph.D., State University of Iowa, 1941); Florence Robinson, "Reform Movements of the Thirties and Forties" (Ph.D., University of Wisconsin, 1925); Frank W. Crow, "The Age of Promise: Societies for Social and Economic Improvement in the United States, 1783–1815" (Ph.D., University of Wisconsin, 1952); William R. Leslie, "The Fugitive Slave Clause, 1787–1842 . . ." (Ph.D., University of Michigan, 1945); Emma Lou Thornbrough, "Negro Slavery in the North. Its Legal and Constitutional Aspects" (Ph.D., University of Michigan, 1946); Margaret L. Plunkett, "A History of the Liberty Party with Emphasis upon Its Activities in the Northeastern States" (Ph.D., Cornell University, 1930); Aaron M. Boom, "The Development of Sectional Attitudes in Wisconsin, 1848–1861" (Ph.D., University of Chicago, 1948); Alto L. Whitehurst, "Martin Van Buren and the Free Soil Movement" (Ph.D., University of Chicago, 1932); Frank L. Byrne, "Neal Dow and the Prohibition Movement" (Ph.D., University of Wisconsin, 1957); Joel Goldfarb, "The Life of Gamaliel Bailey, Prior to the Founding of the *National Era* . . ." (Ph.D., University of California at Los Angeles, 1958); Willis Boyd, "Negro Colonization in the National Crisis, 1860–1870" (University of California at Los Angeles, 1953).

NEWSPAPERS

Such unpretentious items, of which there are too few, as Walter J. Ellis, "Editorial Attitude of the *Onondaga Standard* on Slavery from 1829–1848" (M.A., Syracuse University, 1942), are helpful and suggestive. Joseph A. Del Porto, "A Study of American Anti-Slavery Journals" (Ph.D., Michigan State College, 1953), contains useful survey materials, but is limited by taking the *Liberator* as its "central point of reference." The *Liberator* (1831–65) was indeed a pivot of reform and abolition, but the *National Era* (1847–60) was as indispensable. Benjamin Lundy's *Genius of Universal Emancipation* (1821–38) was a factor in, as well as a precursor of, the reform period. The *Emancipator* (1833–50), the *African Repository* (1825 ff.), and the *Philanthropist* (1836–47) all played individual roles. The British *Anti-Slavery Reporter* (1825 ff.), in several permutations of names and programs, reflects American developments. The *Independent* (1848 ff.) is unequaled for reflecting the transition from abolitionism to free soil. There are numerous specialized publications. *The Hangman,* begun in 1845 by Charles Spear in Boston, opposed capital punishment; it became *The Prisoner's Friend* the following year. *The Lily* (1841–56), Amelia C. Bloomer's famous journal, supported woman's rights and other reforms. Of particular interest are Negro newspapers; see *Negro Newspapers on Microfilm* (Washington, 1953). Horace Greeley's New York *Tribune,* begun in 1841, was not consistently antislavery in tone until antislavery became the northern program. However, it reflected northern sentiments and was cordial to temperance, peace, woman's rights, and other reforms which had their own presses but profited from recognition by so influential a journal.

OFFICIAL DOCUMENTS AND REPORTS

The Annals of Congress (1789–1824) and *The Register of Debates in Congress* (1825–1837), the latter overlapping with *The Congressional Globe* (1834 ff.), are mines of sectional and national discussion on the subject. As important are the legislative records in the states, which plot the changing relations in the North from divisiveness to antislavery unity. They also reveal the political aspects of temperance, peace (as in northern attitudes toward the Mexican War), and other reforms. The official reports and proceedings of the American Anti-Slavery Society, the American and Foreign Anti-Slavery Society, the British and Foreign Anti-Slavery Society, and the state and city societies have been studied for trends in membership, issues, variations in program, and other topics of reform.

FOREIGN TRAVELERS

Of special interest are accounts of the United States by foreign travelers during the Era of Reform. Americans solicited foreign sympathy for their several points of view and showed sensitivity to the opinions and impressions of visitors from abroad. These in turn, though they often brought prejudices and presumptions with them, also often contributed fresh views of American ways and controversies. Their scope and variety are surveyed in Henry S. Commager (ed.), *America in Perspective: the United States through Foreign Eyes* (New York, 1947); see also Henry T. Tuckerman, *America and Her Commentators* (New York, 1864). Of marked significance to the antislavery crusade was British opinion; antislavery was, however, but one theme among many which concerned most influential and representative British travelers; see Allan Nevins (ed.), *America through British Eyes* (New York, 1948 ed.), and also Jane L. Mesick, *The English Traveller in America, 1785–1835* (New York, 1922). Frank Monaghan, *French Travellers in the United States, 1876–1932* (New York, 1933), is purely bibliographical. One of the most famous and influential of all books resulting from visits to the United States is Alexis de Tocqueville, *Democracy in America* (New York, 1945 ed.), originally issued in two parts in 1835 and 1840. For a definitive account of this visit, see George W. Pierson, *Tocqueville and Beaumont in America* (New York, 1938), which is an analysis of the book as well as an account of the tour. Tocqueville's companion, Gustave de Beaumont, did not write an analysis of American society but a novel about America as he had found it, and emphasized that feature, slavery, which was but a facet of Tocqueville's work; see Beaumont's *Marie, or Slavery in the United States* (Stanford, 1958). Of the works which make up the vast literature on foreign travelers, and especially their views on slavery and antislavery, outstanding for their detail are Harriet Martineau's *Society in America* (London, 1837) and *Retrospect of Western Travel* (New York, 1838). Miss Martineau was an antislavery sympathizer as well as a noted scribe and observer; see Vera Wheatley, *The Life and Work of Harriet Martineau* (Fair Lawn, N.J., 1957). Charles Dickens, *American Notes* (London, 1842), continues to merit careful reading for the author's reactions to slavery and related topics. Also of continuing interest are Frances Trollope, *Domestic Manners of the Americans* (New

York, 1927 ed.), originally published in 1832, and Captain Frederick Marryat, *Diary in America with Remarks on Its Institutions* (London, 1839), both vigorous and individual writings. Frances Anne Kemble, *Journal of a Residence on a Georgia Plantation in 1838–39* (New York, 1863), was issued too late to influence opinion during the Reform Era proper, but aids understanding of it. Of special value to the antislavery cause were works by two Quakers, the first a conservative, the second a radical, but both dedicated to reform: Joseph J. Gurney, *A Journey in North America* (Norwich, Eng., 1841), and Joseph Sturge, *A Visit to the United States in 1841* (Boston, 1842).

BIOGRAPHIES

The numerous writings overlap to permit one to discern the most subtle variations in social and personal developments. For best results, they need to be studied in the light of major assumptions in the field. Thus Elizur Wright became the foe of Garrison during the Reform Era, but Wright's biography of Myron Holley (listed in the bibliography for Chapter 4) reveals the author in a more benign mood toward the Boston agitator.

Of general use is Allen Johnson and Dumas Malone (eds.), *Dictionary of American Biography* (20 vols., New York, 1928–36). For worthies who failed to rate inclusion in this dictionary, but who are of importance to antislavery and abolition, the student should also consult James G. Wilson and John Fiske (eds.), *Appleton's Cyclopaedia of American Biography* (New York, 1888–89). Also helpful are works by Edward H. O'Neill, *A History of American Biography, 1800–1935* (Philadelphia, 1935), and *Biography by Americans, 1658–1936: a Subject Bibliography* (Philadelphia, 1939). Marion Dargan, *Guide to American Biography Part II—1815–1933* (Albuquerque, 1952), pp. 141–217, though selective, is useful.

Notable biographies relevant to antislavery and abolition are distributed through the separate chapter bibliographies. By and large, they are noted in chapters dealing with their subjects at strategic points in their careers.

There is need for further work in this field. Thus, Bayard Tuckerman, *William Jay and the Constitutional Movement for the Abolition of Slavery* (New York, 1894), is a faithful work, but inadequate. Lewis Tappan, *The Life of Arthur Tappan* (New York, 1870), is a primary document, but suffices neither for Arthur nor Lewis. The Tappans, including their brother Benjamin, require study as a family; seen together they help clarify relations between abolition and political abolition. Joshua Leavitt, important to both abolition and reform, has received no individualized study whatsoever. The career of Henry B. Stanton, from evangelical abolitionist to machine politician and journalist, is also uninvestigated, as is his relation to his wife E. C. Stanton. One major figure is now reviewed in M. L. Dillon, *Benjamin Lundy* . . . (Urbana, Ill., 1966). However, Charles T. Torrey, William Goodell, Amos A.

Phelps, George F. Simmons, Abby Kelley Foster, John A. Collins, Henry C. Wright, among numerous others, though influential in their own time, have been passed by and can only weakly be brought to bear on our historical appraisals. Happily, Elijah P. Lovejoy's spectacular career has received modern notice; see John Gill, *Tide without Turning: Elijah P. Lovejoy and Freedom of the Press* (Boston, 1959), and Dillon, *Elijah P. Lovejoy, Abolitionist Editor* (Urbana, Ill., 1961). It is not bold to anticipate other useful additions to the literature. Yet even so world-famous a figure as Horace Mann needs work which will bring out the dimensions of his personality and career. True, he was accorded a respectable, if partisan *Life* by his wife, Mary Mann (Boston, 1865), and a publication of his *Works* (5 vols., Boston, 1891); yet in modern times he has received nothing more than the popular treatment of Louise H. Tharp, *Until Victory: Horace Mann and Mary Peabody* (Boston, 1953). Mann's own diary is yet to be published. John Greenleaf Whittier, though famous for more than a century, and much written about, is still to be placed in antislavery perspective.

The greatest loss has been the lack of scholarly attention to white-Negro antislavery relations. Negroes and white people met at sensitive points of colonization, abolition, and political abolition proceedings.

For a survey of personalities along the spectrum of antislavery, see *The Legion of Liberty! and Force of Truth, Containing the Thoughts, Words and Deeds of Some Prominent Apostles, Champions and Martyrs . . .* (New York, 1857). See also, Louis Filler, "Slavery and Antislavery: Subjects in Search of Authors," *Ohio Hist. Qu.,* 69 (1960), pp. 179–182.

II. CHAPTER BIBLIOGRAPHIES

1. THE CHALLENGE OF SLAVERY

Slavery as an institution and as a political force is a vast topic with a full literature of its own. The major historian of slavery is Ulrich B. Phillips: for an introduction to his work, as well as a bibliography of slavery supplementing one of his own, see Introduction by Louis Filler to Phillips, *Plantation and Frontier,* Vols. 1 and 2 of John R. Commons *et al., A Documentary History of American Industrial Society* (New York, 1958 ed.). Notable additions and correctives to the findings in Phillips's work and that of other historians of slavery are contained in Kenneth R. Stampp, *The Peculiar Institution* (New York, 1956), and Herbert Aptheker, *A Documentary History of the Negro People in the United States* (New York, 1951).

Basic works in the early history of slavery include Helen T. Catterall (ed.), *Judicial Cases Concerning American Slavery and the Negro* (5 vols., Washington, 1926–37); Elizabeth Donnan, *Documents Illustrative of the History of the Slave Trade to America* (4 vols., Washington, 1930–35); and W. E. B. Du Bois, *The Suppression of the African Slave-Trade to the United States* of America, 1639–1870 (Cambridge, 1896). See also William F. Poole, *Anti-Slavery Opinions before the Year 1800* . . . (Cincinnati, 1873).

The frontier was, among other things, a problem in reform; it is explicated in Benjamin F. Wright, Jr., "Political Institutions and the Frontier," in *Sources of Culture in the Middle West*, ed. Dixon R. Fox (New York, 1934), pp. 17 ff.; Stanley Elkins and Eric McKitrick, "A Meaning for Turner's Frontier," *PSQ*, LXIX (1954), 321 ff., 565 ff.; cf. Avery Craven, "The 'Turner Theories' and the South," *JSH*, V (1939), 291–314. For the Revolutionary heritage, Herbert M. Morais, *Deism in Eighteenth Century America* (New York, 1934), and Ezra B. Chase, *Teachings of Patriots* . . . *on Slavery* (Philadelphia, 1860). Richard B. Morris, *Studies in the History of American Law* . . . (New York, 1930), develops the content of law in which reformers molded their views.

The poor whites of the South in their relation to slavery deserve extensive consideration. Helpful are Roger W. Shugg, *Origins of Class Struggle in Louisiana* (University, La., 1939); Frank L. Owsley, *Plain Folk of the Old South* (Baton Rouge, 1949); Hugh C. Bailey, *Hinton Rowan Helper, Abolitionist-Racist* (University, Ala., 1965); and Broadus Mitchell, *Frederick Law Olmsted: a Critic of the Old South* (Baltimore, 1924).

2. ABOLITION BEFORE GARRISON

For over-all views, see Mary S. Locke, *Anti-Slavery in America, 1619–1808* (Boston, 1901), and Alice D. Adams, *The Neglected Period of Anti-Slavery in America 1808–31* (Boston, 1908). Thomas E. Drake, *Quakers and Slavery in America* (New Haven, 1950), makes claims which are questioned in Herbert Aptheker, "The Quakers and Negro Slavery," in *Toward Negro Freedom* (New York, 1956), pp. 10 ff. For an alleged antislavery bastion in the South, H. M. Wagstaff (ed.), *North Carolina Manumission Society, 1816–1834* (Chapel Hill, 1934), and John S. Bassett, *Anti-Slavery Leaders in North Carolina* (Baltimore, 1898). Theodore M. Whitfield, *Slavery Agitation in Virginia, 1829–1832* (Baltimore, 1930), and J. C. Robert, *The Road from Monticello: a Study of the Virginia Debate of 1832* (Durham, 1941), describe the collapse of antislavery sentiment in that key state. See also Arthur Zilversmit, *The First Emancipation* . . . (Chicago, 1967).

Early L. Fox, *The American Colonization Society, 1817–1840* (Baltimore, 1919), continues valuable, but is superseded by P. J. Staudenraus, *The African Colonization Movement, 1816–1865* (New York, 1961).

For the Negro, a general guide is Monroe N. Work (comp.), *A Bibliography of the Negro in Africa and America* (New York, 1928). A most helpful study for general purposes is John H. Franklin, *From Slavery to Freedom: a History of American Negroes* (New York, 1947). See also Carter G. Woodson, *The Negro in Our History* (Washington, 1928), and *The Mind of the Negro* . . . (Washington, 1926); George Williams, *History of the Negro*

Race in America, 1619–1880 . . . (New York, 1883). Aptheker, *American Negro Slave Revolts* (New York, 1943), is often guided by wishful thinking, but is a storehouse of investigation. See also Thomas W. Higginson, *Travellers and Outlaws* (Boston, 1889), pp. 189 ff., and Joseph C. Carroll, *Slave Insurrections in the United States, 1800–65* (Boston, 1938). Definitive studies of free Negroes, especially in the North, are still to be attempted. See, however, for useful data and suggestions, McMaster, *History*, V, 184 ff.; Hart, *Slavery and Abolition*, 78 ff.; Bella Gross, *Clarion Call* . . . *the Negro People's Convention Movement in the United States from 1817 to 1840* (New York, 1947); Philip S. Foner (ed.), *The Life and Writings of Frederick Douglass* (New York, 1950–55).

Early white abolitionists have been accorded few ambitious treatments. Ruth A. Ketring, *Charles Osborn in the Anti-Slavery Movement* (Columbus, 1937), suggests what can be done with such figures. [Thomas Earle (comp.)] *The Life, Travels and Opinions of Benjamin Lundy* . . . (Philadelphia, 1847), though a crude compilation, gives more of a sense of Lundy's career than do the excellent essays cited in the text. William Birney, *James G. Birney and His Times* (New York, 1890), is the most important primary source in praise of the early abolitionists.

3. ABOLITIONISTS AND REFORMERS

A valuable essay in the history of American reform (it was originally issued in a limited edition in 1903) is John B. McMaster's *The Acquisition of Political, Social and Industrial Rights of Man in America* (New York, 1961), introduction by Louis Filler. Reformers in and out of the context of society may be compared in George W. Corner (ed.), *The Autobiography of Benjamin Rush* . . . (Philadelphia, 1948), and Arthur E. Bestor, Jr., *Backwoods Utopias* (Philadelphia, 1950). Arthur E. Morgan, *Nowhere Was Somewhere* (Chapel Hill, 1946), seeks to prove that the "social engineer" cannot ignore "utopias"; cf. Louis Filler, "Pilot Plants, Utopias, and Social Reform," *Community Service News,* XII (1954), 45–49.

William W. Sweet's works often relate reform to religion; for an approach to his many writings, see his *Religion in the Development of American Culture* (New York, 1952). Also helpful are Wesley M. Gewehr, *The Great Awakening in Virginia, 1740–1790* (Durham, 1930); Whitney R. Cross, *The Burned-Over District* . . . (Ithaca, 1950); Charles A. Johnson, *The Frontier Camp Meeting* . . . (Dallas, 1955); David M. Ludlum, *Social Ferment in Vermont, 1791–1850* (New York, 1939). See also Timothy L. Smith, *Revivalism and Social Reform in Mid-Nineteenth Century America* (New York, 1957), which supplements and partially corrects Gilbert H. Barnes, *The Anti-Slavery Impulse, 1830–1844* (New York, 1933), also intended to relate religion to reform. Bernard A. Weisberger, *They Gathered at the River: the Story of the Great Revivalists* . . . (Boston, 1958), is secular in its approach.

See also Charles C. Cole, Jr., *The Social Ideas of the Northern Evangelists, 1826–1860* (New York, 1954), and Wilson Smith, *Professors & Public Ethics* (Ithaca, 1956). Robert S. Fletcher, *A History of Oberlin College* (Oberlin, 1943), is an admirable study of that crossroad of reform. See also Hermann R. Muelder, *Fighters for Freedom: the History of Anti-Slavery Activities of Men and Women Associated with Knox College* (New York, 1959). Arthur A. Ekirch, Jr., *The Idea of Progress in America, 1815–1860* (New York, 1944), helps explain the reformer's outlook. E. Douglas Branch, *The Sentimental Years: 1830–1860* (New York, 1934), is a remarkable book by a remarkable author; it argues, tragically, that Americans refused to face realities, even in their best-intended crusades. See also Henry W. Farnam, *Chapters in the History of Social Legislation in the United States to 1860* (Washington, 1938); Alice F. Tyler, *Freedom's Ferment* (Minneapolis, 1944), a survey of enthusiasms, strongest in its treatment of religious movements; and Everett Webber, *Escape to Utopia* . . . (New York, 1959).

Basic to the "woman problem" are Arthur W. Calhoun, *A Social History of the American Family* . . . (Cleveland, 1918), and Elizabeth C. Stanton *et al., History of Woman Suffrage* (Rochester, 1889 ed.). The latter is a mine of useful data, but is partial to the views of Mrs. Stanton and Susan B. Anthony at the expense of others unpleasing to them; cf. Alice S. Blackwell, *Lucy Stone, Pioneer of Woman's Rights* (Boston, 1930); see also Theodore Stanton and Harriot Stanton Blatch, *Elizabeth Cady Stanton* . . . (New York, 1922), and Ida H. Harper, *The Life and Work of Susan B. Anthony* . . . (Indianapolis, 1898). The large and uncritical literature on woman's rights wants review. Helpful has been Eleanor Flexner's *Century of Struggle: the Woman's Rights Movement in the United States* (Cambridge, Mass., 1959). More work, however, will be needed to place in one perspective such disparate writings as Anna D. Hallowell (ed.), *James and Lucretia Mott, Life and Letters* (Boston, 1884); Jane Grey Swisshelm, *Half a Century* (Chicago, 1880); Laura S. Haviland, *A Woman's Life Work* (Grand Rapids, 1881); Helen B. Woodward, *The Bold Women* (New York, 1953); D. C. Bloomer, *Life and Writings of Amelia Bloomer* (Boston, 1895); Margaret F. Thorp, *Female Persuasion: Six Strong-Minded Women* (New Haven, 1949); and Yuri Suhl, *Ernestine Rose and the Battle for Human Rights* (New York, 1959). Sarah J. Hale, *Woman's Record* . . . (New York, 1870) is by an antifeminist. It contrasts suggestively with Hallie Q. Brown, *Homespun Heroines and Other Women of Distinction* (Xenia, Ohio, 1926), a book about Negro women. See also Gerda Lerner, *The Grimké Sisters from South Carolina* (Boston, 1967).

John A. Krout, *The Origins of Prohibition* (New York, 1925), gives the quintessence of a movement which proliferated writings; see also Ernest H. Cherrington *et al., Standard Encyclopedia of the Alcohol Problem* . . . (Westerville, Ohio, 1925–30). *The Reminiscences of Neal Dow. Recollec-*

tions of Eighty Years (Portland, Me., 1898), sheds light, sometimes unconsciously, on an extraordinary career. Walter M. Merrill (ed.), *Behold Me Once More: the Confessions of James Holley Garrison* (Boston, 1954), is a tragic document.

Education as reform is examined in Filler, "Main Currents in Progressivist American Education," *Hist. of Education Jour.*, VIII (1957), 33–57. It is treated in Merle Curti, *Social Ideas of American Educators* (New York, 1935), and Lawrence A. Cremin, *The American Common School: an Historical Conception* (New York, 1951). The lyceum was an instrument of education, as well as communication; see Carl Bode, *The American Lyceum: Town Meeting of the Mind* (New York, 1956). The giant figure of Horace Mann is best approached through the *Selective and Critical Bibliography of Horace Mann, Compiled by Workers of the Federal Writers Project* (Boston, 1937). See also Filler, ed., *Horace Mann on the Crisis in Education* (Yellow Springs, 1965).

The relevant literature on peace begins with William Ellery Channing and ends with Henry C. Wright and Elihu Burritt. It is treated in W. Freeman Galpin, *Pioneering for Peace: Peace Efforts to 1846* (Syracuse, 1933); Curti, *The American Peace Crusade, 1815–1860* (Durham, 1929), and *The Learned Blacksmith* (New York, 1937).

The Indian was one barometer of reform: a test of its sincerity and effectiveness. Roy H. Pearce, *The Savages of America: a Study of the Indian and the Idea of Civilization* (Baltimore, 1953), analyzes the mixed American attitudes toward the Indian; Annie H. Abel, *The American Indian as Slaveholder and Secessionist* (Cleveland, 1915), studies him in a little-known phase. Helen H. Jackson, *A Century of Dishonor* (Boston, 1885), is a classic indictment of government policy and a milestone in its reversal. Marion L. Starkey, *The Cherokee Nation* (New York, 1946), is notable as history and as presentation. Other works covering aspects of Indians and Indian affairs include Grant Foreman, *The Last Trek of the Indians* (Chicago, 1946); Ralph H. Gabriel, *The Lure of the Frontier: a Story of Race Conflict*, Vol. II in *The Pageant of America*, ed. Gabriel (New Haven, 1929); Oliver La Farge, *A Pictorial History of the American Indian* (New York, 1956); Almon W. Lauber, *Indian Slavery in Colonial Times within the Present Limits of the United States* (New York, 1913); Mabel Powers, *The Indian as Peacemaker* (New York, 1932); Paul Radin, *The Story of the American Indian* (New York, 1927); V. W. Crane, *The Southern Frontier* . . . (Durham, 1928).

Institutional reform is best approached in modern versions through its major figures, well treated in Helen E. Marshall, *Dorothea Dix: Forgotten Samaritan* (Chapel Hill, 1937), and Harold Schwartz, *Samuel Gridley Howe, Social Reformer, 1801–1876* (Cambridge, 1956). For other reforms, see Filler, "Movements to Abolish the Death Penalty in the United States," *Annals of the American Academy of Pol. and Soc. Science,* 284 (1952), pp.

124–136; Edwin T. Randall, "Imprisonment for Debt in America: Fact and Fiction," *MVHR,* XXXIX (1952), 89–102, which, however, no more than opens the subject, which wants careful and extended work; and the opposition to poverty, surveyed in Robert H. Bremner, *From the Depths* (New York, 1956), and, by a participant, in C. Loring Brace, *Gesta Christi: a History of Humane Progress under Christianity* (New York, 1882). For a comparison with mere benevolence, see Blanche D. Coll, "The Baltimore Society for the Prevention of Pauperism, 1820–1822," *AHR,* LVI (1955), 77–87. Cheap postage reform, vegetarianism, anti-Sabbatarianism, and other specialized topics are threads which run across most of the references given above. They deserve more analysis than they have received, but in works which treat of reform in general rather than antislavery and abolition in particular.

4. THE ANTISLAVERY CONCERT

A useful work for trans-Atlantic purposes is B. R. Crick and Miriam Alman, *Guide to Manuscripts Relating to America in Great Britain and Ireland* (London, 1961). Also of general interest and use here is Sir Leslie Stephen and Sir Sidney Lee, *The Dictionary of National Biography* (21 vols., London, 1921–22 ed.). For good surveys of British antislavery, see William L. Mathieson, *British Slavery and Its Abolition, 1823–1838* (London, 1926), and *Great Britain and the Slave Trade, 1839–1865* (New York, 1929). Frank J. Klingberg, *The Anti-Slavery Movement in England* (New Haven, 1926), considers itself to be "a Study in English Humanitarianism." Much more substantial is Eric Williams, *Capitalism & Slavery* (Chapel Hill, 1944), which sees the English attack on slavery in the British West Indies as essentially an attack on monopoly by shippers and manufacturers.

For studies which more specifically deal with British antislavery relations with the United States, Michael Kraus, "Slavery Reform in the 18th Century: An Aspect of Transatlantic Intellectual Cooperation," *PMHB,* LX (1936), 53 ff.; Henry B. Stanton, *Sketches of Reform and Reformers of Great Britain and Ireland* (New York, 1850 ed.), indicates the regard of Americans for their opposite numbers abroad; Rev. Thomas Price (ed.), *Slavery in America . . .* (London, 1837), illustrates the attention British accorded Americans. Abel and Klingberg (eds.), *A Side-light on Anglo-American Relations, 1839–1858* (Lancaster, 1927) was assembled out of excellent materials from British abolitionist archives. See also, Frank Thistlethwaite, *The Anglo-American Connection in the Early Nineteenth Century* (Philadelphia, 1959).

Particularly helpful to a grasp of the antislavery position are the works of William Jay and John Greenleaf Whittier, which cover broad areas of controversy and a host of protagonists. In addition, they were both famous in their own time, Jay for his famous family and polemical powers, Whittier as an antislavery journalist, poet, and commentator. Jay, *Miscellaneous Writ-*

ings on Slavery (Boston, 1853), offers entree to his position and includes several of his major works. See also his *Review of the Causes and Consequences of the Mexican War* (Boston, 1849), which integrates numerous events into an abolitionist pattern. Whittier's works are more readily accessible, but are yet to be assimilated into the lore of the Reform Era. In his collected *Works* (Boston, 1892), see especially Vol. 3, "Anti-Slavery Poems" and "Songs of Labor and Reform"; and, in Vol. 7, "The Conflict with Slavery" and "Reform Politics."

The Garrison circle deserves to be recaptured as a whole. Parker Pillsbury, *Acts of the Anti-Slavery Apostles* (Concord, N.H., 1883), is a classic exposition of the Garrisonian crusade; for Pillsbury, see Filler, "Parker Pillsbury: an Anti-Slavery Apostle," *NEQ,* XIX (1946), 315–337. Oliver Johnson, *William Lloyd Garrison and His Times* . . . (Boston, 1880), is by another of the apostles, as is Samuel J. May, *Some Recollections of the Antislavery Conflict* (Boston, 1869). The latter is the subject of Thomas J. Mumford (ed.), *Memoir of Samuel Joseph May* (Boston, 1873), and of W. Freeman Galpin, "God's Chore Boy: Samuel Joseph May" (unpublished, Syracuse University Library, n.d.), which, though lacking scholarly apparatus, is a work of scholarship. *Letters of Lydia Maria Child* (Boston, 1883) worthily introduces this remarkable woman; see also Lloyd C. Taylor, Jr., "To Make Men Free: an Interpretative Study of Lydia Maria Child" (Ph.D., Lehigh University, 1956). John Pierpont, *A Collection from the Newspaper Writings of Nathaniel P. Rogers* (Concord, N.H., 1847), serves numerous purposes. See also, Oscar Sherwin, *Wendell Phillips* (New York, 1956) and Filler, ed., *Wendell Phillips on Civil Rights and Freedom* (New York, 1965). The implications of extremism are reconsidered in Filler, "Garrison Again, and Again," *Civil War Hist.,* XI (1965), pp. 69–75.

The "moderate" abolitionists have been meagerly memorialized. William Goodell, one of them, supplied some of the materials for deeper interpretation in his *Slavery and Anti-Slavery: a History of the Great Struggle in Both Hemispheres* . . . (New York, 1852), but he emphasized struggles rather than personalities. Ralph V. Harlow, *Gerrit Smith: Philanthropist and Reformer* (New York, 1939), exploited the Gerrit Smith Papers at Syracuse University. Useful, rather than definitive, are Luther R. Marsh, *Writings and Speeches of Alvan Stewart* (New York, 1860); Henry B. Stanton, *Random Recollections* (Johnstown, N.Y., 1885); Theodore D. Bacon, *Leonard Bacon: A Statesman of the Church* (New Haven, 1931); Elizur Wright, *Myron Holley: and What He Did for Liberty and True Religion* (Boston, 1882); L. Maria Child, *Isaac T. Hopper: a True Life* (Boston, 1853); P. G. and E. Q. Wright, *Elizur Wright: Father of Life Insurance* (Chicago, 1937).

The 1830's as the "Martyr Age" are treated in Hazel C. Wolf, *On Freedom's Altar: The Martyr Complex in the Abolition Movement* (Madison, Wis., 1952). Though it drives its thesis hard, it provides a roster of abolitionist crises involving Prudence Crandall, Elijah P. Lovejoy, and Charles T. Torrey, among others. Russel B. Nye, *Fettered Freedom* (East Lansing, 1949), which emphasizes southern reactions to abolition and other reforms, sees the abolitionist crusade as one of fundamental rights, but takes some "martyrs" into its purview. See also Eliza Wigham, *The Anti-Slavery Cause in America and Its Martyrs* (London, 1863), and Lorman Ratner, *Powder Keg: Northern Opposition to the Antislavery Movement, 1831–1840* (New York, 1968).

5. The Politics of Freedom

Jacksonian "reform" needs to be winnowed from the political expediences which accompanied it. Marvin Meyers, *The Jacksonian Persuasion* (Stanford, 1957), extracts a sense of its qualities from the viewpoints of James Fenimore Cooper, Martin Van Buren, Theodore Sedgwick, William Leggett, and Robert Rantoul, Jr. The works of Leggett and Rantoul represent, along with William Cullen Bryant's, Jacksonianism in its most persuasive form. See also Joseph L. Blau (ed.), *Social Theories of Jacksonian Democracy* (New York, 1947). Horace Greeley, *Hints toward Reforms* . . . (New York, 1850), is a concentrate of Whig thinking in the field.

The best work on Jackson himself is Marquis James, *Andrew Jackson: Portrait of a President* (New York, 1937). On Arthur M. Schlesinger, Jr., *The Age of Jackson* (Boston, 1945), see Filler, "Tenets of Scientific Skepticism," *Antioch Rev.,* IX (1949), 88 ff.

John R. Commons *et al., A Documentary History of American Industrial Society* (New York, 1958 ed.), and *History of Labour in the United States* (New York, 1918), are storehouses of reform attitudes in labor ranks. They are supplemented by Philip S. Foner, *A History of the Labor Movement in the United States* (New York, 1947–55). See also Bernard Mandel, *Labor: Free and Slave* . . . (New York, 1955); also Walter E. Hugins, *Jacksonian Democracy and the Working Class* (Stanford, 1960) and Edward Pessen, *Most Uncommon Jacksonians* (Albany, 1967), for class and reform analyses. Hannah Josephson, *The Golden Threads: New England's Mill Girls and Magnates* (New York, 1949), helps clarify the role of women in the labor movement. George Henry Evans is in some ways central to the labor movement; he is yet to receive an appropriate portrait. Charles H. Wesley, *Negro Labor in the United States* (New York, 1927), is helpful but insufficient. The strategic role of colored seamen is treated in Philip M. Hamer, especially in his "Great Britain, the United States, and the Negro Seamen Acts, 1822–1848," *JSH,* I (1935), 3–28. Orestes A. Brownson, "The Laboring Classes," *Boston Qu. Rev.,* III (1840), 358 ff., 420 ff., continues to repay reading, though its limitations are not appreciated in the Brownson literature.

A sidelight on labor developments is furnished in W. S. Shepperson, *British Emigration to North America* (Minneapolis, 1957), and Clifton K. Yeardley, Jr., *Britons in American Labor* . . . *1820–1914* (Baltimore, 1957); and for related events abroad, E. L. Woodward, *The Age of Reform, 1815–1870* (Oxford, 1949 ed.), and Elie Halévy, *The Triumph of Reform, 1830–1841* (London, 1950 ed.). See also John Duffy, "Early Factory Legislation: a Neglected Aspect of British Humanitarianism," in *British Humanitarianism, Essays Honoring Frank J. Klingberg,* ed., Samuel C. McCulloch (Philadelphia, 1950), pp. 66–83; B. O. Flower, *How England Averted a Revolution by Force* (Trenton, 1903).

    Samuel F. Bemis, *John Quincy Adams and the Union* (New York, 1956), amply describes its subject's antislavery career. Of particular interest is William H. Seward, *Life of John Quincy Adams* (Auburn, 1849), as reflecting the influence of one statesman on another. The related issues of freedom of petition, freedom of the mails, and slavery in the District of Columbia are treated in W. Sherman Savage, *The Controversy over the Distribution of Abolition Literature, 1830–1860* (Washington, 1938); Mary Tremain, *Slavery in the District of Columbia* . . . (New York, 1922); Robert P. Ludlum, "The Antislavery 'Gag-Rule': History and Argument," *JNH,* XXVI (1941), 202 ff.

6. Schisms and Debates

    John H. Noyes, *History of American Socialisms* (Philadelphia, 1870), and Charles Nordhoff, *The Communistic Societies of the United States* . . . (New York, 1875), are basic studies of American enthusiasms. See also William A. Hinds, *American Communities and Cooperative Colonies* (Chicago, 1902 ed.). Gilbert Seldes, *The Stammering Century* (New York, 1928), is topheavy with Freudian interpretations. For Noyes, see Robert A. Parker, *A Yankee Saint* . . . (New York, 1935). Edward D. Andrews, *The People Called Shakers* (New York, 1953), is a definitive account of that sect.

    Typical socialistic experiments of the era are treated in Clara E. Sears (comp.), *Bronson Alcott's Fruitlands* (Boston, 1915); William S. Haywood (ed.), *History of the Hopedale Community* . . . by Adin Ballou (Lowell, Mass., 1897); John T. Codman, *Brook Farm: Historic and Personal Memoirs* (Boston, 1894). Morris Hillquit, *History of Socialism in the United States* (New York, 1910 ed.), treats them from a Marxist perspective. See also Eunice M. Schuster, *Native American Anarchism* (Northampton, 1932), and Rudolf Rocker, *Pioneers of American Freedom* (Los Angeles, 1949). A modern study is needed of Albert Brisbane, "father" of Fourierism in America; see Bestor, "Albert Brisbane: Propagandist for Socialism in the 1840's," *New York Hist.,* XXVIII (1947), 128–158. Perry Miller (ed.), *The Transcendentalists* (Boston, 1950), treats New England reform on the intellectual level. For an essay in the realities of reform, see Zoltán Haraszti, *The Idyll of Brook Farm* (Boston, n.d.).

    Spiritualism is treated in many accounts, as, for example, in Seldes, *Stam-*

mering Century, pp. 331 ff., but has received no such definitive exposition as has phrenology in John D. Davies, *Phrenology, Fad and Science: a 19th Century American Crusade* (New Haven, 1955).

For church schisms due to antislavery and related causes, see Robert L. Stanton, *The Church and the Rebellion* . . . (New York, 1864), and Willis D. Weatherford, *American Churches and the Negro: an Historical Study* . . . (Boston, 1957); also Goodell's *Slavery and Anti-Slavery.*

The disintegration of the antislavery alliance in 1840 merits separate and detailed treatment. Lerner's *The Grimké Sisters,* previously mentioned, is helpful for a study of the role played by its famous subjects. For a discussion of ultra-reformers who earned the disapproval of moderate antislavery men, see Higginson, "Eccentricities of Reformers," in *Contemporaries* (Boston, 1900), pp. 329 ff., John A. Collins, *Right and Wrong Amongst Abolitionists in the United States* (Glasgow, 1841), is a succinct statement of Garrisonianism. The anti-Garrisonian position has been pieced out by the writer from manuscript and published writings. The British antislavery movement was not similarly disturbed by the "woman question," but for its international repercussions, see *Proceedings of the General Anti-Slavery Convention* . . . (London, 1841) and Frederick B. Tolles (ed.), "Slavery and 'The Woman Question,'" *Lucretia Mott's Diary* . . . (Haverford, 1952).

7. THE RISE OF POLITICAL ABOLITIONISM

William Henry Smith, *A Political History of Slavery* (New York, 1966 ed.), offers the viewpoint of an influential partisan to political abolitionism. Theodore C. Smith, *The Liberty and Free Soil Parties in the Northwest* (New York, 1897), and Margaret L. Plunkett, "A History of the Liberty Party" (cited under unpublished theses), want redoing from a modern perspective. There is at present no fully satisfactory work about Salmon P. Chase. A. B. Hart, *Salmon Portland Chase* (Boston, 1899), and Reinhard H. Luthin, "Salmon P. Chase: Political Career before the Civil War," *MVHR,* XXIX (1943), 517–540, are dependable writings. For Sumner, see David Donald, *Charles Sumner and the Coming of the Civil War* (New York, 1960); for a short view, see Gamaliel Bradford, *Union Portraits* (Boston, 1916), pp. 231 ff. A mine of information, useful in many connections, is Edward L. Pierce, *Memoir and Letters of Charles Sumner* (4 vols., Boston and London, 1877–93).

Joshua R. Giddings has been better served; see the biography by his son-in-law, George W. Julian, *The Life of Joshua R. Giddings* (Chicago, 1892), as well as the excellent theses cited in the text. Julian himself has been pondered to good purpose by Patrick W. Riddleberger in his *George Washington Julian, Radical Republican* (Indianapolis, 1966). The subject, however, requires further study. Greatly needed are studies of William Slade of Vermont among others, as well as careful studies of the political abolitionism of such better-known figures as Horace Mann. Two helpful studies of recent date are Frank O. Gatell, *John Gorham Palfrey and the New England Conscience* (Cambridge, Mass., 1963) and Richard H. Sewell, *John P. Hale and the Politics of Abolition* (Cambridge, Mass., 1965).

For Antimasonry, the standard account is Charles McCarthy, "The Antimasonic Party: A Study of Political Anti-Masonry in the United States, 1827–1840," *AHA Annual Report, 1902* (Washington, 1903), I, 365–574. The relation between Antimasonry and abolition is yet to be fully probed. Most realistic of the biographies of the major figure produced by the movement is Richard N. Current, *Old Thad Stevens: A Study of Ambition* (Madison, Wis., 1942). Major studies of nativism are Ray A. Billington, *The Protestant Crusade, 1800–1860* (New York, 1952 ed.), which emphasizes the anti-Catholic position of nativism, and W. Darrell Overdyke, *The Know-Nothing Party in the South* (Baton Rouge, 1950), which stresses its political purposes.

8. FUGITIVE SLAVES AND POLITICIANS

Fugitive slaves are treated as a humanitarian problem—as distinguished from a constitutional one—in Wilbur H. Siebert, *The Underground Railroad from Slavery to Freedom* (New York, 1899 ed.), and William Still, *Underground Rail Road Records . . .* (Philadelphia, 1883). Marion G. McDougall, *Fugitive Slaves (1619–1865)* (Boston, 1891), is a more formal survey. The subject is best seen against the background of proslavery thought in the North, a subject yet to be fully grasped. See, for example, Howard C. Perkins, "The Defense of Slavery in the Northern Press on the Eve of the Civil War," *JSH*, IX (1943), 501 ff. A related subject, and equally obscure, is anti-Negro feeling and attitudes as a northern phenomenon; see *An Appeal to Pharaoh: the Negro Problem, and Its Radical Solution* (New York, 1889), and John D. Barnhart, *Valley of Democracy* (Bloomington, 1953).

British-American relations over slavery and connected issues in the period following British emancipation—the earlier period is treated in Chapter 4 —are examined in H. G. Soulsby, *The Right of Search and the Slave-Trade in Anglo-American Relations, 1814–1862* (Baltimore, 1933), and Ephraim D. Adams, *British Interests and Activities in Texas, 1838–1846* (Baltimore, 1910). Especially valuable for its revelations of official intrigue over Texas is David L. Child, *The Taking of Naboth's Vineyard . . .* (New York, 1845); see also Elgin Williams, *The Animating Pursuits of Speculation: Land Traffic in the Annexation of Texas* (New York, 1949). Thomas P. Martin has examined economic factors affecting British-American relations, North and South; for a sample of his work, see "The Upper Mississippi Valley in Anglo-American Anti-Slavery and Free Trade Relations: 1837–1842," *MVHR*, XV (1928), 204–220. See also Halévy, *The Liberal Awakening, 1815–1830* (London, 1949 ed.).

A curious product of proslavery opinion is John C. Cobden, *The White Slaves of England,* first issued in Auburn, N.Y., in 1853, and appearing in at least six editions, the last dated 1860. Its 498 pages offered no explanation for its publication, though the occasion was almost certainly British reception of *Uncle Tom's Cabin.* The work, abstracted from Parliamentary hearings, gives evidence of brutal treatment of workers in English mines and factories. Its author has not yet been identified.

For the election of 1840, see Robert G. Gunderson, *The Log-Cabin Campaign* (Lexington, Ky., 1957); A. B. Norton, *The Great Revolution of 1840* . . . (Mt. Vernon, Ohio, 1888), recaptures some of its bizarre, if rugged, enthusiasm. Of general interest is Meade Minnegerode, *The Fabulous Forties, 1840–1850; a Presentation of Private Life* (New York, 1924). The view of Birney cherished by his supporters is displayed in Beriah Green, *Sketches of the Life and Writings of James Gillespie Birney* (Utica, 1844). For other pioneers of political abolitionism, Margaret C. McCullough, *Fearless Advocate of the Right* . . . (Boston, 1941), is more satisfactory for Francis J. LeMoyne than is Edwin B. Bronner, *Thomas Earle as a Reformer* (Philadelphia, 1948), for its subject. For the 1848 elections, Charles B. Going, *David Wilmot: Free Soiler* (New York, 1924); *Oliver Dyer's . . . Report of . . . the National Free Soil Convention at Buffalo, N.Y. . . .* (Buffalo, 1848); George W. Julian, *Political Recollections* (Chicago, 1884); and *Proceedings of the National Liberty Convention . . .* (Utica, 1848).

The one study presently available which includes the work of moral reformers during the Mexican War crisis is Lorenzo D. Turner, *Anti-Slavery Sentiment in American Literature Prior to 1865* (Washington, 1929). This is, however, less analytical than the subject requires, and concentrates on the antislavery "arguments" employed by writers. Thus Herman Melville, despite his profound antislavery content, is treated almost in passing. Materials for proper studies must be sought in biographical writings and works of strategic authors. William Jay and John Greenleaf Whittier have been noted in the bibliography for Chapter 4. Typical authors and relevant works would include James R. Lowell, *The Biglow Papers,* in *Poetical Works* (Boston, n.d.), II; Henry D. Thoreau, *Anti-Slavery and Reform Papers* (London, 1890); and John Pierpont, *Anti-Slavery Poems* (Boston, 1843). Theodore Parker's reform works may be approached through two collections: James K. Hosmer (ed.), *The Slave Power* (Boston, 1916), and Samuel A. Eliot (ed.), *Social Classes in a Republic* (Boston, n.d.). See also Henry S. Commager, *Theodore Parker* (Boston, 1936).

9. THE COMPROMISE OF 1850

Henry H. Simms, *A Decade of Sectional Controversy, 1851–1861* (Chapel Hill, 1942), discusses, on a polemical plane, the issues which were touched off by the great Compromise; see also Mrs. Archibald Dixon, *The True*

History of the Missouri Compromise and Its Repeal (Cincinnati, 1899). Notable figures pushed to the fore by the crisis include those discussed in the following works: Charles F. Adams, *Richard Henry Dana, a Biography* (Boston, 1891), and Harold Schwartz, *Samuel Gridley Howe,* already mentioned as an institutional reformer in the Chapter 3 bibliography. See also Elias Nason and Thomas Russell, *The Life and Public Services of Henry Wilson* (Boston, 1876); Charles F. Adams, *Charles Francis Adams* (Boston, 1900); Henry G. Pearson, *The Life of John A. Andrew* (Boston, 1904); Franklin B. Sanborn, *Recollections of Seventy Years* (Boston, 1909); George F. Hoar, *Autobiography of Seventy Years* (New York, 1903); and Thomas W. Higginson, *Contemporaries* (Boston, 1899).

For a roster of fugitive-slave cases, see Samuel J. May, Jr., *The Fugitive Slave Law and Its Victims* (New York, 1856). A notable example of northern resistance to law is the theme of William C. Cochrane, *The Western Reserve and the Fugitive Slave Law* (Cleveland, 1920). The effect of the measure on Negroes who fled to Canada is shown in Benjamin Drew, *A North-Side View of Slavery: the Refugees . . .* (Boston, 1856), and S. G. Howe, *The Refugees from Slavery in Canada West . . .* (Boston, 1864).

Harriet Tubman has inspired fiction and biography; most substantial, though awkwardly prepared, is Earl Conrad, *Harriet Tubman* (Washington, 1943). A notable case involving resistance to the Fugitive Slave Law and effort to enforce it is the subject of Charles E. Stevens, *Anthony Burns: a History* (Boston, 1856); for a modern review, Samuel Shapiro, "The Rendition of Anthony Burns," *JNH,* XLIV (1959), 34–51.

The controversy over Father Mathew was a link in temperance-and-abolition relations; its effect on political abolitionists is illustrated by Henry Wilson, *Father Mathew The Temperance Apostle: an Address* (New York, 1873). Louis Kossuth, the Hungarian revolutionist, also inadvertently aided northern unity; see Luthin, "A Visitor from Hungary," *South Atlantic Qu.,* XLVIII (1948), 29–34.

The transition of northern opinion from nonslavery to antislavery may be traced in Paxton Hibben, *Henry Ward Beecher: an American Portrait* (New York, 1942 ed.); Robert M. York, *George B. Cheever, Religious and Social Reformer, 1807–1890* (Orono, Me., 1955); Fred H. Harrington, *Fighting Politician: Major General N. P. Banks* (Philadelphia, 1948); and William E. Smith, *The Francis Preston Blair Family in Politics* (New York, 1933). Abraham Lincoln's writings furnish matter for many interpretations. T. Harry Williams, "Abraham Lincoln—Principle and Pragmatism in Politics: a Review Article," *MVHR,* XL (1953), 89–106, fails to distinguish Lincoln's "pragmatism" from that of less vital Northerners. Donald, *Lincoln's Herndon* (New York, 1948), deals with one of Lincoln's more "radical" and influential associates.

The constitutional argument over slavery is seen at its sharpest point of abolitionist antagonism in Wendell Phillips (comp.), *The Constitution a Pro-Slavery Compact* . . . (New York, 1856 ed.); William Goodell, *Views of American Constitutional Law, in Its Bearing upon American Slavery* (Utica, 1845); and Lysander Spooner, *A Defence for Fugitive Slaves* (Boston, 1850). William Jay, in all his works, insisted on distinguishing between the federal government and the Constitution, denying that the latter condoned or accepted slavery. For general purposes, see Charles Warren, *The Supreme Court in United States History* (2 vols., Boston, 1928 ed.). Basic to the constitutional argument are John C. Hurd, *The Law of Freedom and Bondage in the United States* (Boston, 1858), which is a legal study, unlike George M. Stroud, *Sketch of the Laws Relating to Slavery* . . . (Philadelphia, 1827), intended to serve antislavery purposes; see also, William Goodell, *The American Slave Code in Theory and Practice* . . . (New York, 1853). Herman E. von Holst, *Constitutional and Political History of the United States,* noted earlier, will be found most useful in connection with this topic. See also, Julius Yanuck, "The Fugitive Slave Law and the Constitution (Ph.D., Columbia University, 1953).

The literature on Harriet Beecher Stowe and *Uncle Tom's Cabin* rarely grapples with the problems of her personality and the implications of her prose. Forrest Wilson, *Crusader in Crinoline* (Philadelphia, 1941), does this best. Constance M. Rourke, *Trumpets of Jubilee* (New York, 1927), is a strong effort to bind together and to contrast the Beechers; J. C. Furnas, *Goodbye to Uncle Tom* (New York, 1956), ranges through the literature to discover the meaning of the novel; Charles H. Foster, *The Rungless Ladder* (Durham, 1954), is a literary study. Casually written, but suggestive, is Fred L. Pattee, *The Feminine Fifties* (New York, 1940).

10. KANSAS AND ABOLITION: THE IRREPRESSIBLE CONFLICT

Intensified differences between North and South produced new and more popular antislavery proponents, whose voice Horace Greeley became; see Harlan H. Horner, *Lincoln and Greeley* (Urbana, 1953); Glyndon Van Deusen, *Horace Greeley: Nineteenth Century Crusader* (Philadelphia, 1953); and especially Jeter A. Iseley, *Horace Greeley and the Republican Party, 1853–1861* . . . (Princeton, 1947). Others in the widening Republican alliance are treated in A. G. Riddle, *The Life of Benjamin Wade* (Cleveland, 1886); Robert F. Durden, *James Shepherd Pike: Republicanism and the American Negro, 1850–1882* (Durham, 1957); Wilmer C. Harris, *Public Life of Zachariah Chandler 1851–75* (Lansing, 1917). The literature on Stephen A. Douglas is wide; William O. Lynch, "The Character and Leadership of Stephen A. Douglas," *MVHA Proc., 1920–1921* (1923), 454–467, helps explain why conservative Republicans considered him a possible leader for their cause, but hardly establishes his place in antislavery annals. Outstanding in the literature on Douglas are George F. Milton, *The Eve of Con-*

flict . . . (Boston, 1934), and Allen Johnson, *Stephen A. Douglas* . . . (New York, 1908). See also Andrew W. Crandall, *The Early History of the Republican Party, 1854–1856* (Boston, 1930), and Gordon A. P. Kleeberg, *The Foundation of the Republican Party* . . . (New York, 1911).

The gathering crisis is the subject of A. C. Cole, *The Irrepressible Conflict* (New York, 1934). James C. Malin, *The Nebraska Question, 1852–1854* (Lawrence, Kan., 1953), develops a special and complex background for the Missouri Compromise repeal. See also 34th Congress, 1st Session, House of Representatives, Report No. 200, *Report of the Special Committee Appointed to Investigate the Troubles in Kansas* . . . (Washington, 1856). Eli Thayer, *A History of the Kansas Crusade* . . . (New York, 1889), is a valuable but biased primary source; the best of secondary studies is Samuel A. Johnson, *The Battle Cry of Freedom* . . . (Lawrence, 1954).

For antislavery in the border states, of which Kansas became the symbol, John F. Hume, *The Abolitionists* (New York, 1905), deals with Missouri during the Civil War, but reveals its conservative antislavery antecedents. The same is true of the following broader-based studies: Asa E. Martin, *The Anti-Slavery Movement in Kentucky Prior to 1850* (Louisville, 1918); J. Winston Coleman, *Slavery Times in Kentucky* (Chapel Hill, 1940); and Chase C. Mooney, *Slavery in Tennessee* (Bloomington, 1957). The most arresting abolitionist figure in Kentucky, Cassius M. Clay, is self-portrayed in *The Life of* . . . *Clay. Memoirs, Writings and Speeches* . . . (Cincinnati, 1886), I, only one volume being issued. Horace Greeley (ed.), *Speeches and Writings of* . . . *Clay* (New York, 1848), is a valuable supplement.

Antislavery above the Ohio River is depicted in J. P. Dunn, Jr., *Indiana: A Redemption from Slavery* (Boston, 1890); Charles T. Hickok, *The Negro in Ohio, 1802–1870* (Cleveland, 1896); and N. Dwight Harris, *The History of Negro Servitude in Illinois, and of the Slave Agitation in That State, 1719–1864* (Chicago, 1904). There is no published over-all study of antislavery as such in the old Northwest; Helen M. Cavenaugh, "Anti-Slavery Sentiment and Politics in the Northwest, 1844–1860" (Ph.D., University of Chicago, 1938), is weak in analysis. See also Edward Magdol, *Owen Lovejoy, Abolitionist in Congress* (New Brunswick, N.J., 1967).

The best-balanced study of John Brown is Oswald G. Villard, *John Brown, 1800–1859* . . . (London, 1910). Indispensable for the controversial aspects of Brown's career is Malin, *John Brown and the Legend of Fifty-Six* (Philadelphia, 1942); see also Robert P. Warren, *John Brown: the Making of a Martyr* (New York, 1930).

The literature on Dred Scott is very wide; see *Report of the Decision of the Supreme Court of the United States* . . . (New York, 1857). Aspects of the case are covered in Vincent C. Hopkins, *Dred Scott's Case* (New York, 1951), and Elbert W. R. Ewing, *Legal and Historical Status of the Dred Scott Decision* . . . (Washington, 1909).

11. REFORM AND REVOLUTION

The fact that disunion sentiments were not a Garrisonian vagary but a popular northern view has been obscured for decades; for an approach to the subject, see *Proceedings of the State Disunion Convention Held at Worcester, Massachusetts, January 15, 1857* (Boston, 1857). Disunion supplemented rather than contradicted the unionist sentiments developed in Craven, *The Repressible Conflict, 1830–1861* (Baton Rouge, 1939), and probed in Arthur Y. Lloyd, *The Slavery Controversy, 1831–1860* (Chapel Hill, 1939). For studies of the last phases of separation, see Roy F. Nichols, *The Disruption of American Democracy* (New York, 1948); Luthin, *The First Lincoln Campaign* (Cambridge, 1944); David M. Potter, *Lincoln and His Party in the Secession Crisis* (New York, 1942); Charles G. Hamilton, *Lincoln and the Know-Nothing Movement* (Washington, 1954); Kenneth R. Stampp, *And the War Came* (University, La., 1950). See also Jay Monaghan, *The Man Who Elected Lincoln* (Indianapolis, 1956), a biography of Dr. Charles H. Ray, Chicago newspaper editor.

Lewis Tappan, *History of the American Missionary Association* (New York, 1855), describes the work of this important agency; the *American Missionary*, organ of the Association and edited by Tappan, recounts its role in the critical years before the Civil War. See also Frederick I. Kuhns, *The American Home Missionary Society in Relation to the Antislavery Controversy in the Old Northwest* (Billings, Mont., 1959). The American Tract Society and the American Board of Commissioners for Foreign Missions helped crystallize northern antislavery opinion by methods still to be fully deduced from the pamphlet and periodical literature; see Goodell, *American Slavery a Formidable Obstacle to the Conversion of the World* (New York, 1854), which includes a list of societies formed to protest American Board policy, and *Statement and Catalogue of the Western Tract and Book Society for 1866* (Cincinnati, 1866), formed to oppose the American Tract Society.

For the greatest of all debates over northern programs, see Paul M. Angle (ed.), *Created Equal? The Complete Lincoln-Douglas Debates of 1858* (Chicago, 1958). For John Brown's raid, in addition to Villard and Harlow, cited above, see *Report of the Select Committee of the Senate Appointed to Inquire into the Late Invasion . . . at Harper's Ferry. Rep. Com. No. 278, 36th Congress. 1st Session* (Washington, 1860). An abolitionist summary of events preceding the Civil War is contained in *The Anti-Slavery History of the John Brown Year . . .* (New York, 1861). See also French E. Chadwick, *Causes of the Civil War, 1859–1861* (New York, 1906). For some effects, see Charles L. Wagandt, *The Mighty Revolution . . . in Maryland* (Baltimore, 1964); James M. McPherson, *The Struggle for Equality* (Princeton, N.J., 1964); George M. Fredrickson, *The Inner Civil War* (New York, 1965). For some "New Reconstruction" thinking, M. Duberman, ed., *The Antislavery*

Vanguard (Princeton, N.J., 1965), and Howard Zinn, *SNCC, the New Abolitionists* (Boston, 1964).

The antislavery crusade cannot be separated from the numerous social efforts and approaches which it fostered and which spilled over into war and reconstruction. Their forms and leadership retrospectively help clarify the crusade proper. The general problem may be perceived in such a work as C. Vann Woodward, *Reunion and Reaction* (Boston, 1951). An interesting comparison is offered by V. Jacque Voegeli, *Free but Not Equal: the Midwest and the Negro during the Civil War* (Chicago, 1967) and James M. McPherson, *The Negro's Civil War* (New York, 1967). Stanley P. Hirshson, *Farewell to the Bloody Shirt* (Bloomington, 1962) helps define post-War Republicanism, and complements Lerone Bennett, Jr., *Black Power U.S.A. The Human Side of Reconstruction 1867–1877* (Chicago, 1967).

William H. Pease and Jane Pease, *Black Utopia: Negro Communal Experiments in America* (Madison, Wis., 1963) and Willie Lee Rose, *Rehearsal for Reconstruction: the Port Royal Experiment* (Indianapolis, 1964) express tendencies in white and Negro societies. See also, Allan Peskin, ed., *North into Freedom: the Autobiography of John Malvin, Free Negro, 1795–1880* (Cleveland, 1966); Social Science Institute, Fisk University, Unwritten History of Slavery: Autobiographical Account of Negro Ex-Slaves (Nashville, Tenn., 1945), mimeographed; J. H. Cronshore and D. M. Potter, *A Union Officer in Reconstruction* (New Haven, 1948).

Index

305

69 70 71 72 73   12 11 10 9 8 7 6

harper ✦ torchbooks

HUMANITIES AND SOCIAL SCIENCES

American Studies: General

American Studies: Colonial

American Studies: From the Revolution to 1860

† The New American Nation Series, edited by Henry Steele Commager and Richard B. Morris.
‡ American Perspectives series, edited by Bernard Wishy and William E. Leuchtenburg.
* The Rise of Modern Europe series, edited by William L. Langer.
** History of Europe series, edited by J. H. Plumb.
¶ Researches in the Social, Cultural and Behavioral Sciences, edited by Benjamin Nelson.
§ The Library of Religion and Culture, edited by Benjamin Nelson.
Σ Harper Modern Science Series, edited by James R. Newman.
° Not for sale in Canada.
△ Not for sale in the U. K.

American Studies: The Civil War to 1900

American Studies: 1900 to the Present

Anthropology

L. S. B. LEAKEY: Adam's Ancestors: *The Evolution of Man and His Culture.* △ *Illus.* TB/1019
EDWARD BURNETT TYLOR: Religion in Primitive Culture. *Part II of "Primitive Culture."* § *Intro. by Paul Radin* TB/34
W. LLOYD WARNER: A Black Civilization: *A Study of an Australian Tribe.* ¶ *Illus.* TB/3056

Art and Art History

WALTER LOWRIE: Art in the Early Church. *Revised Edition. 452 illus.* TB/124
EMILE MÂLE: The Gothic Image: *Religious Art in France of the Thirteenth Century.* § △ *190 illus.* TB/44
MILLARD MEISS: Painting in Florence and Siena after the Black Death: *The Arts, Religion and Society in the Mid-Fourteenth Century. 169 illus.* TB/1148
ERICH NEUMANN: The Archetypal World of Henry Moore. △ *107 illus.* TB/2020
DORA & ERWIN PANOFSKY : Pandora's Box: *The Changing Aspects of a Mythical Symbol. Revised Edition. Illus.* TB/2021
ERWIN PANOFSKY: Studies in Iconology: *Humanistic Themes in the Art of the Renaissance.* △ *180 illustrations* TB/1077
ALEXANDRE PIANKOFF: The Shrines of Tut-Ankh-Amon. *Edited by N. Rambova. 117 illus.* TB/2011
JEAN SEZNEC: The Survival of the Pagan Gods: *The Mythological Tradition and Its Place in Renaissance Humanism and Art. 108 illustrations* TB/2004
OTTO VON SIMSON: The Gothic Cathedral: *Origins of Gothic Architecture and the Medieval Concept of Order.* △ *58 illus.* TB/2018
HEINRICH ZIMMER: Myth and Symbols in Indian Art and Civilization. *70 illustrations* TB/2005

Business, Economics & Economic History

REINHARD BENDIX: Work and Authority in Industry: *Ideologies of Management in the Course of Industrialization* TB/3035
GILBERT BURCK & EDITORS OF FORTUNE: The Computer Age: *And Its Potential for Management* TB/1179
THOMAS C. COCHRAN: The American Business System: *A Historical Perspective, 1900-1955* TB/1080
THOMAS C. COCHRAN: The Inner Revolution: *Essays on the Social Sciences in History* △ TB/1140
THOMAS C. COCHRAN & WILLIAM MILLER: The Age of Enterprise: *A Social History of Industrial America* TB/1054
ROBERT DAHL & CHARLES E. LINDBLOM: Politics, Economics, and Welfare: *Planning and Politico-Economic Systems Resolved into Basic Social Processes* TB/3037
PETER F. DRUCKER: The New Society: *The Anatomy of Industrial Order* △ TB/1082
EDITORS OF FORTUNE: America in the Sixties: *The Economy and the Society* TB/1015
ROBERT L. HEILBRONER: The Great Ascent: *The Struggle for Economic Development in Our Time* TB/3030
ROBERT L. HEILBRONER: The Limits of American Capitalism TB/1305
FRANK H. KNIGHT: The Economic Organization TB/1214
FRANK H. KNIGHT: Risk, Uncertainty and Profit △ TB/1215
ABBA P. LERNER: Everybody's Business: *Current Assumptions in Economics and Public Policy* TB/3051
ROBERT GREEN MC CLOSKEY: American Conservatism in the Age of Enterprise, 1865-1910 △ TB/1137
PAUL MANTOUX: The Industrial Revolution in the Eighteenth Century: *The Beginnings of the Modern Factory System in England* ° △ TB/1079
WILLIAM MILLER, Ed.: Men in Business: *Essays on the Historical Role of the Entrepreneur* TB/1081
RICHARD B. MORRIS: Government and Labor in Early America △ TB/1244

HERBERT SIMON: The Shape of Automation: *For Men and Management* TB/1245
PERRIN STRYKER: The Character of the Executive: *Eleven Studies in Managerial Qualities* TB/1041

Education

JACQUES BARZUN: The House of Intellect △ TB/1051
RICHARD M. JONES, Ed.: Contemporary Educational Psychology: *Selected Readings* TB/1292
CLARK KERR: The Uses of the University TB/1264
JOHN U. NEF: Cultural Foundations of Industrial Civilization △ TB/1024

Historiography & Philosophy of History

JACOB BURCKHARDT: On History and Historians. △ *Introduction by H. R. Trevor-Roper* TB/1216
WILHELM DILTHEY: Pattern and Meaning in History: *Thoughts on History and Society.* ° △ *Edited with an Introduction by H. P. Rickman* TB/1075
J. H. HEXTER: Reappraisals in History: *New Views on History & Society in Early Modern Europe* △ TB/1100
H. STUART HUGHES: History as Art and as Science: *Twin Vistas on the Past* TB/1207
RAYMOND KLIBANSKY & H. J. PATON, Eds.: Philosophy and History: *The Ernst Cassirer Festschrift. Illus.* TB/1115
ARNALDO MOMIGLIANO: Studies in Historiography ° △ TB/1283
GEORGE H. NADEL, Ed.: Studies in the Philosophy of History: *Selected Essays from History and Theory* TB/1208
JOSE ORTEGA Y GASSET: The Modern Theme. *Introduction by Jose Ferrater Mora* TB/1038
KARL R. POPPER: The Open Society and Its Enemies △
Vol. I: *The Spell of Plato* TB/1101
Vol. II: *The High Tide of Prophecy: Hegel, Marx and the Aftermath* TB/1102
KARL R. POPPER: The Poverty of Historicism ° △ TB/1126
G. J. RENIER: History: Its Purpose and Method △ TB/1209
W. H. WALSH: Philosophy of History: *An Introduction* △ TB/1020

History: General

WOLFGANG FRANKE: China and the West. *Trans by R. A. Wilson* TB/1326
L. CARRINGTON GOODRICH: A Short History of the Chinese People. △ *Illus.* TB/3015
DAN N. JACOBS & HANS H. BAERWALD: Chinese Communism: *Selected Documents* TB/3031
BERNARD LEWIS: The Arabs in History △ TB/1029
BERNARD LEWIS: The Middle East and the West ° △ TB/1274

History: Ancient

A. ANDREWES: The Greek Tyrants △ TB/1103
ADOLF ERMAN, Ed. The Ancient Egyptians: *A Sourcebook of Their Writings. New material and Introduction by William Kelly Simpson* TB/1233
MICHAEL GRANT: Ancient History ° △ TB/1190
SAMUEL NOAH KRAMER: Sumerian Mythology TB/1055
NAPHTALI LEWIS & MEYER REINHOLD, Eds.: Roman Civilization. *Sourcebook I: The Republic* TB/1231
NAPHTALI LEWIS & MEYER REINHOLD, Eds.: Roman Civilization. *Sourcebook II: The Empire* TB/1232

History: Medieval

P. BOISSONNADE: Life and Work in Medieval Europe: *The Evolution of the Medieval Economy, the 5th to the 15th Century.* ° △ *Preface by Lynn White, Jr.* TB/1141
HELEN CAM: England before Elizabeth △ TB/1026
NORMAN COHN: The Pursuit of the Millennium: *Revolutionary Messianism in Medieval and Reformation Europe* △ TB/1037

History: Renaissance & Reformation

5

H. R. TREVOR-ROPER: Historical Essays ○ △   TB/1269
ELIZABETH WISKEMANN: Europe of the Dictators, 1919-1945 ** ○ △   TB/1273
JOHN B. WOLF: The Emergence of the Great Powers, 1685-1715. * Illus.   TB/3010
JOHN B. WOLF: France: 1814-1919: The Rise of a Liberal-Democratic Society   TB/3019

Intellectual History & History of Ideas

HERSCHEL BAKER: The Image of Man: A Study of the Idea of Human Dignity in Classical Antiquity, the Middle Ages, and the Renaissance   TB/1047
R. R. BOLGAR: The Classical Heritage and Its Beneficiaries: From the Carolingian Age to the End of the Renaissance △   TB/1125
RANDOLPH S. BOURNE: War and the Intellectuals: Collected Essays, 1915-1919. △ ‡ Edited by Carl Resek   TB/3043
J. BRONOWSKI & BRUCE MAZLISH: The Western Intellectual Tradition: From Leonardo to Hegel △   TB/3001
ERNST CASSIRER: The Individual and the Cosmos in Renaissance Philosophy. △ Translated with an Introduction by Mario Domandi   TB/1097
NORMAN COHN: The Pursuit of the Millennium: Revolutionary Messianism in Medieval and Reformation Europe △   TB/1037
C. C. GILLISPIE: Genesis and Geology: The Decades before Darwin §   TB/51
G. RACHEL LEVY: Religious Conceptions of the Stone Age and Their Influence upon European Thought. △ Illus. Introduction by Henri Frankfort   TB/106
ARTHUR O. LOVEJOY: The Great Chain of Being: A Study of the History of an Idea   TB/1009
FRANK E. MANUEL: The Prophets of Paris: Turgot, Condorcet, Saint-Simon, Fourier, and Comte △   TB/1218
PERRY MILLER & T. H. JOHNSON, Editors: The Puritans: A Sourcebook of Their Writings
Vol. I TB/1093; Vol. II TB/1094
RALPH BARTON PERRY: The Thought and Character of William James: Briefer Version   TB/1156
GEORG SIMMEL et al.: Essays on Sociology, Philosophy, and Aesthetics. ¶ Edited by Kurt H. Wolff   TB/1234
BRUNO SNELL: The Discovery of the Mind: The Greek Origins of European Thought △   TB/1018
PAGET TOYNBEE: Dante Alighieri: His Life and Works. Edited with Intro. by Charles S. Singleton △   TB/1206
W. WARREN WAGAR, Ed.: European Intellectual History since Darwin and Marx   TB/1297
PHILIP P. WIENER: Evolution and the Founders of Pragmatism. △ Foreword by John Dewey   TB/1212
BASIL WILLEY: Nineteenth Century Studies: Coleridge to Matthew Arnold ○ △   TB/1261
BASIL WILLEY: More Nineteenth Century Studies: A Group of Honest Doubters ○ △   TB/1262

Law

EDWARD S. CORWIN: American Constitutional History: Essays edited by Alpheus T. Mason & Gerald Garvey   TB/1136
ROBERT H. JACKSON: The Supreme Court in the American System of Government   TB/1106
LEONARD W. LEVY, Ed.: American Constitutional Law: Historical Essays   TB/1285
LEONARD W. LEVY: Freedom of Speech and Press in Early American History: Legacy of Suppression   TB/1109
LEONARD W. LEVY, Ed.: Judicial Review and the Supreme Court   TB/1296
LEONARD W. LEVY: The Law of the Commonwealth and Chief Justice Shaw   TB/1309
RICHARD B. MORRIS: Fair Trial: Fourteen Who Stood Accused, from Anne Hutchinson to Alger Hiss. New Preface by the Author.   TB/1335

Literature, Poetry, The Novel & Criticism

JAMES BAIRD: Ishmael: The Art of Melville in the Contexts of International Primitivism   TB/1023
JACQUES BARZUN: The House of Intellect △   TB/1051
W. J. BATE: From Classic to Romantic: Premises of Taste in Eighteenth Century England   TB/1036
RACHEL BESPALOFF: On the Iliad   TB/2006
JAMES BOSWELL: The Life of Dr. Johnson & The Journal of a Tour to the Hebrides with Samuel Johnson LL.D.: Selections. ○ △ Edited by F. V. Morley. Illus. by Ernest Shepard   TB/1254
ERNST R. CURTIUS: European Literature and the Latin Middle Ages △   TB/2015
ADOLF ERMAN, Ed.: The Ancient Egyptians: A Sourcebook of Their Writings. New Material and Introduction by William Kelly Simpson   TB/1233
ALFRED HARBAGE: As They Liked It: A Study of Shakespeare's Moral Artistry   TB/1035
STANLEY R. HOPPER, Ed.: Spiritual Problems in Contemporary Literature §   TB/21
A. R. HUMPHREYS: The Augustan World: Society, Thought and Letters in 18th Century England ○ △   TB/1105
ARNOLD KETTLE: An Introduction to the English Novel. △
Volume I: Defoe to George Eliot   TB/1011
Volume II: Henry James to the Present   TB/1012
RICHMOND LATTIMORE: The Poetry of Greek Tragedy △   TB/1257
J. B. LEISHMAN: The Monarch of Wit: An Analytical and Comparative Study of the Poetry of John Donne ○ △   TB/1258
J. B. LEISHMAN: Themes and Variations in Shakespeare's Sonnets ○ △   TB/1259
ROGER SHERMAN LOOMIS: The Development of Arthurian Romance △   TB/1167
JOHN STUART MILL: On Bentham and Coleridge. △ Introduction by F. R. Leavis   TB/1070
KENNETH B. MURDOCK: Literature and Theology in Colonial New England   TB/99
SAMUEL PEPYS: The Diary of Samuel Pepys. ○ Edited by O. F. Morshead. Illus. by Ernest Shepard   TB/1007
ST.-JOHN PERSE: Seamarks   TB/2002
V. DE S. PINTO: Crisis in English Poetry, 1880-1940 ○   TB/1260
ROBERT PREYER, Ed.: Victorian Literature   TB/1302
GEORGE SANTAYANA: Interpretations of Poetry and Religion §   TB/9
C. K. STEAD: The New Poetic: Yeats to Eliot △   TB/1263
HEINRICH STRAUMANN: American Literature in the Twentieth Century. △ Third Edition, Revised   TB/1168
PAGET TOYNBEE: Dante Alighieri: His Life and Works. Edited with Intro. by Charles S. Singleton   TB/1206
DOROTHY VAN GHENT: The English Novel: Form and Function   TB/1050
BASIL WILLEY: Nineteenth Century Studies: Coleridge to Matthew Arnold △   TB/1261
BASIL WILLEY: More Nineteenth Century Studies: A Group of Honest Doubters ○ △   TB/1262
RAYMOND WILLIAMS: Culture and Society, 1780-1950 ○ △   TB/1252
RAYMOND WILLIAMS: The Long Revolution. ○ △ Revised Edition   TB/1253
MORTON DAUWEN ZABEL, Editor: Literary Opinion in America   Vol. I TB/3013; Vol. II TB/3014

Myth, Symbol & Folklore

MIRCEA ELIADE: Cosmos and History: The Myth of the Eternal Return § △   TB/2050
MIRCEA ELIADE: Rites and Symbols of Initiation: The Mysteries of Birth and Rebirth § △   TB/1236
THEODOR H. GASTER: Thespis: Ritual, Myth and Drama in the Ancient Near East △   TB/1281

C. G. JUNG & C. KERÉNYI: Essays on a Science of Mythology: *The Myths of the Divine Child and the Divine Maiden* TB/2014

DORA & ERWIN PANOFSKY: Pandora's Box: *The Changing Aspects of a Mythical Symbol.* △ *Revised edition. Illus.* TB/2021

ERWIN PANOFSKY: Studies in Iconology: *Humanistic Themes in the Art of the Renaissance.* △ *180 illustrations* TB/1077

JEAN SEZNEC: The Survival of the Pagan Gods: *The Mythological Tradition and its Place in Renaissance Humanism and Art.* △ *108 illustrations* TB/2004

HELLMUT WILHELM: Change: *Eight Lectures on the I Ching* △ TB/2019

HEINRICH ZIMMER: Myths and Symbols in Indian Art and Civilization. △ *70 illustrations* TB/2005

Philosophy

G. E. M. ANSCOMBE: An Introduction to Wittgenstein's Tractatus. º △ *Second Edition, Revised* TB/1210

HENRI BERGSON: Time and Free Will: *An Essay on the Immediate Data of Consciousness* º △ TB/1021

H. J. BLACKHAM: Six Existentialist Thinkers: *Kierkegaard, Nietzsche, Jaspers, Marcel, Heidegger, Sartre* º △ TB/1002

CRANE BRINTON: Nietzsche. *New Preface, Bibliography and Epilogue by the Author* TB/1197

MARTIN BUBER: The Knowledge of Man. △ *Ed. with an Intro. by Maurice Friedman. Trans. by Maurice Friedman and Ronald Gregor Smith* TB/135

ERNST CASSIRER: The Individual and the Cosmos in Renaissance Philosophy. △ *Translated with an Introduction by Mario Domandi* TB/1097

ERNST CASSIRER: Rousseau, Kant and Goethe. *Introduction by Peter Gay* TB/1092

FREDERICK COPLESTON: Medieval Philosophy º △ TB/376

F. M. CORNFORD: Principium Sapientiae: *A Study of the Origins of Greek Philosophical Thought. Edited by W. K. C. Guthrie* TB/1213

F. M. CORNFORD: From Religion to Philosophy: *A Study in the Origins of Western Speculation* § TB/20

WILFRID DESAN: The Tragic Finale: *An Essay on the Philosophy of Jean-Paul Sartre* TB/1030

A. P. D'ENTRÈVES: Natural Law: *An Historical Survey* △ TB/1223

MARVIN FARBER: The Aims of Phenomenology: *The Motives, Methods, and Impact of Husserl's Thought* TB/1291

MARVIN FARBER: Phenomenology and Existence: *Towards a Philosophy within Nature* TB/1295

HERBERT FINGARETTE: The Self in Transformation: *Psychoanalysis, Philosophy and the Life of the Spirit* ¶ TB/1177

PAUL FRIEDLÄNDER: Plato: *An Introduction* △ TB/2017

J. GLENN GRAY: The Warriors: *Reflections on Men in Battle. Intro. by Hannah Arendt* TB/1294

WILLIAM CHASE GREENE: Moira: *Fate, Good, and Evil in Greek Thought* TB/1104

W. K. C. GUTHRIE: The Greek Philosophers: *From Thales to Aristotle* º △ TB/1008

G. W. F. HEGEL: The Phenomenology of Mind º △ TB/1303

F. H. HEINEMANN: Existentialism and the Modern Predicament △ TB/28

ISAAC HUSIK: A History of Medieval Jewish Philosophy JP/3

EDMUND HUSSERL: Phenomenology and the Crisis of Philosophy. *Translated with an Introduction by Quentin Lauer* TB/1170

IMMANUEL KANT: The Doctrine of Virtue, *being Part II of the Metaphysic of Morals. Trans. with Notes & Intro. by Mary J. Gregor. Foreword by H. J. Paton* TB/110

IMMANUEL KANT: Groundwork of the Metaphysic of Morals. *Trans. & analyzed by H. J. Paton* TB/1159

IMMANUEL KANT: Lectures on Ethics. § △ *Introduction by Lewis W. Beck* TB/105

IMMANUEL KANT: Religion Within the Limits of Reason Alone. § *Intro. by T. M. Greene & J. Silber* TB/67

QUENTIN LAUER: Phenomenology: *Its Genesis and Prospect* TB/1169

MAURICE MANDELBAUM: The Problem of Historical Knowledge: *An Answer to Relativism. New Preface by the Author* TB/1338

GABRIEL MARCEL: Being and Having: *An Existential Diary.* △ *Intro. by James Collins* TB/310

GEORGE A. MORGAN: What Nietzsche Means △ TB/1198

H. J. PATON: The Categorical Imperative: *A Study in Kant's Moral Philosophy* △ TB/1325

PHILO, SAADYA GAON, & JEHUDA HALEVI: Three Jewish Philosophers. *Ed. by Hans Lewy, Alexander Altmann, & Isaak Heinemann* TB/813

MICHAEL POLANYI: Personal Knowledge: *Towards a Post-Critical Philosophy* △ TB/1158

WILLARD VAN ORMAN QUINE: Elementary Logic: *Revised Edition* TB/577

WILLARD VAN ORMAN QUINE: From a Logical Point of View: *Logico-Philosophical Essays* TB/566

BERTRAND RUSSELL et al.: The Philosophy of Bertrand Russell. *Edited by Paul Arthur Schilpp*
Vol. I TB/1095; Vol. II TB/1096

L. S. STEBBING: A Modern Introduction to Logic △ TB/538

ALFRED NORTH WHITEHEAD: Process and Reality: *An Essay in Cosmology* △ TB/1033

PHILIP P. WIENER: Evolution and the Founders of Pragmatism. *Foreword by John Dewey* TB/1212

WILHELM WINDELBAND: A History of Philosophy
Vol. I: *Greek, Roman, Medieval* TB/38
Vol. II: *Renaissance, Enlightenment, Modern* TB/39

LUDWIG WITTGENSTEIN: The Blue and Brown Books º TB/1211

Political Science & Government

JEREMY BENTHAM: The Handbook of Political Fallacies: *Introduction by Crane Brinton* TB/1069

C. E. BLACK: The Dynamics of Modernization: *A Study in Comparative History* TB/1321

KENNETH E. BOULDING: Conflict and Defense: *A General Theory* TB/3024

CRANE BRINTON: English Political Thought in the Nineteenth Century TB/1071

ROBERT CONQUEST: Power and Policy in the USSR: *The Study of Soviet Dynastics* △ TB/1307

EDWARD S. CORWIN: American Constitutional History: *Essays edited by Alpheus T. Mason and Gerald Garvey* TB/1136

ROBERT DAHL & CHARLES E. LINDBLOM: Politics, Economics, and Welfare: *Planning and Politico-Economic Systems Resolved into Basic Social Processes* TB/3037

JOHN NEVILLE FIGGIS: The Divine Right of Kings. *Introduction by G. R. Elton* TB/1191

JOHN NEVILLE FIGGIS: Political Thought from Gerson to Grotius: *1414-1625: Seven Studies. Introduction by Garrett Mattingly* TB/1032

F. L. GANSHOF: Feudalism △ TB/1058

G. P. GOOCH: English Democratic Ideas in the Seventeenth Century TB/1006

J. H. HEXTER: More's Utopia: *The Biography of an Idea. New Epilogue by the Author* TB/1195

SIDNEY HOOK: Reason, Social Myths and Democracy △ TB/1237

ROBERT H. JACKSON: The Supreme Court in the American System of Government △ TB/1106

DAN N. JACOBS, Ed.: The New Communist Manifesto *and Related Documents. Third Edition, Revised* TB/1078

DAN N. JACOBS & HANS BAERWALD, Eds.: Chinese Communism: *Selected Documents* TB/3031

7

HANS KOHN: Political Ideologies of the 20th Century
TB/1277
ROY C. MACRIDIS, Ed.: Political Parties: Contemporary
Trends and Ideas   TB/1322
ROBERT GREEN MC CLOSKEY: American Conservatism in
the Age of Enterprise, 1865-1910   TB/1137
KINGSLEY MARTIN: French Liberal Thought in the
Eighteenth Century: Political Ideas from Bayle to
Condorcet △   TB/1114
ROBERTO MICHELS: First Lectures in Political Sociology.
Edited by Alfred de Grazia ¶ °   TB/1224
JOHN STUART MILL: On Bentham and Coleridge. △ In-
troduction by F. R. Leavis   TB/1070
BARRINGTON MOORE, JR.: Political Power and Social
Theory: Seven Studies ¶   TB/1221
BARRINGTON MOORE, JR.: Soviet Politics—The Dilemma
of Power: The Role of Ideas in Social Change ¶
TB/1222
BARRINGTON MOORE, JR.: Terror and Progress—USSR:
Some Sources of Change and Stability in the Soviet
Dictatorship ¶   TB/1266
JOHN B. MORRALL: Political Thought in Medieval
Times △   TB/1076
JOHN PLAMENATZ: German Marxism and Russian Com-
munism. ° △ New Preface by the Author   TB/1189
KARL R. POPPER: The Open Society and Its Enemies △
Vol. I: The Spell of Plato   TB/1101
Vol. II: The High Tide of Prophecy: Hegel, Marx and
the Aftermath   TB/1102
JOHN P. ROCHE, Ed.: American Political Thought: From
Jefferson to Progressivism   TB/1332
HENRI DE SAINT-SIMON: Social Organization, The Science
of Man, and Other Writings. Edited and Translated
by Felix Markham   TB/1152
CHARLES I. SCHOTTLAND, Ed.: The Welfare State TB/1323
JOSEPH A. SCHUMPETER: Capitalism, Socialism and
Democracy △   TB/3008
BENJAMIN I. SCHWARTZ: Chinese Communism and the
Rise of Mao   TB/1308
CHARLES H. SHINN: Mining Camps: A Study in American
Frontier Government. ‡ Edited by Rodman W. Paul
TB/3062
PETER WOLL, Ed.: Public Administration and Policy: Se-
lected Essays   TB/1284

Psychology

ALFRED ADLER: The Individual Psychology of Alfred
Adler. △ Edited by Heinz L. and Rowena R. Ansbacher
TB/1154
ALFRED ADLER: Problems of Neurosis. Introduction by
Heinz L. Ansbacher   TB/1145
ARTHUR BURTON & ROBERT E. HARRIS, Eds.: Clinical
Studies of Personality
Vol. I TB/3075;   Vol. II TB/3076
HADLEY CANTRIL: The Invasion from Mars: A Study in
the Psychology of Panic ¶   TB/1282
HERBERT FINGARETTE: The Self in Transformation: Psy-
choanalysis, Philosophy and the Life of the Spirit ¶
TB/1177
SIGMUND FREUD: On Creativity and the Unconscious:
Papers on the Psychology of Art, Literature, Love,
Religion. § Intro. by Benjamin Nelson   TB/45
C. JUDSON HERRICK: The Evolution of Human Nature
TB/545
WILLIAM JAMES: Psychology: The Briefer Course. Edited
with an Intro. by Gordon Allport   TB/1034
C. G. JUNG: Psychological Reflections △   TB/2001
C. G. JUNG: Symbols of Transformation: An Analysis of
the Prelude to a Case of Schizophrenia. △ Illus.
Vol. I TB/2009;   Vol. II TB/2010
C. G. JUNG & C. KERÉNYI: Essays on a Science of Mytholo-
gy: The Myths of the Divine Child and the Divine
Maiden   TB/2014

KARL MENNINGER: Theory of Psychoanalytic Technique
TB/1144
ERICH NEUMANN: Amor and Psyche: The Psychic De-
velopment of the Feminine △   TB/2012
ERICH NEUMANN: The Archetypal World of Henry
Moore. △ 107 illus.   TB/2020
ERICH NEUMANN: The Origins and History of Conscious-
ness △   Vol. I Illus. TB/2007; Vol. II TB/2008
RALPH BARTON PERRY: The Thought and Character of
William James: Briefer Version   TB/1156
JOHN H. SCHAAR: Escape from Authority: The Perspec-
tives of Erich Fromm   TB/1155
MUZAFER SHERIF: The Psychology of Social Norms
TB/3072

Sociology

JACQUES BARZUN: Race: A Study in Superstition. Revised
Edition   TB/1172
BERNARD BERELSON, Ed.: The Behavioral Sciences Today
TB/1127
ABRAHAM CAHAN: The Rise of David Levinsky: A docu-
mentary novel of social mobility in early twentieth
century America. Intro. by John Higham   TB/1028
KENNETH B. CLARK: Dark Ghetto: Dilemmas of Social
Power. Foreword by Gunnar Myrdal   TB/1317
LEWIS A. COSER, Ed.: Political Sociology   TB/1293
ALLISON DAVIS & JOHN DOLLARD: Children of Bondage:
The Personality Development of Negro Youth in the
Urban South ¶   TB/3049
ST. CLAIR DRAKE & HORACE R. CAYTON: Black Metropolis:
A Study of Negro Life in a Northern City. △ Revised
and Enlarged. Intro. by Everett C. Hughes
Vol. I TB/1086;   Vol. II TB/1087
EMILE DURKHEIM et al.: Essays on Sociology and Philoso-
phy: With Analyses of Durkheim's Life and Work. ¶
Edited by Kurt H. Wolff   TB/1151
LEON FESTINGER, HENRY W. RIECKEN & STANLEY SCHACHTER:
When Prophecy Fails: A Social and Psychological Ac-
count of a Modern Group that Predicted the Destruc-
tion of the World ¶   TB/1132
ALVIN W. GOULDNER: Wildcat Strike: A Study in Worker-
Management Relationships ¶   TB/1176
CÉSAR GRAÑA: Modernity and Its Discontents: French
Society and the French Man of Letters in the Nine-
teenth Century ¶   TB/1318
FRANCIS J. GRUND: Aristocracy in America: Social Class
in the Formative Years of the New Nation △ TB/1001
KURT LEWIN: Field Theory in Social Science: Selected
Theoretical Papers. ¶ △ Edited with a Foreword by
Dorwin Cartwright   TB/1135
R. M. MAC IVER: Social Causation   TB/1153
ROBERT K. MERTON, LEONARD BROOM, LEONARD S. COTTRELL,
JR., Editors: Sociology Today: Problems and Pros-
pects ¶   Vol. I TB/1173;   Vol. II TB/1174
ROBERTO MICHELS: First Lectures in Political Sociology.
Edited by Alfred de Grazia ¶ °   TB/1224
BARRINGTON MOORE, JR.: Political Power and Social
Theory: Seven Studies ¶   TB/1221
BARRINGTON MOORE, JR.: Soviet Politics—The Dilemma
of Power: The Role of Ideas in Social Change ¶
TB/1222
TALCOTT PARSONS & EDWARD A. SHILS, Editors: Toward
a General Theory of Action: Theoretical Foundations
for the Social Sciences   TB/1083
ARNOLD ROSE: The Negro in America: The Condensed
Version of Gunnar Myrdal's An American Dilemma
TB/3048
GEORGE ROSEN: Madness in Society: Chapters in the
Historical Sociology of Mental Illness. ¶ Preface by
Benjamin Nelson   TB/1337
KURT SAMUELSSON: Religion and Economic Action: A
Critique of Max Weber's The Protestant Ethic and
the Spirit of Capitalism. ¶ ° Trans. by E. G. French.
Ed. with Intro. by D. C. Coleman   TB/1131

8

NATURAL SCIENCES
AND MATHEMATICS